Contested Democracy

Contested Democracy

Freedom, Race, and Power

in American History

EDITED BY MANISHA SINHA

AND PENNY VON ESCHEN

Columbia University Press   New York

Columbia University Press
Publishers Since 1893
New York, Chichester, West Sussex
Copyright © 2007 Columbia University Press
All rights Reserved

Library of Congress Cataloging-in-Publication Data

Contested democracy : freedom, race, and power in American history
/ Manisha Sinha and Penny Von Eschen, editors.
p. cm.

Includes bibliographical references.
ISBN 978-0-231-14110-9 (cloth : alk. paper)

1. United States—History. 2. United States—Politics and government. 3. Democracy—United States--History. 4. United States—
Race relations. 5. Power (Social sciences)—United States—History.
6. Radicalism—United States—History. 7. Social movements—United States—History. 8. United States—Social conditions. I. Sinha,
Manisha. II. Von Eschen, Penny M. (Penny Marie) III. Title.

E178.6.C676 2007
973—dc22

Columbia University Press books are printed on permanent and du-
rable acid-free paper

Printed in the United States of America
Designed by Audrey Smith

c 10 9 8 7 6 5 4 3 2 1

References to Internet Web Sites (URLs) were accurate at the time of
writing. Neither the editors, the contributors, nor Columbia University Press is responsible for Web sites that may have expired or changed
since the book was prepared

For Eric Foner

Contents

Acknowledgments

We are happy to acknowledge the help and support of several people who have made this volume possible. We are deeply grateful to Alan Brinkley, provost and Allan Nevins Professor of History at Columbia University, for his generous support of this project. We likewise thank Kenneth Jackson, professor emeritus and director of the Lehman Center for Historical Studies at Columbia University, for hosting the conference "Contested Democracy: Freedom, Race, and Power in American History" in honor of Eric Foner. The conference enabled the contributors to the volume to meet together for presentations and discussion, greatly enriching our book. Warmest thanks to those scholars who joined us as commentators. We thank professors Ira Berlin, Elizabeth Blackmar, Adam McKeown, and Thomas Bender for valuable criticism and feedback. We especially thank Elizabeth Blackmar for her sustained support and encouragement. Both her backing and her astute comments have been very important to us.

We thank Peter Dimock at Columbia University Press for his wisdom, rigorous intellectual engagement, and patience through a protracted process. Thanks also to Anne Routon for expert guidance and Anne R. Gibbons for her excellent copyediting.

We thank all the contributors for their spirited collaboration at every stage of the project. The articles are a testimony to their wonderful scholarship and the manner in which Eric Foner has inspired us all to write on a variety of topics in our own distinct ways. We thank them for their patience as we put this volume together over the last two years. We are honored and delighted that David Blight has contributed a wonderful afterword. His thoughtful tribute has made this a better book.

We also thank our families. We thank Karsten Stueber and Kevin Gaines for their support and engaged editing. Our sons, Sheel Stueber and Maceo Gaines, tolerated and interrupted our work in degrees not of our own choosing. We thank Manisha's baby, Shiv, for sleeping through the night and taking regular morning and afternoon naps so we could work. All of them have nurtured our collaboration by allowing us to continue and enlarge conversations that we began in graduate school.

Most importantly, we thank Eric. He is an inspiration—for this book and much more. His scholarly example has meant the world to us. This volume is a small token of our gratitude for his passionate commitment to history and social justice. We hope this will be the first in a series of books that will honor the work of a master teacher, scholar, and citizen.

Contested Democracy

Introduction

MANISHA SINHA AND PENNY VON ESCHEN

Amid the unprecedented degree of cynical manipulation of U.S. history, the ideals of American democracy, and the tenets of freedom for self-serving political ends, this volume is written with the conviction that history matters. A rigorous engagement with history is essential to a vital democracy, especially as we witness a steady erosion of human rights and civil liberties within the United States and abroad. In the present age of empire, globalization, and the export of American democracy, it is particularly important to reexamine the historically contradictory and exclusionary development of democracy within the United States itself. Historians have always been influenced by contemporary concerns in their writing of history. But if historians talk about the past because of the present, responsible historical scholarship is not "presentist" in misusing history to serve political and ideological agendas. Instead a careful study of history not only illuminates contemporary problems but also serves as a bulwark against history as mythmaking in the service of cynical political ends.[1] The work of Eric Foner has powerfully called on historians and citizens to consider the contradictions of American democracy and to hold the present accountable to the past. Foner's focus on power, the realm of politics itself, and the critical place of ideology in producing political meaning, along with his emphasis on expanding senses of what constitutes political agency, have special merit in pointing the way to writing U.S. history in the age of empire.[2] The profound contemporary challenges to democratic governance as well as intellectual inquiry make this an urgent task for historians and scholars.

An appreciation of the contradictions and limitations of the history of American democracy guards against celebratory mythmaking as well as the nostalgic idea that a previously vibrant democracy has only recently become embattled. Indeed, the birth of the New World was coterminous with the rise of racial slavery and the world market. The deeply entangled history of race and American democracy in many ways is replicated and being played out anew on a global stage today. Since the time of conquest, continental expansion, enslavement, and dispossession of peoples deemed uncivilized, American republicanism has been fully complicit in the history of racial oppression in the modern world. The story of American freedom goes hand in hand with the story of its exclusions and the story of American "unfreedom."

It is essential to realize that the American tradition has been shaped as much by opposition to the broadening of democracy as by movements for social and political change. The essays in this volume seek to examine the internal contradictions and inherent limitations of concepts of American freedom. In emphasizing the deep intertwining of oppression and freedom, we reject not only uncritical accounts of U.S. history but also the inverse teleology that posits an inherently violent and racist logic at work in the unfolding of American democracy. Stories from the margins of U.S. history or alternative and radical visions of American freedom have always challenged the dominant and narrower versions of these ideas. Recentering contradiction and contingency in American history is vitally important to understanding the role of the United States in this latest age of American imperialism and alternative visions of American democracy and freedom.

This volume grew out of conversations between a cohort of U.S. and international scholars, all trained as Americanists at Columbia University in the 1980s and 1990s. We came from diverse democratic movements and intellectual training from Europe, Asia, Africa, and the United States, and we brought these experiences to bear on our study of American history. Our graduate community was enlivened by perspectives ranging from the South African antiapartheid movement, German socialism, international feminist movements, Italian labor, Indian democratic nonalignment, Chinese Marxism, democratic social movements in the United States, and most importantly, by the mentorship of Eric Foner. Foner taught us in the tradition of W. E. B. Du Bois, who understood that the fate of democracy is inextricably bound with questions of race, colonialism, and empire. With diverse political concerns, all of us came to graduate school with the belief that our commitments and responsibilities as citizens were not separate from our vocation as historians. This book is a product of our interactions with—as well as our response to—a particular moment of intellectual fermentation in a postcolonial world. They are, ultimately, historical investigations that chart directions in American history informed by a global milieu and a passionate belief in democratic citizenship and responsible scholarship.

These essays draw on the extraordinarily rich conceptual map laid out by the work of Eric Foner, which has reflected a broad-ranging engagement with the contours of and contestations over American democracy. Foner was foremost among a generation of historians who introduced questions of consciousness, ideology, and culture into historical inquiry. He challenged reductionist notions of politics, insisting that relations of power can only be understood through rigorous inquiry into specific historical contingencies at any given time. His scholarship emphasized the fluidity and the contradictory nature of politics, examining how political blocs have successfully garnered control of state apparatuses by positing their own distinct interests as timeless and real, serving a universal whole.[3]

Unlike historical scholarship that has only emphasized the institutional and cultural practices of the elite, the practices of colonizers rather than the colonized, centers of power rather than oppositional forms, Foner's work has also demonstrated an abiding concern for the agency and subjectivities of peoples dispossessed of formal political and economic power.[4] He has argued that the development of American democracy, liberalism, and citizenship is both enriched and complicated by looking at the ideas and actions of the subaltern, and he has sought to study politics, language, and power at the moments of fissures and collisions between different groups of people. His corpus has provided us with an alternative view of the nature of American democracy, freedom, and citizenship. Such a framework for U.S. history offers us a foundational understanding of the contemporary American drive for empire and the interconnections between the ways in which American power abroad replicates its domestic and especially racial contradictions. As Foner insisted on an engagement with politics that incorporated rather than rejected the contributions of social history, many of the essays in this volume embrace a refocusing on politics through the careful study of culture and discourse.[5]

A U.S. history that is informed by a critical reading of the development of democracy in this country has deep relevance for the unfolding of American hegemony in the world today. Such an approach not only undermines claims to American exceptionalism but also rejects privileging the United States as a site for the production of democratic institutions. Understanding the contested nature of democracy and notions of freedom and citizenship in American history highlights the limitations, failings, and contradictions of U.S. power in the world today. The essays in this volume are informed by an understanding of the problems of the American democratic tradition in addition to advocating the writing of global and transnational histories as so many have done in recent years. Some of the essays represent global and transnational histories; many also insist that these perspectives be informed by a serious engagement with questions of political power, race, and ideology within the metropolis.

Chronologically, these essays span the breadth of U.S. history from the American Revolution to the early twenty-first century. They consider the fault lines of American democracy through such intersecting issues as race, slavery, gender, citizenship, the nation-state, social movements, political economy, immigration, law, empire, and the academy itself. The essays by Tyler Anbinder and Martha Saxton highlight the profoundly exclusionary basis of the early American republic and the white man's democracy of the nineteenth century. They call for renewed attention to contestations over the meanings of democracy, citizenship, and freedom at the moment of their origins. Anbinder and Saxton point to the inherent limitations and failure of early American democracy. Anbinder looks at the contrary and exclusionary vision of an essentially male street politics of intimidation and mob violence in antebellum New York. He reminds us that for hundreds and thousands of white American men, the concept of democracy was tied to their own precious sovereignty and to an intolerant patriotism that repudiated all the rights of democratic dissent. Saxton discusses the political implications of Missouri slave women's resistance that questioned dominant notions of gender and freedom in pre–Civil War America. The labor of black women made it possible for respectable white women to fulfill their obligations of republican motherhood. Free and enslaved black women worked without the visibility and public sanction that secured white women's loyalty and deference to the republican order headed by white men. Both essays reveal the narrowly gendered and racial character of antebellum American democracy.

Essays by Manisha Sinha, Martha Jones, and Xi Wang also reveal the historically racialized nature of freedom and democracy in the United States. All three insist on the importance of black agency in arriving at a broader and more complex understanding of American political and legal history. At a time when racial slavery dominated politics and the economy, the discourse of citizenship and freedom received its fullest expression in black protest thought and action. Sinha argues that African American abolitionists' concept of revolution was not derivative of the American revolutionary tradition but offered a profound critique of it. Black abolitionists developed an oppositional and transnational understanding of revolution that drew its inspiration from the Haitian revolution and slave rebellions in the Western world. Jones looks at African Americans' daily negotiations in a legal culture to define rights and citizenship in mid-nineteenth-century Maryland. She uncovers the rich story of everyday black legal claims amid discussions of colonization, emigration, and citizenship. Xi Wang insists that we center black discourses in the debates over suffrage during the era of the Civil War and Reconstruction. African Americans, he argues, were the strongest exponents of universal suffrage at this time, and they made a seminal contribution to the development of American constitutionalism. These essays highlight the originality of black American thought and protest over the questions of democracy, rights, and citizenship.

Concern over the misuse of the discourse of American freedom and democracy for private and corporate gain has invigorated historical investigations of institutional realms of state formation and the development of liberal ideology. Essays by Michael Zakim and Melinda Lawson consider some of the ways in which such tensions undergirded the development of the nation-state, law, political economy, and liberalism. Zakim examines how the growth of an industrial economy, and attempts to quantify and describe it, contributed to a reformulation of the language of democracy and the legitimization of a market-driven liberalism. While he illuminates the rise of liberal individualism through the reification of the production process, Lawson illustrates the vexed nature of liberal ideology in Western history. She argues that advocates of land reclamation and irrigation in the

West called for the expansion of state power and greater state intervention in the economy, while continuing to use the language of liberal individualism. The notion that the state is just another individual proprietor became a wedge for neoliberal arguments that all the actions of the state should be evaluated according to the precepts of the market economy, and if found to be inefficient, should devolve to private proprietors and contractors, thereby eliminating democratic sovereignty as a defining feature of the American state.

These essays and those by Mae Ngai and Martha Biondi fundamentally challenge romanticized notions of classical, Progressive, and New Deal liberalism that have dealt with the contradictions of liberalism as merely episodic failures. Ngai argues that the internment of Japanese Americans during World War II represented not a lapse in liberalism but was constitutive of it. As liberals conflated culture and loyalty, coercive assimilation was as important to the ideology and implementation of internment as were notions of exclusion. Her examination of the liberal and activist state exposes the inherent flaws of its essentially racialist concept of democracy and citizenship; concepts that would continue to shape a longer trajectory of Americanization policies. Focusing on the college campus as an arena for civil rights activism and the political and legal battles that led to the formation of black studies programs throughout the country, Biondi examines black student activists' critical engagements with liberalism in the late 1960s and 1970s. Armed with Title VII and a liberal judiciary, these African American students helped establish affirmative action, widened access to education, and ultimately translated educational attainment into occupational mobility.

An in-depth comprehension of the internal tensions of democratic discourses and state formation complements our understanding of similarly contradictory international and transnational political and social processes. Sven Beckert's essay reveals how the distinct forces of German imperialism, African American aspirations for racial liberation, and African resistance interacted in the attempt to create a world economy of cotton. He brings alive the economic expansion of the West and the production of agricultural commodities in the global periphery through a narrative involving strange bedfellows. Alessandra Lorini and Lisa McGirr analyze counterhegemonic transnational social movements informed by a politics of labor radicalism and ethnic nationalism. Lorini argues that a transnational Cuba Libre movement situated in New York City grew not only in opposition to Spanish imperialism but also as a rejection of the post–Civil War racial order in the United States. In adapting U.S. republican ideology to the cause of Cuba Libre, such Cuban exiles as Emilia Casanova de Villaverde and Jose Martí developed distinct interpretations of American imperial nationalism. Mc-Girr analyzes the disparate forces and local conditions that comprised the international outcry over the Sacco and Vanzetti case. Galvanizing protest from Mexico City, Buenos Aires, and Montevideo, to Marseille and Casablanca, the Massachusetts trial of the formerly obscure anarchists crystallized a unique moment of international collective mobilization. Penny Von Eschen considers jazz pianist and composer Duke Ellington's 1963 performances in Baghdad, Iraq, to explore the paradox of U.S. ambition and self-absorption in the post-1945 world. Suggesting that "hard and soft power" are not the distinct forces they are often assumed to be, she further argues for the necessity of Americanists broadening their engagement with scholars writing from outside the field of U.S. history in order to comprehend America's global relations. Just as a historical investigation of the domestic development of American democracy, liberalism, and citizenship necessitates a focus on marginalized groups and peoples, any comprehension of the nature of American empire is possible only by studying it from locations around the globe.

This volume concludes with Eric Foner's meditation on questions that have beset American historians in the post-9/11 world. His cautionary words about how to think historically rather than mythically about American freedom are especially pertinent at a time when politicians and public figures justify the brazen use of torture, spying, the undermining of civil liberties, and other undemocratic practices and policies in the name of American democracy. The current dilemma of American democracy has been exacerbated by an accompanying obscurantist attack on science, history, and intellectual inquiry in general. In this dismal moment of our history, the example of Eric Foner's confident scholarship, based on a courageous commitment to historical truth, inspires us to meet the challenges of today. As David Blight notes in his moving afterword, Eric Foner's devotion to the craft of history is as much a product of rigorous archival research as his passionate belief in democracy and equal citizenship. We hope that the essays in this volume are a sufficient tribute to a master practitioner of history "from the archive and from the heart."

NOTES

1. Eric Foner, "American Freedom in a Global Age," in *Who Owns History? Rethinking the Past in a Changing World* (New York, 2002), 49–74, and "Rethinking American History in a Post-9/11 World," in *Liberal Education* (March 2003).

2. Eric Foner, *Free Soil, Free Labor, Free Men: The Ideology of the Republican Party before the Civil War* (New York, 1970; reprint 1995 with a new introduction); Foner, *Politics and Ideology in the Age of the Civil War* (New York, 1980); Foner, *Tom Paine and Revolutionary America* (New York, 1976); Foner, *Nothing but Freedom: Emancipation and Its Legacy* (Baton Rouge, 1983).

3. Foner, "Why Is There No Socialism in the United States?" in *Who Owns History*, 110–45; Antonio Gramsci, *Selections from the Prison Notebooks* (New York, 1971); Louis Althusser, "Ideology and Ideological State Apparatuses," in *Lenin and Philosophy* (London, 1971); Perry Anderson, *Considerations on Western Marxism* (London, 1976); Raymond Williams, *Keywords* (London, 1976); Ernesto Laclau, *Politics and Ideology in Marxist Theory* (London, 1977): Jurgen Habermas, *The Theory of Communicative Action*, 2 vols. (Boston, 1984); Gareth Stedman Jones, *Languages of Class: Studies in English Working Class History, 1832–1982* (Cambridge, Eng., 1984). See also the works of the British school of Marxist historians, such as E. P. Thompson, Eric Hobsbawm, and Christopher Hill, that inspired generations of American historians.

4. Eric Foner, *Nothing but Freedom;* Foner, *Reconstruction: America's Unfinished Revolution, 1863–1877* (New York, 1988); Foner, "Blacks and the U.S. Constitution," in *Who Owns History?* 167–88; Foner, *Forever Free: The Story of Emancipation and Reconstruction*, illustrations edited and with commentary by Joshua Brown (New York, 2005).

5. Eric Foner, *The Story of American Freedom* (New York, 1998) and "Who Is an American?" in *Who Owns History?* 149–66.

Chapter One

· · · · · · · · ·

An Alternative Tradition
of Radicalism

*African American Abolitionists
and the Metaphor of Revolution*

MANISHA SINHA

In recent years, the study of black abolitionism in the United States has come of age. Building on the foundational work of Benjamin Quarles and earlier black historians, scholars have drawn attention to the crucial role of African Americans in the rise of the antebellum abolition movement with its emphasis on immediatism and black rights.[1] We now know in detail the wide array of ideological weapons employed by African American abolitionists in their battle against slavery and racism: the ideas of racial uplift and moral reform, the languages of black nationalism and religious millennialism, the black response to the pseudoscience of race, the cultivation of radical politics, and the debate on the use of violence to resist enslavement.[2] We have for the first time a theoretically sophisticated understanding of the intellectual and political history of black abolitionism. African Americans did not merely add an "experiential" side to abolitionist ideology in recounting their firsthand experiences with slavery and racism, nor were their arguments confined to emotional and sentimental "appeals to the heart." They were original thinkers on the problems of race, slavery, and democracy in antebellum America.

The ever-growing body of historical literature on black abolitionists has finally put to rest the influential yet glib view of black abolitionism as mired in the strictures of middle-class reform and elitism, a reflection of dominant white bourgeois values. However, historians have yet to fully appreciate the alternative and radical nature of black abolitionism. Most still continue to portray black abolitionists not so much as "counterhegemons" but as "cofabricators" of northern political culture. In short, they argue that African Americans appropriated mainstream values and ideas to construct a black protest tradition.[3] From a somewhat different perspective, nationalist scholars have criticized antebellum black thought for its assimilationist tendencies as opposed to allegedly more radical, grassroots, nationalist movements.[4] Thus both the critics and defenders of the black abolitionist tradition have seen it mainly as an offshoot of bourgeois conservatism or radicalism, depending on their particular viewpoint.

In this essay I suggest that we must critically understand the alternative nature of black abolitionism. The terms "adoption," "assimilation," and "appropriation" hardly do justice to the African American ideological engagement with the modern revolutionary tradition. This examination challenges the description of black abolitionist thought as thoroughly integrated into dominant political and intellectual discourses. Revolutionary ideology, as David Brion Davis has pointed out, provided the first comprehensive theoretical challenge to the existence of slavery in the Western world.[5] Black abolitionists pioneered not only in developing a comprehensive critique of slavery in the early republic but also in subjecting the American Revolutionary tradition itself to criticism. They used the metaphor of revolution to argue for a host of ideas and positions, and their arguments involved more than simply the extension of the principles of the American Revolution to black Americans. The idea of revolution became the basis of an oppositional tradition of black radicalism that departed dramatically from American political thought and its premises. Far from simply invoking the promise of the American Revolution, African Americans emerged as its most stringent and vocal critics. Revolution to black abolitionists meant not just the incomplete legacy of the American Revolution but also the Haitian revolution, a way to justify the violent overthrow of slavery through slave rebellion and abolitionist instigation.[6] Their notion of revolution was transnational and expansive, which transcended the narrow and largely uncritical celebration of the American Revolution that became de rigueur in nineteenth-century America. African American abolitionists did not simply indulge in the static invocation of revolutionary principles; they contested the notion and legacy of revolution in the United States.

The black freedom petitions in New England during the Revolutionary era were the first instances of African American use of revolutionary ideology to condemn the existence of slavery. These petitions highlighted the contradiction between the existence of slavery and the colonists' fight for self-government and independence. But by using the language of revolutionary republicanism, they also imbued the black demand for freedom with an immediacy that was missing in the plans for gradual, compensated emancipation advocated by a majority of contemporary antislavery whites in the North. While white Americans dominated the organized revolutionary antislavery movement and saw black slaves as the objects of their benevolence, African Americans developed a distinct and incipient antislavery radicalism outside its organizational boundaries based on revolutionary rhetoric and the insistent plea of the natural rights of man. A 1774 petition of Massachusetts blacks argued for "an act of the Legislative to be pessed that we may obtain our Natural right our freedoms and our children be set at lebety." In 1776, nineteen "natives of Africa" from Portsmouth, New Hampshire, claimed "for the sake of justice, humanity, and the rights of mankind" that "the God of nature gave [us] life and freedom, upon the terms of the most perfect equality with other men; That freedom is an inherent right of the human species."

The freedom petitions also reveal that right from the start African Americans did not hesitate to describe the severity of their situation, and they questioned the Revolutionary assertions of white Americans, which did not encompass them. An early 1773 "petition of many slaves" in Massachusetts to the colony's governor and general court pointed out that they "had every Day of their Lives imbittered with the most intolerable Reflection, That, let their Behaviour be what it will, nor their Children to all generations, shall ever be able to do, or possess or enjoy any Thing, no not even Life itself, but in a Manner as the Beasts that perish. We have no property! We have no Wives! No Children! We have no City! No Country!" The same year, another Massachusetts petition, signed by four slaves—Peter Bestes, Sambo Freeman, Chester Joie, and Felix Holbrook—sarcastically noted, "The efforts made by the legislative of this province in their last sessions to free themselves from slavery, gave us, who are in that deplorable state, a high degree of satisfaction. We expect great things from men who have made such a noble stand against the designs of their *fellow-men* to enslave them."

Despite adopting a deferential tone, these petitions gave notice not just of black condemnation of white hypocrisy but also of a more critical attitude toward American republicanism and the Revolutionary struggle itself. They seemed to imply that compared to the sufferings of black people, the American cause was trivial. A 1777 petition submitted by eight black Bostonians expressed "Astonishment that It have Never Bin Considered that Every Principle from which America has Acted in the Cours of their Unhappy Dificulties with Great Briton Pleads Stronger than A thousand arguments . . . that they may be Restored to the Enjoyments of that which is the Naturel Right of all men." In 1779, a group of Connecticut blacks declared in their petition that it was a "flagrant Injustice" that those "contending, in the Cause of Liberty" deny what "Reason and Revelation join to declare, that we are the Creatures of that God, who made of one Blood, and Kindred, all the Nations of the Earth?"[7] This petition went beyond demanding abolition; it condemned the colonists' racism, which excluded them from the promise of republican citizenship.

During the Revolutionary War, African Americans petitioned, sued, ran away and fought on both sides to gain their freedom. Others wrote autobiographies, poetry, and pamphlets—marking the start of a long tradition of black protest literature.[8] But it is these mostly anonymous black petitioners in New England who laid the foundations of African American abolitionist ideology and its preoccupation with exposing Revolutionary republicanism in this country. Despite the slow demise of slavery in the North, blacks confronted new barriers to their freedom. The dismal days of the early republic, when it became quite clear that racial slavery in the South was an entrenched and expanding institution and when northern states instituted a host of discriminatory laws and practices against free black people, fostered a critical attitude toward the legacy of the Revolution among African Americans. Rather than simply reiterating Revolutionary ideas to condemn slavery, they often challenged and reversed the symbolism of the American Revolution, describing the revolutionaries as tyrants and oppressors and its ideas as, at best, empty rhetoric. In his well-known 1792 letter accompanying his almanac to Thomas Jefferson, the black mathematician and astronomer Benjamin Banneker wrote "how pitiable it is" that he should detain "by fraud and violence so numerous a part of my brethren, under groaning captivity, and cruel oppression, that you should at the same time be found guilty of that most criminal act, which you professedly detested in others, with respect to yourselves."[9]

The United States, in black abolitionist discourse, soon came to represent the land of captivity, of slavery rather than liberty, and the discovery of the New World inaugurated not the founding of the shining city on a hill but the start of the crime against Africans. Prince Hall, founder of the African Masonic Lodge in Boston, recalled how Africans were "dragg'd from their native country by the iron hand of tyranny and oppression . . . to a strange land and strange people, whose tender mercies are cruel; and there to bear the iron yoke of slavery and cruelty till death as a friend shall relieve them." For Daniel Coker, the slave's right to liberty outweighed the slaveholder's right to property, guaranteed by the new American republic and its Constitution. As he wrote in his dialogue between a slaveholder and a black minister, "Shall we hesitate a moment to determine who is the greatest sufferer, and who is treated with the greatest injustice?" Addressing directly "Those Who Keep Slaves and Uphold the Practice," Richard Allen and Absalom Jones, founders of the African Methodist Episcopal Church, clearly state "you . . . have been and are our great oppressors" and imply that America like Egypt would be destroyed for its "oppression of the slaves" by God, "the protector and avenger of slaves." While advocating the gospel of Christian forgiveness and disclaiming any intention to anger white Americans, they nevertheless warn that while slaves may appear contented, "the dreadful insurrections they have made, when opportunity has offered, is enough to convince a reasonable man, that great uneasiness and not contentment, is the inhabitant of their hearts." The reaction of former revolutionaries such as Thomas Jefferson to Gabriel's 1800 conspiracy in Virginia convinced African Americans that Revolutionary professions held no meaning when it came to black people.[10]

Orations on the abolition of the African slave trade in 1808 reveal black abolitionists' concerted attempt to construct a narrative of slavery and freedom to counter the dominant national story of freedom inaugurated by the American Revolution. Some of these, such as those by Adam Carman and Henry Johnson, have been neglected by most historians.[11] It is the slave trade rather than the Revolution that is the starting point of these counternarratives and their main motif is slavery rather than liberty. Russell Parrott of Philadelphia, in his oration on the abolition of the slave trade noted, "It is from this period, that we may date the commencement of the sufferings of the Africans, and the discovery of the new world; which, to one portion of the human family, has afforded such advantages, to the unfortunate African, has been the source of the greatest misery." Recapitulating the history of the Americas in his oration, the Reverend Peter Williams Jr. of New York charged that the first European colonists had enslaved "the harmless aborigines, compelled them to drudge in the mines" and carried Africans "into cruel captivity." In his sermon of thanksgiving on the abolition of the slave trade, the Reverend Absalom Jones asserted that America was the new Egypt. With the abolition of the slave trade the "dear land of our ancestors" would not be stained with the blood "shed by British and American hands." William Hamilton, a carpenter and an early black abolitionist from New York, in his 1815 speech on the abolition of the slave trade wished that "Columbus with his exploring schemes had perished in Europe ere he touched the American Isles." Africa then would have "been spared the terrible calamity she has suffered." By dwelling on the horrors of the slave trade, these early black ideologues exposed the seamier side of Western civilization and American republicanism. Henry Johnson said that he drew attention to the cruelties of the slave trade not to "inflame" the minds of his people but to "cast just obloquy" against "our oppressors." The history of the slave trade and slavery in the United States, according to Henry Sipkins, "a descendant of Africa," was one of "relentless tyranny" and torture.[12]

Instead of singing paeans to American republicanism, Christianity, and commerce, black abolitionists challenged some of the core beliefs and values of early Americans in their attempt to fashion a critique of slavery and racial inequality. In his remarkable oration on behalf of "our injured race," Adam Carman attacked the economic basis of the slave trade and slavery and the system of European commerce that reduced a black person to a "vendible article." He argued that with the institution of slavery in the New World, Africans came to be "viewed and considered as commercial commodities; thus we became interwoven into the system of commerce, and the revenue of nations; hence the merchant, the planter, the mortgagee, the manufacturer, the politician, the legislators, and the cabinet minister, all strenuously advocated the continuance of the Slave Trade." Unlike Paul Cuffee, the black Quaker sea captain and an early pioneer of the Back to Africa movement, and later generations of black emigrationists, Carman argued that Western Christianity, commerce, and civilization did not contain the keys to Africa's redemption but sounded its death knell.[13]

Black abolitionists also developed their exposure of American republicanism in the slave trade orations by criticizing racist thought that justified their enslavement and exclusion from citizenship. Racism, they pointed out, as much as ideals of freedom and independence, was a part of the heritage of the American Revolution. Indeed, if all men were created equal then the persistence of slavery and racial inequality in the American republic implied that black people were less than human. In his speech on the abolition of the slave trade, George Lawrence stressed the problem of American racism and disputed it on intellectual and moral grounds: "Vacuous must the reason of that man have been, who dared to assert that genius is confined to complexion, or that nature knows difference in the immortal soul of man." In a similar vein, Carman asserted "these very savage-like-manstealers, brand us with inferiority of sensibility. My brethren, Africans and descendants of Africans, it would be condescending from the dignity of Africans, to notice what these invidious pedantic nizies have asserted." For him, American racists revealed a "depravity of mind or [profligacy] of morals inferior to that imputed to us."[14] The slave trade orations presented an opportunity for African Americans to publicly express their opinions on slavery. As such, they mark the start of a black abolitionist tradition of protest, unapologetic in tone and highly critical in content.

Speeches in the 1820s on the demise of northern slavery continued the radical tradition of the slave trade orations. The United States in these counternarratives was the site of racist oppression rather than a beacon of liberty. The Reverend Nathaniel Paul of Albany, a confidant of William Lloyd Garrison, pointed out "that in the United States of America, at the extirpation of fifty years after its becoming a free and independent nation, there are no less than fifteen hundred thousand human beings still in a state of unconditional vassalage. Yet America is the first in the profession of the love of liberty, and loudest in proclaiming liberal sentiments toward all other nations, and feels herself insulted, to be branded with anything bearing the appearance of tyranny and oppression. Such are the palpable inconsistencies that abound among us and such is the medley of contradictions that stain the national character, and [render] the American republic a byword, even among despotic nations." In his 1827 speech marking the complete abolition of slavery in New York, Hamilton launched the first full-scale attack on the Jeffersonian legacy of equal rights and racism. Beginning cautiously—"I know that I ought to speak with caution"—he still takes on the racialist arguments of the "ambidexter philosopher" who "kept around him a number of slaves" and who "first tells you 'that all men are created equal, and that they are endowed with unalienable rights of life, liberty, and the pursuit of happiness,'" and "next proves that one class of men are not equal to another, which by the bye, does not agree with axioms of geometry, that deny that things can be equal, and at the same time unequal to one another." For Hamilton, Jefferson was not only illogical, but also immoral, and his immorality infected the very foundations of the American nation: "Does he reason like a man of true moral principles? Does he set a good example? . . . What jargon does the law of the United States form with the principles here laid down, that gives to one class of men, the right to arrest, wherever they may find within its jurisdiction, another class of men, and retain them as their lawful property?" Turning the table on Jefferson and other American republicans, Hamilton asked them to justify their "superior" reasoning and laws. Most black abolitionists were federalists like Hamilton and Joseph Sidney. Sidney developed an extensive criticism of Jeffersonian republicanism, "the Slavery-hole of democracy," in his oration on the abolition of the slave trade.[15]

David Walker's famous 1829 *Appeal* then was not so much an aberration or a lone voice of black militancy but the finished statement of growing African American disenchantment with the United States' Revolutionary tradition. The language of Walker's *Appeal* was uncompromising and its aim was to illustrate black "miseries and wretchedness in this *Republican Land of Liberty!!!!!*" To black Americans, Walker commended resistance, calling whites our "natural enemies," "oppressors," and "tyrants." Like Hamilton, Walker devoted a part of his pamphlet to debunking Jefferson's ideas on race. Jefferson's charges of racial inferiority must be "refuted by the blacks themselves," Walker felt, as he was one "of the great characters" of the American republic and his views would never "pass away into oblivion unobserved by this people and the world." Presciently predicting a Civil War, Walker asked white Americans to "REPENT" or their "DESTRUCTION is at hand." In his lesser known Ethiopian manifesto, published the same year, Robert Alexander Young also warned "the fiendish cast of men" who dared hold men in slavery of divine retribution. Walker ended his pamphlet by quoting from the Declaration of Independence, asking whites to compare their paltry "sufferings under Great Britain" with the "cruelties and murders" inflicted on black people. Walker's use of the Declaration was not so much to appeal to its principles as to reveal its hollowness in the context of black oppression.[16]

On the eve of the start of the abolitionist movement, African Americans continued to expand on this alternative tradition of protest. The Reverend William Paul Quinn of Pittsburgh echoed Walker's call for repentance and destruction and called all talk of liberty in a slave republic, "a burlesque" and an "insult to common sense." And Maria Stewart, inspired by Walker, exhorted black men to act "in the defence of African rights and liberty." Stewart, the first black woman abolitionist to speak in public in the 1820s, declared that the "unfriendly whites first drove the native American from his much loved home. Then they stole our fathers from their peaceful and quiet dwellings, and brought them hither, and made them bond-men and bond-women of them and their little ones." Black abolitionists infused their rhetoric and ideas with vehemence and condemnation. Garrison would soon incorporate their uncompromising style into his movement, even as he rejected their apocalyptic predictions of a violent conflagration that would consume slaveholders and the slaveholding republic.[17]

Increasingly, African Americans portrayed Great Britain, rather than the American Republic as the true exemplar of liberty. Few of them forgot that it was Lord Dunmore, the British governor of Virginia, who had made black emancipation an issue during the Revolutionary War, long before the colonists responded in kind. In a complete reversal of Revolutionary history, they portrayed America rather than Britain as the violator of liberty. After the abolition of slavery in the British West Indies, William Cooper Nell, who celebrated black military service in the War for Independence and the War of 1812 in his writings, asked ironically, "Shall Republican America heed the lessons imparted by Monarchical Europe?" African Americans started celebrating August first, the day of emancipation in the West Indies, rather than July fourth in "slavery-cursed America" as the day of black liberty and freedom. Recalling the services of black soldiers in the Continental Army during the Revolutionary War, Henry Highland Garnet remarked that "they little thought that the power against which they were fighting would one day emancipate all its slaves, while their own country would muster all her power, and make her mightiest effort to blot out the few scattering stars that linger in the horizon of their posterity's hopes." They had fought "the battles of liberty, while their backs were furrowed by the cruel scourge." But Garnet continued, "Unfortunate men!—They knew not that their children were to be immolated upon the altars of slavery—altars erected upon their very graves."[18] Nell and Garnet neglected to mention that more blacks fought as loyalists than as patriots in the Revolution.

As African Americans faced increasing legal and de facto discrimination in the antebellum period, they became more disillusioned with American republicanism. Revolutionary hero and black abolitionist James Forten likened American attempts to disfranchise African Americans as "characteristic of European despotism." As T.V.R. [most likely, black abolitionist Thomas van Rensselaer] put it, "It seems to have been THEN, as NOW, the settled policy of the *white* man, to have permitted the *colored* man, to an equal participation with himself in the dangers to which they are exposed in securing Republican Institutions; but when secured, he is content to enjoy them alone, hence the entire absence (almost) in American History, of any mention of the noble achievements of colored men." Similarly, a Henry Scott of Worcester, Massachusetts, wrote, "My forefathers at the South fought heroically in the revolution for independence. And what did it avail our race, either in the free or slave states. Its fruits were not for us—they were plucked for others—not for us."[19]

The national and state black conventions that met periodically in the thirty years before the Civil War to advocate black uplift and demand citizenship also dwelled on the false hopes American republicanism inspired. According to the address of the first national convention, held in Philadelphia in 1831, "the spirit of persecution" in "this boasted land of freedom" was the cause of its meeting. The 1834 New York convention's Declaration of Sentiment repeated the black abolitionist critique of the American republic, "That we find ourselves, after the lapse of three centuries, on the American continent, the remnants of a nation amounting to three millions of people, whose country has been pillaged, parents stolen, nine generations of which have been wasted by the oppressive cruelty of this nation, standing in the presence of the Supreme Ruler of the Universe, and the civilized world, appealing to the God of nations for deliverance." Again the emphasis was on the "cruelty" of the American republic rather than its promise.[20]

According to the national black conventions of the late antebellum period, not just slaveholders but the United States government itself was complicit in upholding slavery, an abolitionist conclusion that recent historians have seconded. When the national convention convened in 1843 in Buffalo after a hiatus of eight years, Samuel David laid out its purpose in his open-

ing address: "It is our right, our duty, and I hope I may say, our fixed determination, to make known our wrongs to the world, and to our oppressors;
to cease not day nor night to 'Tell, in burning words, our tale of woe.'" At
the 1847 convention in Troy, New York, the report of the Committee on
Abolition argued that "the power of the government, and the sanctity of
religion, church and state, are joined with the guilty oppressor against the
oppressed—and the voice of this great nation is thundering in the ear of
our enslaved fellow countrymen the terrible fiat, *you shall be slaves or die!*"
The 1855 convention at Philadelphia went so far as to address the American people, "in behalf of the sacred cause of HUMAN FREEDOM beaten
down and paralyzed by the force of American Example."[21] Increasingly,
African Americans meditated on the fact that they were in opposition to the
American government and its institutions.

Even the state black conventions, which were far more prone to appeal
to American republicanism and Revolutionary values in their fight for equal
suffrage and against discriminatory state laws, evinced a degree of disenchantment. The history of American slavery, said one report of the New
York state black convention of 1851, was "written in blood and black with
enormities and crimes." During the same year, in his address to the Ohio
state black convention, H. Ford Douglass, an advocate of black emigration,
felt that the history of the slave trade, slavery, and the fugitive slave law
"shrouds our country in blackness; every green spot in nature is blighted
and blasted by that withering Upas." No monument to "American liberty"
or the soils "fertilized by the blood" of Revolutionary heroes was exempt
from its effect. The 1858 Convention of the Colored Men of Ohio resolved
that if the Dred Scott decision was "a true exposition of the law of the land,
then are the founders of the American Republic convicted by their descendants of base hypocrisy, and colored men are absolved from all allegiance to
a government that withdraws all protection."[22] As the official and somewhat
staid voice of black communities, the conventions reveal the extent to which
even moderate black abolitionists had come to question the experiment in
republicanism in the United States.

African American abolitionists would seek to invent their own discourse
of revolution rather than merely appealing to American Revolutionary ideals of which they had grown skeptical. Despite the strong influence of Garrisonian moral suasion and pacifism, black abolitionists starting with Walker used the metaphor of revolution to justify the idea of a slave rebellion.

David Ruggles, who organized the New York Committee of Vigilance in 1835 to help fugitive slaves and free blacks kidnapped by slave catchers, had argued that "self-defence is the first law of nature." The fact that many black abolitionist leaders in the 1840s and 1850s were runaway slaves themselves served to strengthen the link between black abolitionism and slave resistance, giving birth to what Vincent Harding has called the "great tradition of black protest." During the fugitive slave controversy, Samuel Ringgold Ward argued, "Such crises as these leave us the right to Revolution, and if need be, that right we will, at whatever cost, most sacredly maintain."[23]

The most famous instance of a call for a slave rebellion was of course Henry Highland Garnet's *Address to the Slaves of the United States of America*. Repeatedly using the Revolutionary slogan, "Liberty or Death," Garnet urged "RESISTANCE! RESISTANCE! RESISTANCE!" by the slaves. In his pantheon of Revolutionary heroes, Garnet included Toussaint L'Ouverture, Denmark Vesey, Nat Turner, Cinque, and Madison Washington. Even a black Garrisonian such as Charles Remond insisted that Nat Turner should be revered as a revolutionary hero. Though the national black convention rejected Garnet's address in 1843 by one vote, it soon became one of the most influential documents written by a black abolitionist. In 1847, the Troy national convention under Frederick Douglass's leadership condemned advocacy of slave rebellion as "folly" and "suicidal." By the 1850s, however, a majority of African Americans and abolitionists, including erstwhile Garrisonians such as Douglass, openly advocated a violent overthrow of slavery. And while Douglass and his emigrationist rival Martin Delany adopted significantly different programs for black liberation in the decade before the Civil War, both featured a slave rebel as the hero in their works of fiction.[24]

After John Brown's raid on Harper's Ferry, black abolitionists published some of the most thoughtful justifications of the right to rebel against southern slaveholders. Brown, who paid to have Walker's *Appeal* and Garnet's *Address* published in a combined pamphlet in 1848, was clearly influenced by black abolitionists himself. For Ohio abolitionist Charles H. Langston, Brown acted in accordance with biblical precepts "to assist the weak and helpless" and "Revolutionary principles" to resist tyrants. The Reverend J. Sella Martin noted that Brown was condemned because "in America [revolutionary] means have been used for *white* men" but Brown used them for "*black* men." Meetings of "colored citizens" in Detroit and Pittsburgh vowed resistance to tyranny and sang "La Marseillaise" as they commemorated the raid and Brown. In *A Voice from Harper's Ferry*, Osborne P. Anderson, one of the black men who accompanied John Brown in his raid and escaped to tell the tale, invoked the Revolutionary tradition to justify slave rebellions: "There is an unbroken chain of sentiment and purpose from Moses of the Jews to John Brown of America; from Kossuth, and the liberators of France and Italy, to the untutored Gabriel, and the Denmark Veseys, Nat Turners and Madison Washingtons of the Southern American States." Thomas Hamilton, editor of the *Weekly Anglo-African*, published the *Confessions of Nat Turner* in 1859 and in his headnote comparing Brown and Turner baldly predicted, "Emancipation must take place, and soon. There can be no long delay in the choice of methods. If John Brown's be not adopted by the free North, then Nat Turner's will be by the enslaved South." As he argued, "We want Nat Turner—not speeches; Denmark Vesey—not resolutions; John Brown—not meetings."[25]

Douglass reiterated that slavery would be abolished "the John Brown way." In "A letter to the American Slaves from Those Who Have Fled from American Slavery," he asserted, "When the insurrections of the Southern slaves shall take place, as take place it will, unless speedily prevented by voluntary emancipation, the great mass of the colored men of the North, however much to the grief of any of us, will be found by your side, with deep-stored and long-accumulated revenge in their hearts, and with death-dealing weapons in their hands." Comparing the cause of the slave with that of the American Revolution, he pointed out, "If the American revolutionists had excuse for shedding but one drop of blood, then have the American slaves excuse for making blood flow 'even unto the horse bridles.'"[26]

In calling for a revolution against American slavery and slaveholders, black abolitionists drew inspiration from the Haitian rather than the American Revolution. They revealed the enormous ideological influence of the Haitian revolution, the only instance of a successful slave rebellion in world history, exercised on their political imagination. In his oration on the abolition of the slave trade, Jeremiah Gloucester praised the "brilliant exploits" of the Haitians in abolishing slavery and "proclaim[ing] the imprescribable[sic] rights of man." Prince Saunders, an advocate of emigration to Haiti and author of the *Haytian Papers*, related "the traits of bravery and heroism" and "martial valour" of the "Haytien people" who "chose death over slavery." For Saunders, it was grievous that "white men have

hitherto considered it imprudent to acknowledge" the bravery and independence "of their fellow men in Hayti." In his 1826 commencement address
at Bowdoin College, John Russwurm, one of the first black college graduates in the country, extolled the Haitian revolution and the progress of the
black republic. *Freedom's Journal*, the first (and short-lived) black abolitionist newspaper in the late 1820s, devoted several columns to the history of
Haiti and its leader, Toussaint L'Ouverture. The editors, Samuel Cornish
and Russwurm, took it upon themselves to redeem the historical reputation of the Haitian revolution. As they wrote, "The American Revolution
which first led the way in asserting the great principles of liberty, was hailed
with enthusiasm by the wise and the good. . . . But the revolution of St.
Domingo . . . no one wished it well—no fervent prayer was put up for its
success—none bid it 'God Speed.'"[27]

Black abolitionists defended the record of the Haitian revolution from
its detractors, anticipating the efforts of twentieth-century black activists
and intellectuals such as C. L. R. James. According to R. [Charles B. Ray?],
"The immolations and martyrdoms on the plains of St. Domingo, in opposition to cruel and aristocratic oppression, though written as they are on
the pages of history, in characters of blood, should be as 'balm to our souls,
and incense to our worship.' They are sureties to us, that as a race, *we cannot be crushed.* . . . ST. DOMINGO, *the Republic of the sea*, is an altar from
which incense will ever rise to our deliverance, and on which we should
ever delight to look, as a consecrated fane [flame?] in our *liberty-worship*
and our *liberty-efforts.*" In his "Lecture on the Haytien Revolutions; With a
Sketch of the Character of Toussaint L'Ouverture," James McCune Smith,
Glasgow-trained black physician and abolitionist, set out to write a full and
objective history of the revolution. Noting that five thousand African slaves
died each year in Haiti prior to the revolution, Smith compared this holo-
caust in black lives to the casualties of the "*wars, insurrections* and *massacres*"
of the revolution, and he praised Toussaint for abolishing slavery and caste
in the island.[28]

African American abolitionists would use the example of Haiti to write
a different history of revolution for black Americans and to challenge the
revolutionary status of the American War of Independence for not completely ridding the nation of slavery. The Garrisonian William Wells
Brown and the nationalist James Theodore Holly, both of whom spoke and
wrote about revolution in the late antebellum period, usually evoked the

example of the Haitian revolution rather than the American Revolution. In fact, Wells Brown found the latter wanting in comparison to the former. As he wrote, "Would that the fathers of the American Revolution had been as consistent!" Toussaint he argued "liberated his countrymen; Washington enslaved a portion of his, and aided in giving strength and vitality to an institution that will one day rent asunder the UNION that he helped form." Brown not only justified the bloodletting of the Haitian revolution but also wishfully hoped that a similar rebellion would consume the slave South. Holly, who unlike Brown recommended black immigration to Haiti, called the Haitian revolution, "the grandest political event of this or any age. . . . [I]t surpasses the American revolution in an incomparable degree." The "model Republicans" and "*liberty loving* and *democratic* fellow citizens of the United States" were, like "the white colonists of St. Domingo," consumed with race hatred. Haiti, he argued, was the only "black nationality in the New World," "the Fatherland of the race," and there was more freedom for American blacks among the "monarchical Negroes of Hayti" than "in this bastard democracy."[29]

Perhaps the best attempt to view the Revolutionary heritage of the country through the perspective of African Americans remains Douglass's well-known speech "What to the Slave is the Fourth of July," which powerfully and poetically spelled out the black abolitionist critique of the American Revolution. As he famously put it, "The sunlight that brought life and healing to you, has brought stripes and death to me. This Fourth [of] July is *yours*, not *mine*. You may rejoice, I must mourn. To drag a man in fetters into the grand illuminated temple of liberty, and call upon him to join you in joyous anthems, were inhuman mockery and sacrilegious irony." The United States, Delany reiterated was a "*slaveholding, oppressing* country." According to William P. Newman, "the real and true mission" of the American republic is "bonds and death." After the Dred Scott decision, black abolitionists reflected bitterly on the Revolutionary republican tradition in the United States. For Robert Purvis, American claims to ideas of liberty and freedom showed a "sublimity of impudence that knows no parallel."[30]

Douglass would present the finished statement of the black counternarrative of the history of the American republic in his brilliant but lesser-known 1853 speech "A Nation in the Midst of a Nation." It was left to him and a later generation of black abolitionists to criticize the emerging historical reputation of the United States as a New World haven for immigrants fleeing

Old World poverty and tyranny. The history of black people in the United States, he said, using Irish nationalist Daniel O'Connell's allusion, may be traced like the blood of a wounded man through a crowd. "Our wrongs and outrages are as old as our country. They date back to its earliest settlement, and extend through two hundred and thirty years—and they are as numerous and as oft-repeated as the days of all these years." African Americans were "aliens" in their "native land" and treated worse than "strangers" in "the soil of our birth, in a country which has known us for centuries, among a people who did not wait for us to seek them, but a people who sought us, and who brought us to their own chosen land." Americans had sympathy for everyone except African Americans. "The Hungarian, the Italian, the Irishman, the Jew, and the Gentile, all find in this land a home. . . . For these people, the Americans have principles of justice, maxims of mercy, sentiments of religion, and feelings of brotherhood in abundance. But for my poor people enslaved—blasted and ruined—it would appear, that America has neither justice, mercy nor religion. She has no scales in which to weigh our wrongs—she has no standard by which to measure our rights." Douglass spoke he said as "a colored man," a victim of "American oppression," and not as an exemplar of its liberties.[31]

The metaphor of revolution in black abolitionist ideology thus gave birth to an alternative tradition of political radicalism. It allowed African Americans to create an oppositional ideology that not only pointed to the shortcomings of American Revolutionary ideals but also exposed its complicity in upholding racial slavery. Black abolitionists made the heritage of the American Revolution a contested terrain. And some used the metaphor of revolution by alluding not to the American War of Independence but to slave rebellion and the Haitian revolution. African American abolitionists sought to reinvent the idea of revolution in their fight against slavery and racism and to imbue it with new meanings.

ACKNOWLEDGMENTS

Eric Foner's course on the radical tradition in American history inspired this article. I thank Ira Berlin, Iver Bernstein, Richard Newman, Karsten Stueber, and audiences at the 2004 annual meeting of the Organization of American Historians in Boston, the American Antiquarian Society Seminar at Clark University, and the Civil War Institute at Pennsylvania State University for their comments.

NOTES

1. Benjamin Quarles, *Black Abolitionists* (New York, 1969); Donald Jacobs, ed., *Courage and Conscience: Black and White Abolitionists in Boston* (Bloomington, 1993); Paul Goodman, *Of One Blood: Abolitionism and the Origins of Racial Equality* (Berkeley, 1998); Richard S. Newman, *The Transformation of American Abolitionism: Fighting Slavery in the Early Republic* (Chapel Hill, 2002).

2. David W. Blight, *Frederick Douglass's Civil War: Keeping Faith in Jubilee* (Baton Rouge, 1989); Waldo E. Martin Jr., *The Mind of Frederick Douglass* (Chapel Hill, 1984); R. J. M. Blackett, *Building an Antislavery Wall: Black Americans in the Atlantic Abolitionist Movement, 1830–1860* (Baton Rouge, 1983); John Stauffer, *The Black Hearts of Men: Radical Abolitionists and the Transformation of Race* (Cambridge, Mass., 2002); Mia Bay, *The White Image in the Black Mind: African American Ideas about White People, 1830–1925* (New York, 2000); Patrick Rael, *Black Identity and Black Protest in the Antebellum North* (Chapel Hill, 2002); Eddie S. Glaude Jr., *Exodus! Religion, Race, and Nation in Early Nineteenth-Century Black America* (Chicago, 2000).

3. Frederick Cooper, "Elevating the Race: The Social Thought of Black Leaders, 1827–50," *American Quarterly* 24 (Dec. 1972): 604–25. David Blight argues that for black abolitionists such as James McCune Smith, "self-improvement meant black elevation, much more than an emulation of moral values identified as 'white.'" Blight, "In Search of Learning, Liberty, and Self-Definition: James McCune Smith and the Ordeal of the Antebellum Black Intellectual," *Afro-Americans in New York Life and History* 9 (July 1985): 13–14. See also Rael, introduction to *Black Identity and Black Protest.* For an insightful study of class in a black community, see Leslie M. Harris, *In the Shadow of Slavery: African Americans in New York City, 1626–1863* (Chicago, 2003).

4. Vincent Harding, *There Is a River: The Black Struggle for Freedom in America* (New York, 1981); Sterling Stuckey, introduction to *The Ideological Origins of*

Black Nationalism (Boston, 1972). For a criticism of the "assimilationist petite bourgeoisie" strain of pre–Civil War black activism, see Ernest Allen Jr., "Afro-American Identity: Reflections on the pre-Civil War Era," *Contributions in Black Studies* 7 (1985–86): 45–93. For a similar argument, see Steven Hahn, *A Nation under Our Feet: Black Political Struggles in the Rural South from Slavery to the Great Migration* (Cambridge, Mass., 2003).

5. Rael, for example, concludes that African American abolitionists "operated within the paradigm of the continuing revolution. They in fact relied on it so much that they became unparalleled champions of its principles." *Black Identity and Black Protest*, 280; David Brion Davis, *The Problem of Slavery in the Age of Revolution, 1770–1823* (Ithaca, 1975).

6. For the impact of revolutionary ideas on slave resistance, see C. L. R. James, *The Black Jacobin: Toussaint L'Ouverture and the San Domingo Revolution* (New York, 1963); Eugene D. Genovese, *From Rebellion to Revolution: Afro-American Slave Revolts in the Making of the Modern World* (Baton Rouge, 1979); Douglas R. Egerton, *Gabriel's Rebellion: The Virginia Slave Conspiracies of 1800 and 1802* (Chapel Hill, 1993); Laurent Dubois, *Avengers of the New World: The Story of the Haitian Revolution* (Cambridge, Mass., 2004); F. Nwabueze Okoye, "Chattel Slavery as the Nightmare of the American Revolutionaries," *William and Mary Quarterly* 37 (Jan. 1980): 3–28. For a view of the relationship between revolutionary ideas and African American resistance to slavery that is very different from mine, see Francois Furstenberg, "Beyond Slavery and Freedom: Autonomy, Agency, and Resistance in Early American Political Discourse," *Journal of American History* 89 (March 2003): 1295–330.

7. Herbert Aptheker, ed., *From the Colonial Times through the Civil War*, vol. 1 of *A Documentary History of the Negro People in the United States* (New York, 1950), 1–12; Sidney Kaplan and Emma Nogrady Kaplan, eds., *The Black Presence in the Era of the American Revolution, 1770–1800* (Washington, D.C., 1973), 11–15, 26–31; Thomas J. Davis, "Emancipation Rhetoric, Natural Rights, and Revolutionary New England: A Note on Four Black Petitions in Massachusetts, 1773–1777," *New England Quarterly* 57 (1989): 248–64. On black republicanism, see also chapter 2 in John Saillant, *Black Puritan, Black Republican: The Life and Thought of Lemuel Haynes, 1753–1833* (New York, 2003).

8. On the early black public sphere, see Joanna Brooks, "The Early American Public Sphere and the Emergence of a Black Print Counterpublic," *William and Mary Quarterly* 62 (Jan. 2005): 67–98; Vincent Carretta, ed., *Unchained Voices: An Anthology of Black Authors in the English-Speaking World of the Eighteenth Century* (Lexington, Ky., 1996); Vincent Carretta and Philip Gould, eds., *Genius in Bondage: Literature of the Early Black Atlantic* (Lexington, Ky., 2001); Joanna Brooks and John Saillant eds., *Face Zion Forward: First Writers of the Black Atlantic, 1785–*

1798 (Boston, 2002); Dickson D. Bruce Jr., *The Origins of African American Literature, 1680–1865* (Charlottesville, 2001).

9. Joanne Pope Melish, *Disowning Slavery: Gradual Emancipation and "Race" in New England, 1780–1830* (Ithaca, 1998); John Wood Sweet, *Bodies Politic: Negotiating Race in the American North, 1730–1830* (Baltimore, 2003) . Both Melish and Sweet, however, emphasize racism at the cost of black agency. Aptheker, *From the Colonial Times*, 25.

10. Prince Hall, "A Charge," (1797), Absalom Jones and Richard Allen, "A Narrative of the Proceedings of the Black People during the Late Awful Calamity in Philadelphia," (1794), and Daniel Coker, "A Dialogue between a Virginian and an African Minister," (1810) all in *Pamphlets of Protest: An Anthology of Early African American Protest Literature*, ed. Richard Newman, Patrick Rael, and Phillip Lapansky, 41–42, 45, 54 (New York, 2001); Egerton, *Gabriel's Rebellion*.

11. Mitch Kachun, chapter 1 in *Festivals of Freedom: Memory and Meaning in African American Emancipation Celebrations* (Amherst, 2003). Kachun, however, emphasizes the celebratory rather than the oppositional character of the slave trade orations and does not discuss Johnson's or Carman's orations, which have never been reprinted in collections of black abolitionist documents. See also David Waldstreicher, *In the Midst of Perpetual Fetes: The Making of American Nationalism, 1776–1820* (Chapel Hill, 1997); William B. Gravely, "The Dialectic of Double-Consciousness in Black American Freedom Celebrations, 1808–1863," *Journal of Negro History* 67 (Winter 1982): 302–17.

12. Russell Parrot, "An Oration on the Abolition of the Slave Trade" (1814), in *Pamphlets of Protest*, 45, 75, 127; Peter Williams, Jun., "An Oration on the Abolition of the Slave Trade Delivered in the African Church in the City of New York, January 1, 1808," 346, 348; and William Hamilton, "An Oration on the Abolition of the Slave Trade, Delivered in the Episcopal Asbury African Church, in Elizabeth St. New York, January 2, 1815," 396, both in *Early Negro Writing, 1760–1837*, ed. Dorothy Porter (Boston, 1971); Absalom Jones, *A Thanksgiving Sermon Preached January 1, 1808, in St. Thomas's, or the African Episcopal Church, Philadelphia: On Account of the Abolition of the Slave Trade on That Day by Congress of the United States* (Philadelphia, 1808), 7, 14; Henry Johnson, *An Oration on the Abolition of the African Slave Trade with an Introductory Address by Adam Carman Delivered in the African Church of New York January 1, 1810* (New York, 1810), 8, 10; Henry Sipkins, *Oration of the Abolition of the Slave Trade Delivered in the African Church in the City of New York January 2, 1809* (New York, 1809), 13–14.

13. Adam Carman, *An Oration Delivered at the Fourth Anniversary of the Abolition of the African Slave Trade, in the African Methodist Episcopal Church, in Second Street, New York, January 1, 1811* (New York, 1811), 3, 11–13. On Paul Cuffee, see Lamont D. Thomas, *Rise to Be a People: A Biography of Paul Cuffee* (Urbana,

1986). For a different argument, see Philip Gould, *Barbaric Traffic: Commerce and Antislavery in the Eighteenth-Century Atlantic World* (Cambridge, Mass., 2003).

14. George Lawrence, *An Oration on the Abolition of the Slave Trade Delivered on the First Day of January, 1813, in the African Methodist Episcopal Church* (New York, 1813), 13; Carman, *An Oration*, 19. For a view of racism in the early republic that sees black abolitionists as complicit rather than resistant to ideas on race, see Bruce Dain, *A Hideous Monster of the Mind: American Race Theory in the Early Republic* (Cambridge, Mass., 2002).

15. Nathaniel Paul, *An Address Delivered on the Celebration of the Abolition of Slavery in the State of New York, July 5, 1827* (Albany, 1827), 11–12; William Hamilton, "An Oration Delivered in the African Zion Church, on the Fourth of July, 1827, In Commemoration of the Abolition of Domestic Slavery in this State," (New York, 1827); and Joseph Sidney, "An Oration Commemorative of the Abolition of the Slave Trade in the United States; Delivered before the Wilberforce Philanthropic Association in the City of New York, on the Second of January, 1809," both in *Early Negro Writing*, 101, 360–62.

16. *Walker's Appeal and Garnet's Address to the Slaves of the United States of America* (New York, 1969), esp. 11–13, 18, 22–27, 31, 51–66, 76. See also Peter P. Hinks, *To Awaken My Afflicted Brethren: David Walker and the Problem of Antebellum Slave Resistance* (University Park, Pa., 1997). Hinks, however, stresses the Christian evangelical strain in Walker's appeal rather than its critique of revolutionary republicanism. Robert Alexander Young, "Ethiopian Manifesto," (1829) in *Pamphlets of Protest*, 87–88.

17. "The Origins, Horrors, and Results of Slavery, Faithfully and Minutely Described in a Series of Facts, and Its Advocates Pathetically Addressed by the Rev. W. Paul Quinn of African Descent," (Pittsburgh, 1834) in *Early Negro Writings*, 624–25, 630; Maria Stewart, "Productions," (1835) in *Pamphlets of Protest*, 75, 124, 127. For a study of black abolitionist rhetoric, see Jacqueline Bacon, *The Humblest May Stand Forth: Rhetoric, Empowerment, and Abolition* (Columbia, S.C., 2002).

18. *North Star*, May 5, August 11, 1848; *Address in Commemoration of the Great Jubilee, of the 1st of August, 1834*, 2, 4; *Colored American*, May 30, 1840; John R. McKivigan and Jason H. Silverman, "Monarchical Liberty and Republican Slavery: West Indian Emancipation Celebrations in Upstate New York and Canada," *Afro-Americans in New York Life and History* 10 (January 1986): 10–12; Kachun, *Festivals of Freedom*, chapter 2. For the politics of slavery during the American Revolution, see Christopher Leslie Brown, *Moral Capital: Foundations of British Abolitionism* (Chapel Hill, 2006). For the recent literature on black loyalists see Cassandra Pybus, *Epic Journeys of Freedom: Runaway Slaves of the American Revolution and Their Global Quest for Liberty* (Boston, 2006); Simon Schama, *Rough Crossings: Britain, the Slaves, and the American Revolution* (New York, 2006).

19. James Forten, "Series of Letters by a Man of Colour," (1813) in *Pamphlets of Protest*, 69–70. On Forten, see Julie Winch, *A Gentleman of Color: The Life of James Forten* (New York, 2002); *Colored American*, January 29, 1839, February 27, 1841.

20. *Constitution of the American Society of Free Persons of Colour, for Improving Their Condition in the United States; For Purchasing Lands; and for the Establishment of a Settlement in Upper Canada, also the Proceedings of the Convention, with Their Address to the Free persons of Colour in the United States* 9–10; *Minutes and Proceedings of the First Annual Convention of the People of Colour, Held by Adjournments in the City of Philadelphia, From the Sixth to the Eleventh of June Inclusive, 1831*, 12, 15; *Minutes and Proceedings of the Third Annual Convention, For the Improvement of the Free People of Colour In these United States, Held by Adjournments in the City of Philadelphia From the 3d to the 13th of June Inclusive, 1833*, 28, 32–33; *Minutes of the Fourth Annual Convention for the Improvement of the Free People of Colour In the United States, Held by Adjournments in the Asbury Church, New York from the 2d to the 12th of June Inclusive, 1834*, 4, 28, all in *Minutes of the Proceedings of the National Negro Conventions, 1830–1864*, ed. Holman Bell (New York, 1969).

21. *Minutes of the National Convention of Colored Citizens: Held at Buffalo, On the 15th, 16th, 17th, 18th, and 19th of August, 1843. For the Purpose of Considering their Moral and Political Condition as American Citizens*, 5; *Proceedings of the National Convention of Colored People, and Their Friends, Held in Troy, N.Y., on the 6th, 7th, 8th, and 9th October, 1847*, 31; *Proceedings of the Colored National Convention, Held in Rochester, July 6th, 7th, and 8th, 1853*, 16; *Proceedings of the Colored National Convention, Held in Franklin Hall, Sixth Street, Below Arch, Philadelphia, October 16th, 17th, and 18th, 1855*, 30, all in *Minutes of the Proceedings of the National Negro Conventions*. See, for example, Don F. Fehrenbacher, *The Slaveholding Republic: An Account of the United States Government's Relations to Slavery*, comp. and ed. Ward McAfee (New York, 2001), and Leonard Richards, *The Slave Power: The Free North and Southern Domination, 1780–1860* (Baton Rouge, 2000).

22. Philip S. Foner and George E. Walker, eds., vol. 1 of *Proceedings of the Black State Conventions, 1840–1865* (Philadelphia, 1979), 74, 261, 333; Philip S. Foner and George E. Walker eds., vol. 2 of *Proceedings of the Black State Conventions, 1840–1865* (Philadelphia, 1980), 131.

23. Harding, *There Is a River*; David Ruggles to editor, *New York Sun* [July 1836], in *The Black Abolitionist Papers*, vol. 3, *The United States, 1830–1846*, ed. C. Peter Ripley, 169 (Chapel Hill, 1991); speech by Samuel Ringgold Ward delivered at Faneuil Hall, Boston, Massachusetts, March 25, 1850, in *The Black Abolitionist Papers*, vol. 4, *The United States, 1847–1858*, 51.

24. *Walker's Appeal and Garnet's Address*, 84–86. On Garnet, see Joel Schor, *Henry Highland Garnet: A Voice of Black Radicalism in the Nineteenth Century* (Westport, Conn., 1977); Martin B. Pasternak, *Rise Now and Fly to Arms: The Life*

of *Henry Highland Garnet* (New York, 1995); Speech by Charles Lenox Remond delivered at Marlboro Chapel, Boston, Massachusetts, May 29, 1844, in *The Black Abolitionist Papers*, 3:443–44; "Debate over Garnet's 'Address to the Slaves of the United States of America,'" (1843) and "Proceedings of the National Convention of the Colored People," (1847) both in *Pamphlets of Protest*, 157–59, 176.

25. Benjamin Quarles ed., *Blacks on John Brown* (Urbana, Ill., 1972), 4–5, 9, 13, 17–18, 20–25, 27, 38; *New York Weekly Anglo-African*, April 27, 1861, in *The Black Abolitionist Papers*, vol. 5, *The United States, 1859–1865*, 112.

26. *Frederick Douglass' Paper* June 9, 1854; *North Star*, September 5, 1850; Frederick Douglass, *The Frederick Douglass Papers*, ser. 1, *Speeches, Debates, and Interviews*, vol. 2, *1847–54*, 130–32, 148–58, 272–77, vol. 3, *1855–63*, 312–22, 412–20, ed. John W. Blassingame (New Haven, 1979–92).

27. Gloucester is quoted by Kachun, *Festivals of Freedom*, 30; Prince Saunders, *Haytian Papers: A Collection of the Interesting Proclamations and Other Official Documents, Together with Some Account of the Rise, Progress, and Present State of the Kingdom of Hayti* (Boston, 1818), 81, 111, 115, and Saunders, *A Memoir Presented to the American Convention for Promoting the Abolition of Slavery and Improving the Condition of the African Race* (Philadelphia, 1818), 19; John B. Russwurm, "The Condition and Prospects of Hayti," ed. Philip S. Foner, *Journal of Negro History* 54 (Oct. 1969): 393–97; *Freedom's Journal*, March 16, April 20, 27, May 4, 11, 18, June 15, 29, October 12, 1827; all quotations are from April 6, 1827.

28. *Colored American* June 4, August 7, 28, October 2, 9, 1841.

29. William Wells Brown, "The History of the Haitian Revolution" (1855), 243, 249, 252–53, 264–65, and J. Theodore Holly, "A Vindication of the Capacity of the Negro for Self-Government and Civilized Progress" (1857) both in *Pamphlets of Protest*, 278–79.

30. Frederick Douglass, "What to the Slave Is the Fourth of July?" in *Narrative of the Life of Frederick Douglass, an American Slave, Written by Himself, with Related Documents*, ed. and with an introduction by David W. Blight, 156, 158–59 (Boston, 2003); William P. Newman to Frederick Douglass, 1 October 1850; Martin R. Delany, John C. Peck, William Webb, and Thomas Burrows to editor, *Kingston Morning Journal*, 31 May 1853, and speech by Robert Purvis delivered at the City Assembly Rooms, New York, New York, 12 May 1857, all in *The Black Abolitionist Papers*, 4:61, 160, 363.

31. Douglass, *Frederick Douglass Papers*, 2:424–28. For a somewhat different view of African American historical understanding than the one in this essay, see John Ernest, *Liberation Historiography: African American Writers and the Challenge of History, 1794–1861* (Chapel Hill, 2004).

Chapter Two

Isaiah Rynders and the Ironies of Popular Democracy in Antebellum New York

TYLER ANBINDER

The election day scene that brisk autumn day was typical of mid-nine-teenth-century New York City. Hundreds of men, dressed in long, rough overcoats and tall stovepipe hats to ward off the cold, thronged the street outside a polling place in a working-class neighborhood. Many were in a boisterous mood, having fortified themselves at nearby saloons for the an-ticipated rushing and shoving and fighting and brawling—what were popu-larly referred to as "election sports." At booths outside the polls, campaign workers handed out ballots and harangued the crowd with exhortations to vote for their candidates. Voters jostled their way into the line that wound from the ballot box far out into the street.

Suddenly a loud cry pierced the air and all eyes turned to "a lithe, dark, handsome man" standing atop a packing crate. "*I am Isaiah Rynders!*" he shouted, knowing that his name alone would strike fear into the hearts of many within earshot. "My club is here, scattered among you! We know you! Five hundred of you are from Philadelphia—brought here to vote the Whig ticket! Damn you! If you don't leave these polls in five minutes, *we will dirk every mother's son of you!*" New York voters, and even many visitors from Philadelphia, would have known that "Ike" Rynders did not make idle threats. Within minutes, wrote an eyewitness, "five hundred men left the polls, . . . and went home without voting, for fear of assassination."[1]

In his heyday, Isaiah Rynders was one of the best known residents of New York. "He was so conspicuous as to overshadow all the other local leaders of the Democracy," remembered the *Times* years later. During the 1840s and '50s, he and his followers intimidated thousands of voters, dictated Democratic nominations in both the city and state, and instigated what was—up to that time—the most deadly riot in New York City's history. Rynders was even said to have single-handedly determined the outcome of a presidential election. Yet today, only a small handful of historians even know his name.[2]

Rynders and others of his ilk have fallen into obscurity in part because few historians consider local political leaders worthy of careful examination. Rynders and his fellow "ward heelers" are also neglected because few left manuscript collections to facilitate the recovery of their histories. But perhaps the main reason Rynders and politicians like him have been neglected is that Northern Democrats like Rynders are by far the least scrutinized of the major Civil War–era political groups. Admirable Republicans and their Whig and Free Soil predecessors have been thoroughly studied, and the nativist Know Nothing party has been the subject of a number of books and articles in recent years. Southern Democrats and nationalists, as instigators of the Civil War, have always received their fair share of historians' attention, and there has been a recent glut of works on Southern unionism as well.[3] In contrast, no full account of the antebellum Northern Democratic party has been written since Roy F. Nichols's *Disruption of American Democracy* more than half a century ago. The only recent work on Northern Democrats, Jean Baker's excellent *Affairs of Party*, devotes very little attention to urban machine politicians such as Rynders.[4]

As a renowned polling place thug, Rynders hardly seems deserving of the name "Democrat." Yet he and his followers believed wholeheartedly that their tactics were a necessary facet of popular politics. Theirs was democracy in the truest American sense, they thought, for as in the days of '76, the people literally fought for their rights against entrenched elites. It is vital that we recover the forgotten stories of Northern Democrats such as Rynders if we are to better appreciate the many definitions of democracy that coexisted in mid-nineteenth-century America. Rynders's story reveals an alternative conception of citizenship, freedom of speech, and democracy, one that is little appreciated today, but that once represented the views of millions of Americans. Though Rynders is hardly an admirable figure, understanding him, his followers, and their sympathizers is crucial if we are to better comprehend the nature of the antebellum Democratic party and the political dynamics of the Civil War era.

The life of Isaiah Rynders, noted the *New York Times* without exaggeration years later, "forms one of the most romantic of histories." He was born in 1804 in Waterford, New York, a river town along the Hudson ten miles north of Albany, to Protestant parents—a German American father and an Irish American mother. Rynders eventually began to work on the river, earning his lifelong title of "Captain" by commanding a sloop on the Hudson that carried produce and merchandise between New York and upstate river towns. He eventually tired of the waterman's life. By 1830 he had moved to the South, acquiring some notoriety there as a riverboat gambler. In 1832, after allegedly killing a man in a knife duel over a card game in Natchez, he fled to South Carolina. There he became "superintendent" of the racing stables of General Wade Hampton, grandfather of the future U.S. senator of that name. After Hampton died and the panic of 1837 depressed the horse racing business, Rynders returned to New York and settled in Manhattan.[5]

In New York, Rynders became "a thorough-going sporting-man." Sporting men did not hold steady jobs but instead devoted themselves to gambling, politics, boxing, and horses. An entire "sporting" subculture developed in New York, with its own saloons, own patois, even its own newspapers. One, the *Clipper*, noted that Rynders had "a strong love for the card-room and the race-track." Another admiring journalist reported that the Captain was often found dealing faro or "presiding at one of those suppers of oysters, canvas-back ducks, and champagne with which the gamblers of New York nightly regale their friends and customers."[6]

Many sporting men were muscular bruisers, but young Rynders was a man "of medium size and sinewy form, with a prominent nose, and piercing black eyes—a knowing smile, and a sharp look altogether. He was cool and enterprising in his manners, and fluent and audacious in his speech." Unlike others in the "sporting fraternity," Rynders was not an especially skillful pugilist. A tough country minister, Sherlock Bristol, boasted in his autobiography that he fought Rynders to a draw on a Hudson River steamer after defying Rynders by signing an antislavery petition. But as a *leader* of fighters, Rynders was unsurpassed.[7]

It was in that capacity that Rynders rocketed to prominence in 1844. Realizing that Democrats needed to form some sort of organization to rally the faithful during that year's tight presidential race between their candidate, James K. Polk, and the Whig Henry Clay, Rynders established the Empire Club. With a membership dominated by sporting men and prizefighters, the club began to whip up support for Polk. Political veterans believed that whoever captured New York's electoral votes would carry the presidency, and Rynders worked feverishly to turn out the Democratic vote. Led by Rynders on a "white charger," one thousand Empire Club members marched at the head of a Polk parade in New York on the eve of the election, with "music, and thousands of torches, Roman candles, rockets, and transparencies, with never ending hurrahs for Polk and Dallas, Texas, Oregon, Fifty-four-forty-or-fight!" The following day, Rynders and his club worked feverishly to prevent Whigs from casting ballots. New York swung to Polk by just 5,100 votes out of 486,000 cast, and with New York's 36 electoral votes, Polk carried the election.[8]

Although Whigs and Democrats alike gave Rynders credit for Polk's razor-thin margin of victory, and nearly every biographical sketch of Rynders reiterates his central role in Polk's triumph, none of the contemporary newspapers mention any extraordinary scenes of violence or intimidation at the polls on election day.[9] In fact, it would have been perfectly consistent with the sporting men's bragging ways for Rynders to have overemphasized his role in Young Hickory's victory. Many historians now ascribe Clay's defeat in New York to his "flip-flopping" on the annexation of Texas, which could have driven Whigs to vote for the Liberty Party candidate. But contemporaries of both major parties cited Rynders as the cause of Clay's defeat. According to the *New York Herald*'s Washington correspondent, when Clay met Rynders for the first time in 1848, the Kentuckian "inquired, with a smile, 'Have I the honor of an acquaintance with the man who elected Mr. Polk?' The Captain, being a modest hero, blushed, and responded in the affirmative." Polk and his advisers were likewise convinced that Rynders had played a key role in their victory. In gratitude, the new president rewarded Rynders with a lucrative no-show job as "measurer" in the New York customhouse, allowing the Captain to devote his full attention to horses, gambling, and politics.[10]

After 1844, Rynders and the Empire Club became powers in New York politics, dictating the outcomes of primary meetings and disrupting political gatherings of their opponents. Rynders was feared both outside and within the Democratic party. In early 1845, for example, Rynders and his Empire Club compatriots attended a gathering at Tammany Hall (the Democratic headquarters in New York City) organized to discuss the Texas annexation issue. "Aided by a crew of his noisy associates," complained the *Evening Post*, Rynders "took the resolutions prepared by the committee of arrangements and reformed them to suit his own ideas of public policy." His men shouted down speakers and bullied the meeting into adopting a more stridently proannexation pronouncement. No man before Rynders had ever so boldly and impudently dominated Tammany's public gatherings. Yet Rynders was not an ignorant thug. He could recite entire scenes of Shakespeare from memory. Later in life he became intensely interested in the spiritual world and could often be found at New York séances.[11]

By 1848, Rynders had become one of the best known men in New York. Tammany leaders made sure never to enter a meeting or convention without first trying to secure Rynders's support, because his Empire Club bullies could terrorize the participants at virtually any political gathering. But the ambitious Captain wanted to become one of those leaders himself. Newspapers across the Northeast mentioned Rynders as a possible vice presidential nominee; some even wondered if a presidential bid might be in the offing. Rynders realized that such speculation was mere partisan bluster and focused his attention on the New York scene. In a series of audacious moves at midcentury, Rynders thrust himself even more boldly to the forefront of Manhattan civic life, fomenting a deadly riot, throwing an abolitionist convention into chaos, and making his first bid for elective office.[12]

The riot originated in events that today would hardly seem capable of precipitating more than twenty deaths: a dispute between the admirers of two leading actors. In the mid-nineteenth century, however, New Yorkers of all classes were avid theatergoers. Among the favorite leading men of the day were William Macready, an English star who was especially popular in elite New York circles, and Edwin Forrest, an American-born thespian who was the favorite of the working class. In the late 1840s, the two stars became embroiled in a newspaper war of words, accusing each other of butchering the plays they performed. Forrest escalated the dispute by hissing Macready during a performance in London. Macready retaliated by making disparaging remarks about American theatrical audiences, comments many of Forrest's supporters interpreted as insults to all Americans. When it was announced in the spring of 1849 that Macready, after an absence of many years, would perform *Macbeth* in New York at the new Astor Place Opera House, the impending engagement quickly became the talk of the town.

At nineteenth-century American theatrical performances, working-class audience members often interrupted the actors by shouting out comments or hissing the characters on stage. Such behavior was common in the Bowery's cheap theaters, whose customers most admired Forrest's "muscular" style, but was generally frowned upon at the upscale venues whose patrons preferred Macready's more subtle interpretations of the classics. The Astor Place Opera House sought explicitly to attract only these more elite theater-goers, instituting a dress code that required a cleanly shaven face, a "fresh waist coat," and kid gloves. Despite these restrictions, when Macready took to the stage on May 7, he was booed and hissed so incessantly by Forrest's supporters (who had come for that purpose) that he and the other actors soon began acting out the play in pantomime, knowing it was futile to try to be heard above the din.[13]

Leading the hissers was Isaiah Rynders. He later told a crowd that "I had determined from the first to break up this engagement. I used my own money liberally and begged money from others" in order to purchase fifty or sixty tickets for those willing to harass Macready. At the first intermission, Rynders gloated in the lobby about the chaos he and his followers had wrought. When Hiram Fuller, editor of the *Mirror*, a New York literary newspaper, complained to Rynders about the pandemonium, Rynders punched him in the face. (Rynders insisted that it was merely a slap.) When the crowd remained unruly during the second act, Macready left the stage and announced that he would take the next ship back to England. A group of prominent Macready supporters (mostly Whig businessmen but also several leading literary figures, including the young Herman Melville) sent Macready a letter begging him to stay and promising that "the good sense and respect for order prevailing in this community will sustain you on the subsequent nights of your performance." The letter writers were confident that incoming Whig mayor Caleb Woodhull, who would take office on May 9, would guarantee Macready's right to be heard. Macready therefore agreed to resume his engagement on Thursday, May 10.[14]

Rynders, however, was determined to prevent Macready from performing again. Upon learning that Macready would take the stage and that the police would bar from entry any ticket holder who might be expected to disturb the performance, Rynders paid for the printing and posting of two hundred handbills to ensure, at the very least, that a large crowd would be on hand to protest. "WORKINGMEN, SHALL AMERICANS or ENGLISH RULE?" asked Rynders's broadside, adding that the "crew of the English steamer" has "threatened all Americans who shall dare to express their opinion this night at the English Aristocratic Opera House!! We advocate no violence, but a free expression of opinion."[15]

Thousands turned out at the opera house, inspired by Rynders's posters and others that appeared throughout town calling on New Yorkers to "decide now whether English ARISTOCRATS and FOREIGN RULE shall triumph in this, AMERICA'S METROPOLIS." When the performance began, the crowds outside, egged on by the popular pulp fiction writer Ned Buntline, began heaving paving stones through the opera house windows onto the theatergoers. The overwhelmed police called for the aid of the state militia, which had been stationed nearby in anticipation of disorder. The crowd ignored the soldiers' orders to disperse, prompting the troops to fire into the air. When the crowd continued to surge toward the opera house, the militiamen fired several volleys into the crowd. The rioters then fled in panic, but by that point 18 New Yorkers lay dead. Four later died of their wounds, and more than 150 others were injured. The Astor Place Riot was the most deadly episode of civil unrest in New York history until the Draft Riots fourteen years later.[16]

Authorities charged Rynders with conspiracy, for encouraging the protests that led to the violence at the opera house. At his trial in January 1850, prosecutors proved that Rynders had paid for the printing and posting of hundreds of handbills and that he had bought theater tickets for many who hissed Macready. But Rynders's defense attorney, John Van Buren (son of the former president), noted that Rynders's posters had explicitly foresworn violence, and that no witness could place Rynders at the opera house on the night of the riot. The jury consequently found Rynders not guilty. Buntline, in contrast, who had enflamed the crowd outside the theater on the day of the riot, was convicted and sentenced to a year in prison. Insisting that Rynders had been indicted by vengeful Whigs hoping to deflect attention from their incompetent handling of the protests, the *Herald* characterized Rynders's acquittal "a great triumph . . . of justice and right over popular prejudice and political hate."[17]

Though Rynders had been exonerated of criminal wrongdoing, Americans nonetheless considered him the instigator of the deadly affair, an assessment that was not unreasonable. What had motivated Rynders to devote so much energy and money to embarrassing an actor? Rynders was driven in part by the exuberant, jingoistic patriotism that characterized the antebellum "sporting" set. Macready had not merely insulted American theater in his comments about Forrest and his followers, but the United States itself. Men such as Rynders *never* let insults go unpunished. There were unmistakable elements of class conflict motivating the rioters as well, exemplified by Rynders's condemnation of the aristocratic pretensions of Macready and his admirers. At the heart of Rynders's motivation, however, was a belief that freedom of speech was a privilege, not a right, especially if such speech insulted Americans or threatened their values or prerogatives. Rynders also thought that mob action was justifiable if it carried out the will of the majority. If the people who wished to hiss Macready were more numerous than those who wished to hear him, then hissing him was, to Rynders, democracy in its purest form. No act was too extreme, he believed, in order to protect the nation, its honor, or its founding principles.[18]

In February 1850, just a month after Rynders was acquitted of conspiracy, he was convicted of assault for participating in the brutal beating of a fellow politico at a hotel bar.[19] After enduring two trials within a matter of weeks, most men would have chosen to lay low. But Rynders seemed to relish the notoriety. In March 1850, at a Tammany Hall meeting called to express opposition to the Wilmot Proviso, Rynders and fellow Democratic strongman Mike Walsh threw the gathering into "a state of siege" with their violent handling of their Democratic rivals. Like most of the Democrats who attended the meeting, Rynders opposed the Wilmot Proviso's proposed ban on slavery in the territories acquired in the Mexican-American War. Some in Congress were calling for such a ban as part of the legislation that would lead to statehood for California. But Rynders insisted that "Congress has no power to prohibit slavery in the territories." He was willing to admit that slavery was pernicious—"It is an evil in the Southern States," he said, "but we [in the North] have nothing to do with it." Rynders did not mean that the North was blameless, but that slavery was none of their concern, something they had no right to interfere with. He insisted that he did not approve of slavery himself, but was careful to add that he was not "an abolitionist."[20]

Had any doubts about Rynders's stance on abolitionism remained, they were eliminated two months later when he and his followers completely disrupted the annual convention of the American Anti-Slavery Society, which began on Tuesday morning, May 7, 1850, at the Tabernacle, a huge Congregational church at the corner of Broadway and Anthony Street in lower Manhattan. The trouble began during the address of the society's founder, William Lloyd Garrison. When Garrison told the large audience that the abolition movement was "emphatically *the* Christian movement of the day," Rynders interrupted, asking if it were not true that there were churches "whose clergy and lay members hold slaves." Garrison replied that certainly the Episcopal, Presbyterian, Methodist, and Baptist churches were "against the slave, and all the sects are combined to prevent that jubilee which it is the will of God should come." He also noted that President Zachary Taylor, who "believes in Jesus," owned slaves and had, as a soldier, prosecuted an unjust war against Mexico in order to expand slavery.[21]

"The name of Zachary Taylor had scarcely passed Mr. Garrison's lips when Captain Rynders, with something like a howl, . . . dashed headlong down towards the speaker's desk, followed, with . . . a terrifying noise, by the mass of his backers," recalled Garrison's son years later. Shaking his fist in Garrison's face, Rynders said, "I will not allow you to assail the President of the United States. You shan't do it. [I] will not permit you or any man to misrepresent the President." Rynders laced his threats with curses, and when audience members asked him to mind his language for the sake of the ladies, Rynders retorted, "I doubt very much whether white women who cohabit and mix with the woolly-headed negro are entitled to any respect from a white man."[22]

At that point the Hutchinsons, America's most famous folk music group, broke into song from the balcony in an attempt to calm both Rynders and the nervous crowd. But the Captain was not amused. He "marched over to their side of the house," wrote one eyewitness, "and, shaking his fist at them, cried out, 'You long-haired Abolitionist[s], if you don't stop singing, I'll come up there and bring you down.'" Rynders finally allowed Garrison to finish his lecture after the Captain received assurances that he would have the right to speak afterward. He remained on the stage, glaring at Garrison with folded arms as the abolitionist spoke.[23]

When Rynders was told that it was his turn to address the convention, he sent in his place "Professor Grant," "a seedy-looking personage" whom

Garrison recognized as a former pressman from the *Liberator* office. Grant gave a longwinded diatribe in which he argued that blacks were not men at all, "but belonged to the monkey tribe" and were therefore undeserving of rights. Rynders and his followers interrupted Grant during his speech as well, though with laughter and applause rather than with hisses and derision.[24]

Next on the program was Frederick Douglass. As the former slave approached the podium, Rynders warned him that if he spoke "disrespectfully" of the South, or George Washington, or Patrick Henry, "I'll knock you off the stage." Douglass began his oration by reiterating Grant's thesis and insisting that he could prove it was not true. "Look at me," he said to Rynders, "and answer—Am I a man?" "*You* are not a black man," replied Rynders, clearly aware that Douglass's former master was his father. "You are only half a nigger." "Then," replied Douglass, turning to Rynders with a smile, "I am half-brother to Captain Rynders!" The cavernous church exploded with laughter. Rynders admitted years later that Douglass's quip was "as good a shot as I ever had in my life." Later in the address, when Douglass criticized *New York Tribune* editor Horace Greeley for calling blacks inefficient and dependent, Rynders launched into his own screed against Greeley. "I am happy to have the assent of my half-brother here," added Douglass, to the delight of the crowd. Douglass was followed by another black abolitionist, Rev. Samuel R. Ward, and by the end of Ward's lecture Rynders and his supporters did not even bother trying to interrupt him. The eloquent and witty speeches of Douglass and Ward had made a mockery of Grant's racial theories. When the convention adjourned for the day at 1:00 p.m., the abolitionists, who had been aghast just a few hours earlier, were instead delighted. "Never was there a grander triumph of intelligence, of mind, over brute force," wrote the Unitarian minister William H. Furness, who strode up to Rynders afterward and asked, "How shall we thank you for what you have done for us to-day?"[25]

But Rynders and his followers had the last laugh. When the convention resumed the following morning in the New York Society Library lecture room, Rynders was determined not to be outwitted. He packed the room, which held only a couple of hundred people, with his staunchest adherents in order to drown out and overawe the abolitionists. As the meeting was called to order, Rynders and his men began "hooting, screeching, threatening and blaspheming, almost without cessation," Garrison complained in a letter to the *Tribune* a few days later. The police refused to intervene on the grounds that it was a public meeting and that Rynders's men, while loud, were not breaking any law.[26]

Rynders soon strode to the front of the hall and took complete control of the proceedings. He assured the abolitionists that "I am not in favor of slavery. . . . I am willing to give something to buy the freedom of the slaves." But such voluntary, compensated emancipation was "the only honest way to set them free." All other methods, such as those espoused by Garrison and his followers, were unconstitutional and could only lead to the breakup of the Union. Rynders then proposed a resolution stating that Northerners should not interfere with slavery, which carried by acclamation as the terrified abolitionists looked on in stunned silence. Realizing that Rynders would quash any effort the abolitionists might make to take up their own agenda, Garrison announced that the annual meeting of the American Anti-Slavery Society was permanently adjourned.[27]

Rynders's success at silencing Garrison and his organization made the Captain famous nationwide. Newspapers and magazines that sympathized with the antislavery movement, and even some that did not, condemned Rynders's brazen assault on free speech. Having learned his lesson, Garrison stopped holding meetings in New York City, convening his organization's annual gatherings in sympathetic Syracuse instead. Rynders's disruption of the abolition convention was spoken of in the press for years afterward and sealed his reputation as the nation's foremost political thug. He had demonstrated yet again that freedom of speech was for the strong, and that he would stamp out any speech that he believed threatened the harmony of the Union or the racial status quo.[28]

Although Rynders had the power to completely disrupt major New York civic events, his influence within Tammany remained somewhat limited. Because the most important positions within the Democratic organization were chosen by delegates elected from each ward, Rynders needed to establish a power base in one of those districts. He chose to make his bid for office in what he called the "bloody Sixth," a predominantly immigrant ward infamous for its raucous political battles. Five Points, the city's toughest, most impoverished Irish Catholic neighborhood, was situated there. Given Rynders's penchant for violence and intimidation, political weapons that were both accepted and respected in the Sixth Ward, his decision to concentrate his political operations in the district made perfect sense. He moved to the ward in 1847, bought a saloon there called the Star

House to increase his visibility, and, recalled sporting man "Florry" Kernan, "quietly awaited an opening."[29]

Rynders made his move in the autumn of 1850, after his exploits with the Astor Place riot and the abolition convention had brought him to the peak of his fame. His intention, he announced, was to take the district's nomination for the state assembly. Yet Rynders's decision "did not suit the bone and sinew of the ward," Kernan recollected years later, because the ward's Democratic leaders, Con Donoho and Matthew T. Brennan (both Irish Catholics), saw Rynders and his Empire Club thugs as "squatters." Donoho and Brennan were themselves experienced at wielding political muscle. In preparation for the Sixth Ward primary meeting that the two had dominated a year earlier, the police had been ordered "to wear their fire hats to ward off bricks and stones" that would inevitably fly during the electoral battle.[30]

Knowing that he would literally have to fight for the nomination, Rynders arrived at Dooley's Long Room, the site of the primary meeting, accompanied by some of the city's best known fighters—Bill Ford, Tom Maguire, John "Country" McCleester (whose 101-round bare-knuckle prizefight in 1841 with American heavyweight champion Tom Hyer is still considered one of the greatest fights of all time), and "Hen" Chanfrau—"men who seldom met defeat"—as well as hundreds of other supporters. But Brennan, Donoho, and the rest of the ward's Irish Catholics were not about to cede control of the district to these interlopers without a struggle; they came to Dooley's with an equally large contingent of Five Points brawlers. "When the hour came to name the chairman" of the meeting, wrote Kernan, "the fierce onset of Rynders's friends to defeat [Donoho's candidate] was met with a bold response. The ball opened and the strife commenced, and ere ten minutes passed away, the hall was cleared of all who stood in opposition to the regular voters of the ward. Rynders and his men met defeat."[31]

Unaccustomed to losing, Rynders persisted in his attempt to secure the assembly nomination. The candidate would be chosen by delegates from both the Third and Sixth Wards, and Rynders could still capture the nomination if he won support in the other district. He apparently did so, for when the delegates met at Tammany Hall to choose the city's legislative candidates, Rynders prevailed. In New York, winning the Democratic nomination often meant certain victory in the general election, but Five Pointers were determined to keep Rynders from gaining control of their district. Many refused to vote for the Captain on election day, and as a result he received 350 fewer votes in the Sixth Ward than his Democratic running mates. This proved to be decisive; Rynders lost to his Whig opponent by 200 votes. "I am down, and there's no use to try to get round it," said Rynders at Tammany Hall the night of the election. "We are beat, badly beat; and, for myself, it is awful to think about." Realizing that Five Pointers would never accept him as their political leader, Kernan noted, Rynders's "ambition to get a foothold in the glorious old Sixth was quieted ever after." He immediately moved across the Bowery to the Seventh Ward and, stung by his embarrassing defeat, never again ran for elective office.[32]

After his electoral setback, Rynders no longer dominated New York politics with the swagger and impudence that had earlier marked his career. He was forty-six now, and perhaps he was starting to feel too old to bully meetings and conventions the way he once had. Rynders settled down in other ways as well. A few years later, in 1854, he married Phoebe Shortwell (who was twenty when she wed the fifty-year-old Rynders) and this, too, may have curbed his brutish inclinations. But he remained active in Tammany affairs, focusing his efforts on a few increasingly potent issues. One was his belief that the United States ought to continue to expand its boundaries. Many Americans thought that the Manifest Destiny movement had culminated with the Mexican cession, but Rynders sought even more territory for the United States. As a delegate at the Democratic presidential nominating convention in Baltimore in 1852, he tried to secure the nomination for Lewis Cass, the most ardent expansionist among the leading candidates. When his efforts for Cass failed, Rynders lobbied successfully for the selection of a Cass supporter, New Hampshire's Franklin Pierce.[33]

Rynders campaigned earnestly for Pierce, trying to focus New Yorkers' attention on potential targets of expansionism that might be seized should the Democrats triumph. He even organized and headed a New York branch of the Order of the Lone Star, a secret fraternal order whose goal was to free Cuba by filibuster. The *Times* remarked that if Cuba's dictatorial Spanish ruler, Captain-General Don Valentin Cañedo, "should [en]act any more of his capers, . . . *our* Captain undoubtedly would be ready to call in Mose and Sykesy [two "Bowery B'hoys" from a popular play of the day] . . . to teach the Spanish gentry better manners."[34]

Rynders was even more outspoken in support of the American William Walker's filibustering exploits in Nicaragua. He justified his support for Walker on the same Social Darwinist grounds that American expansionists would use to legitimize war and exploitation in the postbellum years. "If there was a country open," argued Rynders, "the Americans or any other people might go there and establish a government and oust what was not a government." Besides, Rynders said, it was a waste not to have "the great resources of that country developed. And who were to develop them? Half-negroes, half-Indians, half-bullfrogs? Why, assuredly not. It was the great persevering industry of the American spirit that was to develop the great resources of that country and to establish a Democratic Republican Government there." Rynders justified filibustering on the same grounds that he defended hissing down an actor or an abolitionist—it was the right and responsibility of the strong to dominate (and in this case exploit and "civilize") the weak.[35]

The pro-Walker meetings at which Rynders spoke were not the huge gatherings that Rynders had once commonly addressed, because by 1856 slavery and its potential extension into the federal territories overshadowed expansionism. Rynders had demonstrated his opposition to the abolition movement through his actions at Garrison's convention in 1850. In a Fourth of July oration delivered a year later, Rynders more thoroughly explained his opposition to the antislavery movement. Having lived in both sections, Rynders said, he could confirm the Southern claim that the "condition of the majority of Northern laborers is worse than that of the Southern slaves. . . . [P]oor white laborers," he insisted, ". . . are not treated with as much humanity as the negro slaves of the South." Rynders also argued that Northerners had no constitutional right to interfere with the South's "local" institutions. "State power is the only agent that can act in the matter." Racism must have also motivated Rynders's views to some extent, though he did not lace his speeches with the racist invective used by so many of his Democratic colleagues. Rynders's primary reason for despising abolitionism, he insisted, was that he opposed "every attempt to agitate questions which tend to diminish the respect and confidence that should be cherished between the people of different sections." Abolitionism might not have many adherents, Rynders admitted, but this "speck of danger" had to be crushed out immediately, before it could grow powerful enough to threaten the nation.[36]

In the end it was Rynders's own Democratic party, and not the abolitionists, who most severely agitated the slavery question. In early 1854, Senator Stephen A. Douglas proposed to repeal the ban on slavery in the Northern portion of the Louisiana Purchase, a prohibition that had been imposed as

part of the Missouri Compromise of 1820. Douglas's bill was wildly unpopular in the North, so Democrats mounted a public relations campaign in
order to ensure the bill's passage. New York City Democrats held their pro-
Nebraska meeting in Tammany Hall on March 16, and the first to address
the crowd was "the inevitable Captain Rynders." He defended the contro-
versial bill on grounds consistent with his lifelong political views. First, anticipating the judgment of the Supreme Court three years later, Rynders
argued that the Missouri Compromise's ban on slavery in most of the Louisiana Purchase was unconstitutional. Just as Congress had no right to force
slavery upon a state, said Rynders, it had no right to ban it from a territory
or state either. Whether or not to have slavery should always be left "to the
people" to decide. Rynders also insisted that the bill's opponents were radicals whose views did not reflect American values. The bill's enemies, insisted Rynders, were merely clergymen who "should stick to the pulpit and
not get involved in politics," as well as "Whigs, Abolitionists, Seward men,
strong-minded women, [applause and laughter,] old grannies, wearing the
habiliments of men, and all the appurtenances belonging thereto, and most
people take them for men. [Laughter.]" By linking the bill's opponents with
women's rights advocates and "old grannies," Rynders sought to emascu-
late those who opposed the Nebraska proposal.[37]

Rynders also justified his support of Douglas's measure on the same
"rights-of-the-majority" grounds that he had used throughout his public career. "In my judgment, it contains the fundamental principles of the
Democratic party; and it is the basis upon which all Republican Governments are founded; the right of the people to self-government, the right and
capacity of the people to govern themselves, and to make all laws relating
to their own domestic institutions for their welfare and their happiness in
the Territories as well as in the States." Rynders might not like slavery, he
admitted, but he could accept it because it was another institution imposed
upon the strong by the weak, by the civilized upon the uncivilized, by the
majority upon the minority.[38]

The Kansas-Nebraska Act did become law, but Rynders and his fellow
New York City Democrats were ill prepared for the political revolution
that the bill's passage would help to foment. While Democrats remained ascendant in New York City, in the rest of the state and country they suffered
unprecedented defeats in 1854 and 1855. Sensing that his party would need
every possible vote in 1856 to carry New York for its presidential nominee,

James Buchanan, Rynders revived the Empire Club, which had become moribund years earlier. Rynders organized a mass meeting held in City Hall Park to ratify Buchanan's nomination and even wrote a letter for publication in Kentucky newspapers lauding the Democratic nominee. Though Buchanan lost New York, he won the election, and he rewarded Rynders for his years of service to the party with one of the most sought after patronage plums, one the Captain had been seeking for years—appointment as U.S. marshal for the southern district of the state of New York.[39]

Rynders relished his role as marshal. He loved careening around the harbor chasing thieves and smugglers. But even hundreds of miles north of the Mason-Dixon line, a significant portion of Rynders's responsibilities as marshal involved slavery. When he first took over the post, the press had asked him if he would return a runaway slave if ordered to do so (marshals in the North were responsible for the return of runaways under the Fugitive Slave Act of 1850). Rynders said he would, and did so on several occasions. Yet Rynders said that he would prefer to devote his energies in this area to the capture of Americans participating illegally in the international slave trade. At first, it appeared that Rynders was assiduously carrying out this obligation as well. South Carolinians even complained about his overzealousness.[40]

It soon became clear, however, that Rynders was not the scourge of the "slavers" after all. After his first year in office, arrests declined dramatically. When slavers were captured, they inevitably seemed to escape (one ran off while the deputy Rynders assigned to guard him was at Brooks Brothers trying on clothes). Rumors that slavers could secure safe passage from the city in return for huge bribes were confirmed when Rynders's own brother Theodore (who worked as one of the marshal's deputies) was caught in 1860 soliciting a fifteen hundred dollar bribe from a slaver captain. The conspiracy only came to light because Rynders was in Charleston attending the Democratic national convention, and the acting marshal, who was not one of Rynders's political appointees, discovered the plot. One can only imagine how many thousands of dollars in bribes Rynders, his brother, and their accessories must have taken from slavers before the practice was uncovered. Theodore Rynders and his accomplice were subsequently indicted for conspiracy and obstruction of justice and pled not guilty, but neither the press nor the minute books of the U.S. Circuit Court that handled the case record any resolution to it. Isaiah Rynders was never charged, and though the *Times* reported that Buchanan might fire him, Rynders held onto his post until Buchanan left office in 1861.[41]

As the secession crisis deepened, Rynders blamed the Republicans for provoking the South to secede. "I have no pecuniary interest in the South," said Rynders referring to his purported Southern sympathies at a public meeting in January 1861. "Nor do I expect to go and live there. I expect to be buried here, where my mother and father are buried; but I would let them be dug from their graves before I could commit oppression against the South. The South asks no concession. She demands justice." Rynders insisted that the Republicans were "trying to conceal their own treason by attributing treason to the South." Democrats who volunteer to fight against the South "are traitors to your country.... If war comes, and I have to fight, I will fight to the death for South Carolina."[42]

Rynders never did take up arms for the South, but he did his best to help the Southern cause within the North, becoming one of New York's best known "Peace Democrats." Whenever antiwar Democrats held public meetings, Rynders was sure to be on hand to deliver a fiery speech condemning the Lincoln administration.[43] Yet much to Rynders's chagrin, few of his fellow Democrats were willing to adopt his antiwar stance. Rynders, who had no ambitions for elective office, could speak his mind. For still-aspiring politicians, antiwar statements usually meant political suicide. But as the war dragged on, Rynders increasingly avoided the Peace Democrats' gatherings. He had used the apparently sizable proceeds from his term as marshal to purchase a large stud farm (worth $29,000 in 1870) in Lodi, New Jersey, where he devoted himself to training and breeding racehorses. Rynders had never lost his eye for equine talent, and he eventually owned some of the most successful trotters of the postwar years, including Widow Mc-Chree, Aberdeen, and Killarney. But he tended to bet recklessly on his trotters. One trainer recalled him wagering $1,700 (equivalent to nearly $40,000 today) on a single race. As a result, he had to return to the city to take minor patronage sinecures, serving as a deputy sheriff in the mid-1860s and as a deputy clerk in the New York county clerk's office from 1873 to 1879.[44]

In February 1882, a few years after Rynders left the county clerk's office, an invitation to a party honoring a former alderman and congressman named William R. Roberts arrived at the office of New York mayor William R. Grace. The highlight of the gathering, the invitation announced, would be the appearance of a seventy-eight year-old Tammany legend, "Captain

Isaiah Rynders," who would prepare his "celebrated . . . Elixir—known as Roman Punch" in the very fourteen-gallon punch bowl used each year by Andrew Jackson at the Hermitage to celebrate the anniversary of the Battle of New Orleans. "It is said the bowl was bequeathed to the Captain by Old Hickory 'as the only man—by the eternal—who knew how to brew a punch fit for gods and men.'"[45]

It made sense that Gilded Age New Yorkers would associate Rynders's name with the bygone era of Andrew Jackson, for New York politics had undergone an utter revolution in the thirty years since Rynders's heyday. Ward primaries were no longer decided by knockdown, drag-out brawls. They had become staid affairs, "usually only a gathering of the clans to get a drink, and incidentally vote the ticket put into their hands," noted one reformer, because by the 1880s the "bosses" handpicked all the candidates for office. And on election day, polling places were no longer dominated by gangs seeking to prevent another faction's voters from casting their ballots. Thuggery was no longer necessary to carry general elections because those same bosses utilized repeat voting and ballot counting fraud to produce the desired results without any embarrassing bloodshed.[46]

While Rynders's once-infamous methods may have been outmoded by 1882, Americans' conception of freedom, democracy, and citizenship had not changed much over the course of the Captain's adult life. Native Americans in the 1880s, like Nicaraguans in the 1850s, were still believed to occupy "empty" space that whites had both a right and an obligation to co-opt. Slaves might have won emancipation and citizenship, but Southern whites had used violence and intimidation even more brutal than Rynders's to effectively disenfranchise the freedmen and make their citizenship virtually meaningless. Democracy was still only for the strong; the Social Darwinism that Rynders had championed still reigned supreme; and despite amendments to the constitution, people of color still had few rights that white men were bound to respect.

We do not know what Rynders thought of the changes that had occurred in urban political tactics over his lifetime. Rynders supposedly bequeathed his political papers, including his own account of the Astor Place Riot, to the editor of a sporting men's newspaper, but they have never been found.[47] Even without such records, the story of Rynders's career teaches us a great deal about antebellum political life. It reminds us, for example, of how important violence was in pre–Civil War urban politics. The more violence Rynders wielded, the greater his power over Tammany grew. Only when

Irish Catholic immigrants in Five Points challenged Rynders fist for fist and club for club did the Captain's power finally begin to wane. Rynders's story also demonstrates that, despite popular belief then and now, Irish Catholics were not the ones who initiated the use of violence as an electoral weapon in New York. Rynders and the primarily native-born members of the Empire Club began to use such tactics in New York in the early 1840s, when the Irish population of New York was still relatively small. Rynders was not the first New Yorker to use intimidation as a political weapon. But he was the first American of national renown whose fame and influence stemmed solely from his success at wielding political violence.

Rynders's life also reveals much about the nature of the antebellum Democratic party in the North. While the Astor Place Riot reflects the elements of class warfare intrinsic in the Democratic appeal, Rynders's avid support for filibustering, expansionism, and slavery demonstrates that maintaining the predominance of white men was just as important as class conflict to Democrats of Rynders's ilk. Rynders was, in a sense, the Preston Brooks of the North. The South Carolinian justified his attack on Charles Sumner on the grounds that the senator's "Crime against Kansas" speech had insulted Brooks's family and state, and that such incendiary utterances had to be stamped out to preserve sectional harmony and the rule of white men. Rynders likewise advocated the use of violence and intimidation at Tammany meetings, abolitionist gatherings, polling places, and in Cuba and Nicaragua to combat national insults, prevent sectional discord, and perpetuate the white man's democracy. This unseemly, undemocratic element within the antebellum Northern electorate has been neglected by historians for far too long.

Finally, Rynders's story provides insight into an alternate conception of freedom and democracy that thrived in the nineteenth century but is barely remembered today. Aggression and intimidation were viewed by many as perfectly reasonable tools if used to implement the will of the majority or protect the honor of the nation or the integrity of the Union. Rynders and his followers viewed these methods as acceptable not only when used against Indians, Mexicans, and Cubans, but against white men and women as well. They considered bullying appropriate not merely in primary meetings and on election day, but also in theaters, saloons, and even churches. To Rynders, freedom of speech and assembly, as well as the supposed rights of citizenship, were privileges for those who wielded power, not inalienable rights for all. Rynders died in New York City in January 1885. Many, many more years would pass before the majority of Americans would finally lay to rest Rynders's narrow definitions of democracy and freedom.

NOTES

1. Thomas L. Nichols, *Forty Years of American Life*, 2 vols. (London, 1864), 2:159 ("lithe, dark, handsome man"); Sherlock Bristol, *The Pioneer Preacher: Incidents of Interest, and Experiences in the Author's Life* (1887; reprint, Urbana, 1989), 66–67 (other quotations).

2. *New York Times*, January 14, 1885.

3. Eric Foner, *Free Soil, Free Labor, Free Men: The Ideology of the Republican Party before the Civil War* (New York, 1970); William E. Gienapp, *The Origins of the Republican Party, 1852–1856* (New York, 1987); Richard H. Sewell, *Ballots for Freedom: Antislavery Politics in the United States, 1837–1860* (New York, 1976); Daniel Walker Howe, *The Political Culture of the American Whigs* (New York, 1980); Michael F. Holt, *The Rise and Fall of the American Whig Party* (New York, 1999); Tyler Anbinder, *Nativism and Slavery: The Northern Know Nothings and the Politics of the 1850s* (New York, 1992); Mark Voss-Hubbard, *Beyond Party: Cultures of Antipartisanship in Northern Politics before the Civil War* (Baltimore, 2002); William J. Cooper, *The South and the Politics of Slavery* (Baton Rouge, 1978); J. Mills Thornton, *Politics and Power in a Slave Society: Alabama, 1800–1860* (Baton Rouge, 1978); John McCardell, *The Idea of a Southern Nation: Southern Nationalists and Southern Nationalism, 1830–1860* (New York, 1979); Manisha Sinha, *The Counterrevolution of Slavery: Politics and Ideology in Antebellum South Carolina* (Chapel Hill, 2000); John C. Inscoe and Robert C. Kenzer, eds., *Enemies of the Country : New Perspectives on Unionists in the Civil War South* (Athens, Ga., 2001); William W. Freehling, *The South vs. the South: How Anti-Confederate Southerners Shaped the Course of the Civil War* (New York, 2001).

4. Roy F. Nichols, *The Disruption of American Democracy* (New York, 1948); Jean H. Baker, *Affairs of Party: The Political Culture of Northern Democrats in the Mid-Nineteenth Century* (Baltimore, 1983); Joel F. Silbey, *A Respectable Minority: The Democratic Party in the Civil War Era, 1860–1868* (New York, 1977).

5. *New York Times*, January 14, 1885; *New York Herald*, November 9, 1853; Nichols, *Forty Years of American Life*, 2:159.

6. *New York Clipper*, January 24, 1885; Nichols, *Forty Years of American Life*, 2: 159.

7. Nichols, *Forty Years of American Life*, 2:159 (quotation); *New York Clipper*, January 24, 1885; Bristol, *Pioneer Preacher*, 66–67.

8. *New York Times*, January 14, 1885; *New York Clipper*, January 24, 1885; Nichols, *Forty Years of American Life*, 2:159–61 (quotation).

9. Matthew P. Breen, *Thirty Years of New York Politics Up-To-Date* (New York, 1899), 307–8; *National Police Gazette*, February 7, 1885, 5; *Frank Leslie's Illustrated Weekly* 59 (January 24, 1885): 380. Neither the *Herald*, the *Tribune*, nor the *Evening Post* mentioned Rynders or the Empire Club in their extensive election-day coverage.

10. *New York Herald*, February 10, 1848, 4; *Doggetts' New York City Directory for 1847–1848* (New York, 1847), 356 ("measurer").

11. *New York Evening Post*, January 25, 27, 1845; *New York Times*, January 14, 1885.

12. *Berkshire County (Mass.) Whig*, February 27, 1845; *Hudson River (N.Y.) Chronicle*, July 8, 1845; *Pittsfield (Mass.) Sun*, January 20, 1848.

13. Edwin G. Burrows and Mike Wallace, *Gotham: A History of New York City to 1898* (New York, 1999), 761–62.

14. Burrows and Wallace, *Gotham*, 761–62; Alvin F. Harlow, *Old Bowery Days: The Chronicles of a Famous Street* (New York: 1931), 331; *New York Herald*, May 12, 1849, January 17, 1850.

15. *New York Herald*, May 11, 1849, January 16, 1850.

16. Burrows and Wallace, *Gotham*, 763–64; *New York Herald*, May 12, 1849.

17. Peter G. Buckley, "To the Opera House: Culture and Society in New York City, 1820–1860" (PhD diss., State University of New York at Stony Brook, 1984), 23–24; *New York Herald*, January 16–20, 1850 (quotation January 20).

18. Rynders justified his role in the riot in the *Herald* and the *Tribune*, May 12, 1849.

19. This second trial stemmed from a bloody affray on the night of July 10, 1849. Rynders and a number of other leading politicos were drinking at the bar of the Carlton House Hotel on Broadway at Leonard Street. When one, Archibald Reynolds, dared to assert that both Forrest and Macready were "knaves," Rynders labeled him "a d——d lying son of a b——t." Reynolds responded that Rynders was a liar and that he could "whip" any of them, prompting Rynders and his friends to beat Reynolds senseless. "Reynolds's condition was pretty bad," testified bartender George J. Smith at Rynders's trial. "His head was covered with blood, and his nose was flattened down." Reynolds's leg was broken too. Rynders was found guilty of assault, but his punishment was a mere fifteen-dollar fine. *New York Herald*, July 12, 1849, February 22–24, 1850.

20. *New York Evening Post*, March 4, 1850; *New York Herald*, March 3, 1850.

21. All quotations from [Wendell P. Garrison], *William Lloyd Garrison*, 4 vols. (New York, 1885–89), 3:285–300. See also *New York Liberator* 20 (May 24, 1850): 81; *New York Herald*, May 8, 1850.

22. *Garrison*, 3:285–300. Rynders was apparently such an admirer of Taylor's that he had crossed party lines to work for the Whig in the 1848 presidential campaign. See the *New Hampshire Patriot*, July 12, 1849, May 30, 1850.

23. Henry W. Smith to the editor, May 10, 1850, in *New York Tribune*, May 11, 1850 ("long-haired"); *Garrison*, 3:285–300 (remaining quotations); *New York Herald*, May 8, 1850; Carol Brink, *Harps in the Wind: The Story of the Singing Hutchinsons* (New York, 1947).

24. *Garrison*, 3:285–300.

25. *New York Liberator* 20 (May 24, 1850): 81 ("look at me and answer"); *New York Times*, January 14, 1885 ("as good a shot"); *Garrison*, 3:285–300 (all other quotations).

26. William Lloyd Garrison to the editor, May 13, 1850, in *New York Tribune*, May 16, 1850 (quotations); *Garrison*, 3:285–300.

27. *New York Herald*, May 9, 1850.

28. *New York Tribune*, May 9, 1850; *Philadelphia Ledger*, May 14, 1850; *National Era* 4 (May 16, 1850): 78; *Philadelphia Saturday Evening Post*, May 18, 1850; *New York Times*, May 12, 1853, 4 (on moving annual meetings). For references years later to Rynders's actions at the abolition convention, see *New York Times*, September 8, 1853, 4; June 1, 1855, 2; and May 14, 1857, 4.

29. Frank Kernan, *Reminiscences of the Old Fire Laddies* (New York, 1885), 53–54. For Rynders's referring to the Sixth Ward as the "bloody Sixth," see *New York Herald*, November 9, 1853.

30. Kernan, *Reminiscences*, 49; *New York Herald*, September 26, 1849. For more on Donoho, Brennan, and the struggles for control of Sixth Ward politics leading up to Rynders's 1850 assembly bid, see Tyler Anbinder, *Five Points* (New York, 2001), 148–66.

31. Kernan, *Reminiscences*, 53–54.

32. Kernan, *Reminiscences*, 53–54; *Manual of the Corporation of the City of New York for 1851* (New York, 1851), 345–46; *New York Herald*, November 6 (election night quotation), November 8 (election results by ward), 1850. Rynders won 967 votes in the Sixth Ward, while the two Democratic candidates for assistant alderman, the highest ward-wide office up for grabs that year, captured 1,328 votes between them. Newspapers reported Rynders's nomination at Tammany Hall without comment (see *New York Herald*, October 10, 1850), so my assessment of how he captured the nomination despite the opposition of Sixth Ward voters is somewhat conjectural.

33. *New York Times*, June 10, 1852, 1; June 14, 1854, 6; census entry for Isaiah and Phoebe Rynders, p. 195, First District, Seventh Ward, New York City, 1860 United States Census, National Archives.

34. *New York Times*, October 20, 1852, 1; December 28, 1852, 6; March 12, 1853, 1 ("Mose"); March 13, 1855, 4; March 16, 1855, 1.

35. *New York Times*, May 10, 1856, 4; December 22, 1856, 2 (quotations) and 4; *New York Herald*, May 24, 1856.

36. Isaiah Rynders, *Oration Delivered July 4th, 1851 . . . before the Old Guard at Their Annual Festival* (New York: 1851), 5–6.

37. *New York Times*, March 17, 1854, 1.

38. *New York Times*, March 17, 1854, 1.

39. *New York Herald*, April 10, 1856 (quotation); *New York Times*, July 9, 1856, 1; October 16, 1856, 2.

40. *New York Times*, May 14, 1857, 4; July 14, 1857, 4; July 15, 1857, 5; May 2, 1860, 2 (fugitive slave cases); July 8, 1858, 4; October 5, 1858, 1 (on capturing slavers).

41. *New York Times*, May 7, 1860, 2; May 9, 1860, 2; June 15, 1860, 3; June 16, 1860, 6 (on Theodore Rynders's arrest); May 21, 1860, 4 (Rynders's possible removal from office); March 18, 1861, 4 (Rynders's record on the slave trade); Minutes of the United States Circuit Court for the Southern District of New York, National Archives, New York City branch.

42. *New York Times*, January 16, 1861, 1.

43. *New York Times*, October 30, November 5, 1862, April 7, May 19, 1863.

44. Hiram Woodruff, *The Trotting Horse of America* (New York, 1871), 342; *The Celebrated Trotting Mare Widow McChree*, Currier and Ives print, 1867, Prints and Photographs Division, Library of Congress; *New York Times*, January 14–15, 1885; entry for Isaiah Rynders, p. 62, Lodi Township, Bergen County, NJ, 1870 United States Census; entry for Rynders, p. 82, Bergen County, N.J., 1880 United States Census.

45. Thomas Ryan et al. to William R. Grace, received 2/1/82, in "Mayor's Drafts and Messages" folder, Box 84-GWR-12, Mayoral Papers, New York Municipal Archives. There is no mention of Rynders in the Jackson will reprinted in Herbert R. Collins and David B. Weaver, *Wills of the U.S. Presidents* (New York, 1976), 68–70.

46. William M. Ivins, *Machine Politics and Money in Elections in New York City* (1887; reprint, New York, 1970), 19; *New York Times*, January 14, 1885; *New York Herald*, January 14, 1885.

47. *New-York Spirit of the Times*, January 17, 1885.

Chapter Three

• • • • • • • • •

Leave of Court

African American Claims-Making in the Era of Dred Scott v. Sandford

MARTHA S. JONES

The beginning of my graduate study of history also marked the end of my career as a public interest lawyer. I had represented, in New York courts high and low, many of the city's most marginalized residents including those who were homeless, mentally ill, and living with HIV or AIDS. Eric Foner was among the first to encourage my career change, and in exchange for his support he extracted only one promise: I would never complain to him when I found myself miserable in my choice to leave law for history. It may please him to know that I have never been miserable—or at least not entirely so. My appetite for our now shared intellectual and professional endeavors has only grown over time. What has surprised me, however, is how the same passage of time did not lead me to forsake my experience as a legal worker. Instead, I have come to see how my sensibilities about law, earned through years of practice rather than study, inform my thinking about African Americans in nineteenth-century legal history.

Thus, this essay begins with an insight from the present rather than an interpretation of the past. In my practice, most poor people and people of color first encountered the law through everyday disputes with seemingly little jurisprudential significance. Many more such people entered legal culture through trial courts, seeking heat and hot water, the custody of children, or public benefits; rarely were they parties to appellate proceedings concerned with constitutional or public policy questions. In my view, any story of poor people or people of color and the law must begin with these encounters in legal culture's "lowest" venues. At first glance, what I term "everyday" proceedings appeared marginal to contests over rights, even as they were critical to the immediate needs of individuals. But this isn't where the story ends. Beyond an understanding of material interests won or lost were interests that linked everyday cases to broader questions. I only had to look around the courthouse. For presiding judges, professional esteem and a seat on an appellate bench were won through decisions that spoke to important jurisprudential issues. For reform-minded lawyers, one case was an element of a broader argument to be made before an appellate court or a legislature. For politically ambitious advocates, reputations earned through a series of cases led to an expanded client base or an appointment to the bench. Just beyond the courthouse door, such cases also had meanings for the communities from which litigants came. Rent strikers, parents' associations, and welfare rights activists heard echoes of the debates they aimed to generate. In this broader context, everyday legal encounters were opportunities to understand more fully what a given case was *about*. Understanding antecedents, dynamics, and the interests of a proceeding's many characters revealed the connections between everyday legal claims-making and broader contests over power and rights.

These insights provide a starting place for this essay's approach to the legal history of African Americans in the pre–Civil War era, suggesting that in the fabric of everyday disputes were the threads of a story about rights and citizenship. Adopting what legal scholar Mari Matsuda terms "looking to the bottom," this essay does not start with high court pronouncements (such as *Dred Scott v. Sandford*), though it is not unconcerned with them. Instead, it begins with the more typical circumstances under which black people entered legal culture, such as applications for marriage licenses, gun permits, and dog licenses, as well as prosecutions for unpaid debts, breaches of the peace, assault, and bastardy. Such a history asks what individual litigants hoped to gain from the proceedings—familial autonomy, a livelihood, their liberty—and then evaluates how they fared. Here, the agency of people often deemed marginal to legal culture is evidenced. Nineteenth-century black Americans maneuvered through the small openings provided by law to renegotiate the material conditions of their lives.

The interests of individual litigants are not the end point of this analysis, however. Remaining grounded in the claims initiated by black Americans, it continues by what historian Elsa Barkley Brown calls "pivoting the center." Brown suggests that historians also consider how black people's lives were part of a broader context comprised of individuals of differing perspectives and interests. In the realm of legal history, this requires looking around the courthouse at the lawyers, jurists, and other litigants present, and beyond it into high court proceedings and the social world. This is a route toward understanding how the modest legal claims of African Americans were re-lated to broader struggles for freedom, rights, and citizenship.[1] Through this approach, cultural history's concerns about everyday lived experience and meaning come together with legal history's interest in the realms of intellect, power, and politics, producing what Ariela Gross terms "cultural-legal" history. Gross advocates analyzing trial court records to understand law from the perspective of judges as well as litigants, witnesses, jurors, and even slaves. In her view, law and social life should not be approached as "separate spheres" because the records of everyday proceedings reflect the social history of ordinary people along with power relations at a level closer to individual confrontations with the state. The aim, Gross explains, is to forge a connection between studies of daily life and inquiries into the relations of power that govern such lives.[2]

This essay examines one such set of cases, applications by free black peo-ple for travel permits in Baltimore, Maryland. It argues that the meanings and interests being negotiated in black Americans' everyday claims-making extended beyond the local courthouse into Supreme Court deliberations, free African American political culture, the aspirations of Baltimore's white civic leaders, and even the infrapolitics of enslaved people on Maryland's eastern shore.[3] Moving between the high and low of legal culture, and from the realm of law to those of politics and society, this essay advocates an approach to legal history that highlights the juridical agency of African Americans, while also revealing how their everyday legal dealings played an integral role in the construction of antebellum American legal culture. The claims of black Americans occupied the center of antebellum legal cul-ture, rather than its shadowy margins.

June 26, 1854, was not a day of particular note in Baltimore. In the city's livestock market, cattle prices continued to decline while hogs were plentiful.[4] The local Board of Health reported that the city's health was overall "very good," though it cautioned that infant mortality was on the rise. Plans were well under way for the city's annual Fourth of July parade. The city council considered matters ranging from fire company petitions to road construction and the erection of a footbridge. A local paper deemed weather the "engrossing topic of conversation"; unseasonable temperatures led to the hottest days in nearly two years.[5] Early on that summer morning, William Henry Calhoun and Charity Govans were among those making their way along the city's busy streets. Their destination was the Baltimore city courthouse; their purpose, to obtain permits for the right to travel. Calhoun likely began the day at his home on Arch Street in Baltimore's densely populated 14th Ward, where he lived with his wife, Mary, and their nine children.[6] This forty-eight-year-old was a member of the city's small class of skilled African American workers, having labored as a blacksmith since at least 1848.[7] Govans traveled from the opposite side of the city, the west side's 5th Ward, with another woman, probably a relative, named Charity Govans Johnson.[8] Govans was also a skilled artisan with a reputation for producing fine gilt objects.[9]

This scene, in which free black Southerners traveled to the courthouse as part of an ordinary day's activities, unfolded in a city located on what historians have termed the "middle ground." Baltimore, in the northern third of the upper South slave state of Maryland, was closer to Philadelphia, Pennsylvania, than Richmond, Virginia. The city's economy had matured along with the expansion of grain production in the region, and Baltimore's shipping industry principally depended on the export of this free labor staple crop.[10] Still the city was not divorced from the South's slave economy. As historian Barbara Fields explains, marketing, processing, the exchange of information, the purchase and sale of slaves, and the provision of food, supplies, and legal advice, linked Baltimore with slave society in Maryland and the rest of the South.[11] It was Baltimore's in-between character that fostered the growth of a substantial free black community.

Govans and Calhoun counted themselves among Baltimore's nearly twenty-six thousand African Americans. But their large numbers do not tell the entire story of Baltimore's black community. Overwhelmingly free rather than enslaved, it was distinct from the South's other urban centers. By 1850, nearly 90 percent of Baltimore's black residents were free.[12] They supported a rich institutional life, with fifteen schools, thirteen churches, and scores of fraternal, benevolent, and social organizations.[13] Theirs was, however, a distinctly poor community that was far less stratified than those of Charleston or New Orleans. For example, less than 1 percent of black Baltimoreans owned property. Most men were employed as laborers and women as domestic workers, and by 1850, even black people in these marginal segments of the labor force faced formidable competition from European immigrants.[14] Just as their associational life, work, and movement along the city's streets and alleyways made African Americans familiar participants in Baltimore's public culture, frequently they could be found in the local courthouse. In 1850, for example, just under six hundred African Americans were convicted of criminal offenses in the City of Baltimore, comprising nearly 25 percent of that year's convictions.[15] These cases covered offenses that ranged from unpaid debts, breaches of the peace, and assault and battery to bastardy, aiding runaways, and selling liquor on Sunday.[16] The sight of Govans and Calhoun, as free black people, in the courtroom that morning would not have given most Baltimoreans pause.

The courthouse was no ordinary meeting place, however. To go "to court" in antebellum Baltimore was to enter a space small in square footage but rich in civic significance. The city's sole courthouse, a modest two-story structure, was centrally located just off of Monument Square.[17] In the city's 10th Ward, Monument Square was also the site of Baltimore's city hall, Masonic Hall, Odd Fellows Hall, the Baltimore Library and Assembly, the post office, the Holliday Theater, and, frequently, mass meetings and rallies. Constructed in 1803, it had a modest footprint of 145 by 65 feet, with one courtroom on each of two floors in which the work of the city's six trial courts took place.[18] On the second floor were public offices that attracted parties never noted in the records of judicial proceedings. The Register of Wills maintained estate-related records; the Commission on Insolvent Debtors processed petitions for debt relief; the sheriff took criminal complaints; the county commissioners reviewed matters of public policy; and the clerk of the court recorded real property proceedings and issued licenses for marriages, the carrying of firearms, the sale of liquor, and the ownership of dogs.[19] The Baltimore city courthouse was a very busy crossroads.

On that particular Monday, Calhoun and Govans were among scores of Baltimoreans taking part in the court's formal proceedings. The docket included a dispute over the opening of a city street, Cecil Alley, and the grand jury's finding in a case of wrongful death. Nearly twenty criminal defendants answered to charges of larceny, intent to commit rape, and murder.[20] Govans and Calhoun each appeared on the docket of the criminal court, scheduled to have their applications for permission to leave the state heard by Judge Henry Stump.[21] It was the terms of an 1844 statute that drew them into legal culture's formal halls. It required those free black Marylanders who wished to leave the state to secure court permission if they planned to return. Specifically, free black Marylanders who intended to leave the state for more than thirty days and later seek reentry were required to secure a travel permit from the criminal court.[22] The statute conferred legal personhood on Govans and Calhoun, paving an avenue by which they achieved some juridical agency. But the law was a double-edged sword. While it conferred legal standing, it also distinguished free black people from their white counterparts, marking them as distinct and indeed inferior. Newcomers were discouraged from entering the state, and longtime residents found their mobility restricted. In both cases, those who entered Maryland without leave of court were subject to arrest, fine, or sale into servitude if apprehended.[23] The statute also required an applicant to provide the written endorsement of "three respectable white persons, known to be such by the judge or judges of said court."[24] Thus, even as the law provided an opening through which African Americans asserted legal standing and a qualified right to travel, it also underscored their debased status as individuals subject to close, racialized scrutiny.

Travel permit requirements were but one part of a legislative scheme designed to establish the inferiority of free black people and curtail their access to social, political, and economic rights throughout the Southern states. The history of such schemes, often termed "black laws," extended back to the post-Revolutionary era when slaveholders argued that free black people would likely encourage slaves to run away or revolt and thus enacted restrictive laws. New statutes prohibited the in-migration of free black people; Maryland enacted such legislation in 1807. This was accompanied by laws requiring registration with local authorities, the posting of bonds for good behavior, and enhanced penalties for vagrancy and the aiding of runaways. Civil rights were curtailed through prohibitions against group meetings, marriage to slaves, and testifying against whites in court. Free black people were also economically marginalized through laws that prohibited them from selling staple crops and restricted their access to certain trades and occupations. The continued growth of the free black populations in upper South states and renewed fears of insurrection, fueled by the Nat Turner revolt of 1831, led Southern lawmakers to strengthen black laws in the 1830s and 1840s. Vagrancy laws were extended, authorizing the forced labor of free black men.

Colonization schemes aimed at removing free black residents to Liberia, as well as other places, received state support. Penalties to which free black people might be subjected were enhanced; whippings and enslavement became likely punishments for African American offenders.[25] Travel restrictions became more complex, penalties became more severe, and individuals such as Govans and Calhoun were forced to navigate a thicket of laws designed to distinguish their rights from those enjoyed by white Marylanders.

While the formal obstacles they faced were formidable, the court record suggests that both Govans and Calhoun were summarily granted the court relief they sought. Separately, they stood before Judge Stump and stated the purpose of their travel, though these details the clerk failed to record. Govans spoke for herself and her companion; perhaps she was traveling to visit family, a reason typically offered by permit seekers. Calhoun proposed traveling alone; perhaps he sought work, another commonly proffered reason. [26] The requisite recommendations were presented, which in both cases were authored by members of the bar. Apparently without further remark, the court granted each the right to leave the state and later return. Of their travels we know little more. Calhoun returned to Baltimore, resuming his work as a blacksmith, though by 1858 his reported occupation was that of a waiter, suggesting that his entrepreneurial aspirations had fallen victim to the difficult economic times that confronted all black Baltimoreans.[27] Govans also returned to Baltimore, resuming life in her Aisquith Street home, where she remained until her death in 1878.[28] Historian Alejandro de la Fuente characterizes such moments as legal claims-making, instances in which those who were structurally marginal to the law used cultural knowledge and skills to gain the "enforcement of potentially favorable laws."[29] Govans and Calhoun successfully furthered their interests in personal and familial well-being, exercised their right to travel, to go and to come, and make their homes in the city of Baltimore.

The nature of the agency being exercised by Govans and Calhoun is further illustrated by an examination of the atmosphere in which free black men and women applied for travel permits. The courtroom itself, despite the relative formality of its proceedings, was a scene in which the open denigration of African Americans was tolerated if not encouraged. A local newspaper reported on such an instance during the trial of an African American man for larceny in the county circuit court. When one witness, described as "a small white boy," was asked if he understood the nature of an oath, the boy reportedly replied "Yes sir—To swear agin the nigger." The questioning attorney's response endorsed the boy's sentiment—"that is the best definition of a State's witness' opinion of the nature of an oath I ever heard"—and elicited a "roar of laughter" from the "bar and spectators."[30] While there is no evidence that either Govans or Calhoun were subjected to such open ridicule, the two must have steeled themselves for the possibility that their dignity and credibility could be undermined by others in the courtroom, even a child.

Beyond the stakes in the courtroom, Govans and Calhoun were surely aware of the risks associated with a decision to travel out of the state without the requisite permit. Stories in which free black people entered the state without permits were common. Among the most notorious was that of Thomas Harvey who was arrested and taken before a local magistrate on his return to Baltimore after a three-month stay in Philadelphia. Harvey allegedly admitted to "temporarily" leaving the state and his accusers sought the imposition of a fifty dollar penalty for every week Harvey had been in Pennsylvania; one half of any fine collected was to be paid directly to the informers, according to law. Harvey's saga, which was chronicled in the local press, included the testimony of supporting witnesses who described him as an "inoffensive, industrious and very worthy colored man." Harvey, whose family remained in Baltimore while he was away, had traveled to Philadelphia "chiefly on account of his health." Facing a fine of some six hundred dollars, the Harvey family faced destitution while Harvey himself faced the prospect of being sold into slavery if unable to pay the fine. The Harveys were spared only when the presiding magistrate, relying on a technicality, dismissed the case "for want of jurisdiction." Ruling that only courts (and by inference not magistrates) could rule in such cases, the magistrate denied his own authority and dismissed the charges. Harvey was fortunate to escape the fate his accusers demanded. However, his circumstances—arrest, trial, and the threat of punishment—were a cautionary tale for all free black Baltimoreans. Travel permits were not mere formalities. To obtain them, petitioners might be subject to racist vitriol in the courtroom. Without them, they were vulnerable to self-serving informants, capricious magistrates, and worse.[31] Thus, when men and women such as Govans and Calhoun entered the courtroom requesting travel permits, their claims-making was neither straightforward nor routine. It required the weighing of a complex set of interests and outcomes.

The individual agency evidenced through travel permit applications is only one dimension of the story, however. Elsa Barkley Brown's "pivoting the center" approach calls for incorporating the perspectives of those standing nearby in the courtroom and just beyond its door in Baltimore's streets. The starting point of this analysis is the meaning of travel for free black people in antebellum America. But examining these issues from the perspective of Baltimore's judges, lawyers, free black activists, and slaves reveals the connections between individual claims-making and broader struggles over rights. The city's judges understood these local proceedings as embedded in an evolving U.S. Supreme Court view of a constitutional right to travel. Those lawyers who supported the requests of free black applicants saw ties between permit proceedings and their standing as civic leaders. Free black activists read such requests against the debates about immigration to Africa in which they were embroiled. And enslaved Marylanders may have perceived a nascent political alliance with free black Baltimoreans through their shared struggles over mobility.

For those in the Baltimore city courthouse who followed developments in the U.S. Supreme Court, such travel permit applications held an additional layer of significance. By the mid-1850s, the Court, in an effort to define Congress's authority pursuant to the commerce clause, was defining the contours of a constitutional right to travel through a series of cases that situated the movement of free African Americans as central to understanding the authority of individual states versus that of the national government. Beginning with the 1841 case of *Groves v. Slaughter*, the Court considered whether the individual states could regulate the interstate travel of free African Americans, but left the question open for the moment.[32] Deliberations on the 1852 case of *Moore v. Illinois* provided an opportunity for the Court to clarify its view. The case took up a review of the state's conviction of a white resident for "harboring and secreting a Negro slave."[33] The defendant, Moore, argued that the state law was preempted and thus void in light of Congress's 1793 fugitive slave legislation. But the Court concluded otherwise, ruling that whatever restrictions the commerce clause might impose on the state, no act of the federal legislature could prohibit the individual states from exercising their police powers and sanctioning those who imported and harbored fugitives.[34] This was consistent, the Court explained, with the right of the individual states to impose regulations for the "restraint and punishment of crime, for the preservation of the health and morals of her citizens, and of the public peace." Among those who might be properly excluded from a state pursuant to such legislation were fugitive slaves, paupers, criminals, and liberated slaves, otherwise known as free African Americans.[35]

The issue of free black travel was again linked to the Court's thinking about the commerce clause in 1849 in what came to be termed the Passenger Cases. Beginning as separate proceedings that reviewed the constitutionality of Boston's poor law and New York's quarantine law, these companion cases reiterated that in the evolving jurisprudence of interstate commerce, the movement of free black Americans and the right to travel were bound up with one another.[36] Contemporary scholars frequently cite these cases as the origin of a constitutionally guaranteed right to interstate travel, relying on the words of Roger Taney's dissent in the Passenger Cases: "For all the great purposes for which the Federal government was formed, we are one people, with one common country. We are all citizens of the United States; and, as members of the same community, must have the right to pass and repass through every part of it without interruption, as freely as in our own States."[37] But Taney's use of the term "citizen" is a sign that the earliest articulations of the right to travel were not unqualified. Indeed, not one of the seven justices who penned opinions in the Passenger Cases argued for an unfettered right to travel. Instead, an increasingly familiar litany of groups excepted from said right was offered up—convicts, felons, vagabonds, paupers, the infirm, and slaves. Not one Justice challenged the view that the exclusion of free African Americans, and hence the curtailment of their right to interstate travel, was a right of the individual states. In Taney's view no scheme, be it a state regulation, an act of Congress, or an international treaty, could permit "Great Britain to ship her paupers to Massachusetts, or send her free blacks from the West Indies into the Southern States or into Ohio, in contravention of their local laws."[38] Essential to the Court's reasoning was the threat that the movement of free black Americans was alleged to pose for the nation.[39]

In the antebellum era's most notorious Supreme Court ruling, *Dred Scott v. Sandford*, Justice Taney's decision was also informed by his thinking about free blacks and the necessity to limit their right to travel. In arguing that Scott, and by extension all African Americans, were never intended to be citizens of the United States, Taney warned that if African Americans were entitled to the "privileges and immunities" of citizens, then state black codes would be invalid. The result, Taney explained, would be to provide African Americans "the right to enter every other State whenever they pleased, singly or in companies, without pass or passport, and without obstruction, to sojourn there as long as they pleased, to go where they pleased at every hour of the day or night without molestation," a circumstance he deemed beyond the pale constitutionally and in practice.[40] Free black people and white slave owners stood on constitutionally distinct grounds. On the substance of Scott's claim, Taney rejected any inference that the right of slave owners to travel could be limited. Invoking his reasoning in the Passenger Cases, Taney explained that the Constitution protected a slave owner's right to interstate travel—the right "to enjoy a common country"—such that movement between two states could not give rise to the deprivation of his property in persons.[41]

Would a local trial court judge, such as Baltimore's Henry Stump, take notice of such Supreme Court decisions and discern the relationship between the dynamics of the local courthouse and the reasoning of high court jurists? (In Stump's case it's difficult to say; by the end of the decade he would be impeached for being intoxicated and sleeping on the bench.) But many of Baltimore city's judges were likely to have followed these developments closely. Taney was a much celebrated Marylander, who continued to preside over Baltimore's U.S. Circuit Court, and whose accomplishments were carefully chronicled in the local press. In the instance of the Passenger Cases, reading of the decision was especially widespread. The text of the Court's ruling was disseminated to an unprecedented extent when Congress had ten thousand copies of the decision reprinted in pamphlet form, an innovation that facilitated a wide reporting on the cases.[42] The Supreme Court discussions of the 1850s provided another frame for understanding the significance of local travel permit cases. The parameters of the Constitution's commerce clause turned, in part, on the desire of free black Americans to travel without restriction between the states, the same desire that undergirded the proceedings initiated by Govans and Calhoun.

While the Supreme Court worked through its concerns about the movement of free black people, African American political leaders also placed travel at the center of their deliberations. Black advocates of emigration—schemes in which black Americans would permanently relocate to more hospitable locales such as Liberia or Haiti—asked whether they shouldn't exercise another dimension of the right to travel. This debate had been prompted by Congress's compromise of 1850, which had included a forceful, new Fugitive Slave Act that empowered slave owners to bypass state due process requirements and enlist the assistance of federal marshals when seeking to take an alleged fugitive into custody.[43] The law's impact was acutely felt in cities like Baltimore, where free black people lived with daily threats of kidnapping and sale into slavery. One response was the

Free Colored People's Convention of 1852.[44] This meeting brought to-gether sixty-one of Maryland's leading black citizens in an unprecedented gathering. (Commentators expressed surprise that such a meeting could be held in a slave state.) The meeting was called in response to a nearly successful attempt by the state's general assembly to pass a new spate of black laws that included a plan for the permanent removal of all free Af-rican Americans from the state.[45] A circular announcing the meeting put the emigration issue up front, inviting delegates to "take into serious con-sideration our present condition and future prospects in this country, and contrast them with the inducements and prospects opened to us in Liberia, or any other country."[46]

Free blacks were not alone in their consideration of emigration. In Mary-land, interest in encouraging free black people to leave the state had long been fueled by the work of the white-led Maryland State Colonization So-ciety, which sponsored schemes that variously advocated the removal of black Americans to Africa, Canada, and the Caribbean. (One of the few exceptions to the state statutes that barred free black people from entering the state was that which permitted them to enter Maryland on their way to Baltimore's ports, if they intended to then board a vessel bound for Libe-ria.) While such emigration proposals had long been the target of African American disdain, by the 1850s, the prospect of making their lives over in a new land—be it by way of colonization or emigration—was embraced by some black activists as a viable solution to the increasingly degraded lives they endured in the United States. [47]

As colonization schemes took on new relevance, black Americans, like those who organized the 1852 meeting in Baltimore, introduced their own emigration proposals. Charity Govans herself became an exemplar of sorts for emigration advocates when, in 1853, directors of the Maryland Institute refused to display her gilt work in their fair, reasoning that it was inadvis-able "to receive contributions to the exhibitions . . . from colored persons, because if their work [was] accepted, they will have to be received by visitors to the fairs." One commentator, a former Baltimore resident and emigration advocate, William Watkins, argued that African Americans should look to places like Canada. They could never expect to find equality and justice in the United States, Watkins stated, if Govans, a woman of talent and accomplish-ment, could not do so. Baltimore's black residents need not, however, have been emigration adherents to understand what such schemes entailed. Their city was the port from which ships carrying black Americans from throughout the north and upper South departed for international destinations.[48]

These issues became the subject matter of a heated public debate. As the 1852 Free Colored People's convention began, delegates found themselves confronted by what the *Baltimore Sun* later described as several hundred "evil disposed and riotous" individuals. Protestors assailed delegates as they entered the hall, while others gained entry, disrupting the proceedings. By the day's end, some delegates so feared for their safety that they abandoned the convention. The local press credited the Baltimore city police with reprimanding the "outsiders" and "rowdies" and preventing a general melee.[49] Such violence was not new in Baltimore; black Baltimoreans were often the targets of mob violence. But the confrontation during the Free Colored People's Convention was different. The outsiders and rowdies set on disrupting the proceedings were African Americans. Emigration was a hotly contested issue in Maryland, leading the city's free black activists to confront one another in meeting halls and in the streets. In the context of ongoing emigration debates, the travel permit applications of Govans and Calhoun might be understood as a commentary of sorts. Their choice to leave and later return to Baltimore—to maintain permanent residence in the city—ran counter to the proemigration views expressed by some black activists.

White Baltimoreans also were concerned with the mobility of free black people and how it might be used toward broader political ends. The work of the Maryland State Colonization Society, in encouraging free black people to leave the country, suggested one perspective. A closer examination of those white men closest to the travel permit applications of Govans and Calhoun, their "respectable white" references, suggests that white civic leaders were not of one mind. Indeed, to ask how it was that some white men came to act as allies to free black claims-makers is complex. Familial ties, commercial interests, patronage, paternalism, antislavery ideals, and nascent civil rights sensibilities were among the various reasons that led white civic leaders to lend their reputations to men and women like Calhoun and Govans.

Charity Govans drew her supporters from a group of men representing the city's mature political leaders. Among the three were brothers David and John Stewart who had long practiced law in Baltimore. David Stewart had served in both the state and the U.S. Senate in the late 1830s and early 1840s, and was well known to the court, but not only as a legislator and practitioner. In the

1830s, he had earned a reputation as a go-between or broker for those Balti-more slaves who sought manumission by way of self-purchase.[50] William Cal-houn procured his recommendations from a younger, but soon to be influential cadre of men. They included forty-two-year-old George Brown, who, just a few years later would be elected Baltimore's mayor. Brown had a reputation as an opponent of slavery that extended back to 1842, when he cut his politi-cal teeth by successfully thwarting the consensus at a Maryland "slaveholders' convention" that would have restricted avenues to manumission and imposed new, more stringent black laws.[51] William Talbott who also supported Cal-houn, later weighed in on the colonization/emigration question by serving on the board of the Maryland State Colonization Society.[52] Calhoun's third spon-sor was Hugh Lenox Bond, a twenty-four-year-old lawyer and Know Nothing Party activist. In the post–Civil War era, Bond would go on, as a state court judge and radical Republican, to advocate for the equal citizenship of black Marylanders. In the legislative realm, Bond became a celebrated advocate of black suffrage and from the bench was a forthright ally to those black Mary-landers making rights claims. In the late 1860s, Bond would declare inden-ture contracts unconstitutional and thus void, a move that buttressed African American claims for familial autonomy in the post–Civil War era.[53]

In securing the support of white allies, free black travel permit seekers navigated one more complex dimension of the proceedings and thereby drew white civic leaders into the question of whether free African Americans should travel and under what circumstances. And while in these cases, all six references clearly signed on to the view that, at a minimum, free black Balti-moreans should be permitted to leave and then reenter the state, their reasons for doing so likely varied. Some may have acted out of long-standing patron-age or familial relationships, and some out of a profit motive, collecting a fee for their services. (The Stewart brothers likely fell into one or the other of these categories.) Others, like George Brown, may have won their political reputations through the championing of a particular point of view. Men such as William Talbott, may have seen their "support" for free black travelers as an extension of their paternalistic relationship to free black people generally. And for still others, such as Hugh Lenox Bond, their associations with free black litigants may have given rise to ideals of racial justice that would not fully bear fruit until the post–Civil War years. The interests of white allies differed from those of the applicants they supported, yet their standing de-pended, in part, on their associations with these everyday legal encounters.

The act of appending one's signature to a permit application was one means by which some white civic leaders arrived at their views about the meaning of free black travel. Other points of view developed as numerous individuals including court personnel and local newspaper writers witnessed the proceedings. As litigants waited for their cases to be heard, among them were enslaved people, some present as criminal defendants and others accused of being fugitives. The right to travel resonated powerfully with the interests of these courtroom figures. Historian Stephanie Camp explains that contests over mobility were central to the infrapolitics of enslaved people.[54] Restrictions on the movement of slaves was a key component of their unfree status. The often clandestine travels of slaves—near and far, temporary and permanent—were an important mode of resistance. Whether enslaved Baltimoreans recognized mobility or travel as a site of political contestation they shared with the city's free black residents is difficult to say. Still the likelihood that African Americans of varied statuses encountered one another in the courthouse suggests the possibility of shared political consciousness born out of the shared interests embedded in the right to travel.

This essay's engagement with both the high and low of legal culture along with the realms of society and culture suggests that African American claims-making was at the center of antebellum legal culture. Their everyday encounters with the law were often related to broader contests of interests and rights. The travel permit applications of Charity Govans and William Calhoun were never merely the proceedings of little note that local newspapers dubbed them. They were one facet of a complex debate over the mobility of free African Americans that was taking place in high courts, local politics, and among black activists. The dynamics we already associate with the Reconstruction era are reframed. The capacity to travel freely—to move from place to place, including from state to state—was among the first rights exercised by former slaves in the postwar era. The capacity to travel facilitated the reunification of families separated under slavery, and the ability to move about at will was among the essences of freedom in a postemancipation world.[55] By challenging segregation in transportation, African Americans continued to use the courts as a battleground, testing the power of the Reconstruction era's Civil Rights Acts and claiming yet another aspect of the right to travel, insisting that they not be segregated from white travelers.[56] While in the postemancipation era contests over the meanings of travel, freedom, and citizenship would take center stage, in 1850s Baltimore, rehearsals for Reconstruction were already under way.

ACKNOWLEDGMENTS

The author thanks this essay's many readers, including the volume editors, Ira Berlin, Susanna Blumenthal, David Bogen, Chris Cappozolla, Jay Cook, and Risa Goluboff. Research for the essay was conducted with the support of grants from an American Historical Association Littleton-Griswold Research Grant and a University of Michigan, Department of History, William T. Ludolph Junior Faculty Development Award.

NOTES

1. Elsa Barkley Brown, "African-American Women's Quilting: A Framework for Conceptualizing and Teaching African-American Women's History," *Signs: Journal of Women in Culture and Society* 14 (1989): 921–29. Brown cites Bettina Aptheker's *Tapestries of Life: Women's Work, Women's Consciousness, and the Meaning of Daily Life* (Amherst, 1989).

2. Ariela Gross, "Beyond Black and White: Cultural Approaches to Race and Slavery," *Columbia Law Review* 101 (April 2001): 640–89, 640.

3. This essay does not consider encounters before justices of the peace, which Michael Willrich suggests were where poor people most frequently encountered nineteenth-century legal culture, *City of Courts: Socializing Justice in Progressive Era Chicago* (New York, 2003), 3–28.

4. "Baltimore Cattle Market," *New York Daily Times*, 27 June 1854.

5. "Local Matters: Mortality of Baltimore," *Baltimore Sun*, 27 June 1854; "Local Matters: Fourth of July," *Baltimore Sun*, 27 June 1854; "Proceedings of the City Council," *Baltimore Sun*, 28 June 1854; "Local Matters: Effects of the Heat," *Baltimore Sun*, 29 June 1854; "Local Matters: The Weather," *Baltimore Sun*, 28 June 1854.

6. Manuscript Census, Town of Baltimore, Baltimore County, Maryland, U.S. Census of Population, 1850, in Ancestry Plus, http://www.gale.ancestry.com/search/rectype/census/usfedcen/main.htm (accessed 31 March 2004).

7. Baltimore's 1848 city directory reports Calhoun as a blacksmith; however by 1858 he is reported working as a waiter *Matchett's Baltimore Directory for 1847–48* (Baltimore, 1847), 375, and *Woods' Baltimore Directory, for 1858–59* (Baltimore, 1859), 445.

8. Manuscript Census, Town of Baltimore, Baltimore County, Maryland, U.S. Census of Population, 1850, in Ancestry Plus, http://www.gale.ancestry.com/

search/rectype/census/usfedcen/main.htm (accessed 31 March 2004); and *Woods'*
Baltimore Directory, for 1858–59, 452.

9. Letter to the editor, *Frederick Douglass' Paper*, 26 August 1853.

10. Barbara Jeanne Fields, *Slavery and Freedom on the Middle Ground: Maryland During the Nineteenth Century* (New Haven, 1985), 4–6.

11. Fields, *Slavery and Freedom*, 7.

12. Christopher Phillips, *Freedom's Port: The African American Community of Baltimore, 1790–1860* (Urbana, 1997), 15, 27, 147. Phillips's excellent social history discusses the emergence of this free black community in Baltimore.

13. R. J. Matchett, *Matchett's Baltimore Directory for 1851* (Baltimore, 1851.)

14. Phillips, *Freedom's Port*, 153–56, 194–95, 203.

15. The precise number of convictions was 578. Baltimore City and County Jail, Proceedings of Visitors, "Report to the City Council . . . ," December 30, 1850, Maryland State Archives, C2045-3. African Americans were disproportionately represented given that they comprised just 17 percent of the city's population. In an average of at least 175 proceedings per term, the defendant was black.

16. Baltimore City and County Jail, Proceedings of Visitors, "Report to the City Council," December 30, 1850, Maryland State Archives, C2045-3. During the July term the court held fifty-four jury trials and three hundred "Saturday" cases (assaults, riots, etc.) over the course of thirty-nine working days, "Business of the Criminal Court," *Baltimore Sun*, 11 July 1854.

17. J. Thomas Scharf, *The Chronicles of Baltimore* (Baltimore, 1874), 535, 595–96; Thomas P. Slaughter, *Bloody Dawn: The Christiana Riot and Racial Violence in the Antebellum North* (New York, 1991); Conway W. Sams and Elihu S. Riley, *The Bench and Bar of Maryland: A History, 1634–1901* (Chicago, 1901), 495; and, "The Fifteenth Amendment. Ratification Celebration in Baltimore," *Baltimore Sun*, 20 May 1870.

18. The Criminal Court, the Orphans Court, the Baltimore City Circuit Court, the City Superior Court, the Court of Common Pleas, and the District Court for the Sixth Judicial District of Maryland sat for terms of varying lengths. Morris L. Radoff, *The County Courthouses and Records of Maryland. Part One: The Courthouses* (Annapolis, Md., 1960), 27–29. Morris Radoff, Gus Skordas, and Phebe R. Jacobsen, *The County Courthouses and Records of Maryland*, pt. 2, *The Records* (Annapolis, Md., 1963). See also, John Carrol Byrnes, "Commemorative Histories of the Bench," *University of Baltimore Law Forum* 27: 3–4.

19. In May 1854 the *Baltimore Sun* noted that the courthouse was particularly crowded with those seeking to renew their "state licenses." "Local Matters: Licenses," *Baltimore Sun*, 6 May 1854. The clerk of the Court of Common Pleas reported having issued 816 marriage licenses during the first half of 1854, "Marriage Licenses," *Baltimore Sun*, 3 August 1854.

20. "Proceedings in the Courts," *Baltimore Sun*, 27 June 1854.

21. Baltimore City Criminal Court; Minutes, 26 June 1854, Maryland State Archives, T483.

22. In 1844 the statute under which Govans and Calhoun made their application was enacted. In that year, the legislature limited the period during which free black residents could leave the state for more than thirty days to May through November, Jeffrey R. Brackett, *The Negro in Maryland: A Study of the Institution of Slavery* (Baltimore, 1889), 177, 179.

23. Since 1807 the state of Maryland had barred the entry of free black people into the state, Brackett, *Negro in Maryland*, 176.

24. Brackett. *Negro in Maryland*, 179, and, *The Maryland Code: Public General Laws and Public Local Laws, 1860*, Article 66, section 50. These restrictions thwarted free black efforts to reunite their families and to obtain gainful employment outside of Maryland. White employers were also subject to the statutes' terms and were thus barred from bringing free black laborers into the state, Brackett, *Negro in Maryland*, 177–83. In the early 1850s the harshest dimensions of these strictures continued to be imposed as in the case of a young man who crossed the border from Pennsylvania into Maryland and was nearly sold into slavery, "Local Matters: Border Kidnapping," *Baltimore Sun*, 17 June 1852. As discussed by Gerald L. Neuman in "The Lost Century of American Immigration Law (1776–1875)," numerous southern states imposed similar restrictions on the movement of free black residents, *Columbia Law Review* 93 (December 1993): 1866–80. Based on his review of the court records, Christopher Phillips reported that between 1832 and 1845, 1,430 free black Baltimoreans submitted travel permit applications, with 55 percent being men. Phillips further noted that just over 27 percent of such applicants were literate enough to write their own signatures, suggesting that permit seekers did not come exclusively from the small skilled artisan class that Govans and Calhoun represented, Phillips, *Freedom's Port*, 168.

25. Ira Berlin, *Slaves without Masters: The Free Negro in the Antebellum South* (New York, 1974), 92–97.

26. Brackett, *Negro in Maryland*, 175–83.

27. *Woods' Baltimore Directory, for 1858-59* (Baltimore, 1858).

28. *Christian Recorder*, 10 October 1863. Charity Govans 1878/10/28 28377 CR 48,054, Maryland State Archives, Maryland Indexes (Death Record, BC, Index) 1875–1880 MSA S 1483.

29. "Slave Law and Claims-Making in Cuba: The Tannenbaum Debate Revisited," *Law and History Review* 22 (Summer 2004): 339. See also Rebecca J. Scott, "Reclaiming Gregoria's Mule: The Meaning of Freedom in the Arimao and Caunao Valleys, Cienfuegos, Cuba, 1880–1899," *Past and Present* [Great Britain] 170 (2001): 181–216. Christopher Waldrep, while not explicitly adopting a claims-making analy-

sis, illustrates this type of freed people's legal agency in the immediate postemancipation era in his examination of Black Code–created courts in Mississippi, "Substituting Law for the Lash: Emancipation and Legal Formalism in a Mississippi County Court," *Journal of American History* 82, no. 4 (March 1996): 1425–51. Waldrep describes postemancipation Black Code restrictions as similar to the statutory strictures imposed on free black Marylanders in the pre–Civil War era. As Ira Berlin explains, "Southern whites developed institutions, standards of personal relations, and patterns of thought which they applied to all blacks after Emancipation," *Slaves without Masters*, xiv.

30. "Nature of an Oath," *Baltimore Sun*, 26 November 1856.

31. "Violating an Act of Assembly," *Baltimore Sun*, 28 December, 1855; "Interesting Question," *Baltimore Sun*, 4 January 1856; "Magisterial Decision," *Baltimore Sun*, 5 January 1856.

32. *Groves v. Slaughter*, 40 U.S. 449 (1841).

33. *Moore v. Illinois*, 55 U.S. 13 (1852) 9, 17, 307.

34. In *Prigg v. Pennsylvania* the Court discussed the tensions between states versus federal statutes related to the recovery of fugitive slaves. 41 U.S. 539 (1842).

35. *Moore v. Illinois*, 18, 11.

36. *Smith v. Turner*, 48 U.S. 283 (1849).

37. *Smith v. Turner*, 472. See, Andrew C. Porter, "Comment: Toward a Constitutional Analysis of the Right to Intrastate Travel," *Northwestern University Law Review* 86 (Spring 1992): 820–57, 820; Heather E. Reser, "Comment: Airline Terrorism: The Effect of Tightened Security on the Right to Travel," *Journal of Air Law and Commerce* 63 (May–June 1998): 819–48; Christopher S. Maynard, "Note: Nine-Headed Caesar: The Supreme Court's Thumbs-Up Approach to the Right to Travel," *Case Western Reserve Law Review* 51 (Winter 2000): 297–352; Jason S. Alloy, "Note: 158–County Banishment" in "Georgia: Constitutional Implications under the State Constitutional and the Federal Right to Travel," *Georgia Law Review* 36 (Summer 2002): 1083–1108.

38. *Smith v. Turner*, 647.

39. Regarding the relationship between ideas about European immigrants and African Americans, both enslaved and free, see, Neuman, "Lost Century of American Immigration Law"; Mary S. Bilder, "The Struggle over Immigration: Indentured Servants, Slaves, and Articles of Commerce," *Missouri Law Review* 61 (Fall 1996): 743–824; and Paul Brickner, "*The Passenger Cases* (1849): Justice John McLean's `Cherished Policy' as the First of Three Phases of American Immigration Law," *Southwestern Journal of Law and Trade in the Americas* 10 (2003–4): 63–79.

40. *Scott v. Sandford*, 60 U.S. 393, 417.

41. *Scott v. Sandford*, 60 U.S. 393, 528.

42. "Opinions of the Judges of the Supreme Court of the United States in the Cases of `Smith v. Turner' and `Norris v. the City of Boston,'" *Southern Quarterly Review* 16, no. 32 (January 1850): 444–502. For one discussion of the significance of this wide dissemination of the case for nineteenth-century legal culture, see, Alfred L. Brophy, "`A Revolution Which Seeks to Abolish Law, Must End Necessarily in Despotism': Louisa McCord and Antebellum Southern Legal Thought," *Cardozo Women's Law Journal* 5, no. 1 (1998): 33–77.

43. Stanley W. Campbell, *The Slave Catchers: Enforcement of the Fugitive Slave Law, 1850–1860* (Chapel Hill, 1970), 23–24. See also, Leon Litwack, *North of Slavery: The Negro in the Free States, 1790–1860* (Chicago, 1961), 248–52.

44. "The Free Colored People's Convention," *Frederick Douglass' Paper*, 30 July 1852; "Free Colored People's Convention" and "Colored Convention Mobbed," *Frederick Douglass' Paper*, 6 August 1852; "The Colored Convention in Session in Baltimore and Mobbed," *New York Daily Times*, 27 July 1852, and "The Free Colored Convention at Baltimore," *New York Daily Times*, 28 July 1852.

45. The proceedings of this convention are also reprinted in "A Typical Colonization Convention," *Journal of Negro History* 1 (June, 1916): 318–38; "The Free Colored People's Convention," *Baltimore Sun*, 29 July 1852; "Oppressive Legislation—Colonization," *National Era*, 27 May 1852; and Philip S. Foner and George E. Walker, eds., *Proceedings of the Black State Conventions, 1840–1865* (Philadelphia, 1980), 2:42–49.

46. "A Typical Colonization Convention," 322.

47. *Frederick Douglass' Paper*, August 26, 1853.

48. Between 1839 and 1860 the colonization society alone successfully arranged the relocation of nearly one thousand black Marylanders to Liberia. See, Penelope Campbell, *Maryland in Africa: The Maryland State Colonization Society, 1831–1857* (Urbana, 1971.)

49. C. Christopher Brown, "Maryland's First Political Convention by and for Its Colored People," 88 *Maryland Historical Magazine* (1993): 325.

50. T. Stephen Whitman, *The Price of Freedom: Slavery and Manumission in Early National Maryland* (Lexington, Ky., 1997), 126.

51. Sams and Riley, *The Bench and Bar of Maryland*, 489–90. Brown discussed this episode in his 1887 memoir, *Baltimore and the Nineteenth of April, 1861: A Study of the War*, ed. Kevin C. Ruffner (Baltimore and London, 1887; 2001); and Brackett, *Negro in Maryland*, 242–46.

52. Phillips, *Freedom's Port*, 233; "George W. Brown," in Sams and Riley, *The Bench and Bar in Maryland*, 484–505.

53. Richard P. Fuke, "Hugh Lennox Bond and Radical Republican Ideology," *Journal of Southern History* 45, no. 4 (November 1979): 569–86. Bond was also among the leaders of the Baltimore Association for the Moral and Educational

Improvement of the Colored People. Richard P. Fuke, "The Baltimore Association for the Moral and Educational Improvement of the Colored People, 1864–1870," *Maryland Historical Magazine* 66, no. 4 (Winter 1971): 369–404.

54. Stephanie M. H. Camp, *Closer to Freedom: Enslaved Women and Everyday Resistance in the Plantation South* (Chapel Hill, 2004).

55. Eric Foner, *Reconstruction: America's Unfinished Revolution, 1863–1877* (New York, 1988).

56. David S. Bogen, "Precursors of Rosa Parks: Maryland Transportation Cases between the Civil War and the Beginnings of World War I," *Maryland Law Review* 63 (2004): 723–34.

Chapter Four

· · · · · · · · · ·

City Women

Slavery and Resistance in Antebellum St. Louis

MARTHA SAXTON

Slave women in pre–Civil War St. Louis were atypical in almost every respect. Before the Civil War, St. Louis was only one of three Southern cities
with a population of one hundred thousand or more (the others being Baltimore and New Orleans). It was an anomaly in an overwhelmingly rural,
agrarian South. Urban slavery moreover, accounted for only 10 percent of
all slaves. Throughout all but the last decade of the antebellum period, St.
Louis slaves, like those in most other Southern cities, although increasing
in numbers, decreased in percentage of the population. After 1830, women
slaves became a growing majority of the slave population, even as that population was diminishing. Their experience, of bearing a premodern status in
a modernizing city, yet being highly useful to the growing middle class, was
another anomalous result of the mixture of city life and slavery.

If anomalous in status, Southern urban bondwomen experienced firsthand the most vexing contradictions of antebellum America. A thriving
market in slaves and goods, as well as proximity to the North, made the
contrast between the ideologies of egalitarian, democratic republicanism
and the racism required to stabilize slavery exceedingly stark. Bondwomen,

who worked almost exclusively as domestics, experienced at close quarters and with added bitterness the ideology that elevated white women at their expense. Enslaved women encountered both unique hardships as well as opportunities. Confronted daily with the ideas that underlay their own exploitation, women slaves resisted slavery, displaying an alternative interpretation of women's potential contributions to the young nation's store of virtue. Instead of submission and dependency, African American slave women struggled for themselves and their children against their condition. Living and working intimately with the privileges of white women, they rejected a moral culture that permitted the ownership and torture of slaves. Like their sisters on plantations, they rejected female weakness as a sign of virtue and admired defiance to oppression and adversity. This essay explores the particular circumstances of slave women in and around St. Louis and how these circumstances shaped their ideas about the responsibilities of womanhood.[1]

Urban slavery in a state in which only seven counties along the Missouri River had a population of 24 percent or more people in bondage, coexisted uneasily with a substantial free black, urban population boasting a "colored aristocracy," a growing market for free laborers, and a rapidly growing immigrant population depressing wages. More than forty years ago, Richard Wade, studying St. Louis, argued that urban life was incompatible with slavery, because hiring out soon caused slave discipline to break down, and slaves began to live like free men. He did not specifically address the experience of women. In the 1980s, Barbara Fields noted that the majority of Baltimore slaves were engaged in domestic labor, and Claudia Goldin later added that the majority of urban slaves, altogether, were women. Enslaved women in St. Louis, as in other cities, offered economic advantages that made them extremely desirable to cost-conscious, ambitious city dwellers and farmers on the periphery of town. While slavery certainly did not organize labor in St. Louis, neither was it about to be overturned.[2]

Elsa Barkley Brown has observed, "White women live the lives they do in large part because women of color live the ones they do." Certainly, in antebellum St. Louis the work of "a girl" permitted prosperous white women and their daughters to lead the lives they did. White families without a girl could not participate in the ideological leadership or the benefits offered the middle class because the women and girls had to work all the time. William Lane, a doctor and the first mayor of St. Louis, wrote to his wife that a mutual friend had made a bad move by marrying an indigent man. "One hardship . . . is the want of a girl: She [their friend] does most of the washing. . . . When I last saw her, she endeavoured to hide her hands, but I distinctly saw that the skin was rub'd off her wrists & fingers." William Lane bought a mother and two daughters and another three-year-old girl named Phillis to protect his own womenfolk's hands and give them the time to perform their roles in the middle class.

The difference between a white home with and without a "girl" was the difference between some leisure for wives and an education for daughters or lives of incessant labor. One rural Missouri white woman, without a girl, wrote a sister back in Kentucky, "The men and dogs have a fine time, but the poor women have to suffer. They have to pack water from one-half to one mile, do all the cooking and washing. So my advice to you is to stay where you are." And Sarah Ewing made the consequences of no "help" clear to one daughter, writing that she had "no apology to make for not knitting . . . socks but Caroline [another daughter] going to school and I had not time." The German immigrant Emil Mallincrodt explained to a relative the particular advantages of an enslaved girl over other kinds of laborers. "We all have reason to be pleased" about Tilly, the black, fifteen-year-old, he had purchased. "In addition to the housework she is able to help me in the fields. That will save me the wages of one hired hand next year." (A hired male hand cost about $43 dollars a year, while a hired girl of twelve hired out for about $34, despite her greater utility. A slave girl could be acquired for between $350 and $400.) As in other parts of the country, enslaved women performed not only housework but also field work, making them uniquely versatile and desirable.[3]

A girl was likely to be somewhere between seven and fifteen, although children as young as three and four appeared on the market. Advertisements for female slaves who were seventeen or eighteen began calling them "women." The territorial governor of Missouri in 1820 bought his sixteen-year-old wife a girl of six when she had her first child. In Boone County, 30 percent of children under fifteen years old were sold. John Mullanphy noted that he owned a four-year-old mulatto girl, whom he had willed to the Sisters of Charity if she should survive him.[4]

When a girl encountered the white family that owned her, she began her education in the interdependence of slavery and republican motherhood and in a moral paradox central to early America. The ideology of republican motherhood, which underlay antebellum attitudes about the duties and

expectations of white women, was first articulated as a post-Revolutionary justification for their education and was to equip them to raise sons and
daughters virtuous enough to ensure the future righteousness of the growing United States. Republican mothers would perform their citizenship at
home and in church by producing morally upright children, while republican fathers participated in politics and the economy on behalf of the family.
To function, this allocation of responsibilities and spheres of action required
dependent family relationships, legitimated and protected by the state.[5]

Thanks to a girl's labor, the majority of white girls in and around St.
Louis, achieved literacy and some facility with arithmetic. Wealthier ones
studied literature, biology, botany, history, philosophy, French, and sometimes Italian. For an extra fee, girls could learn a variety of needlework
and ornamental crafts, from embroidery to "grotto" work, which involved
gluing shells on black velvet. St. Louis had many schools for girls, and
there were academies and colleges as well in Little Dixie, the plantation
counties where slaves cultivated hemp, tobacco, and cotton along the Missouri River.[6]

Mothers, educators, and republican ideologues like Benjamin Rush
agreed that while academic subjects had value, morals were fundamental
to female education. Narrowly construed, this meant self-renunciation and
sexual purity, aspects of the disinterestedness women were supposed to embody, but morality also included an emphasis on the importance of cultivating and sustaining relationships. This training, particularly evident in the
letters girls exchanged with their families and friends, displayed a constant
desire to remain emotionally connected with intimates and exposed the
ways girls learned to cultivate the ties of dependency that they would need
to sustain them throughout their lives.

Republican ideology in the North placed family at the moral center of
the nation. In the North, and to a large extent St. Louis families correspond-
ed to this middle-class model, an absent father left a mother in charge of
the moral care of her young. (In the South the father was usually not absent, and the mother's influence was lessened, both by his presence and by
the greater powers Southern states allocated to patriarchs.) The Northern,
middle-class mother used emotional rewards and punishments to instill an
active, internal moral monitor in her children and to enlist their feelings
in the ongoing shaping of their behavior. Cultivating dependency and the
emotional arts made sense for both middle-class white girls and those of the

Southern elite. Both were destined to rely on their husbands for support and were supposed to guide the family's moral and sentimental life.[7]

The girl on whom the education of white girls depended was much less likely to become literate herself than her white counterpart. Still, the urban setting gave her unusual opportunities to resist the conditions of her subjugation and acquire some education. Black literacy at the time of the Civil War is estimated at 5 percent, but in St. Louis it may well have been higher. Although it was against the law for slaves to learn to read, the free black community in St. Louis helped set up schools wherever they could. Elizabeth Keckley, later Mary Todd Lincoln's dressmaker, ran a school for seamstresses, but it evidently taught much more than sewing. At least five black churches ran schools in their basements throughout the city. If, as historians have claimed, African American education was a form of social and political activism in the postbellum years, it was much more so in the antebellum years. Literacy was, of course, the single most important tool in gathering and disseminating political information. Free blacks and slaves took advantage of the hard-to-patrol confusion of city life to disseminate literacy.[8]

While white girls' education prepared them for leisure, companionship, and the maintenance of dependent relationships, a black girl had to learn to survive slavery while acquiring a variety of skills. The threat or presence of violence punctuated the learning process. Her education frequently coincided with being sold away from her mother, which normally happened around eleven, although it often occurred earlier. This prevalent rite of passage for slave girls forced adulthood on them suddenly and cut off their chances to revisit childhood dependency. As children or early adolescents, girls witnessed the largely private, protected, and dependent lives of their white mistresses. At the same time they were acquiring independence and learning to keep secret the curtailed, precious, private dimensions of their own lives.

Black girls learned to wash and iron, to weed gardens, to work in the fields, to tend poultry and cattle, and to care for white children, sometimes little older than they were. They learned to serve at table, prepare and preserve food, keep a cook fire going, clean the house, and sweep. Some worked making fabric, and sewing. Christian College, a school in Boone County, hired slave girls to cook, wash, and serve the white female students. In her seventh year, Mary Bell of Callaway County, Mo., began being hired out annually to take care of three white children. Lucy Delaney, remembered being whipped as a twelve-year-old slave for stained laundry before learning from her mother the secrets of washing clothes in the muddy waters of the Mississippi. Elizabeth Keckley recalled childcare responsibilities descending upon her at four years old. Mattie Jackson and her mother were sold to a Mrs. Lewis. Mattie's earliest education included learning that Mrs. Lewis had beaten a "little slave girl she previously owned nearly every night . . . [so that she would] wake early to wait on her children." Celia was sold at fourteen to cook and serve the sexual needs of her sixty-year-old owner; she was raped on the day she was purchased.

Mothers like Lucy's helped, when they could, to guide the transition of their daughters from being girls to being a girl. During this transformation, slave girls learned that they could never rely on someone else to shoulder their burdens or responsibilities, and this fundamentally distinguished their outlook from that of white girls. At the center of the white republican marriage was a kind of trade: a husband's economic support in exchange for sex and obedience. As one participant in the debate over the passage of a married women's property act explained, husbands assumed the financial responsibility for their wives voluntarily. In return the wife "guards the home, and, by her presence and affection; gives it a value inestimable and a charm above price." The part of white life that was "above price" began and largely ended within the home. But neither slaves' homes nor their lives were above price, and black mothers and daughters, far from being encouraged to guard their homes, were objects of or vulnerable participants in the market themselves. By marrying, a white woman would see her economic and legal rights transferred from her father to her husband. The process inevitably compromised her moral autonomy. A slave or free black woman did not have this option. She could not surrender the burden of herself even if she had wanted to.

Black girls did not learn the arts of dependency. On the contrary, because young slave girls routinely lost their mothers before or during adolescence, they entered abruptly into what Elizabeth Cady Stanton would later describe as the "solitude of the self." Georgia was the only state that legally restricted the separation of mothers and children, ruling that children under five should not be sold away from their mothers unless estate divisions could not be accomplished in any other way. As historians have observed, slave owners encouraged the establishment of families and the production of children in order to work them or sell them off. There was official disapproval among Catholics over separating slave families in Missouri, but this seems to have slowed down the trade only in the heavily Catholic Perry County. Brenda Stevenson has calculated that before the Civil War, upper South slaves, which included those in Missouri, had about a 30 percent chance of being sold away. The most likely age for sale was twelve to twenty-five. St. Louis was a central exporting location for slaves sent to the lower South.

In addition to loss of family, isolation at work was another factor in the solitude of St. Louis's female slaves. The lively commerce of the city promoted hiring out, thus inhibiting the creation of female networks that might develop on plantation life. Many urban enslaved women lacked the relative stability of extended family on plantation life. They frequently lived in family fragments or even alone and endured unusually prolonged contact with white people. Even in the hinterland of St. Louis, slaveholdings were small. In Callaway County, where Robert Newsom held Celia, he had five other slaves, all male. His holdings were equivalent to or larger than those of his neighbors.[9]

Not only did slavery, particularly urban slavery, shred slaves' family ties, but a racist press also facilitated the shredding by portraying blacks as lacking family feelings. The idea of family bonds, of course, evoked inconvenient sentiments that might hinder the smooth operation of the market in blacks, an important feature in St. Louis's prosperity. A mother, aunt, sister, or daughter is not someone to be forced to work long hours, to be whipped, or to be raped. In addition, the female qualities that defined national virtue—chastity, sacrifice, selfless maternal love, and protection of the pure home—could only occur in the context of republican family life. In republican theory, these were all dependent conditions that required male protection and support to flower. Slavery prevented men from protecting women, and racism represented black women as unchaste, impure, and self-willed.

While the law simply did not recognize slave marriages, the white press worked to erase evidence of slave affection and kinship. Newspaper depictions of slaves almost always stripped them of familial context and, since family relationships were the only virtuous context for girls and women, this automatically characterized slave girls as hard and alien. One newspaper advertised for Louisa (twelve) and Clara (thirteen) as delinquent runaways. Louisa and Clara were probably sisters trying to find their way back to their mother. Since colonial times, this had been the primary motive for girls' flight. Omitting that information cast them adrift from family relationships, without which American females deserved no protection and could not aspire to a moral life.

Like all slaves, they had no claim to a last name, a public reminder of their fatherlessness. While a white child missing a father *or* a mother was an orphan, editors never applied that poignant noun to slave children. The ad for Louisa and Clara cataloged their physical features, emphasizing oddities and supposedly racial characteristics. One was "middle size, African face, heavy built." Clara had "toes somewhat turned inwards and scattering," while Louisa had "slender feet for a negro." Worse, Louisa had a "bad face and bad expression." Simultaneously, their owner (with two names and therefore legitimately fathered or married), Henrietta Jacobs, was a "helpless widow," that is, a woman who had enjoyed the protection of a white man. His death made her and her "three little children," helpless prey to the depredations of the unlovely Louisa and Clara, notwithstanding the fact that they were children themselves.[10]

The prevalence of ideas about the casual family ties and feckless relationships among blacks permitted urban, white slave owners to treat slave mothers outside of any familial context. Pregnancy and childbirth were times when white families tried the hardest to satisfy a prospective mother's needs for the reassurance provided by those on whom she was dependent. The nineteenth century was a period of declining health for women, black and white, and childbirth acquired extra anxiety as women were often weakened for its rigors by ongoing illnesses like malaria. Expectant white women gathered female family members or, short of that, friends and neighbors, in addition to a doctor or midwife.

Slave owners on plantations tended to treat slave mothers marginally better during pregnancy and childbirth to protect their investments and encourage reproduction. But in an urban context, where hiring out was common, slave women had fewer comforts for childbirth than those even a plantation might supply. Dorcas Carr, a St. Louis resident and wife of the extremely wealthy judge Will Carr, hired out her pregnant slave Rachel to her nephew some distance away. Not long after, Rachel, who was ill, delivered a stillborn baby and died ten days later. The letters exchanged about Rachel never mention the baby's father, any relative or friend of Rachel, or any surviving children. They focus on questions of liability. Rachel's renters pointed out (gingerly: these were relatives doing business) that she had never been in shape to do much work and that they had provided her with the best of care: a family member had attended her in childbirth, and a doctor had visited her. They claimed responsibility for her medical care but not for her death.

The Carrs' correspondence memorializes Rachel as a term in a bad bargain. She could deliver neither the work expected of her nor a viable baby slave. Her story illustrates the special risks that enslaved women encountered in urban settings. Renting out slaves in a free labor market encouraged slave owners to abandon those paternalistic responsibilities planters sometimes assumed. The result for slaves was the isolation and exploitation of free labor without any of its rewards.[11]

Urban life highlighted the divergent ways black and white women viewed marriage. Since slavery and racism effectively made married black women's homes porous to the economic and sexual desires of white people, a married slave woman had a deep understanding of the limits of marital dependency. Most married, but they knew that freedom would "change their condition" (as white men often described marriage) more profoundly than marrying. Harriet Jacobs subverted the conventional resolution to a woman's existential fate in her narrative. "Reader, my story ends with freedom: not . . . with marriage. My children and I are now free!" Slave mothers, knowing the pain and fear that could lie ahead of their daughters, did not discourage them from marrying, but encouraged them to put off childbearing as long as possible.[12]

In republican theory, a husband voluntarily assumed the financial responsibility for the family while the wife remained outside of the economy giving the home its priceless charm. Slavery made nonsense of this claim. But even free blacks could rarely manage to divide up responsibilities in the way middle-class whites did. With the exception of a small elite, largely descended from children of Spanish African or French African unions, free black women in St. Louis worked outside the home. The majority worked as washerwomen. Some worked as cooks or nurses or in hotels, on riverboats, in boardinghouses, or in brothels. After 1835, and accompanying the growing conflict over slavery in the nation, free blacks were required to have a white person vouch for them or come up with a thousand dollar bond for a permit to stay in St. Louis. Their children were subject to being bound out from the age of seven to twenty-one. In this increasingly threatening environment, free black women, married or single, had to produce income.

Among free blacks in St. Louis as in other cities like Cincinnati and Petersburg, Virginia, there were a substantial number of woman-headed households and of women property owners, reflecting the prevalent practice of free black widows not to remarry. As widows, they sometimes were able to accumulate a bit of property and dispose of it as they wished. One historian has speculated that in the unusually egalitarian marriages of blacks, in which both spouses had to contribute to keep the family afloat, there was less female deference and more strife. It was, of course, all but impossible for slaves to subscribe to the notion that all sexual relationships should occur within marriage. Free black widows frequently rejected the ideal as well, choosing to remain unmarried to their male companions.[13]

Republican ideology and white society, of course, expected white girls to be sexually pure. It also strongly discouraged any but the most euphemistic discussion of sexuality, thus ensuring widespread female ignorance and compliance with the double standard that allotted sexual guilt and responsibility to women and excused sexual predation in men. The popular moralist Lydia Maria Child carefully referred to the sexual relationship of married couples as "blessed and holy." Republican culture protected the purity of white women legally. States passed legislation to protect them from seduction and abandonment. Moralists advised young white women to "maintain their proper dignity . . . [and] discountenance that familiarity which gives confidence to the other sex." In the newly developing middle class, a young white woman's expression of displeasure or coolness was supposed to be enough to discourage unwonted intimacy.

Historians have argued over just how "passionless" white, middle-class women actually were, but ideology, at least, insisted on and thereby to some extent protected, sexually innocent white girls and women. Even white feminists, who privately discussed men's sexual exploitation of women both outside and inside marriage, had to be cautious about discussing the sexual exploitation that lay hidden behind the ideology insisting on female purity. Women slaves had to grapple with exploitation daily, and this ongoing conflict expanded their ideas about the autonomy they desired and would aim for after emancipation.[14]

Racist ideology projected a picture of black women that was more or less the opposite of that of white women and contributed to the latter's superior status. A news story about an eleven-year-old "coloured girl" who "gave birth to a healthy female child" provided no other context. Without any details about the child's family or her rapist, the story mobilized stereotypes of black female promiscuity, unnatural strength, and unnatural appetites. The rape that certainly caused this birth went unspoken, so a white reader might conclude that this girl desired to become a mother. That her child was "healthy," given what we know about infants born to such young mothers, merely means it survived birth. But the story's subtext was the precocious sexuality, maturity, appetites, and unnatural physical strength of blacks, and the reported health of the child merely reinforced a portrait of amazon-like black females, strong enough to sustain exertions that would reduce white girls to illness or death.[15]

Not only were black women and girls portrayed as available for sexual exploitation, but Missouri also upheld the violation of female slaves as a legal part of their condition. Celia, a fourteen-year-old Missouri slave, became the property of the sixty-year-old Robert Newsom. He raped her on the way back from purchasing her and continued to rape her over the next five years. These rapes produced two children. Celia and a fellow slave, George, became lovers when Celia became pregnant a third time. George pressured Celia to stop Newsom's nighttime visits. Celia warned Newsom that she was sick and he should leave her alone. Newsom's daughters later testified that Celia had threatened to harm him if he did not. He persisted, and Celia clubbed him to death and burned his body in her fireplace. The next day, she asked his twelve-year-old grandson to carry the ashes out and scatter them.

At the time of her trial, her lawyer argued that she, like any woman, had the right to defend herself against rape. The judge, however, warned the jury that a slave woman could not protect herself against sexual assault. Newsom, as her owner, could come into her cabin for any reason, including the intent to have sexual intercourse with her, and she had to obey his command. The jury therefore had to find her guilty of murder, given that she had admitted killing Newsom. Convicted, Celia managed to escape once from jail but authorities caught and imprisoned her again. They waited to hang her until after she gave birth to a child who would have been a slave of the Newsom heirs if it had not been born dead.[16]

The story illustrates how the law underwrote violence against slave women. In addition, it displays not only Celia's reckless defiance but also her claim to pleasure and to what Peggy Davis has called affiliational freedom in the face of Newsom's torture of her. Stephanie Camp has argued that for many slaves the body was the location of important "everyday battles for regaining control" over their lives and their relations with one another. For years, Celia endured the repeated assaults of an old man until she found pleasure in the company of George. Her resistance quickly evolved from claiming pleasure for herself to claiming freedom from sexual slavery, even though it cost her her life.[17]

Celia's desperate defense, like Rachel's death and the news account of the eleven-year-old girl's giving birth, underlies the logic of black women abolitionists who, understanding the sexual abuse of slave women and their vulnerability as mothers, insisted that emancipation would not mean the right of black men to have secure possession of their wives, but the rights of black women to have "self-ownership." As the historian Amy Dru Stanley has observed, they saw personal sovereignty as a universal right that should not depend upon gender. This adds another layer of meaning to Harriet Jacobs's concluding her story with freedom not marriage and may help explain the high rate of free black widows who did not remarry. To the extent that nineteenth-century marriage resembled slavery, black women would reject it.

Black abolitionist women, like men, claimed self-ownership, but extended its meaning to include women's control of their own bodies. The exploitation of slave women's sexuality and reproductive capacity and their experience of the destruction of intimate relationships underlay this enlarged claim. To black women it made little sense to cede to husbands the right to the bodies they were trying to wrest from slave owners. If a master could not, in the eyes of the law, rape a slave, so a white husband could not rape his white wife. Republican ideas of women's purity and "passionlessness" made it shameful for them to allude to this truth, but marital obedience included a husband's right to decide how to use his wife's body. Furthermore, marriage laws in the republic gave husbands not only complete access to their wives' bodies but also custody of their children in the case of separation. Black women's emphasis on freedom and autonomy as of more profound significance than marriage derived from their woman-centered, all-encompassing critique of slavery.[18]

Attacking slavery head-on, enslaved women in St. Louis participated in the extralegal struggles against slavery and were at the forefront of the legal ones. Opportunities in a border state lying just across the Mississippi River from freedom appeared quickly and without warning. Urban practices like hiring out could offer unusual risks but also open windows on autonomy. Not a few black Missouri mothers and fathers, living in circumstances that encouraged flight, saw running away as a possibility for themselves and family members. St. Louis, with a relatively large free black population was a place where slaves could disappear. Crossing the Mississippi landed slaves in the free state of Illinois. (But proximity to the border worked both ways, and while freedom could seem close to Missouri, southern Illinois residents were often proslavery, and some even held illegal slaves there. Runaways were often returned.)[19]

Slaves lived and taught their children to live in a state of readiness for an opportunity. Children understood early that they might have to survive both unwilled separation and freedom. For slave children and parents, separations often meant both liberation and loneliness. A successful fugitive might be separated from the rest of his or her kin and friends, possibly forever, a high emotional price. But some slave children learned early that it might be worth paying.

Historians have noted the strength of mother-daughter bonds in West Africa and in the Deep South. This was no less true in St. Louis. Adding a special weight to this intimacy, colonial laws had made inheriting the status of slave dependent on the condition of the mother: her freedom was crucial to that of her children, and her daughters would bear slave children if they themselves were not free. In Missouri, mothers and daughters went to great lengths to free themselves together. Jenny, whose status as a "free woman of color" was in dispute, sued Ephriam Musick in 1825 for her freedom and that of her daughter, asserting that she and therefore her daughter had been wrongfully held in slavery. From 1805 until 1834, three Scypion women— Catiche, Celeste, and their mother, Marie—all sued for freedom and eventually won.[20]

Polly Wash raised her daughters, Nancy and Lucy, to believe freedom was sufficiently valuable for them to stay alert to take advantage of any opening that offered escape. This involved leading a double emotional life: one genuine and displayed only among trusted family and friends, the other of faked subservience and simulated accord with white rules. The second was a necessary expedient for most slaves, but acutely necessary for those considering escape.[21]

Both the Wash sisters married, but freedom rivaled romance in their lives. Both grew up self-reliant, watchful, brave, and discreet. Lucy Wash

Delaney, who acquired not one but two last names through a two-genera-
tion struggle for freedom, recounted the family odyssey of liberty. Antici-
pated or actual separations punctuated the life of her mother, Polly Wash,
and motivated many of her decisions. Polly Wash was a Kentucky-born
slave purchased at seven. Her owner, Joseph Crockett, took her to Illinois
when she was fourteen and held her there illegally. Therefore, she lost her
mother either at seven or at fourteen. In 1821 Crockett sold her to a St.
Louis resident, Major Berry. Wash married one of Berry's slaves and bore
Nancy and Lucy. After another change of owners, Polly's husband was sold
downriver. In the wake of her father's disappearance, Nancy was sold but
escaped from her new owner into Canada. Polly, too was sold downriver,
but managed to get away and walk to Chicago. Worried that her owners
might mistreat Lucy, now the daughter and sister of runaways, Polly returned to St. Louis. She sued to get her freedom legally, and Lucy's as well,
for having been held as a slave against the law in the free state of Illinois.

Lucy described her mother's elation over Nancy's escape and how she
displayed false irritation and displeasure in front of her owners. But Lucy's
memoir, written fifty years after these events, does not highlight the ex-
quisitely painful separations that motivated and accompanied most of these
comings and goings. Nancy's run for freedom came in the wake of her father's sale. Polly ran for freedom shortly after Nancy's escape, presumably
planning to meet her. And she cut short her journey so as not to endanger or
abandon the child who remained in slavery. Together, she and Lucy made
the final legal offensive. First, she won her own liberty and one dollar in
damages for the four years she had been held illegally in Illinois. Then she
won Lucy's freedom, on the grounds that the child's status follows that of
its mother. In some cases, freedom's attendant price of wrenching separation became more bearable when slave life was most unbearable. Unfulfilled
dependency, despair, and longing for loved ones characterized the lives of
many, if not most, slave mothers and daughters. But a shared belief in courageous female resistance helped mothers and children support heavy loads
of responsibility, pain, sorrow, and loneliness.[22]

Fear of separation motivated other attempts at freedom. Harriet Robinson Scott and Dred Scott's decision about when to sue for his freedom
demonstrate their understanding of the vulnerabilities of "a girl." Harriet and Dred Scott had been married in the free Northwest Territory, and
they could have made a strong case for their freedom much earlier than

1846, when they first brought the matter to court in St. Louis. Scholars have suggested recently that as long as they lived protected by a benign owner, freedom was not essential. But when a new, markedly less benign owner took them over, their two children had become old enough to be considered "girls" and sold. Suddenly it became crucial to a resourceful mother to acquire freedom to fend off the looming, catastrophic separation from her daughters. Using the resources of St. Louis, Harriet Scott apparently found the couple's first lawyer and was decisive in initiating the famous suit.[23]

African American women resisted their subjugation using the unusual opportunities of city life for education, flight, and judicial battles. At the same time, they endured special problems and extra solitude in an economy geared to free labor. Living at unusually close quarters with a growing, white middle class, their situation brought home to them, on the one hand, the terrifying vulnerabilities of their families deprived of the shield of republican ideology, but on the other, the ways in which white republican marriage and slavery resembled one another. This led some to a radical critique of marriage and an understanding of the need for self-ownership for women as well as men. All in all, the conditions of antebellum slavery in a thriving commercial city conditioned bondwomen to independence, self-reliance, and a critical appraisal of the young nation's ideology of republican motherhood. Excluded from the republican family, black women, free and slave, were likely to choose strength over passivity, justice over protection, and autonomy and deliberation over obedience.

NOTES

1. For a more detailed introduction to St. Louis, see Martha Saxton, *Being Good: Women's Moral Values in Early America* (New York, 2003), 173–82. On the urban South population, see Claudia Goldin, *Urban Slavery in the American South, 1820–1860* (Chicago, 1976), 11; see also James Neal Primm, *Lion of the Valley, St. Louis, Mo.* (St. Louis, 1981), 186–88; Jay Gitlin, "'Avec Bien du Regret,' The Americanization of Creole St. Louis," *Gateway Heritage* 9 (1989): 2–11; Charles van Ravenswaay, *St. Louis: An Informal History of the City and Its People, 1764–1865* (St. Louis, 1991); R. Douglas Hurt, *Agriculture and Slavery in Missouri's Little Dixie* (Columbia, Mo., 1992), xi; Cyprian Clamorgan, *The Colored Aristocracy of St. Louis*, ed., Julie Winch (Columbia, Mo., 1999). On urban slave statistics, see Goldin, *Urban Slavery*, 1, 123; for conditions of slaves and free blacks in particular cities, see Christopher Phillips, *Freedom's Port: The African American Community of Baltimore, 1790–1869* (Chicago, 1997), 20–19; Midori Tagaki, "*Rearing Wolves to Our Own Destruction": Slavery in Richmond, Virginia, 1782–1865* (Charlottesville, Va., 1999), and Leonard Curry, *The Free Black in Urban America, 1800–1850: The Shadow of the Dream* (Chicago, 1981). On resistance, see Deborah Gray White, *Aren't I a Woman? Female Slaves in the Plantation South*, rev. ed., (New York, 1985, 1999), 5, 7, 8, 24, and Brenda Stevenson, *Life in Black and White: Family and Community in the Slave South* (New York, 1996), 183.

2. See Richard Wade, *The Urban Frontier: Pioneer Life in Early Pittsburgh, Cincinnati, Lexington, Louisville, and St. Louis* (Chicago, Cambridge, Mass., 1959), 127, 222; Barbara Jeanne Fields, *Slavery and Freedom on the Middle Ground: Maryland in the Nineteenth Century* (New Haven and London, 1985), 25, 40–62; Goldin, *Urban Slavery*, 59–68; Phillips, *Freedom's Port*, 20.

3. Elsa Barkley Brown, "Polyrhythms and Improvization: Lessons for Women's History," *History Workshop Journal* 31 (1991): 86; William Carr Lane to Mary Ewing Lane, April 17, 1819, Carr-Lane Papers, Missouri Historical Society; William Bryan and Robert Rose, *A History of the Pioneer Families of Missouri with Numerous Sketches, Anecdotes, Adventures, etc., Relating to Early Days in Missouri* (St. Louis, 1876), 77–78; Sarah Ewing to Mary Ewing Lane, Sept. 13, 1827, Carr-Lane Papers, Mo. H.S.; Anita Mallincrodt, *From Knights to Pioneers: One German Family in Westphalia and Missouri* (Carbondale, Ill., 1994), 247; Philip Scarpino, "Slavery in Callaway County, 1845–1855," part 2, *Missouri Historical Review* 71 (1977): 270; James McGettigan Jr., "Boone County Slaves: Sales, Estates, Divisions, and Families, 1820–1865," *Missouri Historical Review* 72 (Jan. 1978): 176–96, 274, 285, 287–89; Elizabeth Fox-Genovese, *Within the Plantation Household: Black and White Women of the Old South* (Chapel Hill, 1988), 172–77.

4. Michael Tadman, *Speculators and Slaves, Masters, Traders and Slaves n the Old South* (Madison, Wis., 1989), quotes McGettigan, "Boone County Slaves"; Scarpino, "Slavery in Calloway County," 270; Lorenzo Greene et al. *Missouri's Black Heritage* (Columbia, Mo., 1980), 35, 50. The will of John Mullanphy, 2, Mullanphy Papers, Mo. H.S. See also *St. Louis Beacon*, October 20, 1831, April 30, 1831, July 4, 1829, Feb. 6, 1830; *St. Louis Enquirer*, Sept. 23, 1820, Sept. 30, 1820; Hurt, *Agriculture and Slavery*, 262. David L. Browman, "Thornhill: The Governor Frederick Bates Estate," *Missouri Historical and Genealogical Society Bulletin* 30, no. 2 (Jan. 1974 95; Philips Scarpino, "Slavery in Callaway County, 1845–1855," part 2, *Missouri Historical Review* 3 (April 1977): 270; George Morton, Bill of Sale, June 31, 1837, Mullanphy Papers, Mo. H.S.

5. Linda Kerber, *Women of the Republic: Intellect and Ideology in Revolutionary America* (Chapel Hill, 1980), 200. Jan Lewis, "Motherhood and the Construction of the Male Citizen in the United States, 1750–1850" in *Constructions of the Self*, ed. George Levine (New Brunswick, N.J., 1992), 143–61; Nancy Isenberg, *Sex and Citizenship in Antebellum America* (Chapel Hill, 1998), 7. See also Saxton, *Being Good*, 183–201; Joyce Appleby, *Inheriting the Revolution: The First Generation of Americans* (Cambridge, Mass. 2000), 40–45; Mary Ryan, *The Cradle of the Middle Class: The Family in Oneida County, New York, 1790–1865* (New York, 1981); Stephanie Coontz, *The Social Origins of Private Life: A History of American Families, 1600–1900* (New York, 1988), 116–60; Mary P. Ryan, *The Empire of the Mother: American Writing about Domesticity, 1830–1860* (New York, 1982); A. Mott, *Observations on the Importance of Female Education, and Maternal Instruction, with their Beneficial Influence in Society* (New York, 1827); Lydia Maria Child, *The Mother's Book* (Boston, 1831); Ruth Bloch, "American Feminine Ideals in Transition: The Rise of the Moral Mother, 1785–1815," *Feminist Studies* 4 (June 1971): 101–26; Carroll Smith Rosenberg, "Domesticating 'Virtue': Coquettes and Revolutionaries in Young America," in *Literature and the Body: Essays on Populations and Persons*, ed. Elaine Scarry (Baltimore, 1986); Jan Lewis, "Mother's Love: The Construction of an Emotion in Nineteenth-Century America," in *Mothers and Motherhood: Readings in American History*, ed. Rima Apple and Janet Goldern (Columbia, Ohio, 1997); *The Young Lady's Own Book: A Manual of Intellectual Improvement and Moral Deportment* (Philadelphia, 1832), 32–33, 35, 37.

6. Christie Ann Farnham, *The Education of the Southern Belle: Higher Education and Student Socialization in the Antebellum South* (New York, 1994), 2–80; Anne Firor Scott, *The Southern Lady: From Pedestal to Politics , 1830–1930* (Charlottesville, Va., 1970), 6–9; Hurt, *Agriculture and Slavery*, 199–205; Benjamin Rush, "Thoughts upon Female Education," in *Early American Women: A Documentary History, 1600–1900*, comp. Nancy Woloch (New York, 1997), 137–41.

7. Fox-Genovese, *Household*, 37–99; Peter Bardaglio, *Reconstructing the Household* (Chapel Hill, 1995), 1–55.

8. Norma Basch, *Framing American Divorce: From the Revolutionary Generation to the Victorians* (Berkeley, 1999), 19–67; Hans Hartog, *Man and Wife in America: A History* (Cambridge, Mass., 2000), 167–92; *Laws of the State of Missouri Passed at the First Session of the Sixth General Assembly Begun and Held at the City of Jefferson* (Jefferson City, Mo., 1830), 107–13; The Revised Statutes of the State of Missouri (St. Louis, 1835), 129–38, 66–67, 225; Perry McCandless, *A History of Missouri* (Columbia, Mo., 1971), 2:120; Marlene Stein Wortman, ed. *Women in American Law*, vol. 1, *From Colonial Times to the New Deal* (New York, 1985), 118.

9. On education among free blacks and slaves in Baltimore see Phillips, *Freedom's Port*, 164–69; See Harriet Wilson, *Our Nig, or Sketches from the Life of a Free Black* (New York, 2002), viii, for Henry Louis Gates's suspicion that there was more literacy among antebellum blacks than scholars have thought. Judy Day and James Kedro, "Free Blacks in St. Louis: Antebellum Conditions, Emancipation, and the Postwar Era," *Bulletin of the Missouri Historical Society* 30 (Jan. 1974): 124. Thomas D. Morris, in *Southern Slavery and the Law, 1619–1860* (Chapel Hill, 1996), 348, argues that whites did not really enforce the ban on literacy, but in Missouri they managed to close Mary Sibley's Sunday school (Mary Sibley, "Journal," Mo. H.S., Lindenwood College Collection); Fox-Genovese, *Household*, 148; see Linda Perkins, "Black Women and Racial 'Uplift' Prior to Emancipation," in *The Black Woman Cross-Culturally*, ed. Filomina Chioma Steady, 317–33 (Rochester, Vt., 1981), on African American women's extensive antebellum efforts for education and abolition. See Evelyn Brooks Higginbotham, *Righteous Discontent: The Women's Movement in the Black Baptist Church, 1880–1920* (Cambridge, Mass., 1993), 42. She cites Jacqueline Jones, *Labor of Love, Labor of Sorrow: Black Women, Work, and Family from Slavery to the Present* (New York, 1985)143–44, 147. On training girl slaves, see Marie Jenkins Schwartz, *Born in Bondage: Growing Up Enslaved in the Antebellum South* (Cambridge, Mass., 2000), 107, 109, 111, 113; Jones, *Labor of Love*, 120–21; White, *Aren't I a Woman?* 9. McGettigan, "Boone County Slaves." On Celia, see Melton A. McLaurin, *Celia, a Slave: A True Story* (New York, 1991), 24. William Andrews, *Six Slave Narratives* (New York, 1988), 2–9, 24–25.

Leslie A. Schwalm, *A Hard Fight for We: Women's Transition from Slavery to Freedom in South Carolina* (Urbana, Ill., 1997), 45; Stevenson, *Life in Black and White*, 187; Harry L. Watson, "Slavery and Development in a Dual Economy: The South and the Market Revolution," in *The Market Revolution in America: Social, Political, and Religious Expressions, 1800–1880*, Melvyn Stokes and Stephen Conway, 51 (Charlottesville, 1996); Stevenson, *Life in Black and White*, 183; Tadman, *Speculators and Slaves*, 6–7, 12, 24, 138. Schwalm, *A Hard Fight for We*, 67–68, has argued that slave women on rice plantations in South Carolina sometimes hindered planters from selling off their daughters. Stafford Poole and Douglas Slawson and, *Church and Slave in Perry County, Missouri, 1818–1865* (Lewiston, N.Y., 1986), 156–57; "Narrative of Old Elizabeth," in Woloch, *Early American*, 151–52.

Barbara Fields details the agonizing loneliness of the decline of slavery in the "middle ground" of Maryland, a border state like Missouri, in *Slavery and Freedom*, 24–25. McLaurin, *Celia*, 20.

10. *St. Louis Enquirer*, Dec. 20, 1823.

11. Maria von Phul to Henry von Phul, February 11, 1818, Von Phul Papers, Mo. H.S.; Isabelle de Mun to Jules de Mun, March 20, 1813[?], De Mun Papers, Mo. H.S.; William Lane to his mother, Dec. 13, 1820, and Sarah Ewing to Mary Lane, June 1, 1824, Carr-Lane Papers, Mo. H.S.; Judith Walzer Leavitt, "Under the Shadow of Maternity: American Women's Responses to Death and Debility Fears in Nineteenth-Century Childbirth," *Feminist Studies* 12 (1986): 135; Bryan and Rose, *History of the Pioneer Families*, 101, 303–4; Adele Gratiot to Isabelle de Mun, May 18, 1821, De Mun Papers, Mo. H.S.; Maria von Phul to Rosalie Saugrin von Phul, May 22[?], Von Phul Papers, Mo. H.S.; Sarah Ewing and Rachel Jenckes to Mary Lane, Nov. 28, 18??, Carr-Lane Papers, Mo. H.S.

12. Dorcas Carr to Dabney Carr, January 1850, and Henrietta S. Young to Dorcas Carr, March 11, 1857, Carr Papers, Mo. H.S. See Jenny Bourne Wahl, *The Bondsman's Burden: An Economic Analysis of the Common Law of Southern Slavery* (New York, 1998), 49–76, on liability for hired slaves; on childbirth and health, see White, *Aren't I a Woman?* 82–90, 101–9; on treatment of pregnant slaves, White, *Aren't I a Woman?* 98–99; Wilma King, *Stolen Childhood: Slave Youth in Nine-teenth-Century America* (Bloomington, Ind., 1995), 4–6, 150; Jones, *Labor of Love*, 19; Stevenson, *Life in Black and White*, 248–49; Goldin, *Urban Slavery*, 37. Michael Tadman, *Speculators and Slaves*, has effectively demolished Eugene Genovese's concept of paternalism, although plantation slave owners insisted on it in the posi-tive defense of slavery that emerged in the 1830s. Hiring out effectively disrupted it in urban conditions.

13. Amy Dru Stanley, *From Bondage to Contract: Wage Labor, Marriage, and the Market in the Age of Slave Emancipation* (New York, 1998), 32; White, *Aren't I a Woman?* 101–9; Harriet Jacobs, *Incidents in the Life of a Slave Girl* (Cambridge, Mass., 1987), 201.

14. Clamorgan, *Colored Aristocracy*, intro.; Suzanne Lebsock, *The Free Women of Petersburg: Status and Culture in a Southern Town, 1784–1860*, (New York, 1984), 99, 100–11; James Horton, "Freedom's Yoke: Gender Conventions among Ante-bellum Free Blacks," *Feminist Studies* 12 (1980): 54.

15. John D'Emilio and Estelle Freedman, *Intimate Matters: A History of Sexu-ality in America* (Chicago, 1997), 144; Hartog, *Man and Wife*, 87–91. Fragment of a journal, 1845, Potosi, Mullanphy Papers, Mo. H.S.; *Young Lady's Own Book*,

261–62; Child, *Mother's Book*, 122–28, 151–52, 162–65. See Nancy Cott, "Passion-lessness: An Interpretation of Victorian Sexual Ideology, 1790–1850," in *A Heritage of Her Own: Toward a New Social History of American Women*, ed. Nancy Cott and Elizabeth Pleck (New York 1979), for thoughts on how such a view of women could be useful to them. Recently Karen Lystra, *Searching the Heart: Women, Men, and Romantic Love in Nineteenth-Century America* (New York 1989), has challenged the view that married women were either passionless or sexually ignorant. See Nancy Isenberg, *Sex and Citizenship* ,162–63; 166–67, for white feminists on issues of sexuality.

16. *St. Louis Beacon*, May 24, 1832.

17. A. Leon Higginbotham Jr., *Shades of Freedom: Racial Politics and Presumptions of the American Legal Process* (New York, 1996), 99–101; McLaurin, *Celia*, 16–61; Isenberg, *Sex and Citizenship*, 151.

18. Stephanie Camp, "The Pleasures of Resistance: Enslaved Women and Body Politics in the Plantation South, 1830–1861," *Journal of Southern History*. 63, no. 3 (Aug. 2002): 538; Peggy Cooper Davis, *Neglected Stories: the Constitution and Family Values* (New York, 1997), 38.

19. Stanley, *From Bondage to Contract*, 29–30.

20. Walter Johnson, *Soul by Soul: Life inside the Antebellum Slave Market* (Cambridge, Mass., 1999), 45–49; William Wells Brown, "A Narrative," in Gilbert Osofsky, *Puttin' on Ole Massa* (New York, 1969), 189; Katherine Corbett, *In Her Place: A Guide to St. Louis Women's History* (St. Louis, 1999), 57–58.

21. Joyce Ladner, "Racism and Tradition: Black Womanhood in Historical Perspective," in *The Black Woman Cross-Culturally*, ed. Steady, 274–79; Schwalm, *A Hard Fight for We*, 54, 68–71; Horton,, "Freedom's Yoke," 54, says men initiated most political actions for slaves but that women slaves initiated court suits. Certainly in St. Louis there were many. Jenny, "A Free Woman of Color," St. Louis Circuit Court, 21–23, May 9, 1825, Mo. H.S.; "Jenny v. Ephriam Musick and others," St. Louis Circuit Court, 21–23, June 1835, Mo. H.S., St. Louis Court Records. See also "Marguerite v. Pierre Chouteau, Sieur," St. Louis Circuit Court Records, Nov. 30, 1836, Mo. H.S.; see also Corbett, *In Her Place* , 27–28.

22. Lucy A. Delaney, *"From the Darkness Cometh the Light,"* or *Struggles for Freedom* (St. Louis, 1892?), in Mo. H.S., reprinted in Corbett, *In Her Place*, 57–58. Camp, "Pleasures of Resistance," emphasizes the importance of secrecy in resisting slavery. See White, *Aren't I a Woman?* 5, 7, 8, 24, on the reverence slave women shared for aggression in the defense of self, children, and the care of relationships.

23. Lea VanderVelde and Sandhya Subramanian, "Mrs. Dred Scott," *Yale Law Journal* 106 (1997): 1033–121.

Chapter Five

Free Soil, Free Labor, and Free Markets

Antebellum Merchant Clerks, Industrial Statistics, and the Tautologies of Profit

MICHAEL ZAKIM

On March 30, 1848, nineteen-year-old William Hoffman decided to leave home. "As I had in an early hour dressed myself for the journey," he wrote that evening in his diary, "I stood in the Threshold of the hall and with my eyes bent or turned to the east, looked now and then with steady fixedness for the stage to make its appearance." William spent the next five days traversing the Hudson Valley, trying to "install myself in business." The effort took him from the family farm in Columbia County to the river town of Poughkeepsie, to New York City, then to Brooklyn, Jersey City, and finally back upstate to Albany, where he secured a position as clerk in the dry goods firm of S.V. Boyd & Co. William spent the week, in effect, crossing not only the geographic but the economic, social, and cultural thresholds that divided farm and metropolis, homestead and boarding house, and, most significantly, growing things and selling them. As such, his job search was a personal moment in America's own transformation from agrarian republic to industrial democracy.[1]

The stage was several hours late in arriving—a last frustrating encounter with preindustrial time—and William got only so far as the town of

Hudson the first evening. But he was in Poughkeepsie by next morning, inquiring after work in the first dry goods store he encountered, and at the next several establishments as well. It soon became apparent that employment prospects in Poughkeepsie were dim, however; so William boarded an evening boat that would take him down the Hudson River to New York City, where he arrived just before dawn the following day.

Washing and combing himself in anticipation of another busy effort at self-promotion in the anonymous labor market, William began his search for a New York clerkship on Greenwich Street. He was soon advised to remove himself to Stewart's "great store" on Broadway, which was currently hiring. On the way he stopped into the shop of two acquaintances, Benton Badgley and Lay Bushnell, to borrow an umbrella, for it had begun to rain. At Stewart's, William again discovered, as he had in Poughkeepsie, that his lack of experience was a serious obstacle in securing employment. Selling choice potatoes in town after a day of hoeing, or even purchasing a promissory note from a local merchant for a "slick" one dollar profit, did not apparently qualify William for a place in the metropolitan market. Rebuffed, but not dispirited, he walked east to Pearl, Nassau, and William Streets, the heart of the dry goods trade whose millions of yards of cloths anchored the nation's commodity exchange in the years before Wall Street's ascendance to money market dominance. But he was no luckier there. By late afternoon William was back on Broadway. This time he turned up the avenue, stopping at every dry goods establishment along the way until he reached the northern outskirts of the city. Still no success. He walked back to Greenwich Street, where he had begun his day, and where he now had an unsympathetic encounter with a "Loafer" who played him for a country fool by pretending to be the firm's proprietor and raising false hopes about possible employment.[2]

By this point William had lost track of time. He planned to resume his job search first thing the following day, until someone told him that it was already Saturday night. So he spent Sunday waiting for Monday, at which point William took his efforts to Brooklyn. There, he ran into Jacob Dewith, who had clerked for William's uncle in Hudson, and who told William to proceed forthwith to his former employer's establishment in Manhattan, which was currently seeking to fill a position. Upon arriving there, William discovered another old schoolmate, Bushnell Lumis, already employed at the firm. Lumis informed William that twenty applicants had preceded him that morning and that the position was already filled. Instead of returning to Brooklyn, however, William now crossed the river to New Jersey, determined to try "every store" in Jersey City. There, too, he encountered an acquaintance from home but again "met with but little encouragement" in finding a job. Apparently, Gotham offered few opportunities to a mercantile novice from the provinces. William concluded that it would be best to return upstate and continue his quest for a start in business in Albany. If unsuccessful there, he would then proceed to Troy. He boarded the *Rip Van Winkle* after dark and slept with his head propped up on a table in order to save the extra fifty cents—which would have doubled his fare—that was charged for a berth. By morning he was in Albany. Fixing himself "as slick as possible," he struck out for the city streets. In Albany, William's luck changed, or perhaps his systematic efforts bore their inevitable fruit, for after meeting with a lukewarm response to his supplications in a carpet store, William landed a position in a firm specializing in piece goods. He returned to Hoffman's Gate to pack up his things (and begin planning the sale of the family farm), and was back at Boyd & Co. the following Tuesday, where he was initiated at once into the art of folding up calicos.[3]

The stamina that drove William's search for employment was a testament to his ambition. That ambition, in turn, was testimony to the self-making axioms of an age of free men and free labor. Neither William nor Benton Badgley, Lay Bushnell, Jacob Dewith, or Bushnell Lumis, nor the "countless throng" of other young men being carried along at midcentury by "an increasing centripetal force . . . towards the great emporium," were particularly interested in free soil. They had chosen the yardstick and the scissors over the plough and plane as their "way to wealth." It was a preference with distinct ideological repercussions. "It is a shame," the *New York Tribune* editorialized in 1845, "that fine, hearty lads, who might clear their 50 acres each of western forest in a short time, and have a house, a farm, a wife, and boys about them in the course of ten years, should be hived up in hot salesrooms, handing down tapes and ribbons, and cramping their genius over chintzes and delaines." Chintzes and delaines were clearly not the stuff of manly genius. Free citizens, as the *Springfield Republican* explained in 1856, "work with their hands, . . . live and act independently, [and] hold the stakes of home and family, of farm and workshop, of education and freedom." The merchant clerk satisfied none of these criteria. He snubbed manual labor and often removed himself from home and family in search of a place behind the counter in some distant city. Once having done so, he became a "salaried dependent"—practicing "servile conformity," according to the *Cultivator*—subject to the dictates of his employer and to the caprice of the market, all for the sake of commercial riches that had no obvious connection to either education or freedom. Jesse Chickering, a popular Boston lecturer and amateur statistician, described the resulting perversions: "So many thousands of our ambitious and energetic youths . . . forsake their rural homes, and the half-cultivated farms of their fathers, in the hope of more rapidly achieving independence, and perhaps a fortune, in communities where every branch of trade is already over-crowded with anxious competitors."[4]

"Stay where you are," was the common response, this one proffered by Joel Ross in *What I Saw in New-York* (1852). "Pick greens, weed onions, put faggots under the pot . . . lest when you get down here and open your bundle of luck, you find that you have left the all-important article at home, and you regret exceedingly that it was ever your misfortune to be the smartest man in Podunk!" And yet, the metropolis kept filling up with a peripatetic public of ambitious youth. "Each of them has left behind a beloved circle, which, alas! He has not yet learned to prize, and has entered into a comparatively homeless state," as the Reverend James W. Alexander decried in his "Merchant's Clerk Cheered and Counselled." Their "homelessness" seemed to mimic the perpetuum mobile of the commodity exchange they came to the city to administer. It was no surprise, then, that the clerk became the object of a more general concern regarding "this restless, nervous, bustling, trivial Nineteenth Century," as Henry David Thoreau catalogued his apprehensions of modernity. "Taxes increase, and rents rise, and the goods are marked up again. Upon whom now shall our indignation be expanded? On the clerk, of course. Who got up the war? Who levied the taxes? Who raised the rents? Who, but the clerks?" William Burns offered a portrait in his *Life in New York* of a "strong youth frittering away his strength and emasculating his manhood behind the counters of our retail shops," and Virginia Penny blamed them for female poverty in *Employments of Women*, explaining that "the reason there are so many young men performing the duties of clerks and salesmen, is, that they are lazy, and do not want to perform hard work." Even those entirely sympathetic to the new commercial order, such as the editors of *Hunt's Merchant's Magazine*, cast aspersions on the less than manly nature of the clerk's exertions: "[He] is to business what the wife is to the order and success of the home—the genius that gives form and fashion to the materials for prosperity which are furnished by another."[5]

Indeed, the talking classes fretted incessantly about Americans becoming "impatient of hard work out of doors." There was no one "who will feed his body on a roll of bread," as Horace Mann declaimed in countless appearances before mercantile libraries and young men's associations in protest against the culture of softness, languishing airs, and easier living prompted by material progress. "The stampede towards the golden temple became general," Joseph Baldwin observed in his *Flush Times of Alabama and Mississippi*, while Jesse Chickering, seemingly far removed from the speculative fever of the southwestern frontier, lamented to Boston audiences that "we have become emphatically a commercial community." He meant that the once axiomatic relationship between labor and its fruits was coming undone and that trade now seemed to be the basis of industry rather than the opposite. Francis Walker, superintendent of the federal census after the Civil War, likewise noted how significant it was that the country's industrial output was "conveyed from the producer to the consumer by a series of exchanges which can hardly average less than three in number, and with a percentage of expenses and profits . . . that must amount to fifty per cent upon their original cost. What a tremendous fact!"[6]

Such facts suggested that those "who own the soil, and work it with their own hands" (Thaddeus Stevens), or those whose independent freeholds "incite them . . . to rear families in habits of industry and frugality" (Schuyler Colfax), or those who "tak[e] the whole product to themselves, . . . asking no favors of capital on the one hand, nor of hirelings and slaves on the other" (Abraham Lincoln)—that all these free soil values were increasingly dependent on the "enterprise" of those who produced nothing of value themselves. Republican ideologues might have considered hard work out of doors to be a defining notion of American civic life, as Eric Foner has explained. But all that hard work was increasingly dependent on the offices of those who only knew how to dispose of the surpluses of others' productive efforts, whether by extending credit, closing sales, arranging stock, counting inventories, or keeping accounts, doing so in banks, insurance companies, export firms, import businesses, wholesale houses, jobbing agencies, and proliferating retail "palaces" and "warehouses." "An increased demand for men and money arose," wrote Thomas Kettell, explaining why New York City kept doubling its population during the same years that the city rose to commercial predominance. "Not less than three quarters of a million persons," Francis Walker continued in his analysis of the appearance of a giant class of men responsible for managing the country's market exchange, directly participate in "buying and selling the products of American industry."[7]

The fact that the industrial economy seemed to rest on the labor of some-one who did not satisfy traditional notions of industry was a disconcerting inversion of self-evident truths for a generation of Americans raised on the belief that man should earn his bread "by the sweat of thy brow," and on labor theories of value that continued to inform the writings of most of the country's political economists, who also continued to trace the source of value directly to the land. Emerson summed up the popular creed at mid-century: "No kernel of nourishing corn can come to him but through his toil bestowed on that plot of ground which is given to him to till." But the clerk, in fact, not only snubbed farm work but also repudiated the agrarian order in general. Frederick Marryat observed in 1839 that when a young man went to work for "some merchant, or in some store, his father's home is abandoned, except when it may suit his convenience, his salary being sufficient for most of his wants." That salary now replaced land as both the source of the young man's own livelihood and as the foundation of the economy, for the wage proved to be far more mobile and anonymous and, consequently, instrumental to the requirements of mass exchange. "Young Tradesmen" were advised to "live *totally independent*, in money matters, of all your kindred," the very possibility of which now sundered the tradi-tional dependence of sons on fathers and, with it, the social basis of the re-public. And so it was that the clerk rather than the proletarianized artisan or the New Harmony radical most acutely embodied revolutionary change in industrializing America and personally dismantled the agrarian patriarchy of old. He was brought into existence by market forces and then devoted himself to administering those forces, becoming representative of the indi-viduality, urbanity, mobility, fluidity, autonomy, anonymity, democracy, calculability, and accountability now considered essential to progress.[8]

Like all modern revolutions, there was a powerful dialectic at work in this one as well, for popular suspicions of the clerk's activities were aggravated by the fact that he was as anxious as anyone—and generally more so—to win a position of respect in the existing propertied order. William Hoff-man gave voice to this confusion when, by now a New York City clerk, he complained of the bustle and monotony of life in Gotham, "with all its mammon—its business—its would be luxuries—its plethoric 'markets,'" and ringingly declared his preference for an "ordinary country location and

residence." Preferences aside, Hoffman soon sold off the family farm inher-
ited from his father in an attempt to liquefy his assets. Another New York
clerk, Henry Patterson, attended a Mercantile Association debate in 1841
devoted to the question of whether "Commercial pursuits [are] more favorable to the development of mind than Agricultural" and reported that the
assembled clerks voted at the end of the evening in favor of the agricultural.
Perhaps, it was thought, such pledges of allegiance to country life would
rehabilitate a proprietary tradition that the clerks' own restless ambitions
had so effectively undermined, but which was still considered essential to the
proper workings of a commercial system by which they hoped to get rich.[9]

But the clerks' efforts to resolve the crises and dislocations of their own
making, their attempts to "take the risk out of risk," so to speak, and prove
that personal ambition did not threaten the social order—whether by extol-
ling preindustrial idylls of country living or by championing new techniques
of personal discipline (William Hoffman, for example, became an enthusiastic consumer of Graham bread and early morning saltwater baths, among
other tenets of the era's "self-culture")—were as subjective as the problem
to begin with. In this respect, no measure of individual effort could "naturalize the mania to trade" and recast the clerks' "frittering away" behind counter and desk as legitimate productive labor. That could only happen through
a more structural process, a structure in which the clerk's inverted priorities
would appear as entirely natural and normal. This now took place in a new
form of popular knowledge called statistics. Statistics proved uniquely capable of generating order out of the postpatriarchal commotion without re-
sorting to, or restoring, any of the old hierarchies. Indeed, statistics emerged
at midcentury as a primary means for naturalizing an industrial system in
which making things was subordinated to making a profit, that system which
had brought the new clerking class to the fore of history.[10]

The federal census of 1850 accorded statistics an unprecedented role in
defining American life. It was the first of the decennial enumerations that
counted individuals rather than households as the basis of the population
schedule. Census marshals had always recorded the total number of persons
residing at each "dwelling house" they visited. But the only personal details
that interested them, and the only details they actually collected pertained
solely to the head of the household. This practice was entirely consistent
with a patriarchal order in which all dependents—the overwhelming majority of the population—were subsumed under the civic and personal aegis

of the head of the family. Once this patriarchy became undermined by an economy and a democracy both intent on redistributing power, a new system for counting "the numbers and condition of the American people in all their relations" was required. "The history of each and every individual" consequently became the explicit subject of official inquiry, as Joseph Kennedy, superintendent of the census in 1850, now explained the document's dramatic innovations.[11]

The new census was comprised of six schedules. In addition to the population schedule, there were separate enumerations of slave inhabitants, of the previous year's mortality figures, of the products of agriculture and of industry, and of what was now being called "vital statistics," which encompassed a miscellany of subjects ranging from libraries and religious affiliation to pauperism and crime, all currently deemed necessary for ascertaining the conditions of civic life. The 138 queries included in the seventh census constituted a significant expansion beyond the 6 originally asked of heads of households in 1790. The new scope of inquiry expressed an emerging conviction that the census represented the best means for collecting statistical information. This conviction, in turn, rested on the no less novel belief that statistics were the best means for acquiring systematic knowledge of the variation and fluidity of modern society. As Nahum Capen, a member of Boston's American Statistical Association, wrote to Congress in 1849, the upcoming census should be designed to reflect the "rapid changes constantly taking place in our condition, the unyielding ambition of our people, the irregularity of enterprise, [and] the new and exciting temptations in prospects of wealth." For Capen and his fellow champions of the new science, statistics was an ideal discipline for the exciting, tempting times. The axiomatic proliferation of things and relationships in industrial society constituted the very ontological basis—not to mention the actual subjects of enumeration—of statistics. In this respect, it can be said that statistics made variety into the basis of system, indeed, of uniformity.[12]

Statistics rested on "a number of isolated facts, which thus isolated have little value for human experience," as the political economist Francis Lieber explained in 1836.[13] Only after the facts were collected and classified would they then provide "a more positive knowledge of the real state of things," that is, would they then become statistics. In practical terms, this positive knowledge was created by cross-referencing one fact with another (and another, and another), either over time (comparing, for instance, the

population of New York City in 1850 to the city's population fifty years earlier), over space (comparing the population of New York City to the population of Charleston), or simultaneously over time and space (comparing
the changes in the populations of New York City and Charleston over the
preceding fifty years). The operative principle of the statistical project was
simple: the greater the number and variety of facts that were collected, the
greater the volume of subsequent comparisons that could be made, which
would then yield a better knowledge of "the real state of things . . . in all
their relations." That is why directing all the new census queries to every
family member and not just the head of household offered such significant
statistical advantages.

The near limitless permutations that became possible when cross-referencing the growing number of "isolated facts" became an index of industrial
plenty. Statistics' modernity was further manifest in its nature as a system of
knowledge founded on the conditions of unknowability that prevailed in a
mass society where significant parts of the population now found themselves
living outside traditional networks of household and village. In fact, statistics solved the impersonality and anonymity of modern life that contemporaries found so disturbing by turning the problem into a solution. This was
so because statistical knowledge of social reality no longer depended on
familiarity—which was an increasingly impractical aim anyway—but on
the opposite. "The individual is wholly lost sight of in the average," Nahum
Capen assured skeptical legislators, who worried about a public backlash
against the unprecedented scope and specificity of the questions to be asked
of citizens in 1850. Or, as Robert Chambers wrote a few years earlier, "Man
is seen to be an enigma only as an individual, in mass, he is a mathematical
problem." And while "average man" might be a theoretical fiction, society
itself was also increasingly recognized, since Hobbes, to be an artifice, that
is, a man-made phenomenon. "Beneath this arithmetical exterior," *Harper's
Weekly Magazine* observed in a survey of the census returns published in
1855, "there are found the great cardinal facts of our real life." Statistics was
an artificial method for imposing order on an artificial society, a method that
had no interest in, or need for, traditional, organic hierarchies. Statistics was
not intimidated, in other words, by a market society's tendency to make the
value of everything permanently relative.[14]

Nor was it intimidated by the democratic implications of this relativity. As the historian Theodore Porter has observed, "It makes no sense to

count people if their common personhood is not seen as somehow more significant than their differences." Such equality, in fact, was what made it possible in the first place to translate the plethora of isolated facts into general truths, for comparisons could only be made between members of the same universe. What's more, the statistical goal of generating commonality out of innumerable individualities matched the American understanding of popular sovereignty as a government simultaneously of all and of each. Indeed, while many eighteenth-century republicans had resisted attempts to turn the census into a statistical tool for fear of government abuse of the knowledge that would subsequently be created (James Madison's proposal to include a query on citizens' occupations in 1790 was flatly rejected by the Senate), nineteenth-century republicans now considered statistics to be a means of ensuring proper government. In "dealing with man in the aggregate, and developing results that can be calculated with mathematical precision," the *American Geographic and Statistical Journal* explained in 1859, we move "step by step, to the knowledge of the laws that govern the social system." Likewise, an 1844 report in Congress supporting the establishment of a federal bureau of statistics argued that political oppression was the result of laws enacted upon "partial and imperfect information" that consequently favored the interests of one branch of the community over another. Since government in the United States was supposed to benefit "the *mass* of the people," then the facts informing legislation must likewise embrace "*every interest* and *every class* of the community." It was imperative for democracy to organize an ambitious statistical project (encompassing "every interest . . . every source of revenue . . . every object of expenditure . . . and every question") in order to provide its legislators with the information necessary to make good laws. Archibald Russell argued in his *Principles of Statistical Inquiry* that, in spite of popular prejudice to the contrary, such an aggressive government agenda posed no threat to the citizenry. He predicted that any resistance to an increase in the number of census queries would dissipate once the public was made to understand that such statistics served "all classes and all professions . . . equally. . . . The investigation proceeds from no party feeling . . . [since] all interests, commercial and manufacturing, agricultural and professional, are alike to be represented."[15]

Madison's proposal for classifying the population into agricultural, manufacturing, and commercial sectors so as to better inform the making of economic policy was eventually adopted in the fourth federal census of 1820.

Ten years earlier, a separate schedule for counting the products of industry had been incorporated into the third census. All these early surveys of economic activity, however, were guided by definitions of the public good resting on the tenets of moral economy: an a priori determination of the relative importance of this or that project to the common wealth. The contribution of textile production to the republic, for example, was very important. The contributions of upholsterers were far less so. This hierarchy then guided the actual collection of census information, for upholsterers were nowhere to be found in the resulting economic record. The stated goal of the industrial schedule of the third census might have been to present "the actual condition of manufactures" in the nation at large, but in 1810 this referred solely to those enterprises capable of replacing imports with domestically produced goods during the embargo, or to those directly contributing to settlement in the West.[16]

In 1820 an attempt was made to introduce greater system into the census's manufacturing schedule. Fourteen standard queries were formulated, inquiring into the quantities and costs of raw materials, of labor, of machinery, and of the goods consequently produced. The goal was to pose the same set of queries to all the country's enterprises, which would then result in a comparable—comparisons, of course, being the crux of the statistical project—abstract of the assets and expenditures of all the nation's manufacturing establishments. In addition, the census office printed an alphabetical catalog of manufacturing activities to be included in the enumeration. This was a further attempt at systematization, but one that nevertheless remained true to an a priori logic that predetermined the subjects of enumeration. Nor, apparently, was this extensive list of manufactures binding, for the 1820 census returns were no less partial and haphazard than those in previous surveys. Eventually, the same inventory of textile, metal, leather, soap, glass, and ship-building industries that were to be found at the heart of the traditional mercantilist production economy was reproduced. In this respect, the 1820 innovations could still not be described as statistical, for they continued to count what was already known rather than to discover a new reality beneath the "arithmetical exterior." These were, as Joseph Kennedy later acknowledged, closed systems informed by ideological habits that were no better than diversions and illusions.[17]

The 1840 census was supposed to be different. It consciously aspired to achieve a *"full view"* of the nation's industry. Two years earlier, in his presidential address, Martin Van Buren had explicitly endorsed suggestions for turning the census into a statistical digest. The purview of the upcoming federal enumeration was duly extended to include "all such information in relation to mines, agriculture, commerce, manufactures, and schools, as will exhibit a full view of the pursuits, industry, education, and resources of the country." The results, however, were so flawed that an 1843 memorial presented to the House of Representatives by the American Statistical Association actually regretted "that such documents [the census totals] have the sanction of Congress." This was, in part, a bureaucratic problem. The apparatus of census taking had not been revised to match its vastly expanded program. Egregious discrepancies were discovered between the published tabulations and the actual numbers appearing in the manuscript returns sent from the field, the result of a lack of supervision in the Washington office, where all the returns were collated. But the sixth census suffered from structural flaws as well. There was, for instance, still no attempt to establish a universal definition of what qualified as industry, that is, what qualified for inclusion in a census that aspired to achieve a "full view" of the resources of the country. Numerous irregularities were caused by the continued reliance on the personal discretion of marshals in the absence of detailed instructions. What's more, in being told to count what they considered to be a manufacturing or commercial enterprise, marshals often simply reported on what was already commonly defined as such. The result was both arbitrary and conventional, making most of the census's numbers statistically useless. Ultimately, the historical significance of the unprecedentedly ambitious 1840 census was the conclusion drawn by disappointed contemporaries, namely, that any serious attempt to survey the nation's industrial life would require a wholly new paradigm for counting.[18]

This paradigmatic breakthrough occurred in 1850. The first practical indications came in memorials sent to Congress in 1848 by the New-York Historical Society and the American Statistical Association that continued to criticize the 1840 debacle but now also called for a mobilization of expert advice in preparing the next census. Such advice was soon offered. Referring to the failures of 1840, for instance, Jesse Chickering advised Congress that "it is better to have a few leading facts clearly and accurately ascertained, than to attempt a great number and obtain only loose returns." Chickering contended that what had doomed the statistical agenda of the sixth census was its lack of any "clear and definite" idea of what was to be counted. He pointed as an example to the attempt to quantify commercial activities. "What is meant by those employed in *commerce*?" Chickering asked. "Did it include the itinerant pedlar, the small retailer, or the whole-sale merchant?" The failure to decide on uniform definitions had led to pre-dictably sorry results. Thus, 796 persons were listed in the returns as being engaged in commercial occupations in Troy, New York, while in Albany, a city twice the size of Troy, the total reported by the census was 35. In order to avoid such failures, Chickering concluded, it was necessary to standard-ize terms. And the best way to do that was by limiting the number of sub-jects to be counted by the census.[19]

Nahum Capen took issue with Chickering's proposal to reduce the scope of subjects included in the census's statistics. He argued that such a quan-titative sacrifice would not lead to a qualitative improvement in accuracy but would, in fact, have the opposite effect. "A work is generally executed with care," he argued, "according to the degree of its magnitude and im-portance." Capen was critical of the tendency "to reduce the objects of the census by making inquiries upon some subjects, and omitting others." This would be an arbitrary selection of subjects that would mar the statistical enterprise, that is, its inclusionary, nondiscriminating nature. He proposed, instead, to widen the scope of the census in order to bring statistical am-bitions in line with the ever-growing number of subjects that constituted economic life in the industrial age. Capen thought the best way to carry out such an expansion was by means of a system of multiple schedules, each with its own discrete set of queries specifically tailored to various branch-es of industry. This would simultaneously allow for improved accuracy, through more searching and minute questioning, without also sacrificing the establishment of standards.[20]

At this point, J. D. B. DeBow, editor of one of the country's most widely read economic journals, joined the debate in a series of "letters" published in the *New Orleans Daily Picayune*, which he addressed to the Census Board recently established by Congress. DeBow, who had taken part in the state census project in Louisiana and was destined to replace Joseph Kennedy as superintendent of the federal census in 1854, recognized that the old para-digm, by which census categories were based on existing hierarchies, had lost its relevance once it was decided to make the census a tool of statistics. He exposed the circular nature of a system that "makes indispensable to the taking of the census the very information which the census itself can alone give!" What's more, DeBow argued, no amount of more specific definitions could resolve what was, in essence, an epistemological problem. But DeBow was more concerned with the political than the philosophical implications of this question, and he was clearly troubled by Nahum Capen's proposal to institute a system of multiple manufacturing schedules. Such a plan, DeBow warned, would undermine the "rule of uniformity" that was essential to the statistical project and that was no less essential to national unity, which could not be taken for granted in the current era of escalating sectional conflict. It followed that a universally applicable set of queries for the entire manufacturing economy was necessary in order to generate usable results of general relevance. Designing separate schedules for separate economic sectors would be a self-realizing prophecy, DeBow argued, and would further divide the country into autonomous social units. Queries regarding rice, cotton, and sugar cane, for instance, would be exclusively directed toward the South, even though traces of these crops were to be found in almost all the states of the union. (True, they might often still be in an infant condition, DeBow conceded, but so was manufacturing in Massachusetts in 1790, which everyone now regretted not having been included in the census.) Likewise, schedules devoted to counting industrial production would be restricted to Northern states. As a consequence, the census, originally intended as "the great common measure of our representative system," would become no less than a vehicle of disunion. Ironically, then, the most insistent advocate of standardization and universality—the desiderata of the industrial market—was motivated by a desire to protect the position of slavery within the Union.[21]

The new plan ultimately adopted for the 1850 manufacturing schedule simultaneously incorporated Jesse Chickering's endorsement of a stricter definition of the subjects of inquiry, Nahum Capen's proposal to enlarge the scope of the census, and J. D. B. DeBow's argument on behalf of uniformity. The seventh census, in fact, was another great compromise of 1850—another project for creating unity in a fragmenting reality—and a far more successful one than Henry Clay's attempt in the same year to preserve the slave republic. (The first significant changes in the structure of the manufacturing schedule would only be made in 1880.) The revolutionary new industrial taxonomy—"constructed on entirely different principles from any ever used previously for a like purpose"—rested on the lone instruction to census marshals to count every "corporation, company, or individual producing articles to the annual value of $500." This single criterion immediately annulled all preexisting, predetermined productive hierarchies.

The census now presented a summary view of the economy's innumerable particulars that did not rest on any a priori plan or permanent social order. The economy was no longer governed by a supra authority. It was, rather, a sphere of life in which everyone was doing business with everyone else, and they were, therefore, governing themselves. In such a scheme, no branch of industry was inherently more or less important to the nation's material life than any other. Textile magnates in Lowell and furniture upholsterers on Manhattan's South Street qualified for inclusion in the same economic universe. While the special status or transcendent identity of certain manufactories had determined their position in (or exclusion from) the official record of productive enterprise in the past, the 1850 schedule generated an inclusive catalog consisting of a greatly expanded quantity of facts whose importance could only be determined after the returns were all in. As such, the industrial enumeration was analogous to the postpatriarchal individualism that lay at the heart of the new population schedule.[22]

The five-hundred-dollar definition of an industrial enterprise resulted in a far more extensive and variegated assemblage of "facts" than anything seen before. The businesses of confectioners, looking glass makers, tailors, milliners—and upholsterers—among others, some qualifying as industrial giants on the basis of the aggregate value of their product or the size of their labor force, appeared for the first time in the nation's record of material progress. Indeed, the massive presence in the census of so many types of manufacturing, let alone manufacturers, seemed to be incontrovertible proof that the discipline of statistics was exactly what it claimed to be, namely, "a neutral ground on which all parties may cordially meet."[23]

They met over a bargain. Statisticians claimed to have discovered a classification system that reflected the natural affinities of the material world. In so doing, they helped to naturalize a man-made reality in which apples and oranges, let alone tailored suits and iron ore, were entirely analogous components of a single "living economy." Gilbert Currie explained how the "mere facts and figures presented in the official tables gradually take on the form, substance, and habiliments, and become animated with something of the life, activity, and beauty" of material life. This realistic picture was based on a common monetary denominator—an "annual value of $500"— that effectively turned money into the foundation of statistical neutrality, untainted as it was by narrow political interests, by traditional hierarchies, or as improbable as it may seem, by "diversions and illusions." Markets and statistics shared the fundamental axiom of analogy—the desideratum of making everything comparable. This common nature now turned the manufacturing schedule of the census into a mirror of the business ledger. Business logic, in short, was reified as statistical truth.[24]

The new industrial taxonomy did not just generate a commercial order of unprecedented scope. It also transformed the nature of classification because the fixed sum of five hundred dollars actually constituted a highly fluid boundary. Without needing to be revised every ten years, it would yield a consistently varied picture of industrial activity in accordance to the constantly shifting conditions of doing business. The money standard, in other words, was as elastic as the market it measured. This did not, of course, mean that it lacked a stable point of reference. The five hundred dollar figure was strictly applied, not in the least because it could be. But in contrast to the strict notions of a permanent public good that informed previous census taxonomies, the 1850 model did not reproduce itself in the results. The opposite was the case, in fact. The returns now reflected the fluctuations and relativities endemic to the volatility of a growing market. The census was able to document the rise of new industries and the demise of old ones without requiring any prior knowledge of them. The five hundred dollar threshold thus became the foundation of an autonomous model of knowledge, one based on the presumption that change was a permanent condition. And so, a taxonomy that abolished stable hierarchies and certain results became the basis of statistical stability and predictability. In this respect, the census offered a structural solution to the bourgeois dilemma of having to bring order and control to industrial revolution without, at the same time, having to sacrifice the profits to be accumulated from the constant movement and flux. Money was credibly promoted to Archimedean status, the relativity and fluidity of exchange becoming the basis of "a harmonious whole in which all interests, commercial and manufacturing, agricultural and professional, are alike to be represented." In contrast to preindustrial visions of the common wealth, this harmony was not the result of a transcendent vision of the public good that would then be applied to the realm of material relations. Harmony, instead, would be achieved by the opposite method: first, the facts of material relations would be ascertained; only then would it be possible to begin to determine what they had in common.[25]

This, at least, was the conceit. But was the census's collection of facts as categorically free of a priori impositions as the advocates of statistical truth contended? Was the new census really so much more universal than its "crude" predecessors? Did statistics, in other words, really contain the source of its own meaning, constituting a system invulnerable to opinion and passion, a matter for "accountants, book-keepers [and] school-teachers, used to figures?" Archibald Russell was certainly aware of the tautological predisposition of the new science when he compared the statistician to a compiler of dictionaries in his 1839 work, *Principles of Statistical Inquiry.* "It is quite possible," he confessed, "to arrange a detail of facts as to bias the reader towards one or other of the leading political creeds of the day."[26]

In truth, of course, no fact could be collected without first deciding what qualified as a fact. The census could not be carried out, therefore, without a "leading idea," as was explained in an address to the American Statistical Association in 1844; otherwise it would be fruitlessly trapped in a loop between a preconception of economic life that informed the collection of facts and a collection of facts intended to inform a conception of economic life. Russell himself supplied such a "leading idea" in his aptly entitled *Principles* when he contended that manufacturing is "the fabrication for *wholesale trade* of any species of raw material." This meant that the transformation of nature into instruments of practical use would not be counted as an industrial activity until those instruments began to circulate as goods for purchase.

On one level, Russell's definition was sharply anti-intuitive. He acknowledged as much himself when he noted that manufacturing "conveys readily to the mind the general impression that it is the perfecting of raw materials." However, as he replied to his own admonition, "that is not the sense in which the [statistician] uses it." For Russell and his colleagues, aspiring as they did to invent a system of knowledge capable of epitomizing the "rapid changes ... [the] unyielding ambition ... the irregularity of enterprise, [and the] new and exciting temptations" of the age, knitting stockings at home in the winter was of such "trifling" economic significance that it could rightly be left out of the system. So could the productive efforts of the village shoemaker. "What sort of return can he make, he knows not how many boots he has made, nor the value of those he has repaired but working for minute gains he does not keep accurate accounts of the progress of his business." There was simply no practical way, in other words, to translate all these private undertakings into a public account of industry.[27]

If all manufacturing activities whose value fell below five hundred dollars were included in the census, Gilbert Currie wrote in the *Material Progress of the United States* in 1862, the result would be "of startling magnitude." Francis Walker, analyzing the 1860 census returns in the *Atlantic Monthly*, was more specific. "Of 43,624 coopers working at their trade," a figure Walker derived from the population schedule, where each person's occupation was recorded, "the production of only 13,750 is accounted for among the 'products of industry,'" whose numbers were based on the number of hands employed by firms that qualified for inclusion in the manufacturing schedule. "Of 112,357 blacksmiths enumerated, only 15,720 . . . contribute to the reported production of their craft; of 242,958 carpenters, only 9,006, and of 51,695 painters, only 913." A giant gap, in other words, had emerged between what was now counted as "industry" in the census's record of industry and what was otherwise still recognizable as productive labor. It was one thing to ignore family manufactures, which had clearly lost their place in an advancing industrial society. But Walker complained that the census's production taxonomy erased the artisan from the official record.[28]

The new statistical language, in other words, which proved so adept at narrating the growing complexity of the industrializing economy, had no place for the producerist grammar of free soil ideologues such as Walker. Instead, it turned industry into a process in which value valorizes itself, which, as Marx explained at the time, is how capitalism invents truth. This made statistics equivalent to other market tautologies, such as the merchant who misrepresents himself as solvent in order to obtain the credit that then makes him so. Counting industrial activity on the basis of the "leading idea" of producing for exchange meant, in short, that business had become synonymous with industry. Consequently, industriousness—the physical act of transforming nature into objects of use—was no longer the defining act of what could now be called an industrial economy. Such labor—unless it was wage labor—could not be integrated into a modern universe of common values.

And so it was that industrial revolution first of all revolutionized the very meaning of "industrial." It did this by means of new census categories for counting, which promoted the commodity to epistemological status. The result was an economy that only worked for profit. The yeoman republic, which was founded on the alienability of property as the guarantor of property's wide distribution, had bitten off the hand that fed it.[29] Buying and selling were no longer just the means for disposing of the products of labor. They were now products themselves. The merchant clerk could now assume his place in the pantheon of industrial labor.

NOTES

1. William Hoffman, Diary, New-York Historical Society, March 30, 1848.

2. Hoffman, Diary, April 17, 1847; March 1, 30, 31, April 3, 1848.

3. Hoffman, Diary, April 3, 6, 10, 1848; Toby Ditz, "Ownership and Obligation: Inheritance and Patriarchal Households in Connecticut, 1750–1820," *William and Mary Quarterly* 47, no. 2 (April 1990): 258–62.

4. James W. Alexander, "The Merchant's Clerk Cheered and Counselled," in Alexander et al., *The Man of Business, Considered in his Various Relations* (New-York, 1857), 8; Richard Poe, B.L.E.S.Q., Etc., "Modern Clerks—How Made Up," *United States and Democratic Review* 35, no. 2 (February 1855): 119; *New York Tribune*, Mary 7, 1845; Eric Foner, *Free Soil, Free Labor, Free Men: The Ideology of the Republican Party before the Civil War* (New York, 1970), 34; *American Whig Review* 15, no. 89 (May 1852): 471; *Cultivator*, June 1854; Chickering Papers, Duke University Special Collections, box 4, writings and speeches, Misc. 1821–1851, n.d.

5. Joel H. Ross, *What I Saw in New-York* (Auburn, N.Y.:, 1852), 136–42; Alexander, "The Merchant's Clerk," 8–9; Michael T. Gilmore, *American Romanticism and the Marketplace* (Chicago, 1985), 44; T. De Witt Talmage, *Behind the Counter: A Sermon to Clerks* (Philadelphia: George H. Hartman, 1866), 14; Burns quoted in John B. Andrews and W. D. P. Bliss, *History of Women in Trade Unions*, 61st Congress, 2nd Session, Senate Document 645 v. 95, 235; Virginia Penny, *The Employments of Women: A Cyclopaedia of Woman's Work* (Boston, 1863), 126; *Hunt's* quoted in Angel Kwolek-Folland, *Engendering Business: Men and Women in the Corporate Office, 1870–1930* (Baltimore, 1994), 56.

6. Horace Mann, *A Few Thoughts for a Young Man: A Lecture* (Boston, 1850), 29; Joseph G. Baldwin, *The Flush Times of Alabama and Mississippi* (New York, 1957); Jesse Chickering Papers, Box 4, writings and speeches, Misc. 1821–1851, n.d.; Francis Walker, "American Industry in the Census," *Atlantic Monthly*, 24, no. 146 (December 1869): 691–2.

7. Foner, *Free Soil*, 17, 29, 30–31, 45. T. P. Kettell, "The Commercial Growth and Greatness of New York," *Commercial Review of the South and West*, 5 (January 1848): 32; Francis Walker, "American Industry in the Census," *Atlantic Monthly*, 24, no. 146 (December 1869): 691–92. See also, in general, Mary Ryan, *Cradle of the Middle Class: The Family in Oneida County, New York, 1790–1865* (New York, 1981); Allan Stanley Horlick, *Country Boys and Merchant Princes: The Social Control of Young Men in New York* (Lewisburg, Pa., 1975); Stuart M. Blumin, *The Emergence of the Middle Class: Social Experience in the American City, 1760–1900* (New York, 1989).

8. Robert V. Remini, *The Age of Jackson* (New York, 1972) 185; Emerson quoted in Michael T. Gilmore, *American Romanticism and the Marketplace* (Chicago, 1985), 21; Marryat quoted in Burton J. Bledstein, *The Culture of Professionalism: The Middle Class and the Development of Higher Education in America* (New York, 1978), 214; Paul K. Conkin, *Prophets of Prosperity: America's First Political Economists* (Bloomington, 1980); James L. Huston, *Securing the Fruits of Labor: The American Concept of Wealth Distribution, 1765–1900* (Baton Rouge, 1998), 3–80; *Hints to Young Tradesmen, and Maxims for Merchants* (Boston, 1838), 53; Samuel Roberts Wells, *How to Do Business: A Pocket Manual of Practical Affairs* (New York, 1857), 53–54; Thomas Augst, *The Clerk's Tale: Young Men and Moral Life in Nineteenth-Century America* (Chicago, 2003) 1–2; Amy Dru Stanley, *From Bondage to Contract: Wage Labor, Marriage, and the Market in the Age of Slave Emancipation* (New York, 1998); Christopher Clark, *The Roots of Rural Capitalism* (Ithaca, 1990).

9. Hoffman, Diary, Aug 31, 1850, n.d.[late June 1850]; Henry A. Patterson, Diary, New-York Historical Society), January 1841, vol. 3, p. 47.

10. Colin Gordon, "Governmental Rationality: An Introduction," in *The Foucault Effect: Studies in Governmentality*, ed. Graham Burchell, Colin Gordon, and Peter Miller (Chicago, 1991), 39–41; Hoffman, Diary, June 26, July 1, 14, 1849; July 3, Aug 25, 1850; Michael Newbury, "Healthful Employments: Hawthorne, Thoreau, and Middle-Class Fitness," *American Quarterly* 47, no. 4 (December 1995); Mary Poovey, *A History of the Modern Fact: Problems of Knowledge in the Sciences of Wealth and Society* (Chicago, 1998), 90; William Ellery Channing, *Self-Culture* (London, 1844); Vincent J. Bertolini, "Fireside Chastity: The Erotics of Sentimental Bachelorhood in the 1850s," *American Literature* 68, no. 4 (December 1996).

11. J. D. B. DeBow, *The Seventh Census of the United States, 1850* (Washington, D.C., 1853); Joseph Kennedy, "The Origin and Progress of Statistics," *Journal of the American Geographical and Statistical Society* (1860): 109; see also Carroll D. Wright, *The History and Growth of the United States Census* (Washington, D.C., 1900), 39–50.

12. Nahum Capen in "Letters Addressed to the Hon. John Davis Concerning the Census of 1849, by Nahum Capen and Jesse Chickering," 30th Congress, 2d Session, Miscellaneous, No.64 (Senate), 1, 4.

13. "Memorial from Francis Lieber," 24th Congress, 1st Session, Senate, doc. 314, 3.

14. Capen, "Letters Addressed to the Hon. John Davis"; Theodore M. Porter, *The Rise of Statistical Thinking, 1820–1900* (Princeton, 1986), 57, 25; *Harper's Weekly*, February 1855, 334; C. B. McPherson, *The Political Theory of Possessive Individualism: Hobbes to Locke* (Oxford, 1962), 80.

15. Porter, *Rise of Statistical Thinking*, 25; *American Geographical and Statistical Journal* (February 1859): 56; "Bureau of Statistics and Commerce" (28th Congress,

1st Session, House of Representatives, Rep. No. 301), 1–3; Patricia Cline Cohen, *A Calculating People: The Spread of Numeracy in Early America* (Chicago, 1982), 154–56; Archibald Russell, *Principles of Statistical Inquiry; as Illustrated in Proposals for Uniting an Examination into the Resources of the United States with the Census to Be Taken in 1840* (New York, 1839), 10–11; James H. Cassedy, *Demography in Early America: Beginnings of the Statistical Mind, 1600–1800* (Cambridge, 1969), 215–16; Robert C. Davis, "The Beginnings of American Social Research," in *Nineteenth-Century American Science: A Reappraisal*, ed George H. Daniels (Evanston, 1972). 154–55.

16. *A Statement of the Arts and Manufactures of the United States of America, for the Year 1810*, digested and prepared by Tench Coxe (Philadelphia, 1814), xxvii; Alexander Hamilton, "Reports on Manufactures," *Annals of Congress* (1791), 971; Wright, *History and Growth of the United States Census*, 135; Russell, *Principles*, 52–58; Kennedy, "Origin and Progress of Statistics," 94. See too Timothy Dwight, *A Statistical Account of the City of New-Haven* (New Haven, 1811), vi–xi; D. B. Warden, *A Statistical, Political, and Historical Account of the United States of North America* (Edinburgh, 1819), 3:264–71; Timothy Pitkin, *A Statistical View of the Commerce of the United States* (Hartford, 1816), 56–73.

17. Secretary of State, *Digest of Accounts of Manufacturing Establishments* (Washington, D.C., 1823); Kennedy, "Origin and Progress of Statistics."

18. Wright, *History and Growth of the United States Census*, 36, 144; John Cummings, "Statistical Work of the Federal Government of the United States," in John Koren, *The History of Statistics: Their Development and Progress in Many Countries* (New York, 1918), 672–74.

19. Chickering, in "Letters Addressed to the Hon. John Davis," 19–30.

20. Capen in "Letters Addressed to the Hon. John Davis," 1–19.

21. *New Orleans Daily Picayune*, Sept. 27, Oct. 6, Oct. 7, Oct. 10, Oct. 13, Nov. 10, 1849.

22. Gordon, "Governmental Rationality," 14–16, 22; Victor L. Hilts, "Aliis Exterendum, or, the Origins of the Statistical Society of London," *Isis* 69, no. 246 (1978); Porter, *Rise of Statistics*, 61–62; Laura Rigal, *The American Manufactory: Art, Labor, and the World of Things in the Early Republic* (Princeton, 1998), 10; Poovey, *History of the Modern Fact*, 278; Daniel Roche, *A History of Everyday Things: The Birth of Consumption in France, 1600–1800*, trans. Brian Pearce (Cambridge, UK, 2000), 74.

23. J. D. B. DeBow, *The Seventh Census of the United States, 1850: An Appendix* (Washington, D.C., 1853).

24. Talmage, *Behind the Counter*, 12–13; "meet" in "The Approaching Census," *United States Magazine and Democratic Review* 5 (January 1839): 77; Gilbert E. Currie, *The Material Progress of the United States during the Past Ten Years* (New York,

1862), 6; A. Hunter Dupree, "The Measuring Behavior of Americans," in *Nineteenth-Century American Science*, ed. George H. Daniels 32; Poovey, *History of the Modern Fact*, 70–76, 126–29; Peter Buck, "Seventeenth-Century Political Arithmetic: Civil Strife and Vital Statistics," *Isis* 68, no. 241 (1977): 73–74; also see Peter Buck, "People Who Counted: Political Arithmetic in the Eighteenth Century," *Isis* 73, no. 1 (March 1982).

25. Jack Amariglio and Antonio Callari, "Marxian Value Theory and the Problem of the Subject: The Role of Commodity Fetishism," in *Fetishism as Cultural Discourse*, ed. Emily Apter and William Pietz, 201–2 (Ithaca, 1993); Russell, *Principles*, 10–11.

26. Edward Jarvis, The *Autobiography of Edward Jarvis*, ed. Rosabla Davico (London, 1992), 99; Rigal, *American Manufactory*, 8; Russell, *Principles*, 11–12, 55–6; *Constitution and By-Laws of the American Statistical Association . . . and an Address* (Boston, 1844), 16; DeBow in *New Orleans Daily Picayune*, Oct. 13, 1849.

27. Russell, *Principles*, 50–51, 121–22. An echo of Russell's thinking can be found in Wells's *How to Do Business* (15): "The manufacturer buys materials, changes their forms, and adds to their value, by means of the labor and skill which he applies to them, and then sells the results. He is one who makes something to sell. It may be a willow basket, or it may be a rosewood piano, a rag-carpet, or a piece of broadcloth; the process is manufacturing, and he is a manufacturer, and, incidentally, a trader."

28. More than half of the northern nonfarm population lived in rural areas in 1860. Jeremy Atack and Fred Bateman, *To Their Own Soil: Agriculture in the Antebellum North* (Ames, 1987), 202; Currie, *Material Progress*, 5; Francis Walker, "American Industry in the Census," *Atlantic Monthly* 24, no. 146 (December 1869): 689, 691–92; Secretary of the Interior, *Manufactures of the United States in 1860; Compiled from the Original Returns of the Eighth Census* (Washington, D.C., 1865), iii; see also "Memorial of the American Statistical Association, Praying the Adoption for the Correction of Errors in the Returns of the Sixth Census," December 10, 1844, 28th Congress, 2nd Session, no. 5 (Senate), 4–8; Martin J. Lee, *Consumer Culture Reborn: The Cultural Politics of Consumption* (London, 1993), 59–60; Poovey, *History of the Modern Fact*, 64; Cohen, *Calculating People*, 150–51, 164–68.

29. Gregory S. Alexander, *Commodity and Propriety: Competing Visions of Property in American Legal Thought, 1776–1970* (Chicago, 1997); Jeffrey Sklansky, *The Soul's Economy: Market Society and Selfhood in American Thought, 1820–1920* (Chapel Hill, 2002).

Chapter Six

· · · · · · · ·

Make "Every Slave Free, and Every Freeman a Voter"

*The African American Construction of Suffrage
Discourse in the Age of Emancipation*

XI WANG

The irony of the American Civil War, Eric Foner observed in 1980, was that "[e]ach side fought to defend a distinct vision of the good society, but each vision was destroyed by the very struggle to preserve it." Abraham Lincoln would certainly appreciate this observation as it echoed his own reflections about the paradox of the war: "We all declare for liberty; but in using the same *word* we do not all mean the same *thing*." Indeed, instead of preserving either antebellum version of American liberty, the bloodiest military conflict in American history produced "a new birth of freedom" that neither the North nor the South had ever imagined before the war. From the moment when the "contraband" slaves voluntarily entered the Union army lines near Fortress Monroe in May 1861, the foundations of antebellum American freedom had been shattered. The Civil War and the ensuing Reconstruction became essentially a struggle to redraw the boundaries of American freedom and to rebuild a new American nation-state. This struggle called not only for the bloodshed in the battlefields and legislative debates in Congress but also for the construction of a new political language that would capture the aspirations and imaginations of the nation's second revolution and translate them into a new constitutional order.[1]

The enfranchisement of African Americans, former slaves in the South and disfranchised free blacks in the North, was a major step toward a critical transformation of American democracy that, until the time of Reconstruction, had largely been race and gender based. Granting voting rights to African Americans shortly after their emancipation, as Foner has argued, "fundamentally altered the terms of the post-emancipation conflict in the United States" and distinctively set apart the U.S. experience of emancipation from that of Latin American nations. Establishing black suffrage as a political principle and a constitutional practice required not only a restructuring of the original constitutional order but also a novel political discourse to ideologically justify and sustain the constitutional undertaking. While debates over black suffrage have long been recognized as central to the politics of Reconstruction, historians have focused far more attention on the legislative work of Republican lawmakers than on African American advocates of black suffrage. The fact that no African American sat in Congress when critical black suffrage legislation was made—in particular, the Reconstruction Act of 1867 and the Fifteenth Amendment—may have justified the neglect for some. But overlooking the contributions of African Americans has impoverished our understanding of this process and continues to reinforce the impression that the freed people played no part in the construction of the post–Civil War American constitutionalism and were simply the beneficiaries of the new American democracy that was single-handedly designed by Republican lawmakers at the national level.[2]

This essay argues that African Americans took the lead in framing the nation's constitutional order in the post–Civil War era. It presents the neglected story of how African Americans seized the opportunity of emancipation to push for a fundamental transformation of American democracy. The evolution of the African American discourse on black suffrage from the antebellum period to the ratification of the Fifteenth Amendment in 1870 demonstrates the persistence and creativity of what might be called African American constitutional thinking or African American constitutionalism. The relationships between the Constitution, suffrage, citizenship, nationality, and democracy were debated by black leaders, black intellectuals (such as newspapers editors), and ordinary black folk across the nation. Such thinking was profoundly rooted in the American political, ideological, and constitutional traditions, but also charged that contemporaneous political consensuses or habits of mind had explicitly and implicitly reduced the inspiring principles of universal freedom to legal mechanisms used to enforce racial hierarchy before the Civil War. Indeed it was African Americans who first foresaw the Civil War not as a chance to save the old Union but to make a new nation, not to preserve the old freedom but to imagine and create a new freedom. The first to articulate the necessity of black voting rights and link it to the rebuilding of a new American nation-state, African Americans drew inspiration from American political traditions and their own experience of liberation during the Civil War era to invent a new political language of transformative constitutionalism that generated and sustained the democratic dynamics that led to the first nationwide experiment in racial democracy.

Black discussions of political equality originated in African Americans' struggle against voting discriminations before the Civil War. During what might be called the nation's first black disfranchisement movement, the voting rights of free blacks had been either restricted, taken away, or denied entirely by a majority of states in the Union—including those that had originally permitted them to vote and those that joined the Union after the enactment of the Constitution. On the eve of the Civil War only the five New England states—Massachusetts, New Hampshire, Rhode Island, Vermont, and Maine (where only about 7 percent of the black population in the nonslaveholding states lived)—allowed blacks to vote. In the meantime, Congress had prohibited blacks from voting in the unorganized territories under its control.[3] Although disfranchised, black citizens in the North never stopped protesting against voting discriminations.

Conducted primarily as uncoordinated efforts at the state and local levels, early black protests nonetheless shared ideological and political similarities. From the 1830s through the 1850s blacks in New Jersey petitioned the state legislature to repeal the state's 1807 law that had barred both women and blacks from voting. Under the pressure mounted by the black state convention of 1849–50, the state legislature considered amending the state constitution's disfranchisement clause, but the proposal was narrowly defeated. African Americans in Pennsylvania issued protests against the "Reformed Constitution" of 1838 that disfranchised the state's 5,000 black citizens.[4] Letters published by the *Colored American* in 1837 and 1838 protested the disfranchisement constitution and collectively documented legislation and speeches by the Founding Fathers to challenge the notion that free blacks were not citizens. Making "whiteness a qualification for the exercise of suffrage" in the North, one *Colored American* correspondent wrote, was a "wicked and shameful" outrage that could only be used to "sustain slavery at the South."[5] Organizers of the 1841 black Philadelphia state convention, including Martin R. Delany, called for the restoration of suffrage, defining it as "a right paramount in vitality and importance to all political rights."[6] In New York, where the state's black-only voting qualification of $250 in property had disfranchised the majority of the state's otherwise eligible black citizens, blacks had organized statewide conventions to protest. Addressing the state's white voters in 1840, a group of black leaders cited the Declaration of Independence and the Constitution as the embodiment of "the primary ideas of American republicanism" and called the right to vote "a republican birthright."[7] Indeed, many antebellum black advocates of political equality relied heavily on the Constitution in support of black citizenship rights. In responding to the Dred Scott ruling, one black correspondent argued that "colored citizenship" had been confirmed by Congress and presidents and could not simply be annulled by "various rulings of the minions of slaveholders."[8]

Frederick Douglass's powerful critique of the Constitution developed in tandem with his advocacy of black suffrage. Douglass's unconventional interpretation of the Constitution—emphasizing its general objectives to "establish justice" and "secure the blessings of Liberty" instead of its sanction of states' rights—attempted to compel the federal government state to take the lead on suffrage.[9] The Union, not states, embodied American nationhood and national values. For Douglass national welfare, prosperity, reputation, and honor laid the foundations for Americans' "common rights, common duties, and common country."[10] In an 1847 address in Norristown, Pennsylvania, Douglass argued that suffrage was "essential to citizenship" and that black disfranchisement had violated the fundamental principle upheld by the American Revolution of no taxation without representation. He further emphasized that excluding blacks from political participation would create hostility and alienation among blacks toward the state government.[11] In his 1855 speech against New York State's discriminatory property qualification, Douglass invoked "nativity" to identify blacks as politically "native Americans" who had helped found the American republic and gave utterance to their sentiments "in precisely the same language" of the Declaration of Independence. Conferring equal voting rights on blacks, he told the state lawmakers, would only make them more attached to "your institution" and gave them more reason "to love your government."[12]

Douglass's consistent references to the American governments—national and state—as "your," instead of "our," institutions, revealed a profound sense of alienation; such alienation resulted from antiblack suffrage sentiment prevalent among the Northern populace and Northern politicians. Lincoln, the rising star of the Republican party, aptly declared that "as a nation" the United States could not "continue together *permanently forever* half slave, half free" in the mid-1850s, but he would not oppose the feeling of "the great mass of white people" to even imagine the possibility for social and political equality between blacks and whites.[13] The Republican Party platform of 1860 kept silent on black rights, fearing being labeled problack by its opponents. In 1860, New York Republicans elected Lincoln but defeated the proposal to remove property qualifications for voting imposed on blacks in the state, leading to charges of hypocrisy. "The black baby of Negro Suffrage," Douglass chided in *Douglass' Monthly*, "was thought too ugly to exhibit on so grand an occasion" by the Republican party that claimed to be antislavery.[14]

By linking suffrage to citizenship, Douglass challenged the dominant nineteenth-century theory of citizenship, which separated the two. Douglass's view that the right to vote was an indispensable and universal right of the citizenship in a republic was rejected by important Republican leaders during the Civil War. Edward Bates, Lincoln's attorney general, issued an opinion on the definition and boundaries of national citizenship, insisting that citizenship and suffrage were separated as the former was a "political status" or legal belonging of an individual in a nation-state whereas the latter was a privilege accorded by an individual state at its own discretion.[15]

If, for Lincoln, the Confederate attack upon Fort Sumter on April 12, 1861, buried "the last ray of hope for preserving the Union peaceably," for African Americans, it opened the possibility of emancipation. Black leaders challenged Lincoln's policy of gradual and compensated abolition and defined the conflict as "essentially an abolition war." There was "no escape" from choosing freedom over slavery in the war, Douglass declared in January 1862, almost a year before Lincoln argued in his second annual message that "we cannot escape history" in terms of abolishing slavery.[16] In the meantime, Douglass seized the opportunity to affirm a new political relationship between African Americans and the federal government. Abandoning his deliberate use of "your" in reference to government, he told his Boston audience in February 1862, that "our Government . . . is still our Government" in spite of all its defects, and "in birth, in sentiment, in ideas, in hopes, in aspirations, and responsibilities, I am an American citizen."[17]

Lincoln, too, felt the need to break away from antebellum constitutionalism in order to preserve the Union. "The dogmas of the quiet past, are inadequate to the stormy present," he told Congress in 1862, "[we] must think anew, and act anew." By issuing the Emancipation Proclamation he committed the Union to "a new birth of freedom," for both free and enslaved Americans, a position from which he did not retreat throughout the remainder of the war.[18] He also recognized that black soldiers, who "stake their lives for us," had acted on "the promise of freedom."[19] Nonetheless, when it came to reconstructing "the republican form of government" in the Confederate states, Lincoln relied entirely on white voters.[20]

African American visions for reconstructing "the republican form of government," as outlined by Douglass in a number of his wartime speeches, were different. Because slavery had "stamped its character too deeply and indelibly" in American society, emancipation must be followed by a national action to "conquer its prejudice."[21] "Break[ing] the chains of their bondage" was not enough, Douglass reasoned. "To make slaves truly free, the nation must admit them to the full and complete enjoyment of civil and political Equality." Only by "saving the Negro, [could] the nation be saved, but only Liberty and equality without distinction of color could save both." Shortly after Lincoln delivered the Gettysburg Address on November 19, 1863, Douglass gave his definition of the nation's "new birth of freedom": a new American nation that was to be a "unity of object, unity of institution, in which there shall be no North, no South, no East, no West, no black, no white, but a solidarity of the nation, making every slave free, and every freeman a voter."[22] For Douglass, Reconstruction was a new nation-building process, dependent on former slaves and a democratizing process: "We are not to be saved by the captain this time, but the crew."[23]

Indeed, a national groundswell of demands for suffrage came from ordinary folk across the nation. In December 1862, T. P. Saunders and his brother, P. H. B. Saunders, two black tailors in Hartford, Connecticut, petitioned the U.S. Senate, protesting that because of their color they had been deprived of the "privilege of taking part whatever in matters of Government—both State and National." A black convention in Kansas in December 1863 demanded that the restoration of the Union go hand in hand with black voting rights. Black residents in the District of Columbia initiated at least two petitions in 1863 for voting rights, one asserting that it was only at the polling place that "a man confirms his manhood; and defends, supports and preserves his country."[24]

New Orleans blacks began their campaigns for suffrage shortly after the Union army had taken control of the city in 1862. Frustrated with local whites' hostility and Union generals' indifference toward their demands, blacks sent two representatives—Jean-Baptiste Roudanez and Arnold Bertonneau, editors of the city's black newspapers—to Washington, D.C., in March 1864, in hopes of persuading Lincoln and congressional Republicans to take national action to grant them suffrage. Presenting a petition signed by more than one thousand black citizens in the city, they challenged the notion that the federal government had no power to interfere with state regulations of suffrage.[25] Although generating little concrete results, their lobbying strengthened their Northern comrades' argument that politically conscious and active blacks represented the future South and were "a natural counterpoise" to the South's "malignity and enmity" to the national government. James Jones, a black soldier stationed in New Orleans, confirmed "strong opposition" in the state constitutional convention to black suffrage but also noted that the military advances of the Union forces had caused a "change in public opinion" in the city and that blacks in Louisiana had begun "to think of our race as something more than vassals, and goods, and chattels."[26]

The Civil War also revived Northern blacks' fight for equal suffrage. In October 1864 African Americans in New York used their state convention to launch a nationally collaborative effort, making black suffrage an issue for the year's presidential election. The convention created a National Equal Rights League and empowered its executive board to "take steps necessary to secure the rights and improvements in the conditions of life of Blacks everywhere."[27] Speaking at the convention, Douglass and other black leaders welcomed the proposed Thirteenth Amendment, but warned that, without suffrage, black freedom could not be permanently maintained. Douglass reminded the Republicans that two hundred thousand black soldiers had defended the Union "as volunteers" and that in "a republican country, where general suffrage is the rule," blacks wanted "to have a voice in making the laws of the country."[28]

Indeed, the most frequent argument for black suffrage during wartime, especially after the issuance of the Emancipation Proclamation, advocated rewarding blacks for their sacrifices to defend the Union with voting rights. In his recruitment speeches in 1862 and 1863, Douglass had urged blacks to adopt the "great national family of America" by joining the Union army, but reminded the federal government of its obligation to reward black soldiers with full and equal rights. Wm. P. Allen, a black minister from St. Louis, Missouri, also linked blacks' sacrifice in war to their right to political equality in peace. Intelligence and loyalty, not color, qualified a citizen for voting: "You permit the black man to fight for the Union, why not allow him to vote for the Union?"[29]

Other arguments linked black suffrage to "fundamental truths" as established by the Revolution of 1776: the right to self-government and no taxation without representation. African Americans in Missouri argued that they alone had paid a huge portion of the state's taxes and yet they had "never been permitted to taste the sweets of their labor."[30] Blacks in the District of Columbia complained that they had no right to voice their opinion of how the taxes they paid should be used. Black advocates regarded suffrage as an embodiment of a uniquely American civic identity and value, signifying one's national belonging and existence. Blacks especially valued suffrage because the American government was "based upon a peculiar idea and that idea is universal suffrage." If the United States were a monarchical, autocratic, or aristocratic polity, the deprivation of suffrage would "do me no great violence." But in a republic, the exclusion from political participation meant nothing but "to brand us with the stigma of inferiority." Blacks also rejected the Northern presses' frequent accusations that blacks were too ignorant and degraded to intelligently exercise the right to vote. "If we know enough to be hung, we know enough to vote," Douglass said. The ironic juxtaposition of black men's services in all major national wars—the War of Independence, the War of 1812, and the Civil War—and blacks' disfranchisement revealed a profound hypocrisy of American republicanism. "Shall we be citizens in war, and aliens in peace?" he asked, "would that be just?"[31]

African American arguments for suffrage and black soldiers' devotion had a strong impact on Lincoln and the Republican lawmakers.[32] For Lincoln, black soldiers had "heroically vindicated their manhood on the battlefield" and "demonstrated in blood their right to the ballot." Hence, he concluded, the restoration of the Union must "rest upon the principle of civil and political equality of both races."[33] Lincoln received Roudanez and Bertonneau in the White House on March 12, 1864. The day after, he wrote to Louisiana governor Michael Hahn, "privately" suggesting the enfranchisement of intelligent blacks and black soldiers because these people, Lincoln noted, "would probably help, in some trying time to come, to keep the jewel of liberty within the family of freedom."[34] The letter, made known to some leading Republicans in Congress as well as some members of the Louisiana state constitutional convention, prompted the state convention to empower the state legislature to enfranchise citizens on the basis of intelligence and military service.[35] Toward the end of the war, it was clear that Lincoln had come to accept the principle of black suffrage, but nonetheless wanted black enfranchisement implemented as a state-initiated action.[36]

Events in early 1865 intensified black activism on black suffrage. Lincoln's assassination had saddened and agitated the black community. For Douglass, Lincoln's death was "a personal as well as national calamity" especially in thinking of "the deep interest" he had taken in "the elevation" of the black race. While blacks were translating sorrow for Lincoln into support for the Republicans, there was growing frustration with President Andrew Johnson, whose Reconstruction plan excluded blacks but opened doors for former rebels. In mid-1865, the *Christian Recorder*, the influential Philadelphia-based AME church newspaper, published a series of editorials and letters criticizing Johnson's policy. Drawing on Lincoln's acknowledgment of blacks' loyalty and contributions to the war, the *Recorder* urged Johnson to work with radical Republicans in Congress to enfranchise blacks and appealed to Northern states to "remove the word 'white' from your State constitutions." Declaring that it could not "remain silent," the *Recorder*'s July 1, 1865, editorial attacked the widespread practice of black disfranchisement "in the free north as well as the slave south." White Americans, who had "sadly degenerated from their first principles" and created "a system of proscription against the black man," the editorial charged, had been "guilty of a great theft." Unless white America relinquished its "hold upon what is not your own and restore to us, unabridged, our God-given rights," God would bear "wrath against you, and score you with many stripes."[37]

The harsh tone of the editorials reflected blacks' frustration with and indignation at Johnson's indifferences toward the danger that freedmen faced daily in the South, which the *Recorder* had reported through letters from the

South. One correspondent from Natchez, Mississippi, in reporting one of many tales "of horror, violence and injustice, done to colored people," told Northern audiences that slavery was not dead in Mississippi and that emancipation was "only to have been a ruse, a base ruse to secure the triumph of the Union arms." While as slaves, the correspondent wrote, "we had some protection from our masters from the interest they had in us," but now "as freemen, we have none from the law." For self-defense as well as for the outcome of the war, the writer demanded "*complete personal* enfranchisement." Without the right of suffrage, all other privileges were "as baseless as a shadow." The writer asked the federal government not to leave freedmen "to the mercies of men guilty of the crimes of the celebrated Libby or Andersonville Prisons, or the cold-blooded murders of Fort Pillow, and the assassination of Lincoln." To deal with "the enfranchised traitors" the government must enfranchise freedmen.[38]

The political terrorism against freedmen in the South pushed the black suffrage discourse beyond the conventional "reward" or "citizenship" arguments. While Johnson claimed to defend the Constitution and the states' rights protected by the Constitution, the *Recorder* saw the Constitution and antebellum federal and state laws as deeply flawed. To secure freedmen's emancipation and the possibility of constructing a new democratic nation, a revolutionary constitutionalism must be imagined and put into practice. The *Recorder*'s editorial of July 15, 1865, declared that the Civil War was indeed "a revolution" that had destroyed not only slavery but also "all the law, which pertained to it." Blacks were now citizens "made so by no state laws, but by a revolution." The Emancipation Proclamation had made slaves "citizens and nothing else" and this compelled Congress to treat blacks as citizens and confer upon them the rights of citizens. "If they are not citizens, they are nothing;" the editorial argued. "If they cannot vote, they cannot be represented."[39] This editorial contained two original and radical arguments: (1) the constitutional machineries that had been made to sustain the old Union of incomplete, race-based freedom could not be used to construct a new nation of complete freedom; (2) former slaves must immediately be made equal citizens and empowered with equal political rights after their emancipation. No halfway house was possible between slavery and freedom because incomplete freedom, or freedom without suffrage, meant no freedom at all.[40]

Advocates of black suffrage discourse also placed America's reconstruction and blacks' fight for voting rights in the international context of nation-building. Rejecting the South Carolina governor's use of the Dred Scott decision to define American government as a white man's government, a black correspondent of the *Recorder* equated American blacks' struggle for suffrage with the struggles of various Europeans, arguing that blacks had the same desire for liberty as the Hungarians, Italians, and other European nationalities.[41]

At the first state convention of North Carolina, black leaders firmly demanded the right to testify, sit on juries, "act as counsel in the courts for the black man," and "carry the ballot." Blacks in Kentucky issued several petitions pressing the state legislature to grant full equality. Although radical Republicans' first attempt to enfranchise blacks in D.C. was defeated in January 1866, the issue of equal suffrage had "created a sensation among our people second only to the famous Proclamation of Emancipation."[42]

Black leaders' meeting with Andrew Johnson in the White House on February 7, 1866, and their ensuing reply to the president marked an unprecedented and bold act of political participation, by which black leaders, although disfranchised, acted as democratic nation-builders to directly challenge the president's policy of reconstruction without black suffrage. The black delegation, which included Douglass and his son Lewis, praised Lincoln for having "placed in our hands the sword to assist in saving the nation" and asked Johnson to place "in our hands the ballot with which to save ourselves." Johnson refused, saying federally imposed black suffrage would cause "a contest between races" and would not "ameliorate" the conditions of great masses of blacks. He claimed that "the first principle" of the American government was "the right for people to govern themselves," which prevented him from imposing black suffrage upon Southern whites "without their consent." Possibly unaware of imitating Lincoln's language, Johnson told his black guests that he did not "assume or pretend to be wiser than Providence, or stronger than the laws of nature" but was simply following "the nature of things." Johnson's rationale was dismissed by black leaders as "entirely unsound and prejudicial to the highest interests of our race, as well as our country at large." Since Johnson had declared his intent to be a "freedmen's Moses," black leaders asked in a written reply to Johnson, why would you want to deprive blacks of "all means of defence" while clothing their former masters "in the panoply of political power?"[43]

Johnson's veto of the civil rights bill in March 1866 triggered another round of protests from the *Recorder* and its readers. Calling Johnson "a

James Buchanan," the newspaper expressed confidence that his antiblack policy would be overridden by Republicans in Congress. Although the President was "Judas-like," one reader was equally dismayed by the Republican party, which, in his view, had betrayed Lincoln and treated blacks as "truly a troublesome thorn." Even with the civil rights bill, the *Recorder* still found the party's Reconstruction plan "very strongly objectionable" for failing to include in the bill the right to vote, "the right to breathe" for blacks in the South.[44] For Douglass, Johnson's power had become a destructive force in the new American democracy, and the anachronistic state was destroying the prospect of the new nation: "It is sad to think that half the glory, half the honor due to the great act of emancipation was lost in the tardiness of its performance. It has now gone irrevocably into history—not as an act of sacred choice by a great nation, of the right as against the wrong, of truth as against falsehood, of liberty as against slavery—but as a military necessity."[45]

Johnson's intransigence deepened Douglass's resolve to challenge the built-in constitutional constraint and inertia that had obstructed and dismantled blacks' and radical Republicans' struggle for black suffrage. Speaking at the Southern Loyalists' Convention in early September 1866, Douglass envisioned the new American nation-state not as a mechanical entity of institutions but as an embodiment of morality and values corresponding to "the unity of sentiment" that he had earlier articulated.[46] It was, however, his speech delivered in St. Louis a few weeks before Congress enacted the Reconstruction Act of 1867, that revealed his fuller and more thorough thinking on revolutionary constitutionalism. The ballot box was supposed to be "the safety valve of our institutions," but the South's abuse of it had produced "a formidable rebellion" against the Constitution; the Union survived the rebellion not because of the legal technicalities and designs of the Constitution but because of "an honest President backed up by intelligent and loyal people—men, high minded men that constitute the State, who regarded society as superior to its forms, the spirit as above the letters." To "the defective ship" of the antebellum Constitution, Douglass declared, "we owe nothing ... for our preservation as a nation." Furthermore, the original Constitution itself was not truly republican because it had been "framed under conditions unfavorable to purely republican results." Douglass advocated the construction of "a genuine democratic republic" that would "keep no man from the ballot box or jury box or the cartridge box, because of his color—exclude no woman from the ballot box because of her sex." Articulating his expansive vision of a democratic society, he advocated abolishing a number of the executive privileges and powers, including presidential patronage, control of federal appointments, the two-term system, pardoning power, and the office of vice president.[47]

In 1866, Republicans in Congress managed to insert a restrictive provision into the proposed Fourteenth Amendment (sec. 2) that threatened to reduce a state's House representation if the state disfranchised its adult male citizens. As ratification was pending at the end of February 1867, Republicans had enacted four other laws that enfranchised blacks in the District of Columbia, unorganized federal territories, Nebraska, and Colorado.[48] With all legislation passed over Johnson's vetoes, Republicans in Congress had finally taken concrete steps to respond to African Americans' call for breaking away from antebellum constitutionalism.[49] Applying the same logic, that Congress had the power to set up conditions in new states that guaranteed "the republican form of government," Republicans overrode Johnson's veto to create the Reconstruction Act of 1867. The act rejected Johnson's reconstruction plan and made black enfranchisement a precondition for the readmission of the former Confederate states (except for Tennessee, which had already been readmitted by Congress). Calling the act "the rising sun of pure Republicanism," the *Recorder* interpreted the message of the law simply as: former slaveholders "shall not form a government without consulting those whom they once held in bondage."[50] In other words, for blacks, the Reconstruction Act of 1867 redefined "We, the People"—the basis and source of the American "republican form of government."

Southern blacks greeted the Reconstruction Act of 1867 with joyful celebrations. Blacks in Columbia, South Carolina, felt "gratified with the spirit of political affiliation with which they have been met" while in Newbern, North Carolina, blacks were "determined to cast their votes in accordance with the provisions of the Reconstruction law."[51] Blacks in Louisiana, now enfranchised, formed political clubs "in every parish throughout the State." Black New Orleans quickly sent greetings to "the friends of the Reconstruction under the terms of said Military Bill." In Alabama, black leaders, previously moderate with their political demands, were encouraged by the act to demand a wide range of rights, including the right to hold office, sit on juries, and use public facilities. In Florida, a "rash of Negro political meetings" occurred after passage of the act was announced.[52]

In the meantime Southern blacks lost no time in joining the Republicans in shaping the cause of Reconstruction. Of more than 100,000 registered black voters in Mississippi, 90 percent identified themselves as Republicans and helped elect Hiram Rhodes Revels, who took Jefferson Davis's Senate seat in 1870, as the first black U.S. senator. Black voters in Florida helped elect a Republican-dominated state constitutional convention that drafted a new constitution offering universal amnesty for former rebels and universal manhood suffrage. Blacks' votes ensured that the majority of the delegates for the state constitutional convention in Louisiana were Republican and half were black.[53]

The Reconstruction Act produced a chain reaction in Northern and border states. In spite of the state Republican party's refusal to face the issue, black Kentuckians joined a small group of radical Republicans who had pushed for equal suffrage in the state since 1867.[54] When blacks in Kentucky were told the ballot would never come to them, they laughed and replied, "It's a comin' massa."[55] In New York after the state's Republican party officially endorsed black suffrage for the state constitutional convention, blacks held a convention on October 6, 1868, in Utica to design measures for the "recovery and protection of their rights."[56]

A number of black woman abolitionists, most notably Sojourner Truth, had been active in the woman suffrage movement before the war.[57] By 1866, Truth and other black women abolitionists and suffragists—Harriet Purvis, Sarah Remond—joined the newly organized American Equal Rights Association to push for universal suffrage. Before the New York state constitutional convention in 1867, Sarah Remond joined her brother, Charles, and traveled throughout New York state to lobby for the enfranchisement of women and blacks. In New Jersey about 170 women staged an 1868 protest by casting ballots in the presidential election. Four of these women were black.[58] But black women suffragists were placed in a difficult position when the woman suffrage movement, led by Elizabeth Cady Stanton and Susan B. Anthony, rejected the notion that black men should be enfranchised first. The bitter clash of the movements' paramount objectives—in part the result of political conservatism in the Republican party—as demonstrated in the 1867 Kansas campaign for woman suffrage, would eventually divide the effort for universal suffrage. When Stanton refused to endorse a constitutional amendment guaranteeing only black suffrage, Frances Ellen Watkins Harper, who represented the younger and more radical generation of black women activists, retorted, "Black women would not put a single straw in the way, if only the men of the race could obtain the vote." Harper's view was shared by Sojourner Truth and Mary Ann Shadd Cary when the movement for universal suffrage came to the point of division in 1869.[59]

Black enfranchisement in the South also raised fears of retaliation against black communities. "What guarantee have we that that act will not be repealed or modified?" asked the *Christian Recorder*. The newspaper urged enfranchised Southern blacks to throw their support behind the Republican party." But despite black votes, Ulysses S. Grant's modest victory over his Democratic challenger in the presidential election of 1868 and the defeat in a number of Northern states made Northern Republicans worried about the continuation of the party's supremacy in national politics. In fact, as a number of historians point out, without Southern blacks' votes, Grant's victory would have been doubtful if not impossible. Serious concerns about the party's future, coupled with the desire to resolve the ideological and constitutional double standards on black voting in the North and elsewhere propelled the Republicans in Congress, in early 1869, to propose the Fifteenth Amendment to nationalize black male suffrage.[60]

Although the so-called liberal class of politicians in the North had endorsed black suffrage in the South, as an Indiana correspondent of *Christian Recorder* wrote, they became "weak-kneed" and "water and milk" when facing black suffrage in the North. But Northern blacks did not stop putting pressure on Northern Republicans. Even before the presidential election of 1868, a black convention of the border states called for a national convention of colored people to discuss "the partial or total exclusion of colored citizens from the exercise of the elective franchise and other citizen rights in so many States of the Union."[61]

When the convention took place on January 12, 1869, in Washington, D.C. it was regarded as "a truly national convention" of black people with delegates from twenty-two states. John Mercer Langston, one of many presenters, gave a speech that highlighted black critiques of the undemocratic nature of the old "republican forms of government." American blacks' degradation, historical and present, had been the result of the long deprivation of voting rights, which was "the dearest treasure in the gift of any government" and "the strongest weapon in the procession of the subject." He argued that "most of our State governments," instead of being republican or democratic, were in fact "mere aristocracies" by which the "insignia of (so-called) republican notability" had been selectively conferred upon and withheld from their citizens.[62]

As soon as Congress passed the Fifteenth Amendment, on February 25, 1869, black leaders launched a campaign for its ratification in Northern and western states. Speaking at an American Anti-Slavery Society meeting in New York in May 1869, Douglass urged the state to help put the Fifteenth Amendment, which he called the "keystone of the arch," into "the organic law of the land." Ratification of the Fifteenth Amendment on March 30, 1870, was celebrated with a nationwide jubilee among blacks.[63] Speaking to four thousand black citizens in Macon, Georgia, Henry M. Turner called the amendment "the crowning event of the nineteenth century."[64] The Fifteenth Amendment also encouraged blacks outside the United States. As John G. Urling, editor of the West Indies–based *Liberator*, told the readers of the *Christian Recorder*, the amendment had "opened a door for the races, all over the world." For Douglass, one of the most eloquent but generally unacknowledged intellectual framers of the era's black suffrage laws, it simply meant that "color is no longer to be a calamity; that race is to be no longer a crime; and that liberty is to be the right of all."[65]

The evolution of African American discourse on black suffrage during the Civil War era offers a critical perspective on America's post–Civil War state- and nation-building. Largely excluded from participation in government, African Americans seized the age of emancipation to redefine the meaning of freedom and the boundaries of citizenship. In doing so they created a new political language of "a genuine democratic republic." For African Americans, enfranchisement was as much an opportunity to create a new American political nation as it was an institutional leverage needed to secure their other rights as freemen. While many Republicans, including Lincoln, attempted to construct the "new birth of freedom" on the basis of antebellum constitutionalism, African Americans envisioned and articulated a much bolder and more genuinely democratic "new birth of freedom." Their experience with slavery, as well as their penetrating observation of how antebellum American constitutionalism worked, told them that freedom was not given freely and that, in a democracy, freedom could not be maintained permanently without possessing a firm, equal, and well-guarded right to political power.

With the Fifteenth Amendment, Douglass optimistically declared, the American people had "undertaken an experiment—a new experiment" of government. The experiment in interracial democracy of the Reconstruction era did not survive the racism and the politics of retreat, the betrayal and the compromises of the late nineteenth century. But the idea of democracy, creatively articulated and gloriously fought for by African Americans, had taken root in the hearts of African Americans and created a powerful political legacy with which they would renew the struggle in the twentieth century, not only to regain their voting rights but also to once again reform and regenerate American democracy. For modern students of the history of American democracy, the African American construction of black suffrage discourse provides a powerful illustration of how contested ideas have been translated into law and public policy that eventually transformed the nation's history.[66]

ACKNOWLEDGMENTS

I have intentionally incorporated several themes of Eric Foner's major works into this writing, not only because they are thematically relevant but also because they have inspired my thinking of the current subject. I thank Manisha Sinha, Penny Von Eschen, and Ira Berlin for their insightful comments on various drafts of the essay.

NOTES

1. Eric Foner, *Politics and Ideology in the Age of Civil War* (New York, 1980), 33; Lincoln, "Address at Sanitary Fair, Baltimore, Maryland, April 18, 1864," in Abraham Lincoln, *The Collected Works of Abraham Lincoln*, ed. Roy P. Basler, 8 vols. (New Brunswick, 1953), 7:301; hereafter cited as *CW*.

2. Eric Foner, *Nothing but Freedom: Emancipation and Its Legacy* (Baton Rouge, 1983), 46. For recent reviews of the historiography of constitutional reconstruction during the Civil War and Reconstruction era, see the introduction in Xi Wang, *The Trial of Democracy: Black Suffrage and Northern Republicans, 1860–1910* (Athens, Ga., 1997); see also Richard M. Valelly, *The Two Reconstructions: The Struggle for Black Enfranchisement* (Chicago, 2004). The rewriting of Reconstruction history with an emphasis on black agency began with W. E. B. Du Bois's *Black Reconstruction* (New York, 1935) and has been effectively advanced by Eric Foner's *Reconstruction: America's Unfinished Revolution, 1863–1877* (New York, 1988), which treats black activism as a central theme of Reconstruction. On African Americans and the constitutional order, see Donald G. Nieman, *Promises to Keep: African-Americans and the Constitutional Order, 1776 to the Present* (New York, 1991), esp. chapters 3 and 4.

3. Phillis F. Field, *The Politics of Race in New York: The Struggle for Black Suffrage in the Civil War Era* (Ithaca, 1982), 187–219; Alexander Keyssar, *The Right to Vote: The Contested History of Democracy in the United States* (New York, 2000), 6, 20, 54–55; Wang, *The Trial of Democracy*, 4–7. See, *Historical Statistics of the States of the United States: Two Centuries of the Census, 1790–1990*, comp. Donald B. Dodd (Westport, Conn., 1993).

4. George Fishman, *The African American Struggle for Freedom and Equality: The Development of a People's Identity, New Jersey, 1624–1850* (New York, 1997), 241–44, 246–47. The quote is from Keyssar, *The Right to Vote*, 57. See *Colored American*, January 13, 27, March 22, April 15, 19, May 3, June 2, July 14, November 3, 1838.

5. "Colored People of Pennsylvania," *Colored American*, April 19, 1838; see also *Colored American*, January 13, 27, March 22, April 15, 19, May 3, June 2, July 14, and November 3, 1838.

6. Victor Ullman, *Martin R. Delany: The Beginnings of Black Nationalism* (Boston, 1971), 40–45, quote on 41. See also reports of the *Colored American*.

7. A. Steward, C. L. Reason, H. H. Garnet, and Wm. H. Topp, "Address of the New York State Convention of Colored Citizens, to the People of the State," *Colored American*, December 19, 1840; see also Joel Schor, *Henry Highland Garnet: A Voice of Black Radicalism in the Nineteenth Century* (Westport, Conn., 1977), 47–49, 70–71, 143. Interracial efforts for black suffrage in Michigan, Wisconsin, New York, Connecticut, and Ohio were unsuccessful. Only in Rhode Island did blacks, who had been barred from the polls since 1822, regain suffrage through a new state constitution enacted after the Dorr Rebellion in 1841. Eric Foner, *Free Soil, Free Labor, Free Men: The Ideology of the Republican Party before the Civil War* (New York, 1970), 281–87; Richard H. Sewell, *Ballots for Freedom: Antislavery Politics in the United States, 1837–1860* (New York, 1976), 97–98, 173–82, 335.

8. Wm. G. Nell, "Colored American Patriots," *Anglo-African Magazine* 1, no.1 (January 1850) (reprint, New York, 1968), 30–31; Smith, "Citizenship," 149.

9. Douglass, "The Political Response to Slavery's Aggressions: Addresses Delivered in Syracuse, New York, on 28 May 1856," *FDP*, 3:134–42; hereafter cited as *FDP*.

10. Douglass, "The Dred Scott Decision: Addresses Delivered in Part, in New York, New York, in May 1857," *FDP*, 3:163–83, quote on 173.

11. Douglass, *The Frederick Douglass Papers*, ser. 1, *Speeches, Debates, and Interviews*, ed. John Blassingame, 5 vols. (New Haven, 1979–92), 2:89–90.

12. Douglass, "We Ask Only for Our Rights: An Address Delivered in Troy, New York, on 4 September 1855," *FDP*, 3:91–96.

13. Lincoln to George Robertson, Springfield, Illinois, August 15, 1855, *CW*, 2:317–18; Lincoln, Speech at Peoria, Illinois, October 16, 1854, *CW*, 2:247–83, quote on 256. For Lincoln's repeated opposition to black political equality, see *CW*, 2:519–20, 541; 3:16, 79, 403.

14. The reaction of the *St. Louis Democrat* was reprinted in *National Anti-Slavery Standard*, 70, no. 29 (Dec. 1, 1860): 1, col. 2; Douglass, "Equal Suffrage Defeated," *Douglass' Monthly* (December 1860)[, 369].

15. James M'Cune Smith argued that the right to vote was one of the "public rights" of Roman citizenship, from which modern citizenship and its rights were derived. See, Smith, "Citizenship," *Anglo-African Magazine* 1, no.5 (May 1850) (reprint, New York, 1968), 144–50. See also, *Colored American*, December 19, 1840. For Bates's opinion, see *National Anti-Slavery Standard* 23, no. 35 (January 10, 1863): 1, cols. 1–5.

16. Lincoln, Annual Message to Congress, 3 December 1861, *CW*, 5:35–53; David W. Blight, *Frederick Douglass' Civil War: Keeping Faith in Jubilee* (Baton Rouge, 1989), 79; Douglass, "Fighting the Rebels with One Hand: An Address Delivered in Philadelphia, Pennsylvania, on January 14, 1862," *FDP*, 3:473–88, quote on 481, 488; Lincoln, Annual Message to Congress, December 1, 1862, *CW*, 5:518–37, quote on 537.

17. Douglass, "The Black Man's Future in the Southern States: An Address Delivered in Boston, Massachusetts, on 5 February 1862," *FDP*, 3:489–508, quote on 493.

18. Lincoln, "Annual Message to Congress," December 1, 1862, *CW*, 5:537. Lincoln had repeatedly affirmed that he would not retract his emancipation proclamation in 1863 and 1864. Lincoln to Stephen A. Hurlbut, Washington, 31 July 1863, *CW*, 6:358–59; Lincoln to Nathaniel P. Banks, Washington, August 5, 1863, *CW*, 6:364–65.

19. Lincoln to James C. Conkling, Washington, August 23, 1863, *CW*, 6:409.

20. Lincoln, "Proclamation of Amnesty and Reconstruction," December 3, 1863, *CW*, 7:53–56; Lincoln to Thomas Cottman, December 15, 1863, *CW*, 7: 66–67.

21. Douglass, "The Day of Jubilee Comes: An Address Delivered in Rochester, New York, on 28 December 1862," *FDP*, 3:543–46; Douglass, "The Proclamation and a Negro Army: An Address Delivered in New York, New York, on 6 February 1863," *FDP*, 3:549–69.

22. Douglass, "The Present and Future of the Colored Race in America: An Address Delivered in Brooklyn, New York, on 15 May 1863," *FDP*, 3:570–84, quote on 572, 575. Douglass, "The Mission of the War: An Address Delivered in New York, New York, on 13 January 1864," *FDP*, 4:3–24, quote on 11–12.

23. Douglass, "The Mission of the War: An Address Delivered in New York, New York, on 13 January 1864," *FDP*, 4:3–24, quote on 11–12; Douglass, "Emancipation, Racism, and the Work before Us: An Address Delivered in Philadelphia, Pennsylvania, on 4 December 1863," *FDP*, 3:598–609, quote on 608–9. Eric Foner, *Politics and Ideology in the Age of Civil War* (New York, 1980).

24. Benjamin Quarles, *Lincoln and the Negro* (New York 1962), 225; Wang, *The Trial of Democracy*, 12. In most of the early black discourse on suffrage, the right to vote was closely linked to the idea of masculinity or manliness.

25. Donald E. Everett, "Demands of the New Orleans Free Colored Population for Political Equality, 1862–1865," *Louisiana Historical Quarterly* 38 (April 1955): 41–64; see also Charles Vincent, *Black Legislators in Louisiana during Reconstruction* (Baton Rouge, 1976), 16–47; C. Peter Ripley, *Slaves and Freedmen in Civil War Louisiana* (Baton Rouge, 1976), 161–64; Wang, *The Trial of Democracy*, 12.

26. Douglass, "Representatives of the Future South: An Address Delivered in Boston, Massachusetts, on 12 April 1864," *FDP*, 4:24–31, quote on 29; James Jones,

"A Letter from a Soldier in New Orleans," letter to the editor, *Christian Recorder*, July 16, 1864.

27. About 140 delegates representing eighteen states attended the Syracuse convention. Other black leaders present at the convention included William Wells Brown, Henry Highland Garnet, Peter H. Clark, George L. Ruffin, Robert Hamilton, William Howard Day, George T. Downing, John M. Langston, Jonathan C. Gibbs, William Keeling, and A. H. Galloway. *A Documentary History of the Negro People in the United States*, ed. Herbert Aptheker (New York), 511–15; Ena L. Farley, *The Underside of Reconstruction New York: The Struggle over the Issue of Black Equality* (New York, 1993), 8–9.

28. *Proceedings of the National Convention of Colored Men Held in Syracuse, New York, October 4–7, 1864*, in Philip S. Foner, *The Life and Writings of Frederick Douglass*, vol. 3, *The Civil War, 1861–1865* (New York, 1952), 418–23; Wang, *The Trial of Democracy*, 11–12.

29. For example, Douglass, "Fighting the Rebels with One Hand" (January 14, 1862), *FDP*, 3:473–88; Douglass, "The Present and Future of the Colored Race in America" (May 15, 1863) *FDP*, 3:570–84, quote on 572. "Negro Suffrage," editorial, *Christian Recorder*, April 1, 1865.

30. Douglass, "Black Freedom Is the Prerequisite of Victory: An Address Delivered in New York, New York, on 13 January 1865," *FDP*, 4:51–59; "Negro Suffrage," *Christian Recorder*, April 1, 1865.

31. Douglass, "What the Black Man Wants: An Address Delivered in Boston, Massachusetts, on 26 January 1865," *FDP*, 4:59–69, quotes on 61–63, 67.

32. Lincoln had repeatedly acknowledged the contributions of black soldiers during wartime. See Lincoln "Address at Sanitary Fair, Baltimore, Maryland," April 18, 1864, *CW*, 7:301; Lincoln to Charles D. Robinson, Washington, August 17, 1864, *CW*, 7:499–500; Lincoln, speech to the One Hundred Sixty-fourth Ohio Regiment, August 18, 1864, *CW*, 7:504–5; Lincoln, interview with Alexander W. Randall and Joseph T. Mills, August 19, 1864, *CW*, 7:506–8. For the influence on the Republicans in Congress, see Wang, *The Trial of Democracy*, 11–13.

33. Lincoln to James S. Wadsworth, January 1864?, *CW*, 7:101–2. The letter was published by the *New York Tribune* on September 26, 1865, but it was believed that Lincoln wrote this letter sometime in January 1864 before Wadsworth was killed in the Battle of the Wilderness (May 5–7, 1864).

34. Lincoln to Michael Hahn, March 13, 1864, *CW*, 7:243; Wang, *The Trial of Democracy*, 19; Quarles, *Lincoln and the Negro*, 227–28.

35. Lincoln's letter was published by the *New York Times* on June 23, 1865.

36. Lincoln, "Address at Sanitary Fair, Baltimore, Maryland," April 18, 1864, *CW*, 7:301. See, also, Lincoln to Albert G. Hodges, Washington, D.C., April 4, 1864, *CW*, 7:281–83.

37. Douglass, "On Martyred President: An Address Delivered in Rochester, New York, on 15 April 1865," *FDP*, 4:74–79, quote on 76. See, also, Douglass, "The Freedmen's Monument to Abraham Lincoln: An Address Delivered in Washington, D.C., on 14 April 1876," *FDP*, 4:427–40, quote on 440; "The Right of Franchise," editorial, *Christian Recorder*, June 10, 1865; "Suffrage for Our Oppressed Race," editorial, *Christian Recorder*, July 1, 1865.

38. Emphasis in the original. P. Houston Murray, "Negro Suffering and Suffrage in the South," letter to the editor, *Christian Recorder*, July 1, 1865.

39. "Dynamics of the Ballot," *Christian Recorder*, July 15, 1865. The piece was mistaken about Johnson's position and thought Johnson was in favor of black suffrage.

40. See, Robert Purvis's response to Bates's letter on citizenship. *National Anti-Slavery Standard* 24, no. 1 (May 16, 1863): 3, cols. 4–5.

41. C., "Our Charleston Letter" letter to the editor, *Christian Recorder*, September 30, 1865.

42. "The Congressional Reconstruction Plan," *Christian Recorder*, October 28, 1865; Victor B. Howard, *Black Liberation in Kentucky: Emancipation and Freedom, 1862–1884* (Lexington, Ky., 1983), 146–47; W. W. H., "Letter from Washington, D.C.," letter to the editor, *Christian Recorder*, February 3, 1866.

43. Douglass, "The Claims of Our Race: An Interview with President Andrew Johnson in Washington, D.C., on 7 February 1866," *FDP*, 4:98–99; Andrew Johnson, "Response of the President," *FDP*, 4:100–104; Lincoln to Albert G. Hodges, Washington D.C., April 4, 1864, *CW*, 7:281–82; "Reply of the Colored Delegation to the President," *Christian Recorder*, February 17, 1866. In his April 4 letter to Hodges, Lincoln wrote, "I claim not to have controlled events, but confess plainly that events have controlled me."

44. "The Veto—The Nation Aroused," editorial, *Christian Recorder*, March 31, 1866; Simon Peter Barjona, "Our Republic," letter to editor, *Christian Recorder*, July 21, 1866; "The Congressional Reconstruction Plan," editorial, *Christian Recorder*, May 19, 1866.

45. Douglass, "Sources of Danger to the Republic," *FDP*, 4:171.

46. Douglass, "Govern with Magnanimity and Courage: An Address Delivered in Philadelphia, Pennsylvania, on September 6, 1866," *FDP*, 4:143.

47. Douglass, "Sources of Danger to the Republic: An Address Delivered in St. Louis, Missouri, on 7 February, 1867," *FDP*, 4:149–72, quotes on 150, 156–58.

48. For the legislative history of these legislations, see Wang, *The Trial of Democracy*, 28–39.

49. "The Southern Loyalists' Convention," *Christian Recorder*, September 15, 1866. See also *FDP*, 4:123–33. "The Signs of the Times," editorial, *Christian Re-*

corder, March 9, 1867. For radical Republicans' thinking on this and relevant issues in 1866–67, see Wang, *The Trial of Democracy*, 28–39.

50. "The Signs of the Times," editorial, *Christian Recorder*, March 9, 1867.

51. "The Signs of the Times," editorial, *Christian Recorder*, March 23, 1867.

52. C. F. C. South, "From Louisiana," letter to the editor, *Christian Recorder*, June 29, 1867; Peter Kolchin, *First Freedom: The Responses of Alabama's Blacks to Emancipation and Reconstruction* (Westport, Conn., 1972), 152–67; Joe M. Richardson, *Negro in the Reconstruction of Florida, 1865–1877* (Tallahassee, 1965), 145.

53. Vernon Lane Wharton, *The Negro in Mississippi, 1865–1890* (1947; New York, 1965), 157, 172; Buford Satcher, *Blacks in Mississippi Politics, 1865–1900* (Washington, D.C., 1978), 1, 18–19; Richardson, *Negro in the Reconstruction of Florida*, 148, 151–60; Vincent, *Black Legislators in Louisiana*, 16–47.

54. Farley, *The Underside of Reconstruction*, 29, 50–53.

55. Victor B. Howard, *Black Liberation in Kentucky: Emancipation and Freedom, 1862–1884* (Lexington, Ky., 1983), 149, 168–70; Stella, "A Letter from Columbus," letter to the editor, *Christian Recorder*, March 20, 1867; Farley, *The Underside of Reconstruction*, 29, 50–53.

56. Douglass, speech in Albany on November 20, 1866, *FDP*, 4:148; Douglass, speech in New York City, May 14, 1868, *FDP*, 4:173–75. See also Douglass's other speeches on the same issue, *FDP*, 4:180–86.

57. *The History of Woman Suffrage, 1848–1920*, ed. Elizabeth Cady Stanton et al., 6 vols. (New York, 1969), 2:182–83, 3:457; Rosalyn Terborg-Penn, *African American Women in the Struggle for the Vote, 1850–1920* (Bloomington, 1998), 14–16, 21–26; Willie Mae Coleman, "Keeping the Faith and Disturbing the Peace, Black Women: From Anti-Slavery to Women's Suffrage (PhD diss., University of California, Irvine, 1982), 90–91.

58. When Lucy Stone complained that black leaders in Kansas did not give enough attention to white woman suffrage, a correspondent of the *Christian Recorder* called it "simply absurd." S.A.D., "Letter from Chicago," letter to the editor, *Christian Recorder*, July 27, 1867; Terborg-Penn, *African American Women*, 28; see also Philip N. Cohen, "Nationalism and Suffrage: Gender Struggle in Nation-Building America," *Signs* (Spring 1996): 707–27.

59. *History of Woman Suffrage*, 2:382–92; Coleman, "Keeping the Faith and Disturbing the Peace," 91–92; Terborg-Penn, *African American Women*, 26–27; for the split of the woman's suffrage movement in 1869, see Ellen Carol DuBois, *Feminism and Suffrage: The Emergence of an Independent Women's Movement in America* (Ithaca, 1978).

60. "The Enfranchised Freedmen," editorial, *Christian Recorder*, April 20, 1867; Foner, *Reconstruction*, 338–45; James M. McPherson, *Ordeal by Fire: The Civil*

War and Reconstruction (New York, 1982), 544–45; Wang, *The Trial of Democracy*, 39–43.

61. W.S. Lankford, "Indiana Correspondence," letter to the editor, *Christian Recorder*, July 6, 1867; the convention was held in Baltimore on August 4–5, 1868, and was attended by representatives from Delaware, Maryland, Virginia, West Virginia, Tennessee, Missouri, New York, New Jersey, and Pennsylvania. "Call for a National Convention," *Christian Recorder*, October 24, 1868.

62. "The National Address," *Christian Recorder*, February 6, 1869.

63. Douglass, "Let the Negro Alone: An Address Delivered in New York, New York, on 11 May 1869," *FDP*, 4:199–213; quote on 201. For Douglass's other major speeches on the Fifteenth Amendment, see Douglass, "We Are Not Yet Quite Free: An Address Delivered at Medina, New York, on 3 August 1865," *FDP*, 4:240; see, "Celebration in Camden, N.J.," *Christian Recorder*, May 7, 1870.

64. "Fifteenth Amendment," *Christian Recorder*, May 14, 1870.

65. John G. Urling, "Letter from the West Indies," Buxton, East Coast, Demerara, W.I., June 6, 1870, quoted in *Christian Recorder*, July 6, 1870; Douglass, "At Last, At Last, the Black Man Has a Future: An Address Delivered in Albany, New York, on 22 April 1870," *FDP*, 4:271.

66. Douglass, "We Need a True, Strong, and Principled Party: Address Delivered at Washington, D.C., on 29 March 1871," *FDP*, 4:281–89, quote on 283. For the contested history of American freedom, see Eric Foner, *The Story of American Freedom* (New York, 1998).

Chapter Seven

• • • • • • • • • • •

Making It Fit

The Federal Government, Liberal Individualism, and the American West

MELINDA LAWSON

In 1899, six years after the publication of Frederick Jackson Turner's *Significance of the Frontier in American History*, Nebraska journalist William E. Smythe put his own ideas about the impact of the West on the American character in writing. Like Turner, Smythe argued that the western landscape had a transformative power. The challenges and adversities inherent in remaking vast regions of wilderness into an agrarian idyll had the capacity, Smythe wrote, to change men: the West would shape a new American identity.[1]

But there the similarities ended. For Turner, the settling of the West had transformed the civilized, urbane European into a rugged, individualistic American. This transformation had been in process as long as there had been a frontier. Thus the challenge to American identity lay in the closing of the frontier—a closing the 1890 census had announced. But to Smythe, the West had barely begun to work its magic—a magic of a very different sort. If the humid West—the portion of the United States east of the 100th meridian, where natural rainfall fed fertile farmland—had been settled, the arid West had not. Beyond this marker, from the middle of Kansas to the

Pacific Coast, lay vast areas of desert, useless for American farmers if not irrigated. Here was how the West would shape the American character; this was the gift the West offered the nation. To irrigate the arid West, Americans would have to work together as a unit, in cooperative enterprises. The product would be "the finest flower of Anglo-Saxon civilization, with . . . everything beyond the sphere of the individual firmly held by associated man." If for Turner the West had engendered American individualism, for Smythe it would create a cooperative American, less concerned to prove his individual mettle, more aware of his dependence—economically and socially—on his fellow citizens.[2]

In the years since, Turner has come under attack by historians, not the least for his argument about the West and American individualism. The West, as it turns out, was not conquered by individuals. Wagon roads, railroads, Indian removal, and, in the end, irrigation, bear witness to the influence of both associative enterprise and the federal government. In fact, in stark contrast to the Turnerian image, the nineteenth-century West was, as historian Richard White argues, "the kindergarten of the American state."[3]

The new western history suggests that Smythe had one thing right: the West would not be conquered by individuals. But Smythe's larger vision was never realized. The challenges of the western landscape did not inform a new associative American identity. In spite of the numerous cooperative enterprises that arose to take on the challenges of the West; in spite of the vast extension of the federal government into the affairs of the West, Turner's image of western rugged individualism persisted. The West continues to be seen as the embodiment of American individualism.[4]

Given the inadequacies of laissez-faire individualism to the demands of settling the West, the persistence of this image presents a paradox. How, in the face of evidence that would seem to undermine the illusion of rugged individualism, has the illusion endured? If the building of the West shaped American identity, and that building required cooperative enterprises and the federal government, why do cooperation and a celebration of the national state not form central components of American national identity?

This essay explores one aspect of that question. It examines attitudes toward individualism and an active national state in the West, focusing on the debate over irrigation between 1870 and 1902, the year Congress passed the Newlands Reclamation Act. It examines the campaigns of the advocates of reclamation, paying particular attention to the language they used as they discussed the need for new approaches to the problem of the arid West. Advocates of a planned system of irrigation confronted three separate but related tenets of American national identity: individualism, private property, and a limited role for the federal government. How did they deal with these challenges? What alternatives to laissez-faire individualism did they propose? What alternative meanings did they assign American freedom? And what does this tell us about American national identity, both in the West and in the nation as a whole?

Americans have always struggled to find an appropriate role for the federal government in creating what Eric Foner calls "the social pre-conditions of freedom." Thomas Jefferson's ideas are illustrative: Jefferson shared his fellow Revolutionaries' fear of centralized power and argued for a limited role for the national state. But Jefferson also proposed that the government provide land for its citizens so they could achieve the economic autonomy he believed to be a requisite of real freedom. The tension between the idea that freedom meant limited government and the notion that freedom could only flourish in the presence of certain social conditions, themselves requiring government intervention, became a mainstay of American political culture.[5]

In the West, the need for the national state to create the conditions for freedom as Americans understood it was particularly salient. There the federal government conducted surveys, built wagon roads, subsidized railroads, and distributed land. And, since the land this benevolent state distributed to its yeoman farmers in the name of freedom was not vacant, the federal government assumed an active role in Indian removal. Even after Reconstruction, when the former slaves' arguments that freedom entailed economic autonomy failed to withstand the rollback of the wartime activist state, the federal government vigorously pursued Indian removal, driving the Nez Perce Indians seventeen hundred miles from their Oregon home.[6]

By the late nineteenth century, the idea that American freedom meant freedom of contract was ascendant. But this definition was still contested. Industrialization, economic consolidation, a growing disparity between rich and poor, and increasing labor unrest raised questions about the ability of laissez-faire to sustain democracy. As Americans debated the role that the national state should play in the regulation of industry, in the West a debate arose over the uses of the federal government in irrigation—a debate that included a challenge to the notion that the self-sufficient individual must form the basis of American national identity.[7]

The notion that much of the land beyond the 100th meridian would not yield its fruits to the West's yeoman farmers without substantial planning and corporate or government intervention did not come easily to Americans. In the years following the Civil War, as exploration of the far West accelerated, it became clear that western aridity was obstructing settlement. The government responded with acts designed to facilitate that settlement. In 1873, Congress passed the Timber Culture Act, which granted 160 acres to any person who planted and maintained 40 acres of timber for ten years. While clearly designed to remedy the shortage of timber in the West, framers of this act also hoped to alleviate western aridity: proponents subscribed to the speculative theory that "rain follows the plow"—that cultivation of the land would alter the climate. In 1877, Congress passed the Desert Land Act, which granted 640 acres for $1.25 per acre to any person committing to irrigate the land within three years. Both acts had as their premise a belief that individuals could settle the arid West. Neither act worked, and both laid the West open to speculation and monopoly.[8]

In 1878, college professor, Civil War veteran, and western explorer John Wesley Powell challenged the federal government's commitment to a land policy informed by individualism. In *A Report on the Lands of the Arid Regions of the United States*, Powell argued that the United States was in reality two sections: the first, comprising three-fifths of the national land mass, was humid; the remaining two/fifths was arid. The western portion could only be settled if it was irrigated, but the nation's traditional land distribution system was inadequate to the task. Increasingly, the idea that Americans could settle the West as they had the East came under fire. In 1877, an article in the New York *Daily News* expressed concern about "the fitness of our present system of public land distribution. . . . We have very little public land of value left." In 1894, *Harper's Weekly* called the effort to farm the arid West by traditional means "a sad and pathetic failure."[9]

If the individual could not farm the land by traditional methods, what was to be done? Between the 1878 publication of Powell's book and the passage of the 1902 Newlands Act, a debate raged: if the American farmer could not irrigate this land alone, how should it be done? And what would the solution say about American ideas of individualism, private property, and laissez-faire? The leading participants in this debate were rarely farmers themselves; rather the advocates of reclamation were primarily reformers, scientists, and political leaders who viewed the irrigation of the West as the means to larger political and social ends.

If the current land distribution system was not opening the West to settlement, it was in part because the job was simply too big. By the 1880s, the small streams in the arid region that could be easily diverted by individuals had, for the most part, been tapped. If the remaining land was to be settled, it would have to be irrigated from large, often distant bodies of water. But this was a daunting task: dams must be built, reservoirs dug, and canals constructed—tasks requiring intensive capital, scientific knowledge, and planning. Individuals could not do this on their own, as a board commissioned by President Grant in 1874 acknowledged. "If left to themselves," the board's report read, "the farmers in any county of large extent can never execute such a system." In 1884, prominent sociologist Lester F. Ward was still arguing the point: "It is in the nature of things, that the settlers themselves . . . can never carry out this extensive system of irrigation. . . . To be made a practical success, it would require an immense outlay of capital. . . . Under the ordinary laws of supply and demand it can never be accomplished."[10]

As the inadequacies of America's land distribution system became apparent, irrigation proponents began to search for other models. Scientists, commissioners, and politicians studied irrigation arrangements in England, France, Spain, Italy, Egypt, India, the Sandwich Islands, Mexico, and Peru. Turning to models within the American West, Powell and Smythe studied the Mormons. Taken as a whole, these irrigating societies offered a myriad of models for western irrigation.[11]

But if they differed in their arrangements, these societies had one thing in common: none had the attachment that mainstream Americans had to the ideals of individualism. Describing a system it deemed effective in India, one commission noted that the entire system was financed and run by the government. But "In India," the report continued, "the government does everything and the people do nothing in the management of the canal system. On the other hand, in our country, we expect the people to do everything and the Government nothing." Other countries that had successfully irrigated—some of which, as the *Independent* noted, "we are pleased to call less enlightened than our own"—had not been fettered by the principles of individualism. As the *Irrigation Age* explained, "In all the great irrigation systems of ancient times . . . rules and laws . . . were framed in such a manner as to ensure the greatest good to the largest number."[12]

To irrigate the arid West, then, Americans would have to move beyond their traditional notions of individualism and embrace associative enterprise. While the authors of these studies did not agree on the locus of power within these associations—variously advocating private, district, state, or national planning—many recognized that the shift away from competitive individualism might itself prove a challenge to Americans. Smythe assured his readers that in turning to one another to meet the demands of western irrigation, they would be none the weaker as a people. "What is needed," he wrote, "is a true adjustment of the relations of individual to associated man."[13]

If the demands of settling the arid West pointed up the inadequacies of American individualism, they also challenged notions of private property. To be sure, water rights had never fit comfortably with the concept of private property. Over the years, property rights in water had been regularly renegotiated, changing with the needs of an expanding nation. The British North American colonists had brought with them an English tradition of water rights, the "riparian doctrine," which stated that a landowner could use the water that bordered his property provided he did not interrupt its flow. This doctrine worked for a humid nation of small farmers, where those who did not live at the water's edge could depend on rainfall and the village well. But it was not conducive to arid farming or to industry. In the antebellum era, as mining and lumber companies looked to exploit the resources of the West, water laws adapted to accommodate their needs. In some areas, "appropriative rights," which allowed individuals who did not own adjoining land to divert a stream as long as they put the water to use, replaced "riparian" rights. In time, the doctrine was amended to one of "prior appropriation." Under this doctrine, the person who first asserted a use for the water could claim it as a form of personal property. It did not matter how much water he diverted, or how far away he diverted it, or whether he left any for farmers downstream. If he was "first in time," he was "first in right." The doctrine of prior appropriation encouraged industry, but it also encouraged land monopolies and took its toll on small farmers. Even those fortunate enough to settle near a body of water might find that in times of low rainfall, the water supply ran dry.[14]

In the 1870s, as small farmers continued the struggle to irrigate their land, private business stepped in. Corporations built dams, dug canals, distributed water, and, in the spirit of American enterprise, hoped to turn a profit. But with few exceptions, these hopes were dashed. Irrigation companies overestimated settlement, built canals for settlers who never arrived, priced their water out of reach, and spent precious resources fighting each other and their customers in court. One economist estimated that 95 percent of the money invested in canals between 1885 and 1895 produced no profit and that much of it was lost altogether. By 1900, 90 percent of canal companies were failing or near failing.[15]

Increasingly it was clear that in the western experience, treating water as a commodity to be appropriated by private interests led to privation and suffering for small farmers. As the *Overland Monthly* reported, in most western states speculators had "grabbed the land" and "gobbled the water" and farmers had been left out in the cold. By the 1890s, many irrigation advocates argued that Americans needed to rethink the whole concept of private property as it related to water. In 1897, a report written by Hiram M. Chittenden, captain of the Army Corps of Engineers, was submitted to Congress. "Water," wrote Chittenden, "is perhaps the most elusive of all forms of property. . . . It is becoming more and more apparent in the course of irrigation development in the West that the waters in the streams should not be made the subject of private property, but that they should inhere in the land to which they are applied, and that purchase or sale of water as a commodity should not be allowed." Chittenden advocated "the doctrine of the public character of all streams." Nelson A. Miles, brigadier general in the U.S. Army, concurred: citing an unnamed state party's platform, he wrote, "We believe the water is the property of the people, and that it should be so used as to secure the greatest good to the greatest number of people."[16]

For some, the issue seemed particularly urgent: democracy—even American freedom—were at stake. Fearing that ideas of "water rights" and "water rent" would become the norm in the West, Smythe warned that millions of men would find themselves tenants, not proprietors, and democracy as Americans understood it would be jeopardized. Smythe recognized Americans' deep attachment to private property, and acknowledged that there had been "no deep design—no premeditated effort" to "enslave or exploit those who should come to till the soil. . . . By instinct and training the Anglo-Saxon sees value in land." But "radically different conditions" had been encountered in the far West, and these conditions were not conducive to real freedom. If water continued to be considered a private commodity, Americans would face "all the conditions for a hateful economic servitude."[17]

The difficulties of irrigating the West challenged notions of property rights in land as well. "Land is not property like other property," wrote John E. Bennett in support of an organized district irrigation system, "and . . . owners cannot 'do as they please with their land.'" George Julian, former Indiana congressman and radical Republican, believed the distribution of the remaining western lands to be "the overshadowing question of American politics. . . . The unrestricted monopoly of the soil is as repugnant to republican government as slavery is to liberty; and we hold, therefore, that the right of individual property in land . . . must be subordinated to the natural rights of man and the public welfare." Julian called for a thorough revision of land laws, including government intervention in irrigation. For these men, America's blind commitment to individualism and private property could cost its farmers their freedom. How, after all, could a farmer maintain his freedom if he could not afford the water that alone rendered his land productive?[18]

Since traditional notions of private property were proving an obstacle to the settling of the West, and private enterprise was proving an ineffective irrigator, reclamation reformers began calling for the communal development of irrigation. Powell's 1878 book had proposed one solution—planning on a massive level combined with cooperation on a smaller scale. Powell called for a government-financed survey of the West to classify the land according to its potential use. Once irrigable farmland had been identified, the land would be divided into districts, within which cooperatives would organize and carry out irrigation. Each farmer would be limited to an 80-acre farm and would receive an allotted share of the water. The farmers as a group—not private "water companies"—would own the water.[19]

Powell pointed to an existing irrigation colony as a model for westerners: the Mormons in Salt Lake Valley, Utah. As a young western explorer, Powell had traveled to Utah and befriended Brigham Young, the president of the Mormon church. Under Young's direction, the Mormons had migrated to Utah in the 1840s, squatted on land whose legal status was unclear, and divided the land among their members. Though this division was by no means democratic—the church elite received disproportionate shares—every head of household received enough for a viable farm. The average farm ranged between 10 and 50 acres, well below the 160 acres the Homestead Act allowed.[20]

To irrigate these small farms, Mormons had developed a system of water rights based on a principle they had learned from Hispanic communities in the Rio Grande Valley: water was not considered personal private property but was shared for the good of all. Mormons built communal canals that distributed the water to all the community's farmers, bringing each only what he needed for his farm. Thus Mormons had rejected the doctrine of prior appropriation and placed the good of the community before that of the individual. Their grazing system reflected these same communal values: they established a village herd, to which each contributed a few cattle. This herd grazed together on commonly held land.[21] Powell's book included an article by Captain C. E. Dutton, who described the success of the colony: "The communal arrangement has been attended with great success. . . . The general welfare has immensely benefited." Thus, even as the nation celebrated laissez-faire individualism as the fullest expression of freedom, Powell called on Americans to emulate the Mormon model: to embrace co-operation and place the community before the individual.[22]

William E. Smythe, who had traveled through the Southwest and observed the Hispanic irrigation system, shared Powell's admiration of the community model. But for Smythe it was not just the effectiveness of the irrigation system that was inspiring. Smythe pointed to the Mormon community as a perfect illustration of the *social* benefits of irrigation. "Irrigation," he wrote, was not "merely an adjunct to agriculture. It is a social and economic factor in a much larger way. . . . It shapes and colors . . . civilization after its own peculiar design." In the East, vast acreage was coveted; it was a sign of a successful farmer. But the price eastern farmers paid for that success was high: disconnected from one another, miles from the nearest town, they lived their lives in isolation. "The bane of rural life," Smythe observed, "is its loneliness." Irrigation shaped a different life. Because it was costly and laborious, it necessitated the adoption of the small farm unit—a large farm in the arid West was a burden. The irrigation communities Smythe studied situated farmers on small lots in town; adjacent to those lots were their modest farms. The benefits were incalculable: "Compared with the familiar conditions of country life . . . in the East and central West, the change which irrigation brings amounts to a revolution. . . . Even food, shelter, and provision for old age do not furnish protection against social discontent where the conditions deny the advantages which flow from human association. Better a servant in the town than a proprietor in the country! . . . The starvation of the soul is almost as real as the starvation of the body."[23]

The combination of the irrigation model and the social arrangements that accompanied it attracted Smythe to Holland as well. The founders of the "wonderful civilization of the Netherlands" faced a different problem than that with which the West struggled: they worked to keep the water from flooding the land. But Smythe was impressed by the level of organization and cooperation shown by the Dutch as they mastered this task. Quoting from a book describing Holland's work culture, he wrote, "Labor here has never been selfish and individual. . . . A single man laboring on a dike would accomplish nothing; the whole population must turn out and act together. . . . The people are a vast civic army."[24]

Smythe admired the Hispanic, Mormon, and Dutch models of water regulation and believed that Americans had much to learn from them. But he was careful to couch his admiration in a framework that confirmed for white Americans the superiority of their own Anglo-Saxon way of life. He was not, he assured them, asking them to jettison their individualistic ways all together. In fact, even as he waxed eloquent about the virtues of community life, he continually asserted the value of American individualism: "The surpassing virility of our race and people . . . is doubtless largely due to . . . private initiative, energy, and ambition." Arguing in a racial vein common to his time, Smythe asserted that individualism was a valued racial trait. It simply needed to be modified in order to realize the full Anglo-Saxon potential. In building cooperative colonies, he asked, "do we depart from the traditions of the race?" Smythe believed not. Acknowledging the limits of individualism did not entail abandoning it. [25]

The demands of the West challenged notions of individualism and private property; they inspired ideas about community and cooperation and a new associative American. And, as the debate progressed and increasing numbers of supporters began to suggest that federal intervention was necessary, they also challenged the nation's commitment to the idea of a limited national government.

Not all irrigation supporters advocated federal intervention. Many explicitly eschewed the notion of national involvement right up to the passage of the Newlands Act. Opponents of federal intervention feared the corruption and monopoly that had accompanied federal land policies; they predicted competition for midwestern farms; they believed that the federal government did not have the constitutional authority to finance or oversee the operation; they asserted states' rights. And there were ideological objections: "Why call on the national government to enter a field which so far has been entirely the theater of individual effort?" asked Congressman Frank Mondell of Wyoming. As a report of the Public Land Commission explained, "such a method is not in consonance with the traditions of the American people, but is utterly opposed to the prevalent theories of wise legislation."[26]

As an alternative to federal involvement, state governments moved into the field of irrigation. In 1886, California passed the Wright Act, which granted farming communities the authority to form districts authorized to collect money and construct irrigation works. In 1894, the Carey Act authorized the cession of 1 million acres to each desert state; the states were to irrigate the land, sell it to farmers, and reimburse the national treasury. The Carey Act produced scant results: lacking the funds to pay for the projects, the states were unable to construct the works. By 1910, the Carey Act had been responsible for irrigating fewer than 300,000 acres.[27]

The late 1890s witnessed a severe drought, underscoring the need for irrigation. In 1897, Hiram M. Chittenden issued a report that represented the first prominent call for federal provision of irrigation. Two years later, California lawyer and irrigation lobbyist George Maxwell formed the National Irrigation Association to rally support for the cause. A growing campaign for a national irrigation policy challenged notions of laissez-faire as it called on the national government to step in and reclaim the arid West.[28]

Advocates of national reclamation argued, first of all, that irrigation was a job of "considerable magnitude." Large sums of money would have to be furnished, and the states simply did not have the resources. Moreover, while states might be able to mediate disputes concerning a stream or river that lay within its boundaries, there were too many cases where the bodies of water in question ran through more than one state. Who would build the reservoirs? Who would get the water? Who would mediate disputes concerning prior appropriation? Already this issue had engendered a number of lawsuits. As the *Irrigation Age* explained, "Everything in the United States has been left to individual enterprise and to state regulation, until in many of the state and territories, water rights . . . have come to be in a badly tangled condition."[29]

National irrigation was touted for another reason: only the federal government could take the long-term view. Irrigation had failed as a suitable project for private interests because it required enormous overhead but did not show a profit in short order. As an article in *Scribner's Magazine* explained, private enterprise asked, "Will it pay, and pay quickly?" Government was not fettered by such concerns. *Scribner's* recommended "the building of permanent dams on a large scale at public expense" because "it is not absolutely necessary that their work should pay dividends from the first or second year, nor that it should pay at all, in the strict commercial sense." Return for the government would be defined differently. The government would not, as Chittenden explained, "seek its return in the form of levy or toll" but rather "in the general enrichment of the people and increase of national wealth. . . . A work may be entirely justifiable as a public enterprise which would be ruinous as a private investment."[30]

In 1902, Congress passed the Newlands Reclamation Act, and President Theodore Roosevelt signed it into law. The act set aside monies received from the sale of western lands, placing them in a fund for the construction and maintenance of irrigation projects throughout the arid West. The government was then to sell the irrigated land, and proceeds from those sales would refurbish a revolving reclamation fund. The act limited the size of farms to 160 acres and required that most of the money received from the sale of land be expended in the state where that land was located.[31]

One might think that when the Newlands Reclamation Act was passed, it was with recognition of the inadequacies of individualism and private property. After all, proponents had acknowledged that help was needed—the individual could not do this, neither could private enterprise, neither could the states. Perhaps the act might even suggest a celebration of the associated man, per Smythe, or an acknowledgement of the new, expanded role that government would play in the lives of westerners.

But federal intervention in the West in the form of irrigation and the Newlands Act did not help create a new associated American, nor did it undermine the image of western individualism. In fact, though in retrospect the act is viewed as a turning point in the role of the federal government in western affairs, the language that surrounded it gave no such indication. Instead, arguments for federal intervention placed the reclamation act—with its challenge to individualism, private property, and laissez-faire—in the framework of those same traditional American values. Proponents worked to make the new irrigation policies fit American ideology.

By the 1890s, the political groundwork was being laid for the acceptance of a national plan. Between 1889 and 1896, five western territories were admitted to statehood. Western representation in Congress increased accordingly—by

1896, the West had 30 percent of the votes in the Senate—and petitions to Congress demanding assistance with irrigation escalated.[32] In 1901, Nevada Congressman Francis G. Newlands, a Democrat who had campaigned for free silver, introduced the National Reclamation Act. That same year, with the assassination of President McKinley, Theodore Roosevelt became the twenty-sixth president of the United States. Unlike his predecessor, Roosevelt was known as a nationalist. The political machinery was primed.[33]

But a shift in the political climate did not alone explain the ultimate acceptance of federal reclamation. Past plans for national involvement had made little headway in part because the West was not united—many westerners feared federal involvement would bring corruption, monopolies, and the surrender of state sovereignty—and the East was not interested. A campaign to yoke national reclamation to the Rivers and Harbors Bill had gotten the East's attention—but something more was needed.

One of the chief leaders of reclamation by the late 1890s was lobbyist George Maxwell. Backed by railroad companies and joined by land promoters and eastern investors, Maxwell waged a campaign that differed markedly from those of his predecessors. Instead of trying to unite the West, Maxwell set out to make reclamation palatable to eastern politicians. Whereas Smythe's vision bore a suspicious resemblance to radical calls for the cooperative commonwealth, in Maxwell's more conservative appeal, a federal system of irrigation would not create a new, communitarian America; it would rescue the old, individualistic one from ruin.[34]

Reclamation advocates had painted a picture of a new West—an agrarian idyll, offering small, fertile farms, creating a new sense of community and cooperation among Americans. These men focused on the hopes of the potential settlers of the West. But as historian Donald J. Pisani has suggested, the campaign run by Maxwell appealed not to westerners' hopes but to easterners' fears. Maxwell argued that with burgeoning industrialization and escalating radicalism threatening American democracy, the only hope for American institutions was the opening of western land through reclamation.[35]

The rhetoric of the West as safety valve was by no means new. Republicans in the Civil War era identified the territories as the sole hope for the perpetuation of a free labor society, and irrigation proponents had often invoked this language. As early as 1878, the *Nation* had called for reclamation of the West so that the thousands of easterners who were "not obtaining the rewards of labor" and were "becoming a burden and a danger in the east" might enjoy homes and prosperity. The theme of the West as safety valve gained momentum over the years. "When the great Mississippi Valley begins to feel some of the European evils of over population," wrote Walter Gillette Bates in 1890, " . . . and cannot relieve itself, as the East has always done, by drafting off its surplus population to the West, the Government may well ask itself whether it can any longer afford to leave one third of its domain a desert."[36]

Maxwell and his supporters seized the rhetoric of the West as a "safety valve" and used it to enlist eastern support for irrigation. If industrial consolidation, urban instability, and agrarian and labor radicalism were threatening to undermine order in the East, the West offered an escape. As long as farmers could head west, they would not disturb the status quo in the East. Senator Henry Teller had expressed this conviction years earlier: "The man who lives upon the farm is never an anarchist," he argued, "he is never a communist, he is never a revolutionary." In the debates over the Newlands Reclamation Act, this notion was repeated time and again. Irrigation would "solve the social problems of discontent that agitate our cities" and "kindle anew the fires of patriotism almost smothered by poverty and distress." National reclamation would not change American society—it would preserve it on its own individualistic terms.[37]

Agrarianism was not the only way that federal reclamation was made to fit with American ideals. The Newlands Act could still be said to pose challenges to notions of private property, individualism, and laissez-faire. But in the rhetoric surrounding the federal reclamation act, the issues were reframed. In a creative application of the language of individualism, reclamation proponents recast the government itself as an individual whose actions were consistent with—even representative of—American traditions of individualism, private property, and laissez-faire.

In this analysis, the federal government was essentially a large landowner, with the right, indeed, the obligation to improve its property. If, as the Chittenden Report had argued in 1897, the federal government was the "largest landowner in the arid West," then surely the government should act as any private owner of land would. In early 1901, this is the argument that began to accompany calls for federal irrigation. As Newlands himself explained in a speech before Congress, "the Government . . . occupies the position of proprietor of the public lands," and thus has "the usual obligations of land proprietors." Senator Joseph E. Ransdell, a Democrat from

Louisiana, concurred: "Our government is the owner of 600,000,000 acres of land in the arid region," he argued. "It has the same right to improve its property that any private owner has. . . . Being a large proprietor of worthless land, which brings no revenue . . . it would seem the part of wisdom to improve this land and have it settled. . . . This is what any prudent businessman would do. . . . If this be true of an individual it must be true of the government, because its inherent powers over its own property are certainly as great as one of its citizens."[38]

Moreover, like any individual, the federal government was looking to become self-reliant. In an era when debates were swirling about expanded internal markets versus "open doors" abroad, North Dakota senator H. C. Hansbrough drew on Americans' concern for reliable markets. Foreign markets waxed and waned with variables beyond U.S. influence; thus, "the best market is the home market." But Hansbrough's argument tapped more than the nation's interest in markets. In a creative approach to making federal intervention in the West fit with a commitment to individualism, he compared the self-reliance that would result from opening the western market to that of the individual: "A policy of self reliance is the best policy with nations as with men," he avowed. "It was this thought, I am sure, that inspired Charles Sumner to declare, 'the true greatness of nations is in those qualities which constitute the greatness of the individual.'"[39]

The notion that the government was simply acting as an individual preserved, on some level, both the idea of individualism and the idea of private property; it also reassured those Americans who feared centralized power. The federal government was not violating its proper role, and there was no need to fear an expanding state: "The operations contemplated under the bill will be carried on by the secretary of the interior, acting for the government as a large landholder and proprietor. No action is contemplated by the measure which could not be undertaken by an individual or corporation if it were in the position of the government as regards the ownership of its lands." Lester Ward suggested that the government was acting only as a normal, responsible businessman would. "The nation is the largest of all capitalists," he wrote, "and, at the same time, has no tendencies toward monopoly." The planning that the national government was called upon for in reclamation was "the same degree of collective foresight . . . as exists in the average capitalist." The United States was merely "acting as a businessman, seek[ing] only its own interest."[40]

Casting the federal government as an individual, acting as any landowning individual would—improving its property, in search of a profit, which it defined a bit differently than did other landowners—allowed Americans to avoid the implications, on a rhetorical level at least, of government intervention in western affairs. A related image further promoted the notion that the federal government was not violating dearly held notions of laissez-faire: at times, the image of government as businessman gave way to one of government as banker. In this image, the government was merely lending westerners money that they would soon pay back. As the governor of Arizona explained, "this plan avoids the vice and evil tendencies of subsidy by government, for the relationship between the government and the owner of the reclaimed land is essentially that of creditor and debtor.... The government gets back the money expended, and the settler retains his self-respect." Since the federal government would not be officially taxing U.S. citizens to pay for reclamation, but simply advancing the money received from sales of western land, westerners could claim that they themselves bore the cost. "What, then, is the demand of the West?" Newlands rhetorically demanded of the House. "It is that the West should be enabled to reclaim itself." If there was tension between the notion that the federal government might improve the land because it owned the land, and the idea that the land situated in the West belonged to the West, proponents did not acknowledge it.[41]

In 1905, William E. Smythe published a revised version of his book *The Conquest of Arid America*. On the frontispiece appeared a poem titled "Emancipation." "The Nation reaches its hand into the desert," Smythe wrote,

> and Lo! Private monopoly in water and in land is scourged
> from the holiest of temples—the place where men
>   labor and build their homes! . . .
>   The Nation reaches its hand into the desert
>   That which lay beyond the grasp of the individual yields
>   To the Hand of Associated Man. Great is the
> Achievement—Greater the Prophecy![42]

Ever the visionary, Smythe still hoped that national reclamation would inspire the nation to come to terms with the limits of laissez-faire and to recognize the social conditions requisite for a meaningful freedom. He urged Americans to embrace community and cooperation as fundamental American values. The result, he suggested in his accounts of irrigating communities and his poem's title, would be freedom in a different sense than that to which Americans were accustomed: freedom from indigence; freedom from monopoly; freedom from isolation.

But Smyth did not capture the mood of the day. Though the challenges posed by the West brought numerous people, both westerners and easterners, to recognize the inadequacy of Americans' traditional modes of thought, the language that ultimately justified the Newlands Act did not challenge American individualism, or the notion of private property, or laissez-faire. Rather, couched securely in terms of the status quo, the rhetoric of federal reclamation encouraged Americans to continue to believe, with Frederick Jackson Turner, that the West had shaped a nation of rugged individuals who did not need help from the government. The men who passed the Newlands Act imposed the framework of laissez-faire individualism on an active national state and ignored the poor fit.[43]

The Newlands Act of 1902 prefigured the Progressive agenda. In 1906, Roosevelt would sign into law the Hepburn Act, the Meat Inspection Act, and the Food and Drug Act. During the following decade, the Progressives would encourage Americans to rethink their commitment to laissez-faire and strengthen the national state. But the history of the Newlands Act foreshadowed more than the Progressives' activist state. It also foreshadowed the fate of Progressive hopes that constructive national action would engender a corresponding public consciousness devoted less to pursuit of individual economic well being and more to national ideals and the welfare of one's countrymen. Captured by Herbert Croly in his 1909 book *The Promise of American Life*, these hopes echoed Smythe's vision of a new national identity. "There comes a time," Croly argued, "in the history of every nation, when its independence of spirit vanishes, unless it emancipates itself from traditional illusions." Croly encouraged Americans to abandon their attachment to laissez-faire individualism and undertake "experimental collective action aimed at the realization of the collective purpose." Only then, he believed, would Americans "obtain a sufficiently complete sense of self-expression."[44]

Croly's activist national state would be built by Progressives and later by New Dealers. But the social consciousness that was to be engendered by constructive national policies would rest uneasily atop a traditional individualistic faith that was deeply rooted in American political culture and buttressed by the superior economic resources of dominant elites. Even as Americans recognized the inadequacies of laissez-faire individualism and embraced national policies designed to address those inadequacies, they would eschew the corresponding national ideal. If, as Richard White has argued, westerners have been in denial about the role the federal government played and continues to play in western affairs, the terms in which reclamation finally came to the West set the tone for this denial—not just for the West, but for the nation as a whole.

ACKNOWLEDGMENTS

I thank my research assistant, Jeff Roffman, the Humanities Faculty Development Fund at Union College, and participants in the Herbert H. Lehman Center for American History conference "Contested Democracy: Freedom, Race, and Power in American History," especially Elizabeth Blackmar.

NOTES

1. Frederick Jackson Turner, *The Significance of the Frontier in American History*, ed. Harold P. Simonson (New York, 1963); William Ellsworth Smythe, *The Conquest of Arid America* (New York, 1900), in *The Evolution of the Conservation Movement, 1850–1920*, Library of Congress, General Collection and Rare Books Division, http://lcweb2.loc.gov/ammem/amrvhtml/conshome.html.

2. Smythe, *Conquest*, 302. Turner later acknowledged that the West might shape a community identity. See Turner, "Contributions of the West to American Democracy," *Atlantic Monthly*, Jan. 1903.

3. Richard White, *"Its Your Misfortune and None of My Own": A New History of the American West* (Norman, Okla., 1991), 58. For more on the federal government in the West, see Patricia Limerick, *Legacy of Conquest: The Unbroken Past of the American West* (New York, 1988); Clyde A. Milner II, "National Initiatives," 155–94, and Carl Abbott, "The Federal Presence," 469–500, both in *The Oxford History of the American West*, ed. Milner et al. (New York, 1994).

4. For more on the new western history, see *Trails: Toward a New Western History*, ed. Patricia Limerick, Clyde A. Milner II, and Charles E. Rankin (Lawrence, Ky., 1991); Donald Worster, "New West, True West: Interpreting the Region's History," *Western Historical Quarterly* 18 (Apr. 1987).

5. Eric Foner, *The Story of American Freedom* (New York, 1998), 20–21.

6. Foner, *The Story of American Freedom*, 101–13; Eric Foner, *Reconstruction: America's Unfinished Revolution, 1863–1877* (New York, 1988), 583.

7. Foner, *The Story of American Freedom*, 115–37.

8. White, *"It's Your Misfortune,"* 151–52. For general histories of irrigation in the American West, see Donald Worster, *Rivers of Empire: Water, Aridity, and the Growth of the American West* (New York, 1985); Marc Reisner, *Cadillac Desert* (New York, 1986); Donald J. Pisani, *To Reclaim a Divided West: Water, Law, and Public Policy, 1848–1902* (Albuquerque, 1992); Donald J. Pisani, *Water and American Government: National Water Policy and the West, 1902–1935* (Berkeley, 2002).

9. John Wesley Powell, *A Report on the Lands of the Arid Regions of the United States* (Belknap Press, 1962); *New York Daily Tribune*, Apr. 28, 1877; *Harper's Weekly*, Sept. 29, 1894.

10. "Message from the President of the United States Transmitting the Report of the Commissioners on the Irrigation of the San Joaquin, Tulare, and Sacramento Valleys in the State of California," HR Ex. Doc. 290, 43rd Cong., 1st sess., 39; Lester F. Ward, "Irrigation in the Upper Missouri and Yellowstone Valleys," *Science* 4, no. 82 (Aug. 29, 1884): 167, *JSTOR*, Schaeffer Library, Union College, http://www.jstor.org/. See also *Harper's Weekly*, Sept. 22, 1894; "Preliminary Report of the Public Land Commission to the Senate and House of Representatives," *HR Ex. Doc. 46*, 46th Cong., 2nd sess., xxviii.

11. William E. Smythe, "Ways and Means in Arid America," *Century* 51, no. 5 (March 1896): 742–58, *Making of America*, Cornell University Library, http://cdl.library.cornell.edu/moa; *New York Tribune*, Apr. 4, 1878; Nelson Miles, "Our Unwatered Empire," *North American Review* 150, no. 400 (March 1890): 374–75, *Making of America*, Cornell University Library, http://cdl.library.cornell.edu/moa; "Message from the President," HR Ex. Doc. 290, 40–73.

12. "Message from the President," HR Ex. Doc. 290, 48; *Independent*, Feb. 16, 1893; *Irrigation Age* 14, no. 11 (Aug. 1900): 305. See also *New York Times*, Oct., 29, 1873; *Irrigation Age* 14, no. 11 (Aug. 1900): 388–89.

13. Smythe, *Conquest*, 300–302. See also John E. Bennett, "The District Irrigation Movement in California," *Overland Monthly and Out West Magazine* 29, no. 171 (March 1897): 248, *Making of America*, University of Michigan Library, http://www.hti.umich.edu/m/moagrp. For more on Smythe, see Lawrence B. Lee, "William Ellis Smythe and the Irrigation Movement: A Reconsideration," *Pacific Historical Review* 41, no. 3 (Aug. 1972).

14. Worster, *Rivers of Empire*, 88–92; John T. Ganoe, "The Origins of a National Reclamation Policy," *Mississippi Valley Historical Review* 18, no. 1 (June 1931): 34–52.

15. White, *"It's Your Misfortune"*, 403; Pisani, *To Reclaim a Divided West*, 69–108.

16. John E. Bennett, "The District Irrigation Movement in California," 248; "Preliminary Examination of Reservoir Sites in Wyoming and Colorado," HR Doc. 141, 55th Cong., 2nd sess., 52–53.; Miles, "Our Unwatered Empire." For a discussion of debates over defining property rights in land see Maria E. Montoya, *Translating Property: The Maxwell Land Grant and the Conflict over Land in the American West, 1840–1900* (Berkeley, 2002).

17. Smythe, "The Struggle for Water in the West," *Atlantic Monthly* 86, no. 517 (Nov. 1900): 648, *Making of America*, Cornell University Library, http://cdl.library.cornell.edu/moa.

18. Bennett, "The District Irrigation Movement in California," 248; George Julian, "Our Land Policy," *Atlantic Monthly* 43, no. 257 (March 1879): 336–37, *Making of America*, Cornell University Library, http://cdl.library.cornell.edu/moa. For the struggle over the meaning of freedom to padrones and immigrant workers in the West, see Gunther Peck, *Reinventing Free Labor: Padrones and Immigrant Workers in the North American West, 1880–1930* (Cambridge, UK, 2000).

19. Powell, *Report*, 8, 35–49, 52–56; Worster, *A River Running West: The Life of John Wesley Powell* (New York, 2001), 337–59; John Upton Terrell, *The Man Who Rediscovered America: A Biography of John Wesley Powell* (New York, 1969), 196–204; Everett W. Sterling, "The Powell Irrigation Survey, 1888–1893," *Mississippi Valley Historical Review* 27, no. 3 (Dec. 1940): 421–34; White, *"It's Your Misfortune,"* 152.

20. Worster, *A River Running West*, 351–54; Terrell, *The Man Who Rediscovered America*, 114.

21. Worster, *A River Running West*, 351–54.

22. C. E. Dutton, "Irrigable Lands of the Valley of Sevier River," in Powell, *Report*, 142.

23. Smythe, "The Struggle for Water in the West," 653; Smythe, *Conquest*, 45.

24. Douglass Campbell, cited in Smythe, *Conquest*, 32–33.

25. Smythe, *Conquest*, 300–302. See also Smythe, *Conquest*, xiii: "Their true mission is . . . to work out the highest forms of civilization for their own race and nationality."

26. *Congressional Record*, 57th Cong., vol. 35, 6675; "Preliminary Report," HR Ex. Doc. 46, 46th Cong., 2nd sess., xxviii. See also *New York Times*, Jan. 10, 1892.

27. Donald Pisani, *From the Family Farm to Agribusiness: The Irrigation Crusade in California and the West* (Berkeley, 1984); Reisner, *Cadillac Desert*, 114.

28. Ganoe, "Origins."

29. "Reclamation of Arid Lands," HR Doc. 794, 57th Cong., 1st sess., 3, *The Evolution of the Conservation Movement, 1850–1920*, Library of Congress, Law Library, http://lcweb2.loc.gov/ammem/amrvhtml/conshome.html; Miles, "Our Unwatered Empire," 376; Elwood Mead, cited in Albert Perry Brigham, "Notes on the Recent Progress of Irrigation in the United States," *Bulletin of the American Geographical Society*, 33, no. 1 (1901): 77, *JSTOR*, Schaeffer Library, Union College, http://www.jstor.org/; *Irrigation Age* 14, no. 11 (Aug. 1900): 388–89. See also Ward, "Irrigation"; "Preliminary Exam of Reservoir Sites in Wyoming and Colorado," 55th Cong., 2nd sess., HR Doc. 141, 1897.

30. Walter Gillette Bates, "Water Storage in the West," *Scribner's Magazine* 7, no 1, (Jan. 1890): 16, in *Making of America*, Cornell University Library, http://cdl.library.cornell.edu/moa; "Reclamation of Arid Lands," HR Doc. 794, 57th Cong. 1st sess., 7–8; "Preliminary Examination of Reservoir Sites," HR Doc. 41 55th Cong., 2nd sess., 58.

31. *U.S. Statutes at Large*, vol. 32, pt. 1, ch.1093, 388–90; Francis G. Newlands, *The Public Papers of Francis G. Newlands* (Boston, 1932), 1:64.

32. Pisani, *To Reclaim a Divided West*, 274; Ganoe, "Origins," 34–52.

33. Stanley Roland Davison, *The Leadership of the Reclamation Movement 1875–1902* (New York, 1979), 252–59.

34. Davison, *The Leadership of the Reclamation Movement*, 252–59; Pisani, *To Reclaim a Divided West*, 273–325; Samuel P. Hays, *Conservation and the Gospel of Efficiency* (Cambridge, Mass., 1959), 9–15. According to Worster, *Rivers of Empire*, 161–62, historians have argued that the passage of the Newlands Act was due either to political skill or a wave of progressivism. Worster disagrees with both theories and argues that it was passed to promote "the accumulation of profit and power."

35. Pisani, *To Reclaim a Divided West*, 273–325.

36. *Nation*, May 2, 1878; Bates, "Water Storage," 16. See also Julian, "Our Land Policy"; Bennett, "The District Irrigation Movement in California," 248–57; Carl Snyder, Founding a New Empire," *Harper's Weekly*, Oct. 14, 1893; *New York Times*, Apr. 7, 1895; *Science* 12, no. 297 (Oct. 12, 1888): 169, *JSTOR*, Schaeffer Library, Union College, http://www.jstor.org/. Mary E. Young studies agrarian rhetoric in public land policy in "Congress Looks West: Liberal Ideology and Public Land Policy in the Nineteenth Century," in *The Frontier in American Development*, ed. David M. Ellis, 74–112 (Ithaca, 1969).

37. Teller cited in Pisani, *To Reclaim a Divided West*, 294; Wesley Jones, in "Irrigation of Arid Lands," Senate Doc. 446, 57th Cong., 1st sess., 2–30, *The Evolution of the Conservation Movement, 1850–1920*, Library of Congress, Law Library, http://lcweb2.loc.gov/ammem/amrvhtml/conshome.html. See also "Reclamation of Arid Lands," HR Doc. 794, 57th Cong. 1st sess., 15, and Senate Doc. 446, 2–30, which records congressional speeches and letters from the debate over the Newlands Act.

38. "Preliminary Examination of Reservoir Sites," HR Doc.141, 55th Cong., 2nd sess., 56; Francis G. Newlands, *The Public Papers of Francis G. Newlands* (Boston, 1932), 1:64; Joseph Randall, in "Irrigation of Arid Lands," Senate Doc. 446, 21–22.

39. H. C. Hansbrough, in "Irrigation of Arid Lands," Senate Doc. 446, 7–9. For the need for markets and its impact on internal expansion, see William Appleman Williams, *The Tragedy of American Diplomacy* (New York, 1988).

40. "Reclamation of Arid Lands," HR Doc. 794, 57th Cong. 1st. sess., 8; Ward, "Irrigation," 168.

41. "Report of the Governor of Arizona," *Reports of the Departments of the Interior* (Aug. 26, 1905), cited in *Reading the American West*, ed. Michael Roth, 272 (New York, 1999); Newlands, *Public Papers*, 1:69.

42. Smythe, *Conquest*, ix.

43. Some of the government-sponsored irrigation systems that were the product of the Newlands Act did assume cooperative approaches. For irrigation following the Newlands Act, see Worster, *Rivers of Empire*, 191–334. But the rhetoric surrounding the act was individualistic, not cooperative.

44. Herbert Croly, *The Promise of American Life* (New York, 1965), 279, 407–9.

Chapter Eight

· · · · · · · · · ·

Reconstructing the Empire of Cotton

A Global Story

SVEN BECKERT

The worldwide decline of bonded labor was one of the key economic, social, and political changes of the nineteenth century. If in the early nineteenth century the vast majority of agricultural commodities imported into the industrializing economies of the North Atlantic were produced by slaves and serfs—ranging from Caribbean sugar to American cotton to Russian wheat—by the end of the century, slavery and serfdom had all but disappeared as labor systems for agricultural production. The tight and long-lived connection between slavery and capitalism had been severed. To be sure, indentured labor, repressive credit arrangements, and all kinds of legal and extralegal violence persisted in the global countryside. Yet the forms and intensity of coercion had shifted.[1]

The struggles that resulted in abolition were drawn out and often violent.[2] Labor lords throughout the world resisted the emancipation of their workers, but faced with the determined resistance of slaves, declining support from metropolitan elites, diminishing influence over national governments, and a growing abolitionist movement, they gave way—some of them, like the planters of Saint Domingue, quite early; others, such as the planters of Brazil, much later. As one bastion of bonded labor after another fell, a global discourse emerged among capitalists and bureaucrats on how to reconcile the continued needs of metropolitan economies for cheap and plentiful agricultural commodities from the periphery with new forms of labor. This discussion stretched from Saint Domingue to London, from New Orleans to St. Petersburg, from Berlin to London, from Paris to Calcutta, from Boston to Washington, and from São Paulo to Madrid. In Boston, experts such as Massachusetts cotton manufacturer Edward Atkinson spoke on the promises of free labor; in Manchester, the members of the English Ladies Free Grown Cotton movement glowingly believed in the opportunities of new systems of labor; in Paris, the experts at the Ministry of Colonies issued in the 1840s "Rapport sur l'organisation du travail libre" and constituted in 1873 a commission aptly named the "commission du régime du travail aux colonies"; and in Berlin and Chicago budding social scientists explored the possibilities of free labor regimes in securing access to agricultural commodities.[3] Bureaucrats, planters, industrialists, as well as former slaves learned from one another's experiences, carefully following the spread of freedom. In the 1790s, for example, American slaves observed the revolutionary upheavals on Saint Domingue.[4] American, Cuban, and Brazilian planters worried in the 1830s about the impact of emancipation in the British West Indies, as when they observed that in British Guyana, upon emancipation, freedpeople had moved into subsistence farming, "with evil consequences."[5] In 1865, the Spanish ambassador to Paris asked the French minister of colonies to report on the French experience with emancipation and its effect on labor supply. In the 1890s, the British colonial authorities in Bombay inquired into the mobilization of labor in Russian central Asia. And in the 1910s, the Japanese Ministry of Agriculture and Commerce, set on expanding cotton production in colonial Korea, investigated the efforts of European nations to use free labor for the growing of cotton in their colonial possession.[6]

By the last third of the nineteenth century, with bonded labor clearly diminishing in importance, the debate shifted ever more to the issue of how—in the face of the slow disappearance of slavery and the firm resistance to new forms of bondage and wage labor by agricultural cultivators from western Africa to Pernambuco, from Berar to South Carolina—the production of agricultural commodities could be secured. The new intensity of the discussion was related to two factors. First, emancipation in the United

States in 1865 had given new and unprecedented urgency to the question of how cotton, a core commodity at the center of nearly all Western economies, was to be produced. Who would grow cotton, if not American slaves? Second, as European powers and Japan captured new territories, they faced the question of how to organize labor in these colonies. In the following decades, a global struggle unfolded between landowners, imperial bureaucrats, metropolitan capitalists, and intellectuals about how to reconcile commodity production for export with the desire of rural cultivators the world over to remain free and retain or acquire control over their labor and land. The outcome of these struggles, which stretched from India to central Asia, from the American South to Brazil, varied from region to region, but by the early twentieth century new systems of labor had emerged that became the cornerstone of the production of agricultural commodities and of a new global political economy.[7]

The transition from bonded labor took place in a global process in which the ideas, politics, and strategies of distant protagonists informed one another. The emergence of new forms of agricultural labor, moreover, was embedded within a continued tight relationship between economic expansion of the West and the production of agricultural commodities in the global periphery. In this essay, I suggest some of the complexities of this struggle by telling a story that illuminates some of its basic dynamics. It is a story that touches on an unlikely combination of places, ranging from Alabama to Saxony and Togo, and reports on what seems like a fantastic experiment that features, among others, a German aristocrat, Beno von Herman auf Wain; a freed slave and director of an important educational institution in the American South, Booker T. Washington; and a West African chief, Akpanya von Boem.[8]

The story begins in January 1901, when four African Americans from Alabama—James N. Calloway, John Robinson, Allen Burks, and Shepherd Harris—arrived on the beach at Lomé, the capital of the fledgling German colony of Togo. All four were the sons of slaves, and all were connected to Booker T. Washington's Tuskegee Industrial and Normal Institute. Calloway was a teacher; Robinson, Burks, and Harris were students or recent graduates. The four had come to the western coast of Africa to instruct the German colonialists and their subjects on how to grow cotton for export—an experiment that was to last until 1909, when the last of the African Americans, John Robinson, drowned.

Why did the four embark on this extraordinary journey? It had begun in Berlin a few years earlier, when cotton industrialists and government bureaucrats made plans to lessen Germany's dependence on American grown cotton. They resented the dependence on what they feared could be an economic and political competitor on the world stage, and they realized that Germany's economy remained exceedingly dependent on its cotton industry. Securing a reliable and cheap supply of raw cotton was, therefore, centrally important to economic prosperity and social peace. With newly acquired colonies at hand, the idea to turn them into major producers of cotton was embraced in the cotton districts of Saxony, Bavaria, and elsewhere, as well in the corridors of power in Berlin. In 1900, the Kolonialwirtschaftliches Komitee (KWK, Colonial Economic Committee), a semiprivate organization of industrialists including four hundred cotton manufacturers, began a concerted push for the production of cotton within the German colonial empire. Neither they nor anyone else in Germany, however, had any significant experience with growing cotton, so they looked to others for that expertise—to the United States in general and African Americans in particular. They considered "cotton culture since time immemorial the Negro's favorite culture" and saw African Americans as the world's most experienced and significant cotton farmers; indeed they had proven themselves to be the world's most successful commodity producers of African heritage anywhere.[9] Moreover, the German advocates for colonial cotton had learned that the head of one of the most important educational institutions for African Americans, Booker T. Washington, had widely advertised his belief in scientific agriculture, the "new Negro," and his support for Western imperialism, promising a role model for Africans that combined political accommodation with an eagerness to produce commodities for world markets, a combination that made him an ideal partner for the Germans. To the Germans' liking, Washington believed that Africa was backward and therefore in need of civilization, a civilization that colonial powers, foremost among them Germany, would dispense on their imperial missions. European states promised to uplift the "weaker races" by spreading capitalism and Christianity, and Washington agreed with the German colonialists that cotton would play an important part in this project. Because one of the members of the association that pushed for colonial cotton, Beno von Herman auf Wain, was the agricultural attaché at the German embassy in Washington D.C., he contacted Washington at

Tuskegee in the summer of 1900 and asked him for help in securing cotton experts for Togo.[10]

Thus it was that in January 1901 a group of Tuskegee cotton experts, personally chosen by Booker T. Washington, began their advisory role to the German colonial administration. The experiment, which lasted eight years, ended when John Robinson, on a mission to spread cotton commerce into the Togolese hinterland, drowned in a "swift river." During these years, as another member of the group, Shepherd Harris, put it in May 1901, "we [will do] all that there is in our power to reflect credit upon our race in America, and above all, credit upon Tuskegee our dear old Al."[11]

The journey of African Americans from Tuskegee to Togo illuminates a small but telling part of the global nature of the struggle to reconcile the decline of slavery and the expansion of commodity production. The Alabamians were able to embark on the journey only because their parents had been set free by the convulsions of the American Civil War. Reflecting post-Reconstruction notions of race, they saw their African sojourn as part of a larger struggle for black emancipation and themselves as the vanguard of the "black race." As experts on both the Negro and cotton, the Tuskegee experts seemed to their German hosts to promise extraordinary insights into how Africans could be turned into commodity producers. Their German employers were interested in hiring them because that same Civil War—which historians have called the "industrial world's first raw materials crisis"—had made European statesmen and industrialists deeply concerned about their continued dependence on a single supplier for their most crucial raw material. In the process of expanding cotton production, these German colonialists learned from British cotton-growing efforts in India as well as Russian ventures in central Asia and were connected to a global discourse on the Negro that ascribed specific characteristics to people of African heritage. The Germans' African subjects, in the meantime, like their counterparts in the American South, northeastern Brazil, and western India, understood that a radical expansion of commodity production would threaten their cherished way of life, including control over the way they worked, how they organized their reproduction, and how they defined their relationship to the rest of the world. Thus they resisted it.[12]

For eight years, the Tuskegee experts, German colonialists, and African rural cultivators struggled to reconcile their particular understandings of freedom and commodity production in Togo. They all wanted Togolese cotton to be exported, but they sharply disagreed about the conditions of its production. For the German colonialists, maximizing cotton exports stood at the center of their agenda: They believed that Ewe cultivators, working their own land, could be persuaded, and, if need be, coerced, to produce more of the white gold using American agricultural methods. The Ewe responded by taking advantage of a rapidly expanding market for one of their cash crops but also diligently safeguarded the production of subsistence crops, thus in effect limiting their output. The Tuskegee experts, in turn, were caught in the middle. They agreed with the German colonialists that cotton production should increase, believing that production for world markets could help make Africans and people of African heritage central to a core Western industry, thus securing their freedom. However, the Tuskegee experts held that the recasting the social structure of the Togolese countryside should be affected through a slow, evolutionary process, with as little coercion and violence as possible. In their disagreements, Tuskegee experts, the Ewe, and the German colonialists all drew on lessons learned from distant locales. And, perhaps surprisingly, in the end, the Africans managed to retain significant control over their lives—including their own vibrant cotton industry—at least in the short term. At the same time, Calloway, Robinson, Burks, and Harris, from their ambivalent position between German employers and African rural producers, negotiated the treacherous shoals of a new and increasingly virulent discourse on race that stretched from Tuskegee to Berlin to Togo. The contradictions between their aspirations for recognition and African improvement, the aims of the German colonialists for integrating metropolitan economies with commodity producers in the periphery, and the self-interest of African cultivators in retaining control over their land and labor were at the core of this novel project of bringing cotton, civilization, and colonialism together.

"I cannot say the trip was very agreeable," reported John Robinson to Booker T. Washington only days after arriving in Togo. "Within a few degrees of the equator—beneath a parching sun, after such a prolonged ride from America . . . all foot sore, lame and weary we reached our destination. . . . After three days we went out to locate the place of action and on the fourteenth Jan. 1901, we made a desperate attack upon the mighty African forest."[13]

The KWK's operations unfolded in grand style right from the beginning. On land once owned by the king of Tove, Calloway, Robinson,
Burks, and Harris ventured to build a cotton farm much like the ones they
had left behind in the United States. With the help of two hundred local
men, they cleared the high grass and trees, while women and children collected the remaining roots for burning. By May they had planted about
twenty-five acres in cotton and by July about a hundred acres. Virtually
ignoring the accumulated experience of the people of Tove, Calloway and
his colleagues systematically planted fields with various kinds of cotton
at different times to investigate what cotton would grow best and when it
should be sown. By April, Calloway reported proudly to Booker T. Washington, "Our work looks quite promising . . . and we believe that we will
make cotton."[14]

Despite these energetic beginnings, the Tuskegee experts soon encountered numerous difficulties. For the African American planters, operating a successful cotton farm without draft animals was unimaginable.
But the rural cultivators around Tove, reported John Robinson in astonishment, "were as afraid of a horse or cow as a common American youth is
of a 'mad dog.'" In addition, the animals themselves did not survive long
in the environment.[15] Unknown rainfall patterns also created problems.
When the rains started in July, the cotton the Tuskegee experts had planted right after their arrival rotted.[16] They could have learned as much from
local cultivators, but their firm belief in the superiority of their own methods, and their inability to communicate in the local language, precluded
such lessons. While for John Robinson "it was more difficult to train the
boys than it was to train the horses," for local cotton growers it was at
first impossible to penetrate the beliefs of the Americans.[17] The Tuskegee
experts also faced nearly insurmountable problems because of the lack of
infrastructure. To get their ginning equipment from the beach near Lomé,
where they had left it upon their arrival, to Tove they first had to widen
the road to make it passable for their wagons.[18] Then thirty people took
two weeks to pull the wagons to Tove. Such reliance on human muscle
power also hindered the ginning process: "24 natives were required to
operate the power [of the gin]; this number was necessary to take the place
of two horses and nevertheless only one bale of cotton could be ginned
in one day."[19] The African Americans, meanwhile, were isolated, lonely,
and deprived of the most basic comforts. As James Calloway reported to

his wife back home in Alabama a few weeks after arriving, "You cannot imagine how we are short here, no beds, no houses, no horses, no cows, no water fit to drink, no vegetables for civilized man. No Dr. when you are sick."[20]

Despite these frustrations, the Tuskegee experts on their experimental farm harvested one bale of Egyptian cotton and four bales of American cotton in the early summer and five more bales of American cotton in November and December.[21] Considering the enormous input of labor, land, and expertise, this was a meager harvest, but both Calloway and the KWK considered it a success. The KWK concluded that the local climate was indeed, as expected, favorable for the growing of high quality cotton, that the indigenous population was willing to embrace the crop, and that plenty of land was available to grow cotton, perhaps as much as in Egypt. Calloway concurred, suggesting that production could be expanded further by creating markets where indigenous people could bring their cotton for sale and by educating rural producers in agricultural techniques, especially the use of plows and draft animals. If these reforms were embraced, Calloway expected that "in a few years we shall be able to export many thousands bales of cotton from this colony. This will not have an effect on the market of the world; it will nevertheless be of great advantage to Germany and especially to the 2½ millions of natives of this colony."[22]

The amount of cotton grown by the Tuskegee experts during their first year in Togo may have been exceedingly small, but the goal of the KWK had never been to make Calloway and his colleagues into major cotton growers. What German industrialists had hoped for was to learn from these experienced cotton farmers and then to transfer that knowledge to local growers.[23] Their goal, from the beginning, was to make cotton production in Togo a *Volkskultur*—a people's culture—and not, as elsewhere in the German colonial empire, a *Plantagenkultur*—a plantation culture. This decision was based partly on the tremendous problems German cotton interests had encountered with the mobilization of labor for their plantations in German East Africa. These plantations, many of them run by German textile industrialists, had had trouble securing a sufficient number of African laborers. Though local German planters had tried to persuade the colonial administration to raise taxes in order to force rural producers to work for wages, the government had been reluctant to do so, fearing open rebellion.[24]

Moreover, German cotton policy was influenced by its encounter with the Ewe's old and thriving indigenous cotton industry. For centuries, rural cultivators had interspersed their fields with cotton plants, which was spun into yarn by local women and woven into cloth by men. Some of this cotton had also been traded across substantial distances.[25] It was this thriving domestic industry that the German colonialists had encountered when they expanded their influence into the Togolese hinterland during the 1890s. They hoped to recast this industry by changing its internal orientation to an external one—just like the British had done in India, and the Russians in central Asia. Thanks to the exposure to "scientific" agriculture, infrastructure improvements, and free market incentives, indigenous farmers were expected to grow more cotton of a uniform quality and then sell it to German merchants—just like former slaves had done in the United States.[26]

Unable to mobilize labor for colonial production on plantations, and inspired by the expansion of free labor cotton in the United States as well as the seemingly successful transmission of these experiences to Togo by the Tuskegee experts, German cotton interests hoped to set up a small number of model farms to serve as examples for the Ewe. Calloway himself returned to Alabama in 1902 to get four more Tuskegee graduates for the Togo project. Unfortunately, two of the prospective farmers, Hiram Dozier Simpson and William Drake, drowned when they arrived in Lomé.

When persuading more African Americans to travel to Togo proved difficult, the KWK, the German colonial administration, and the Tuskegee experts developed a number of policies to promote their common goals. To improve the quality of cotton, the KWK, along with private German investors such as the Deutsche Togogesellschaft, set up gins throughout the cotton-growing areas of Togo so growers need not gin the cotton themselves or transport the much heavier raw cotton over long distances. Purchasers, meanwhile, gained control of the cotton much earlier in the production process. Moreover, the colonial government tried to make the cotton more uniform in appearance by distributing seeds to growers. Here, the expertise of the Tuskegee advisers mattered a great deal: They had experimented with Egyptian, American, Peruvian, and Brazilian seeds and cataloged existing seeds in Togo. After 1911, an American variety mixed with Togo strains was marketed under the name "Togo Sea-Island"; it was the only strain distributed by the German authorities. In addition, to encourage rural cultivators to grow more cotton, the colonial government set minimum prices for the purchase of cotton, presumably making it less risky for growers to plant cotton. To export this cotton, a concentrated effort was made to gain control of the cotton market, at the beginning mainly by sending members of the cotton expedition, including Calloway and Robinson, to remote areas to purchase cotton from growers. By 1902, the Tuskegeans had fanned out over a large area of Togo, running various experimental farms and purchasing cotton whenever possible. They were also instrumental in building and supervising cotton-collecting stations in Klein Popo, Kpeme, Ho, Kete Kratchi, Kpandu, and Yendi.[27]

Price guarantees, ginning facilities, seed selection, and control over markets were critical measures to make more cotton available to German merchants. Even more crucial was the rapid development of an infrastructure to move cotton to the coast. When Calloway and his colleagues first arrived in Togo, it took fifteen days to go to Lomé and return—with hand-drawn wagons. By 1907, when a railroad connected the most important cotton areas to the coast, transportation time was cut to a few hours.[28]

In all these measures, the colonial state played a central role. Indeed, prices, markets, and infrastructure were creations of the colonial administration. And the colonial state's role went further. By taxing rural cultivators and making these taxes payable in labor, the state coerced them to, among other things, carry cotton from Tove to the coast, build railroads, and even clear land for cotton.[29] *Volkskultur*—people's culture—in the end had little to do with the choices of the Ewe cultivators and everything to do German colonialists' efforts to redirect labor toward the production of commodities for world markets.

The Tuskegee experts, as invested as the colonial state in the success of the project, were driven by a different motivation. They believed that their efforts to spread modern agricultural knowledge would improve Africans' well-being and secure their freedom. Moreover, by making themselves as well as African cultivators indispensable to the world economy, they believed they could secure the "advancement of the race." As a result, they—and especially Calloway and Robinson—took great pride in their work. They dedicated themselves wholly to the undertaking, so much so that Calloway resisted pleas from his wife to come home, postponing his return to prolong his project of "bringing civilization to Africa," as he put it. As late as August 1909, shortly before his death, Robinson explained that though "I am conscious of growing weaker. . . . I see no other way but to spend and be spent. My whole desire is to accomplish something."[30]

Taken together, the efforts of the Tuskegee experts and the colonial government were spectacularly effective. Cotton exports from Togo rose from virtually nothing in 1900 to 14,453 kg in 1902, 108,169 kg in 1904, and 510,742 kg in 1909, most of which was comparable in quality to "good American middling." This was only a minuscule part of German cotton imports (indeed, Germany never got more than half a percent of its cotton supply from its colonies).[31] But the rate of expansion (increasing by a factor of thirty-five in seven years) suggested that colonial cotton would have a bright future.[32]

Despite such a spectacular beginning, after 1909, further increase in cotton exports eluded the Tuskegee experts, the cotton commission, and the German colonial administration. In 1913, the last year of German colonial rule in Togo, cotton exports were slightly lower than they had been in 1909.

What were the reasons for such stagnation? While the sudden availability of vastly expanded markets did encourage rural cultivators to significantly increase their cotton production, there were limits to such expansion. These limits were largely rooted in the ways cotton fitted into the agricultural schemes of local producers. Ewe cultivators, after all, had their own ideas about the relationship between freedom and commodity production, which did not necessarily correspond with those of the Tuskegee experts or the German colonialists.

At the core of cultivators' resistance was their desire to maintain older economic and social patterns that gave them control over their work, subsistence, and lives. Traditionally, women had interspersed their corn and yam fields with cotton plants, providing them with an additional crop without much additional labor, as the land had to be hoed and weeded in any case. At first, the production and export of cotton did not disrupt these agricultural patterns. But cotton occupied a definite place within traditional work patterns and a long-standing, gendered division of labor, however, placed severe limits on how much this culture could be extended. To the chagrin of German colonial authorities, Togolese peasants refused to engage in the monocultural production of cotton. According to a German colonial report the peasants disliked growing only cotton because it was much more labor intensive and not necessarily more profitable. Corn and yams, moreover, provided cultivators with food, no matter how low the price of cotton might fall. The prices offered for raw cotton were too low to persuade peasants to abandon their subsistence crops and engage in the backbreaking work of cotton monoculture. The local peasants preferred growing food crops to expanding their cotton production, a preference shared by cotton growers the world over—from Demerara to the United States, from Brazil to India.[33]

Cotton exports were also limited by keen competition from indigenous spinners for the white gold. And the fact that most native cultivators remained far removed from world markets and experienced little if any commercialization of their lives meant they felt little economic pressure to produce cash crops, unlike, for example, upcountry farmers in the United States. The Ewe could back up their preference for mixed farming with their ability to maintain it. The "dread of starving" that British abolitionists had hoped would replace the "dread of being flogged" as a motivation for colonial people to produce crops for world markets failed in Togo in the face of plentiful alternatives.[34]

German colonial authorities understood these forces well. Even before Togo's cotton cultivation stagnated, the authorities began to investigate how rural producers elsewhere were pressured to increase their production of cotton. KWK member Karl Supf, clearly comprehending the tensions between subsistence and world market production, suggested that the goal of colonial policy should be "to bring the Natives into economic dependence upon us." One way to do so, he suggested, was to increase local taxes and make them payable in cotton.[35] Alternatively, the governor of Togo suggested in December 1903 that small sums of money, secured by future cotton harvests, be advanced to peasants to enable them to focus on cotton as "an emphatic influence of the governmental agencies on the natives at least for a number of years is essential." He thought the government should explicitly look for ways to "pressure those natives, who took on responsibilities by voluntarily accepting seeds, credit or advances or other support for cotton growing."[36] Free labor cotton depended on turning labor into a marketable commodity and divorcing growers, willingly or through coercion, from their control of land and labor. But the relatively weak presence of the German colonial state left the resilient social structure of rural producers, predicated on the continued access to plentiful land, largely untouched.[37]

Railroads, markets, and price guarantees were not sufficient to persuade growers to abandon subsistence agriculture.

With efforts to involve rural cultivators in debt schemes faltering and outright expropriation of land beyond the power of the colonial administration, other forms of coercion moved ever more into the center of the German colonialists' project to grow cotton. Colonialists systematically undermined markets by fixing prices, compelling cultivators to bring their cotton to market in particular ways, eliminating middle men, forcing certain cotton strains on producers, and extracting labor from peasants by force. Extraeconomic coercion was central to the colonial "free labor" cotton project—but, in the end, it was not sufficient to persuade rural growers to reconsider the allocation of their labor and crop choices. Not only were roads, railways, and cotton gins built by forced labor, colonial authorities also asserted ever tighter control over cotton production and marketing. Local government officials supervised the planting of cotton, tried to make sure that fields were regularly weeded, and secured a timely harvest. By 1911, for example, the German administration had created forty-seven authorized buying stations throughout the cotton-growing areas to ensure that cotton sales occurred only under the watchful eyes of the government; indeed at times, soldiers were employed to purchase cotton. In January 1912, they further ordered that every ginning or mercantile company send only government-licensed purchasers to markets. Sellers also had to separate good and poor quality cotton. By 1914, rules as to how cotton was to be treated were honed further and now included corporal punishment for indigenous growers who violated them. Force, violence, and coercion became ever more central to German policy. In Togo, as elsewhere in Africa, compulsion accompanied the spread of colonial cotton growing, setting the continent apart from most other cotton-growing places in the world, where physical violence had been replaced by other, and ultimately more successful forms, of coercion. Africans, the colonial powers believed, needed to be forced into accepting the "natural laws" of the market. As a result, the people of Togo suffered unprecedented violence at the hands of a deeply racist regime.[38]

But none of these efforts resulted in a further expansion of cotton production after the peak year of 1909, mirroring the maddeningly difficult experiences of other colonial powers in Africa. Meanwhile, the German colonial authorities watched with envy the expansion of cotton production in central Asia and western India, where Russian and British colonialists had virtually recast local social structures to make them conducive to cash crop production. Clearly, market integration and commercialization of agriculture went hand in hand with growing cotton for export. To reorient an internal economy to an external one in the absence of clear-cut economic incentives, social relations in the countryside had to be drastically recast—a process that usually took several decades or ruthless violence. To be sure, Africans could adopt rapidly to a new set of incentives—as the pioneering efforts of Gold Coast peasants in the 1890s and 1900s to produce cocoa for world markets show.[39] But the Germans in Togo could not wait long enough, nor did they have the administrative, economic, or military capacity to shorten the process.

Not only did the German colonial administration, after its first spectacular successes, fail in expanding cotton production for German markets, but its experiment of working with the Tuskegee experts was ultimately a disappointment. The relationship grew increasingly tense as the Germans and African Americans diverged in their understanding of how freedom and commodity production could be reconciled. Not that the Tuskegee experts and the German colonialists disagreed on everything. Robinson believed that Togolese cultivators in general and his students in particular should use modern agricultural methods to increase cotton production—the plow instead of the hoe, animal instead of human power. In this way, they would improve their economic well-being and show that Africans were capable of embracing superior techniques of agricultural production. German cotton interests agreed with these goals and lauded the Tuskegee experts for their work.[40]

Admiration stopped there, however. In contrast to the German colonialists, Robinson strongly believed in the importance of growing subsistence crops along with cotton. He advocated the joint development of cotton and food crops in "harmonious ways," and his teachings reflected Washington's concern that rural African Americans focused too much on the growing of cotton and too little on providing their own subsistence.[41] When Robinson outlined his plans for a cotton school in Nuatjä in early 1904 he asserted that "I stand for more than Cotton, and am sure that the government will not assume to take a stand so narrow and biased." In an exceptionally wide-ranging letter, Robinson opined that "[t]he source and life of all governments are its people, and the first duty of the government is to maintain this life and source. Consequently, the people are its first and Chief Concern. For that same reason we wish to teach the people cotton culture, because it is good for *them*, they will gain wealth thereby and the Colony grow richer. . . . But the people cannot live by Cotton alone. Therefore we should begin now to teach them. Where they grow only maize we will teach them to grow more maize and better maize, and also Cotton. Where they grow now Yams and Cotton they must be shown how to grow larger Yams and finer Cotton."[42] To effect such a transition, Robinson believed, peasants must not be coerced but should be involved with "as little excitement and inconvenience" as possible.[43]

The position of the African American experts was always threatened by German racism. The German colonial administration feared from the beginning that the Tuskegee experts' primary loyalty would be to the people of Togo. They remained ambivalent about being dependent on African Americans, particularly since Calloway and Robinson had a wealth of knowledge about cotton planting unrivalled among German experts.[44] This dependence on the Tuskegee expertise, of course, secured the experts' position. But it also created fears among German colonialists that the visitors from Tuskegee would fraternize with the local population.[45]

For the German colonial administration, the tensions between their dependence on black expertise and their need to see people of African heritage as inferior to themselves—along with a concern that visible dependence on black people might not be the image that they wanted to project to the Africans they dominated—led them to slowly move away from the experiment. But the project of colonial cotton growing itself remained a central element in the agenda of colonial domination and industrial policy.

For Booker T. Washington and the Tuskegee experts who ventured to Togo in the early years of the twentieth century, the self-improvement of their race was at the core of their understanding of the project. They were pleased that the German colonial administration had sought them out. Colonization of Africa was the spirit of the age, and Tuskegee proudly played its role within it. As James N. Calloway observed in June 1901: "If you could see this land and know these people you would have even a greater zeal for your work. If Africa is ever reclaimed it will be through such missionary work as is done in school, shops, and farms at Tuskegee."[46]

For years to come, Washington and Tuskegee proudly forged this episode into an important part of their public image. A song was even com-
posed celebrating "Tuskegee's first martyrs," Hiram Simpson and William
Drake, "who gave up school and native land, for their race and country's
sake," and whose "monument stands unveiled . . . in every Tuskegee
heart."[47] The work in Togo, they all believed, not only shed glory on
Tuskegee but also played an important part in the larger project of uplifting the black race. Calloway, Burks, Harris, Robinson, Byrant, Griffin, and
Simpson's widow brought modern agriculture, indeed modernity itself, to
what they perceived to be a part of the world in desperate need of such uplift. Just like the German colonizers, though with a very different agenda,
they perceived their excursion as a "civilizing mission." They could not
understand why the Ewe might resist such a seemingly benevolent project,
because they failed to see that the Ewe—unlike most former slaves in the
southern United States—continued to enjoy access to land, the tools of subsistence, and power, and therefore did not perceive a reallocation of their
labor to commodity production as emancipatory. Ignoring such fundamental differences, Calloway proclaimed that "if I did not know I am in Africa
I could easily believe myself in Alabama."[48]

Whereas German colonialists willingly resorted to economic coercion—corvée, taxation, and other devices—and physical force to compel
Africans to produce cotton, the Tuskegee experts believed that growing
cotton would awaken the Togolese to a whole world of modern products
they would then willingly work hard to acquire. "The natives," argued Calloway in 1903, "learn from the Americans about the wants, namely in clothing and tools, that have eluded them so far," making them "better consumers than before" while they "must at the same time, work more to supply
themselves with these objects."[49] Not only was Tuskegee at the forefront of
the uplift of the black race in the United States, it was also a beacon of light
in the "African darkness."

The venture of a small group of Tuskegee cotton experts in Togo speaks
also to a story larger than itself. The encounter between African Americans
one generation removed from slavery, German colonial authorities, and
Togolese rural cultivators illuminates a vast recasting of the global empire of cotton—and, with it, global capitalism—in the last decades of the
nineteenth century. States had now taken on unprecedented importance
in structuring global cotton markets: Colonial cotton growing was only

one facet of a policy that included import duties, imperial preferences, and powerful national industrial policies. But perhaps even more important in the long run, the empire of cotton had survived a dramatic transformation of its dominant system of labor. Not long before the Germans began thinking about colonial cotton in Togo, African slaves who had worked the cotton plantations of the American South for more than half a century had finally won their freedom. Now, throughout the world, nominally free but often highly indebted cultivators grew cotton for world markets under new systems of social relations. Colonial powers such as Germany tried to spread this system, with mixed success. Peasant resistance to a radical recasting of their economies proved to be a powerful, if temporary, barrier to complete world market integration. People with little access to economic, social, and political power helped shape the social relations in which cotton for world markets was produced, retaining at least temporary control over their own lives.[50]

The significance of the cotton experiment in Togo comes into even sharper relief when compared to the cotton-growing efforts of French, British, Russian, Belgian, and Portuguese colonial authorities. After 1861, French, Russian, and British manufacturers started pressuring their governments to draw more cotton out of their various colonial possessions in India, central Asia, and North Africa. By the early twentieth century, they had embarked upon a concerted effort to grow more colonial cotton. British cotton manufacturers founded the British Cotton Growing Association in 1902 in the cotton metropolis of Manchester, which also hired five Tuskegee graduates to support their cotton-growing endeavor in the Sudan. Less than a year later, the Association Cotonnière Coloniale was founded by French textile entrepreneurs to encourage colonial cotton production and promote "the independence of our national cotton industry." By 1906, Russian cotton entrepreneurs followed suit. These early twentieth-century efforts at colonial cotton growing were inspired by the activities in Togo. The French and British associations, in fact, sent representatives to meet with John Robinson. The 1904 International Cotton Congress in Vienna featured a special session examining German cotton-growing efforts in Togo, and the 1907 congress emphasized once more the importance of colonial cotton for the future health of the industry. Even the Japanese cotton spinners in distant Osaka kept taps on German efforts in Togo, hoping to replicate their work in Korea.[51] Though all these efforts were fundamentally about isolating national industries from the vagaries of the world market, they themselves formed part of a new cotton international. People from all over the empire of cotton engaged with these institutions and tried to learn from each other's experiences.[52]

It was a volatile encounter between Booker T. Washington's pan-Africanism and zeal for self-improvement and the desire of German colonial authorities to recast Togo into a major source of raw cotton for German industry that resulted in the meeting of African American farmers, German textile industrialists and bureaucrats, and Togolese cultivators in the early twentieth century. This encounter was possible only because of the vast restructuring of the global empire of cotton in the wake of the American Civil War, with states and nonbonded labor moving to center stage, where once slavery had stood. Around the world, peoples' desire for the freedom to control their own land and labor clashed with the needs of industrialists and statesmen for increased commodity production. These struggles inaugurated a new and different phase of capitalist globalization. And while, as in Togo, rural cultivators tried their best to protect their subsistence agriculture and resist the monocultural production of cash crops for world markets, in the long term they could not defy the two-pronged assault on their traditional economy by powerful capitalists and imperial states. As a result, nonbonded cultivators, in Togo as elsewhere, ultimately produced huge quantities of cotton for world markets. The story of cotton in Togo underscores what scholars have learned from investigations into the history of the postbellum American South, nineteenth-century India and Egypt, as well as twentieth-century Africa: the process of divorcing rural producers from control over their own labor and land often involved significant violence. Free labor production of commodities for world markets, in effect, frequently depended on the destruction of subsistence economies and older patterns of trade by powerful colonizing states—in other words, on coercion.

Although Booker T. Washington and his disciples had witnessed the tremendous legal and extralegal coercion that had descended on freed slaves in the American South, they worked to secure freedom for Africans and African Americans by accommodating themselves to powerful capitalists and statesmen within the United States and beyond. By becoming indispensable and remaining independent, Washington believed, people of African heritage could secure their freedom as small but indispensable wheels in the machinery of global capitalism—namely, in the reconstruction of the worldwide web of cotton production. Half a century later, the civil rights movement and efforts to achieve national independence in Africa followed a different path—a path that eventually led to political emancipation. Economic emancipation, however, which had been so crucial to Washington's agenda, remains an elusive goal, as Africans and African Americans remain on the margins of the capitalist world economy.

ACKNOWLEDGMENTS

Thanks to Natsuko Kitani, Erin Sprague, Luise Tremel, and Carsten Vogelpohl for their terrific research assistance, Cynthia Wilson at Tuskegee for her help in locating records on the Tuskegee students who went to Togo, and Freiherr von Herrman auf Wain for providing me with copies of his grandfather's papers. Thanks also to Emmanuel Akyeampong, Caroline Elkins, Deborah Gesensway, Lisa McGirr, Julia Rosenbaum, Manisha Sinha, Cyrus Veeser, Penny von Eschen, and the members of the seminar on the political economy of North America at the Charles Warren Center at Harvard University for their helpful comments on an earlier draft of this essay. Many thanks also to the Alexander von Humboldt Foundation, the Kittredge Fund, and the Weatherhead Center for International Affairs at Harvard University, whose generous support made the research possible. Parts of this essay have been reprinted with the permission of the Organization of American Historians.

NOTES

1. Elisée Reclus, "Le Coton et la crise americaine," *Revue des Deux Mondes* 32 (1862): 176–208 ; J. T. Danson, "On the Existing Connection between American Slavery and the British Cotton Manufacture," *Journal of the Statistical Society of London* 20 (March 1857). Some historians have agreed with this assessment. See, among others, Kenneth Pomeranz, *The Great Divergence: China, Europe, and the Making of the Modern World Economy* (Princeton, 2000); Joseph E. Inikori, *Africans and the Industrial Revolution in England: A Study in International Trade and Economic Development* (Cambridge, UK, 2002).

2. Eric Foner, *Nothing but Freedom: Emancipation and Its Legacy* (Baton Rouge, 1983); Robert Steinfeld, *Coercion, Contract, and Free Labor in the Nineteenth Century* (New York, 2001); Nan Elizabeth Woodruff, *American Congo: The African American Freedom Struggle in the Delta* (Cambridge, Mass., 2003); Eric Foner, *Reconstruction: America's Unfinished Revolution, 1863–1877* (New York, 1988); Jonathan M. Wiener, *Social Origins of the New South: Alabama, 1860–1885* (Baton Rouge, 1978); Barbara Jeanne Fields, "The Advent of Capitalist Agriculture: The New South in a Bourgeois World," in *Essays on the Postbellum Southern Economy*, ed. Thavolia Glymph (Arlington, 1985); Gavin Wright, *Old South, New South: Revolutions in*

the Southern Economy since the Civil War (New York, 1986); Sugata Bose, *Peasant Labour and Colonial Capital: Rural Bengal since 1770* (Cambridge, UK, 1993); *South Asia and World Capitalism*, ed. Sugata Bose (Delhi, 1990); Laxman D. Satya, *Cotton and Famine in Berar, 1850–1900* (New Delhi, 1997); *Cotton, Colonialism, and Social History in Sub-Saharan Africa*, ed. Isaacman and Roberts; Richard L. Roberts, *Two Worlds of Cotton: Colonialism and the Regional Economy in the French Soudan, 1800–1946* (Stanford, 1996).

3. Commission Coloniale, "Rapport Sur L'Organisation Du Travail Libre," in 317/Gen 40/472, Fonds Ministérielle, Centre des Archives d'Outre Mer, Aix en Provence (henceforth CAOM); Procès verbaux des séances de la commission du travail aux colonies, 1873–1874, 1105/Gen 127/473, Fonds Ministérielle, CAOM; "Régime du Travail dans les colonies, rapport, 1875," in 1152/Gen 135/475, Fonds Ministérielle, CAOM; *Liverpool Mercury*, Sept. 23, 1863, 6; Edward Atkinson, *Cheap Cotton by Free Labor: By a Cotton Manufacturer* (Boston, 1861), 478. Atkinson is here not identified as the author, but his authorship becomes clear from his correspondence with Charles E. Norton. See box N 297, Letters, 1861–1864, Edward A. Atkinson Papers, Massachusetts Historical Society, Boston, Mass. See also John Bright to Atkinson, London, May 29, 1862, box N 298, Edward A. Atkinson Papers.

4. Ira Berlin, *Generations of Captivity: A History of African-American Slaves* (Cambridge, Mass., 2003), 128–29.

5. W. H. Holmes, *Free Cotton: How and Where to Grow It* (London, 1862), 18.

6. Note from the Ambassade d'Espagne a Paris, no date, 994/Gen 117/474, Fonds Ministérielle, CAOM; copy of a report by R. B. D. Morier to the Secretary of State, the Marquis of Salisbury, Oct. 12, 1889, Revenue Department, Compilations, 1890, vol. 51, Compilation No. 476, "Establishment by the Russian Government of a Model Cotton Plantation in the Merva Oasis," Maharashtra State Archive, Mumbai, India; Rinji Sangyo Chosa Kyoku [Special Department of Research on Industries], "Chosen ni Okeru Menka ni Kansuru Chosa Seiseki" [The Research on Cotton in Korea] (Aug., 1918); No-Shomu Sho Nomu Kyoku [Ministry of Agriculture and Commerce, Department of Agriculture], "Menka ni Kansuru Chosa" [The Research on Cotton] (March, 1913).

7. For an account of this transition, in regard to cotton, see also Sven Beckert, "Emancipation and Empire: Reconstructing the Worldwide Web of Cotton Production in the Age of the American Civil War," *American Historical Review* 109 (Dec. 2004): 1405–38.

8. *Baumwoll-Expedition nach Togo, Bericht 1901* (Berlin, 1901), 4. On the journey, see also James N. Calloway to Booker T. Washington, Nov. 20, 1900, Booker T. Washington Papers, Manuscripts Division, Library of Congress, Washington, D.C., (hereafter BTW Papers); Kolonial-Wirtschaftliches Komitee to Washing-

ton, Oct. 10, 1900, and Dec. 11, 1900, BTW Papers. On the episode, see also Sven Beckert, "From Tuskegee to Togo: The Problem of Freedom in the Empire of Cotton," *Journal of American History* 92 (Sept. 2005): 498–526; Booker T. Washington, *Working with the Hands* (New York, 1904), 226–30; Louis R. Harlan, "Booker T. Washington and the White Man's Burden," *American Historical Review* 71 (Jan. 1966): 441–67; Edward Berman, "Tuskegee-in-Africa," *Journal of Negro Education* 41 (Spring 1972): 99–112; W. Manning Marable, "Booker T. Washington and African Nationalism," *Phylon* 35 (Dec. 1974): 398–406; Louis R. Harlan, *Booker T. Washington: The Wizard of Tuskegee, 1901–1915* (New York, 1983), 266–95; Michael O. West, "The Tuskegee Model of Development in Africa: Another Dimension of the African/African-American Connection," *Diplomatic History* 16 (Summer 1992): 371–87; Milfred C. Fierce, *The Pan-African Idea in the United States, 1900–1919: African-American Interest in Africa and Interaction with West Africa* (New York, 1993), 171–97; Donna J. E. Maier, "Persistence of Precolonial Patterns of Production: Cotton in German Togoland, 1800–1914," in *Cotton, Colonialism, and Social History in Sub-Saharan Africa*, ed. Allen Isaacman and Richard Roberts (Portsmouth, N.H., 1995), 71–95; Kendahl L. Radcliffe, "The Tuskegee-Togo Cotton Scheme, 1900–1909" (PhD diss., University of California, Los Angeles, 1998).

9. *Baumwoll-Expedition nach Togo, Bericht 1901*, 3.

10. Karl Supf, "Zur Baumwollfrage," in Kolonial-Wirtschaftliches Komitee, *Baumwoll-Expedition nach Togo* (n.d., but probably 1900), 10, file 332, record group R 150F, Fonds Allemand 1 (henceforth FA), Papers of the Administration of the German Protectorate Togo (L'Administration du Protectorat Allemand du Togo) (Archives Nationales du Togo, Lomé, Togo, microfilm copy in Bundesarchiv Berlin, Germany); *Baumwoll-Expedition nach Togo, Bericht 1901*, 3; Radcliffe, "Tuskegee-Togo Cotton Scheme," 37.

11. Okon Edet Uya, ed., *Black Brotherhood: Afro-Americans and Africa* (Lexington, Ky., 1971), 134; Shepherd Lincoln Harris to Washington, May 15, 1901, BTW Papers.

12. Allen Isaacman and Richard Roberts, "Cotton, Colonialism, and Social History in Sub-Saharan Africa: Introduction," in *Cotton, Colonialism, and Social History in Sub-Saharan Africa*, ed. Isaacman and Roberts, 7.

13. Robinson to Washington, May 26, 1901, BTW Papers.

14. For the quote see Calloway to Washington, April 30, 1901, BTW Papers. See also Calloway to Kolonial-Wirtschaftliches Komitee, 12 March 1901, file 8221, record group R 1001, Papers of the Deutsche Kolonialgesellschaft; Darkoh, "Togoland under the Germans," 112; Calloway to Kolonial-Wirtschaftliches Komitee, Feb. 3, 1901, file 8221, record group R 1001, Papers of the Deutsche Kolonialgesellschaft; Calloway to Washington, Feb. 3, 1901, BTW Papers; Calloway to Kolo-

nial-Wirtschaftliches Komitee, May 14, 1901, file 8221, record group R 1001, Papers of the Deutsche Kolonialgesellschaft.

15. Robinson to Washington May 26, 1901, BTW Papers; Calloway to Kolonial-Wirtschaftliches Komitee, June 13, 1901, file 8221, record group R 1001, Papers of the Deutsche Kolonialgesellschaft; Calloway to Mr. Schmidt, Nov. 11, 1901, file 1008, R 150 F, FA 3, Papers of the Administration of the German Protectorate Togo.

16. Calloway to Mr. Schmidt, Nov. 11, 1901, file 1008, R 150 F, FA 3, Papers of the Administration of the German Protectorate Togo; Calloway to Kolonial-Wirtschaftliches Komitee, Sept. 2, 1901, file 8221, record group R 1001, Papers of the Deutsche Kolonialgesellschaft.

17. Robinson to Washington, May 26, 1901, BTW Papers.

18. Calloway to Kolonial-Wirtschaftliches Komitee, March 12, 1901, file 8221, record group R 1001, Papers of the Deutsche Kolonialgesellschaft.

19. Eventually, one source reports that 105 men were involved in moving the wagons to the plantations. See *Baumwoll-Expedition nach Togo, Bericht 1901*, 24.

20. Calloway to his wife, March 17, 1901, quoted in Radcliffe, "Tuskegee-Togo Cotton Scheme," 74.

21. *Baumwoll-Expedition nach Togo, Bericht 1901*, 26.

22. For the quote see *Baumwoll-Expedition nach Togo, Bericht 1901*), 28–36, quote is on 36; F. Wohltmann, "Neujahrsgedanken 1905," *Der Tropenpflanzer* 9 (Jan. 1905), 5; *Baumwoll-Expedition nach Togo, Bericht 1901*, 4–5; Karl Supf, Kolonial-Wirtschaftliches Komitee, to Kolonial-Abteilung des Auswärtigen Amtes, Berlin, Aug. 15, 1902, file 8221, record group R 1001, Papers of the Deutsche Kolonialgesellschaft.

23. *Der Tropenpflanzer*, 7 (Jan. 1903), 9.

24. Kolonial-Wirtschaftliches Komitee, *Deutsch-koloniale Baumwoll-Unternehmungen, Bericht* XI (Frühjahr 1909), 28; Thaddeus Sunseri, "The Baumwollfrage: Cotton Colonialism in German East Africa" *Central European History* 34 (2001): 46, 48.

25. Kolonial-Wirtschaftliches Komitee, *Verhandlungen der Baumwoll-Kommission des Kolonial-Wirtschaftilichen Komitees vom 25. April 1912*, 169; Doran Ross, *Wrapped in Pride: Ghanaian Kente and African American Identity* (Los Angeles, 1998), 126–49; Agbenyega Adedze, "Cotton in Eweland: Historical Perspectives," in Ross, *Wrapped in Pride*, 132; Maier, "Persistence of Precolonial Patterns of Production," 73–76.

26. John Robinson, in Kolonial-Wirtschaftliches Komitee, *Baumwoll-Unternehmungen 1902, 1903* (Berlin, 1903), 18; *Zeitfragen: Wochenschrift für deutsches Leben* (Mai 1, 1911), p. 1.

27. German cotton merchants in particular were active in creating these ginning and pressing operations, helped by the Tuskegee experts, and as early as 1902 the Deutsche Togogesellschaft established itself in Berlin, a private enterprise that was to build gins and cotton-buying agencies in Togo. See "Prospekt der Deutschen Togogesellschaft," Berlin, April 1902, private archive, Freiherr von Herman auf Wain, Schloss Wain, Wain, Germany, copy in author's possession; Karl Supf, *Deutsch-Koloniale Baumwoll-Unternehmungen*, Bericht IX, 1907, 304. See also Pape to Bezirksamt Atakpame, April 5, 1909, file 1009, record group R 150F, FA 3, Papers of the Administration of the German Protectorate Togo. During the 1908–9 season, for example, they stipulated the minimum price for ginned cotton, delivered at the coast, to be 30 Pfennige per pound. See Verhandlungen des Kolonial-Wirtschaftlichen Komitees und der Baumwoll-Komission, Nov. 11, 1908, file 8223, record group R 1001, Papers of the Deutsche Kolonialgesellschaft; Kolonial-Wirtschaftliches Komitee, *Baumwoll-Unternehmungen 1902, 1903* (Berlin, 1903), 17; Radcliffe, "Tuskegee-Togo Cotton Scheme," 103.

28. Calloway to Kolonial-Wirtschaftliches Komitee, June 13, 1901, file 8221, record group R 1001, Papers of the Deutsche Kolonialgesellschaft. In 1903 Robinson reported that transporting cotton from Tove to Lomé would take ten to twelve days. Kolonial-Wirtschaftliches Komitee, *Baumwoll-Unternehmungen 1902, 1903* (Berlin, 1903), 21; Karl Supf, Kolonial-Wirtschaftliches Komitee, to Auswärtiges Amt, Kolonial-Abteilung, May 10, 1902, file 8221, record group R 1001, Papers of the Deutsche Kolonialgesellschaft.

29. German cotton interests appealed to the Kolonial-Abteilung of the Auswärtiges Amt that *Steuerträger*, in effect forced laborers, should carry the cotton from Tove to the coast without pay. See Karl Supf, Kolonial-Wirtschaftliches Komitee, to Auswärtiges Amt, Kolonial-Abteilung, Nov. 15, 1901, 8221, record group R 1001, Papers of the Deutsche Kolonialgesellschaft. See also note "Station Mangu No. 170/11, May 8, 1911, file 4047, record group R 150F, FA 3, Papers of the Administration of the German Protectorate Togo; Karl Supf, "Zur Baumwollfrage," in Kolonial-Wirtschaftliches Komitee, *Baumwoll-Expedition nach Togo* (no date, but probably 1900), p. 12, file 332, record group R 150F, FA 1, Papers of the Administration of the German Protectorate Togo.

30. Calloway to his wife, Nov. 2, 1902, quoted in Radcliffe, "Tuskegee-Togo Cotton Scheme," 118. On Calloway's reluctance to return to the United States see ibid., 81. John W. Robinson, "At Work in West Africa," *Southern Letter* (Aug. 1909): 3.

31. Radcliffe, "Tuskegee-Togo Cotton Scheme," 107; Verhandlungen des Kolonial-Wirtschaftlichen Komitees und der Baumwoll-Komission, Nov. 11, 1908, file 8223, record group R 1001, Papers of the Deutsche Kolonialgesellschaft.

32. Metzger, *Unsere Alte Kolonie Togo*, 245, 252. For further statistics on the export of cotton from Togo after World War I, see "Togo: La Production du Cotton," *Agence Extérieure et Coloniale*, Oct. 29, 1925. The expansion of cotton production continued throughout the twentieth century, and in 2002–3, Togo produced 176 million pounds (80 million kg) of cotton, about 19 times as much as in 1938 and 160 times as much as in 1913. See Reinhart. "Cotton Market Report" 44, Jan. 23, 2004, at www.reinhart.ch/pdf_files/marketreportch.pdf.

33. Maier, "Persistence of Precolonial Patterns of Production," 77. Moreover, large areas of Togo were also sparsely settled, lacking surplus labor for cotton production. See Pape, "Eine Berichtigung zu dem von Prof. Dr. A. Oppel verfassten Aufsatz "Der Baumwollanbau in den deutschen Kolonien und seine Aussichten," file 3092, record group R 150f, FA3, Papers of the Administration of the German Protectorate Togo. On intercropping see also Thomas J. Bassett, *The Peasant Cotton Revolution in West Africa: Côte d'Ivoire, 1880–1995* (New York, 2001), 57; "Bericht über den Baumwollbau in Togo," Enclosure in Kaiserliches Gouvernement Togo, Gouverneur Zech to Reichskolonialamt Berlin, Nov. 23, 1909, 2, file 8223, record group R 1001, Papers of the Deutsche Kolonialgesellschaft; Beckert, "Emancipation and Empire."

34. *Deutsch-Koloniale Baumwoll-Unternehmungen, Bericht XI* (Frühjahr 1909), file 3092, record group R 150F, FA 3, Papers of the Administration of the German Protectorate Togo. James Stephen quoted in Davis Brion Davis, *Slavery and Human Progress* (New York, 1984), 218.

35. Supf, "Zur Baumwollfrage," in Kolonial-Wirtschaftliches Komitee, *Baumwoll-Expedition nach Togo* (n.d., but probably 1900), 9, 12, file 332, record group R 150F, FA 1, Papers of the Administration of the German Protectorate Togo.

36. Gouverneur of Togo to Herrn Bezirksamtsleiter von Atakpame, Dec. 9 (no year), file 1008, record group R 150 F, FA 3, Papers of the Administration of the German Protectorate Togo; "Massnahmen zur Hebung der Baumwollkultur im Bezirk Atakpakme unter Mitwirkung des Kolonialwirtschaftlichen Komitees," Verwaltung des deutschen Schutzgebietes Togo, file 1008, record group R 150 F, FA3, Papers of the Administration of the German Protectorate Togo. For the quote see Kolonial-Wirtschaftliches Komitee, *Baumwoll-Unternehmungen 1902, 1903* (Berlin, 1903), 57–59.

37. John Robinson remarked as early as 1904 that the "habits [of the people of Togo] cannot be changed in a day." See "Baumwollanbau im Schutzgebiet Togo, Darlegungen des Pflanzers John W. Robinson vom 26. 4. 1904 betr. die Voraussetzungen, Boden- und Klimaverhältnisse, Methoden und Arbeitsverbesserung, Bewässerung," Fragment, file 89, record group R 150F, FA 1, Papers of the Administration of the German Protectorate Togo.

38. Supf quoted in Supf, "Zur Baumwollfrage," Kolonial-Wirtschaftliches Komitee, *Baumwoll-Expedition nach Togo* (no date, but probably 1900), 12, file 332, record group R 150F, FA 1, Papers of the Administration of the German Protectorate Togo. Schmidt is quoted in Peter Sebald, *Togo, 1884–1914: Eine Geschichte der deutschen "Musterkolonie" auf der Grundlage amtlicher Quellen* (Berlin, 1988), 436; Governor Zech quoted in Sebald, *Togo, 1884–1914*, 439; *Amtsblatt für das Schutzgebiet Togo*, 6, Jan. 11, 1911, Number 2, "Sonderausgabe." On soldiers buying cotton see Sebald, *Togo, 1884–1914*, 441; Paul Friebel, Togo Baumwollgesellschaft to Togo Baumwollgesellschaft Bremen, April 7, 1911, box 1, record group 7,2016, Papers of the Togo Baumwollgesellschaft (Staatsarchiv Bremen, Bremen, Germany); Maier, "Persistence of Precolonial Patterns of Production," 92; Frederick Cooper, "Conditions Analogous to Slavery: Imperialism and Free Labor Ideology in Africa," in Cooper et al., *Beyond Slavery*, 113.

39. For an excellent survey, see *Cotton, Colonialism, and Social History in Sub-Saharan Africa*, ed. Isaacman and Roberts. Yet German cotton experts were still envious of British successes in Africa. See O. Warburg, "Zum Neuen Jahr 1914," *Der Tropenpflanzer*, 18 (Jan. 1914), 9. See Polly Hill, *The Migrant Cocoa-Farmers of Southern Ghana: A Study in Rural Capitalism* (Cambridge, UK, 1963).

40. Graf Zech, Kaiserliches Gouvernement Togo to Kolonial-Wirtschaftliches Komitee, Aug. 22, 1904, file 8673, record group R 1001, Papers of the Deutsche Kolonialgesellschaft. Kolonial-Wirtschaftliches Komitee, *Baumwoll-Expedition nach Togo, Bericht 1901* (Cotton Expedition to Togo, Report 1901), 6.

41. See "Baumwollanbau im Schutzgebiet Togo, Darlegungen des Pflanzers John W. Robinson vom 26. 4. 1904 betr. die Voraussetzungen, Boden- und Klimaverhältnisse, Methoden und Arbeitsverbesserung, Bewässerung," Fragment, 49, file 89, record group R 150F, FA 1, Papers of the Administration of the German Protectorate Togo; Anson Phelps Stokes, *A Brief Biography of Booker Washington* (Hampton, 1936), 13.

42. John Robinson to Graf Zech, Jan. 12, 1904, file 332, record group R 150F, FA 1, Papers of the Administration of the German Protectorate Togo.

43. See "Baumwollanbau im Schutzgebiet Togo, Darlegungen des Pflanzers John W. Robinson vom 26. 4. 1904 betr. die Voraussetzungen, Boden- und Klimaverhältnisse, Methoden und Arbeitsverbesserung, Bewässerung" (Fragment), 13, file 89, record group R 150F, FA 1, Papers of the Administration of the German Protectorate Togo.

44. See the letters in Bundesarchiv Berlin, "Maßnahmen zur Hebung der Baumwollkultur im Bezirk Atakpame unter Mitwirkung des Kolonialwirtschaftlichen Komitees," in Verwaltung des deutschen Schutzgebietes Togo, file 1008, record group R 150F, FA3, Papers of the Administration of the German Protectorate Togo.

45. Graf Zech, Kaiserliche Gouvernement Togo to Kolonialwirtschaftliches Komitee, Feb. 7, 1904, file 8222, record group R 1001, Papers of the Deutsche Kolonialgesellschaft. "Der Baumwollbau in Togo, Seine Bisherige Entwicklung, und sein jetziger Stand," undated draft of an article, file 8224, record group R 1001, Papers of the Deutsche Kolonialgesellschaft.

46. Calloway to Washington, June 2, 1901, BTW Papers; Booker T. Washington, *Up From Slavery: An Autobiography* (Garden City, N.Y., 1901), 267.

47. Harlan, "Booker T. Washington and the White Man's Burden," 444–45.

48. *Tuskegee Student*, Aug. 24, 1901, 1.

49. Calloway, "Inspection der Baumwollfarmen und Baumwollmärkte in Togo" in *Deutsch-Koloniale Baumwoll-Unternehmungen, 1902–1903* (German Colonial Cotton Ventures 1902–3) (Berlin, 1903), 42.

50. For the general argument see also Foner, *Reconstruction*; Fields, "The Advent of Capitalist Agriculture."

51. No-Shomu Sho Nomu Kyoku [Ministry of Agriculture and Commerce, Department of Agriculture], "Menka ni Kansuru Chosa" [The Research on Cotton] (March 1913), 450–53.

52. *Cotton, Colonialism, and Social History in Sub-Saharan Africa*, ed. Isaacman and Roberts; Bassett, *The Peasant Cotton Revolution*; Cyril Ehrlich, "The Marketing of Cotton in Uganda" (PhD diss., London University, 1958), 28–33. On the Association Cotonnière Coloniale see Kolonial-Wirtschaftliches Komitee, *Baumwoll-Unternehmungen 1902, 1903* (Berlin, 1903), 66–68. As to the Sudan, see Booker T. Washington to Gladwin Bouton, May 6, 1915; Leigh Hart to Washington, Feb 3, 1904, BTW Papers; Radcliffe, "Tuskegee-Togo Cotton Scheme," 3. See also Kolonial-Wirtschaftliches Komitee, *Baumwoll-Unternehmungen 1902, 1903* (Berlin, 1903), 69–71. Karl Supf, *Deutsch-Koloniale Baumwoll-Unternehmungen, Bericht IX*, 1907, 297; Radcliffe, "Tuskegee-Togo Cotton Scheme," 133, 135; Karl Supf, *Deutsch-Koloniale Baumwoll-Unternehmungen, Bericht IX*, 1907, 295. German colonial cotton activists often referred to the experiences of the French, British and Russians. See, for example, Kolonial-Wirtschaftliches Komitee, *Baumwoll-Unterneh-mungen 1902, 1903* (Berlin, 1903), 66–71; "Anlage zum Bericht des Kaiserlichen Generalkonsulats in St. Petersburg," Dec. 26, 1913, sent to Reichs-Kolonialamt and the Governor of Togo, 360, record group R 150F, FA 1, Papers of the Administration of the German Protectorate Togo; Copy of a report by R. B. D. Morier to the Secretary of State, the Marquis of Salisbury, Oct. 12, 1889, Revenue Department, Compilations, 1890, vol. 51, Compilation No. 476, "Establishment by the Russian Government of a Model Cotton Plantation in the Merva Oasis" (Maharashtra State Archive, Mumbai, India).

Chapter Nine

• • • • • • • • • •

Cuba Libre and American Imperial Nationalism

Conflicting Views of Racial Democracy in the Post-Reconstruction United States

ALESSANDRA LORINI

On the night of July 3, 1876, the celebrations in New York for the centennial of the Declaration of Independence included a large march of foreign political refugees living in the city. Cubans marched as a subdivision of the Italian group.[1] This parade, which occurred in the eighth year of the Cuban "Ten Years' War" (1868–78), revealed the social, political, racial, and national relations existing in cosmopolitan New York at that time.[2]

The parade also demonstrated that the Cuba Libre movement had stirred a great deal of support among political refugees in the United States, and that the centennial of American independence saw Cuban and American flags waving united. At that time, Cuban exiles considered the United States, a modern, free country welcoming exiles in her bosom, as the example to follow in order to achieve their independence. One component of the Cuban community was in favor of annexation by the United States, while another group interpreted the idea of freedom in terms of a fully independent Cuban republic. Cuban immigration to the United States had grown, and the class background of immigrants had changed profoundly from midcentury, when the small number of Cubans in New York belonged to the white Creole elite. The growing number of those leaving Cuba after 1868 and settling in the North included businessmen, workers, artisans, free blacks, and fugitive slaves.[3]

Recent scholarship has shown that the U.S. military intervention of 1898, publicly justified as a means of defending Cuban human rights from Spanish cruelty, actually blocked the pursuit of Cuba Libre.[4] What has not been explored is the complex interaction between post-Reconstruction views of racial reconciliation and the transnational political culture of a North American city like New York, where groups of German, Italian, and other European socialists, anarchists, exiles of the 1848 revolutions, and Latin American anticolonialist intellectuals lived. The leaders of Cuba Libre who fought against Spanish domination and fled to the United States in the second half of the nineteenth century interpreted the American antislavery and abolitionist movements and the Civil War in distinctive ways by adapting American republican ideology to the cause of Cuban independence. They also witnessed the powerful ideology of "national reconciliation" in the 1880s and 1890s. As proponents of reunification forged a memory of the Civil War in which both North and South had shown military courage, and slavery had not been such a bad form of control of an inferior race after all, Cubans further witnessed Americans interpreting the ideals of Cuba Libre by racializing Cuban insurgents. Exploring these mirroring images sheds light on the origins of American imperial nationalism and the nature of humanitarian military missions.[5]

In the post–Civil War community of Cuban exiles in New York, Emilia Casanova Villaverde boldly crossed the boundaries of the restricted male "public sphere" to become an important voice of Cuba Libre. The founder of the first women's club in New York, Villaverde was also the first Cuban woman to write political essays and to address the U.S. Congress on Cuban independence.[6] In January 1869, at an early stage of the Ten Years' War, the former Cuban plantation mistress and now New York exile wrote a letter to the Italian hero Giuseppe Garibaldi. Believing that his silence on Cuba was due to lack of information on Cuban political aspirations, and eager to hear "a word of approbation and support from the legendary Garibaldi," Villaverde explained that "the beginning of our revolution means the freedom of our slaves, giving them arms and incorporating them in our patriotic ranks." While it took the Italian hero a full year to write two courteous and short notes to *señora* Emilia, he explained that his soul was with Cuba Libre, that he would always be on the side of the oppressed "whether the oppressors are kings or nations," and that he wished that beautiful Cuba would gain its independence.[7]

In 1872 Villaverde traveled to Washington to petition the U.S. Congress to grant Cuban insurgents the status of belligerents. Speaking as the representative of the Liga de Las Hijas de Cuba, she eloquently explained (in English) that what was happening in Cuba was "a popular, political and social revolution" against Spanish colonial domination. Garnering evidence on continued U.S. support for Spain, she argued that from the 1820s to the 1850s any attempt to abolish slavery in Cuba had faced the opposition of the United States, and that in the last fifty years the American government had opposed any idea of making Cuba independent because independence meant the abolition of slavery in the island. If Congress recognized the status of belligerency for Cubans, she argued, it would help to terminate a war that was ruining the country.[8] With the economic interests of the United States in Cuba better preserved by a weak colonial power than a new, independent republic with a large population of black former slaves, Villaverde's arguments did not gain any support from the U.S. Congress. That "popular, political and social revolution"—the Ten Years' War—ended in 1878 with the Pact of Zanjon, the defeat of Cuban insurgents, and the immigration of many of them to the United States, where they continued to organize for Cuba Libre.

In 1880, the New York community of Cuban exiles warmly welcomed José Martí, who would spend the next fifteen years of his life in the metropolis.[9] Martí had been charged with conspiracy against the colonial government and deported from Havana to Spain in 1879. From Spain, he traveled to France before arriving in New York. An eloquent and charismatic speaker, writer, and political leader, and an extraordinary chronicler, Martí offered firsthand information and precocious insights into the intersection of U.S. white supremacy, expansionist ideology, and the material culture of the Gilded Age to Latin American newspapers such as *La Nación* (Buenos Aires), *La República* (Honduras), *La Opinion Pública* (Uruguay), and *El Partido Liberal* (Mexico). The intense literary work of the most popular Cuban exile in North America gained him an international reputation as one of the best Latin American essayists and poets of his generation. His death in 1895 in Cuba at the age of forty-two—riding his horse under the Spanish fire even though his fragility, health, and complete lack of military experience made him a most unsuitable soldier—turned the intellectual political activist into the "apostle," the embodiment of civic virtues, and a symbol of personal integrity and patriotic love.[10]

In 1883, writing from the perspective of a New York Cuban exile for *La Nación* on the meeting held at Cooper Union to honor the memory of the recently deceased Karl Marx, Martí expanded on his first impressions of the city: "New York is becoming a kind of vortex: whatever boils over anywhere else in the world spills into New York. Elsewhere they make men flee, but here they welcome the fleeing man with a smile. From this goodness has arisen the strength of this nation." *El cronista* Martí was interested in the large crowd of ten thousand people gathered at Cooper Union. The crowd he portrayed for his Latin American readers represented a rich New York internationalism. This experience led him to conclude that Marx's concept of "class war" could not grasp the complexity of economic, political, and social conflicts in the New World.[11] By developing a profoundly severe and yet constructive criticism of the United States, Martí created a political language of autochthony that rejected European theoretical imports and devised a continental and democratically inclusive concept of *Patria* "with all, and for the good of all," to make Cuba an independent republic. This would have blocked what he came to see as the threat of North American expansion into Latin America. Through the lens of an exile living in the United States and politically committed to the cause of Cuba Libre, Martí strengthened that cause by articulating an early and thorough analysis of the forces operating in the northern colossus that led to its expansion by virtue of its materialistic degeneration. At the same time, he also saw the other major danger to the idea of the new egalitarian society in the Latin American military actions run for the sake of the *caudillos*.

Martí spent the next few years forging continental political alliances by covering diplomatic offices for Latin American countries. Becoming a transnational figure, Martí served as the New York consul for Uruguay (1884, 1887) and for Argentina and Paraguay (1890). As the delegate of Uruguay he participated in the Inter-American Conference (1889–90) and the International Monetary Conference (1891). At the same time, he worked steadily to unite the communities of Cubans and Puerto Ricans in the United States across class, racial, and gender boundaries. Forging political alliances by using the powerful eloquence of his speeches and writings, Martí reached various benefit and literary associations, labor societies, and the New York City garment workers, as well as Florida cigar manufacturers, rich indi-

vidual benefactors, and poor tobacco workers. In 1884, when the two charismatic military leaders of the Ten Years' War, the Dominican general
Máximo Gómez and the Cuban mulatto general Antonio Maceo, traveled to
New York to organize another war of independence in Cuba, Martí had the
opportunity to discuss the ideas he had developed in close contact with the
communities of Caribbean exiles in the United States.[12]

From his New York exile Martí created a new style of leadership that
was politically grounded in the mobilization of a network of clubs that led to
the founding of the Cuban Revolutionary Party (PRC) in 1892. For Martí
the numerous associations created by the community of Cuban exiles in the
United States were the instrument for creating the particular kind of partici-
patory democracy that he envisioned in a truly independent Cuba. Strongly
rooted in these communities, although highly centralized in its direction, the
PRC was to provide funds and direction for the invasion and insurrection
of Cuba. At that point, with the strength of substantial community support,
Martí could invite Gómez, Maceo, and the old leadership of Cuba Libre to
direct the new and final war. At that point, in Martí's view, the war would
not be a military coup but the necessary and brief step needed to bring about
Patria, a new egalitarian society "with all, and for the good of all."[13]

These associations of Cuban exiles attracted the attention of the New
York press, which regularly reported on their numerous and lively public
meetings in which club members pledged allegiance to the Cuban flag by
standing and singing the Cuban anthem. The records of clubs and educational institutions of the Cuban community reveal a group of people who
were able to turn their exile into an uplifting experience of group solidarity
in the name of Cuba Libre. Members of these clubs saw themselves as part
of the tradition of the American Revolution and praised the U.S. as "the
greatest, the freest and the most prosperous and glorious republic of the
civilized world."[14]

Cuban women's clubs in New York date as far back as 1869, when Emila
Casanova Villaverde founded the Liga de las Hijas de Cuba. Women's clubs
boomed after 1892, the year of the founding of the PRC, reaching eighty in
number by 1898. Most of the leaders of these clubs, in New York as well as
in Florida, were the wives, widows, sisters, mothers, or daughters of the
male leaders of the PRC, and the names of the clubs reflected this dependency: *Hijas de . . .* , *Hermanas de . . .* , and so on.[15] After the 1895 insurrection
most women's clubs provided services for widows, orphans, and prisoners

of war and developed autonomous and creative forms of fund-raising such as picnics and theatrical events. The leadership of a women's club was under the supervision of a male figure—the husband, father, or the brother of one of the principal ladies—elected as the club's representative to the PRC.[16] Although *Patria*, the official organ of the PRC, always highlighted women's traditional relationships to the family, more and more women had left the domestic circle over the course of the Ten Years' War, and many engaged in new forms of public, and explicitly political action.[17]

Like the large majority of nineteenth-century male intellectuals, Martí believed that men and women had separate spheres and that the maternal role of women was the source of their moral strength. Therefore, it was imperative that women pursue the welfare of the family and forsake individual aspirations that would distract them from their fundamental role. Martí's idea of Cuban nation included gender differences but excluded racial ones. This was largely due to Martí's observation of the transforming gender roles in the United States, of the women's suffrage movement, and of women's leading role in reform associations. At a time when Spencerism and Darwinism had pushed racial and gender hierarchies and the notion of the inferiority of women and darker races onto the political agenda and into popular perceptions, the idea that women, by virtue of their nature, were morally superior to men appealed to someone like Martí.[18] His idea of healthy nations consisted in balancing feminine and masculine traits. He considered violence, energy, and action masculine traits; arts and sentiments, feminine. He elaborated this idea in his best-known essay, "Nuestra America," which was published in New York's *La revista illustrada* and Mexico City's *El Partido Liberal* in 1891. Publishing "Nuestra America" in both countries showed that Martí read national events as part of transnational forces and that he considered Latin American states to be agents of the unification effort to protect their populations and sovereignty from the economic and political expansion of the United States.

"Nuestra America" is undoubtedly Martí's most powerful analysis of the intersections of U.S. expansionism, allegorized as "the giant with seven-league boots," and a Cuban national identity defined through the use of gender differences for a racially egalitarian society. In a creative effort to devise what sociologist Benedict Anderson would call "an imagined community," Martí invented a source of identity for those American societies produced by Iberian colonialism. He called it "Our America," assuming the existence of a geocultural distinction from those American societies produced by British colonialism. By then he was convinced—and his view was confirmed during his participation in the pan-American and international monetary conferences called by the U.S. secretary of state James Blaine in order to unify the American continent under U.S. hegemony—that the philosophy of Manifest Destiny, which led to annexation and colonization of half of Mexico's territory by midcentury, would now pursue new lands and markets. As European powers were colonizing Africa and Asia, the United States was looking south to Latin America and the islands of the Pacific. Having lived for many years in the United States, and being familiar with American political culture, it was clear to Martí that early 1890s expansionism, powerfully devised in terms of Anglo-Saxon racial superiority, was becoming mainstream national identity. Martí wrote this essay as a manifesto addressed to Hispanic intellectuals; he believed that the members of the criollo elite should no longer think of themselves as extensions of the European bourgeoisie. There was a difference, Martí argued, between the ability to assimilate foreign ideas in a healthy manner and a shallow imitation pretending that these ideas had universal validity. Echoing his favorite North American writers, Walt Whitman and Ralph Emerson, Martí declared: "In America the natural man has triumphed over the imported book. Natural men have triumphed over an artificial intelligentsia. The native mestizo has triumphed over the alien, pure-blooded criollo. The battle is not between civilization and barbarity, but between false erudition and nature."[19]

Besides the inner danger of Eurocentric artificiality, Martí saw another powerful, external danger for Nuestra America. Evoking the image of a possible rape that could be prevented by developing mutual knowledge, Martí warned: "The hour is near when she will be approached by an enterprising and forceful nation that will demand intimate relations with her, though it does not know her and disdains her." The attraction might be fatal: "virile nations self-made by the rifle and the law love other virile nations, and love only them." Locating such violence in racial thought that prevented genuine mutual knowledge, Martí called for the erasure of racial hatred: "There is no racial hatred, because there are no races. . . . The soul, equal and eternal, emanates from bodies that are diverse in form and color. Anyone who promotes and disseminates opposition or hatred among races is committing a sin against humanity."[20]

In 1893, in an article entitled "Mi raza," Martí claimed that racial distinctions undermined the project of building a nation. Speaking both to his fellow Cubans and to those North Americans afraid that an independent Cuba would become a new black Haiti, Martí assured them that in Cuba there was no fear of a "race war" as "Cuban" meant more than white, mulatto, or Negro: "affinity of character," according to Martí, was "more powerful than affinity of color."[21]

Martí formulated such a no-race argument from the United States of the 1880s and early 1890s, a period in which the most vicious racist theories and practices had gained widespread legitimacy. The sanitized portrayal of slavery as an institution that had produced a civilizing impact on Africans transplanted to America encouraged even progressive northerners to rationalize lynching as a backward and lawless southern punishment of the unleashed beast of the black rapist, ravaging purity and other virtues of white womanhood.[22] In this context, it was easy for Spanish anti–Cuba Libre propaganda to feed North Americans' fear that a "racial war" would inevitably break out in an independent Cuba. Indeed, the language that American imperial nationalism used to define the U.S. "humanitarian mission" in Cuba employed the same metaphors of southern chivalry that condoned racial lynching.[23]

Martí masterfully used the press as a venue to challenge such racist fears. On March 21, 1889, the *New York Evening Post* published "A Protectionist View of Cuban Annexation" in response to a recent article in the *Philadelphia Manufacturer* that expressed a strong antiannexation view. The anonymous *Post* author shared the assessment in the *Manufacturer* article that Cubans' "unmanliness" made them unfit for self-government, like "the freemen of our Northern Sates." He went on to say that Cubans of Spanish descent added to all other Spanish vices "effeminacy and a distaste for exertion," and were "helpless, idle, of defective morals, and unfitted by nature and experience for discharging the obligations of citizenship in a great and free republic." The "Southern question," the author warned, would be aggravated by annexing Cuba to the Union with its "near a million blacks, much inferior to our own in point of civilization, who must, of course, be armed with the ballot and put on the same level politically with their former masters." This writer was relieved to know that Spain had refused to sell the island to the United States.

In his March 25 letter to the *Post*, Martí contested the racial bias of the article and opposed any idea of annexation. Conceding that there were some Cubans who "from an ardent admiration for progress and liberty" wanted to see Cuba annexed to the United States, he argued that they were certainly not those who had fought in the Ten Years' War and had learned in exile "by the work of hands and mind" to be successful. Although they admired the United States as "the greatest ever built by liberty," they disliked "the evil conditions that, like worms in the heart, have begun in this mighty republic their work of destruction." Martí stressed that proindependence Cubans loved the country of Lincoln, but they did not like its excessive individualism and reverence of wealth. These people were certainly not the "destitute vagrants or immoral pigmies" portrayed in the *Manufacturer*. Martí cited Cuban achievements in exile to prove that they were far from helpless and idle people. Women, whose husbands were at war, ruined, dead, or imprisoned in Spain, arrived in the United States and went to work. The former *señora* who had owned slaves "became a slave, took a seat behind the counter, sang in the churches, worked button-holes by the hundred, sewed for a living, curled feathers, gave her soul to duty, withered in work her body." Far from having "defective morals," unfit for citizenship in a free country, Cubans showed a "passion for liberty," both in the island and in exile. The lessons of the Ten Years' War had made them ready "for free government" as they were free from religious intolerance, familiar with the laws and the processes of liberty, and could rebuild their country from the ruins its oppressors had left behind. It was inconceivable for Martí that "the nation that was rocked in freedom, and received for three centuries the best blood of liberty-loving men, will employ the power thus acquired in depriving a less fortunate neighbor of his freedom."[24]

By 1895, New York public opinion was sharply divided over the Cuban question. Unlike previous uprisings, the insurgents had reached the western areas of the island. While the Cleveland administration actively cooperated with the Spanish government to defeat clandestine organizations organized by Cuban exiles in the States, it hoped that Spain would concede some reforms to make the island more autonomous and therefore defeat Cuba Libre.[25] But this time Spain used the hardest stick possible against the revolution. By the time of the 1896 presidential campaign, American opposition to the ferocious methods of "total war" that the Spanish general Valeriano Weyler inflicted on Cuban civilians was growing, buoyed by the fear that American property would be destroyed during the insurgency. Weyler's military tactics included partitioning up the island with barbed wire fences and blockhouses; civilians suspected of sympathizing with the rebels were forced into "reconcentration" camps.[26] News of these practices inflamed a large portion of American public opinion between 1896 and 1898 and convinced many Cuba Libre supporters that this movement should become a U.S. humanitarian mission. By this logic, Cuba needed to be independent on American terms. If Cuba was lost to Spain, and Washington did not act, it would also be lost to the United States. The Cleveland and the McKinley administrations shared a similar belief that an independent Cuba, "full of Negroes," would turn into a second Santo Domingo.[27]

On October 16, 1897, an immense crowd in and around Madison Square, Manhattan, greeted nineteen-year-old Evangelina Cisneros, the beautiful Cuban woman officially "rescued" from the Havana prison Las Recogitas where she had been awaiting trial on charges of conspiracy and attempted murder. Her official rescuer was Karl Decker, a reporter for Hearst's *New York Journal*.[28] Who was Evangelina Cisneros? Was her rescue from the Havana prison merely a sensationalist story orchestrated by the *New York Journal* to promote the American humanitarian military mission in Cuba? Did her real story fit the image of a poor white girl whose virtue was threatened by a Spanish brute and who was rescued by a brave American? The story is a puzzle with several missing pieces. Generally regarded as a mere example of Hearst's yellow journalism, the Cisneros case has recently attracted the interest of a few historians looking at the gender representations of Cuba Libre.[29] New evidence suggests that reporter Karl Decker was not alone in planning Cisneros's rescue. His accomplice may have been Carlos Carbonnell, a Cuban American banker closely connected to Fitzhugh Lee, the U.S. general consul in Havana. A year after Cisneros's rescue, Carbonnell proposed marriage to her at Lee's home in Virginia. Most media historians and biographers of Hearst have dismissed the escape as a farce, claiming that the *Journal* bribed the jailers to free the young woman. Recent scholarship indicates that U.S. diplomatic personnel and their associates based in Cuba may have played a role in the rescue, a role that has remained hidden for more than a hundred years.[30]

The protection of women was a recurrent theme of prointerventionist press, and the case of Evangelina Cisneros is indicative of existing racial and gender perceptions that made southern chivalry compatible with the national ideology of sectional reconciliation. This, more than the shrewd mass-manipulation techniques of "yellow journalism" may have been the motivating force behind Cisneros's dramatic rescue.

Evangelina Cisneros was the daughter of a Cuban officer of the Ten Years' War and an insurgent in the revolution of 1895. When her father was deported to the Isle of Pines, she offered to lead his group of insurgents. Betrayed by one of them, she too was sent to the Isle of Pines. According to her story, she and her father planned to use the governor's infatuation with her in order to free the Cuban prisoners. The attempt failed, and both Evangelina and her father were sent to Havana prisons. Charged with conspiracy against the Spanish crown and an attempt to murder the governor of the Isle of Pines, the young woman was sent to Las Recogitas, where Fitzhugh Lee, the U.S. general consul, visited her. The *Journal* reported that "this tenderly nurtured girl was imprisoned at eighteen among the most depraved Negresses of Havana." As rumors circulated that she would be deported to a penal colony in Morocco, the *Journal* encouraged Americans to see in Cisneros the representative of all Cuban women.

This view was disputed from the beginning. According to Lee, she was not badly treated while she was awaiting her trial. In an interview with Pulitzer's *World*, the former Confederate officer said that the case had been "much magnified and exaggerated," assuming "a sensational aspect before the American public that it was not entitled to."[31] Nonetheless, the *Journal* instigated a campaign to free her. Striking a sentimental chord by mixing the perfect romantic ingredients (a tropical island; a cruel war; a spirit of patriotism and liberty; a beautiful, persecuted maiden) the *Journal* appealed to prominent American women to sign a petition for Cisneros's release. According to the *Journal*'s estimate, some fifteen thousand women, including President McKinley's mother and the wives of many politicians, signed the petition. The widow of Confederate president Jefferson Davis appealed to the queen regent of Spain; the reformer Julia Ward Howe, author of the "Battle Hymn of the Republic," wrote to the pope; and many women's organizations sent telegrams to the queen regent and to the American consul general Lee. This extraordinary mobilization merely made Spanish authorities more resentful of "American propaganda" and Cisneros was not released.

As public interest in the case began to wane, Hearst decided to send one of his reporters, Karl Decker, to free Cisneros from the Havana prison. According to the story recounted in the *Journal*, Decker rented a house next to the jail, entered the prison, rescued the damsel in distress, and brought her to the United States. The young Cuban woman, who in Decker's words was a "fairylike little Cuban maiden," was idealized as the model of femininity: beautiful, charming, and compliant. Decker, furthermore, became the ideal American man who demonstrated his manliness if an appropriate cause was at hand.[32]

Other papers rendered a more complex tale, reporting that Decker received help from several people in Havana and that Evangelina had reached the U.S. ship *Seneca* disguised as a young man smoking a cigar. Reports provided details of her change of clothes on the ship and the time she spent during the sailing with Walter Baker, the U.S. consul at Sagua. The *World* reported that the Spanish minister Dupuy de Lóme had sent a letter to every person who signed the petitions to the pope and the queen regent of Spain on behalf of Cisneros, stating that they had been deceived, and he wanted to tell the true version of Cisneros's case, with information derived directly from the words of the highest U.S. official power in Cuba, the consul general Lee. Upon Lee's arrival in New York, after he had visited the imprisoned Evangelina, he described her as a plucky Cuban girl, "brave enough to lead a regiment on horseback." Although this image of a courageous Cuban *patriota* was closer to that of Emilia Villaverde than that of a devoted daughter and helpless girl fighting to save her virtue from a Spanish brute, the *Journal* turned the image of the rescued Cuban girl into the symbol of Cuba: "We have freed one Cuban girl—when shall we free Cuba?"[33] Lee believed that General Valeriano Weyler would have eventually released Cisneros to please the Americans. He further suspected that while the Spanish authorities had not helped her escape from Las Recogitas, "they must have winked at her leaving the island, which could never have been accomplished without their permit." The next day, Lee contradicted himself, rejecting as "absurd" the idea of Spanish collusion in the escape and saying that it took "brave, resolute and fearless men to plan and carry out the scheme."[34] Why did Lee change his statement? According to a media historian, it was because of politics: Lee was a Democrat, and the McKinley administration had promised the Havana consul-generalship to a former Republican congressman. Only after Lee conferred with the president and the State Department while home on leave was his return to Havana guaranteed. Given the uncertainty of his post in Havana, "it is not unconceivable that Lee . . . encouraged the conspiracy to free Cisneros." Indeed, evidence demonstrates that Decker received the support he needed from U.S. diplomats in Havana.[35]

U.S. mainstream media then erased Cuban men from their war for independence and talked of the United States "rescuing" Cuba—creating the image of a masculine country saving a feminine one incapable of self-government. But by 1897 insurgents in Cuba felt strong enough to turn down any concession or reform that Spain offered. [36] "Spain has exhausted her resources, and her civil and military power in Cuba surely will collapse if hostilities continue," the chairman of the U.S. Senate Committee on Foreign Relations remarked. This meant establishing the independent republic of Cuba under the actual or implied protection of the United States, in accordance "with the Monroe doctrine," though he believed that annexation would not be desirable until 250,000 Americans lived on the free island.[37] After several units of Spanish troops had mutinied and joined the growing riots against autonomy in Havana, Fitzhugh Lee cabled Washington requesting the presence of a U.S. warship. The *Maine* entered the Havana harbor on January 25, 1898.[38]

Although the story of yellow journalism bringing the country to war has been exaggerated, writer-observers such as Richard Harding Davis and artists like Frederic Remington, whose talents were put into Hearst's service, did produce extraordinary evidence of "journalism that gets things done," inspiring readers to action in the name of Anglo-Saxon American manhood, honor, courage, and boldness, and in defense of a "feminine" Cuba.[39]

An early example of the embedded journalist, Richard Davis was attached to the First U.S. Volunteer Regiment popularly known as the Rough Riders. A well-known writer of adventure stories at the time the Cuban revolution broke out, Davis published works such as *Cuba in War Time* (1898) based on his reports for Hearst's *New York Journal*. A self-fashioned American Rudyard Kipling, Davis believed that the age of rapid industrialization and urbanization still needed the values of strenuous living, courage, and boldness. Kipling's India became Davis's Cuba: English-speaking people had the duty to bring the best of their civilization to people of lower races, and in so doing, they would remain morally and physically superior. Describing the desperate conditions of the Cuban civil population in the "reconcentration camps" where women and children starved to death, Davis's muscular prose represented the drama of Cuban revolution as a manly mission. The Cuban-Spanish conflict, as Davis reported it, required the intervention of morally superior Americans: "Before I went to Cuba I was as much opposed to our interfering there as any other person equally ignorant . . . but since I have seen for myself I feel ashamed that we should have stood so long idle. We have been . . . too fearful that as a younger nation, we should appear to disregard the laws laid down by older nations. We have tolerated what no European power would have tolerated; we have been patient with men who have put back the hand of time for centuries."[40]

Davis portrayed the Rough Riders as the incarnation of the best fighting spirit of eastern men like Theodore Roosevelt and himself and of western men grown up in the hardship of the frontier. Davis's descriptions of Roosevelt's prodigious military leadership turned the colonel into a star of American popular culture and paved his path from San Juan Hill to the White House.[41] Although Roosevelt defined himself "a quietly rampant Cuba Libre man," as he wrote to his sister early in 1897, he never believed in Cuban independence and never mentioned the name of Martí in any of his writings.[42] He looked at Cuba Libre as an opportunity to deploy "muscular" and vigorous U.S. expansionism. An immediate bestseller, Roosevelt's book *The Rough Riders* (1899) was an extraordinary piece of narcissistic and self-congratulatory male patriotism that portrayed a volunteer regiment as an ideal, masculine, reunified American nation. In the epic report that Colonel Roosevelt made of his Rough Riders, Cuban insurgents did not exist.

By not even mentioning Cuba Libre, or the explosive domestic social conflicts of the 1890s, Roosevelt's "Rough Riders" text set the stage for the nation's sectional reunion as a ritual of male bonding representing all classes of a masculine nation: "Easterners and Westerners, Northerners and Southerners, officers and men, cowboys and college graduates, wherever they came from, and whatever their social position, possessed in common the traits of hardihood and a thirst for adventure." Roosevelt's description of the regiment's trip to Tampa to embark for Cuba depicted war as the best route to reunification. In his account of the regiment sailing to Cuba there is no word about the island, its history or geography, or the cause of Cuba Libre.[43] For page after page Roosevelt depicted Cuba as a jungle being tamed by mighty American soldiers, without mentioning Cuban insurgents on the scene. Such erasure of Cubans from their war paralleled, in Roosevelt's prose, the portrayal of African American soldiers as lacking bravery and therefore manhood.[44]

Roosevelt was not alone in erasing black manhood from his reunified country and in representing Cubans as former slaves, ill equipped for the task of their own liberation and unable to compete with the masculine valor of white American soldiers in Cuba. American officers portrayed Cuban soldiers as bandits, specialists in guerrilla warfare but not the military art of open battling, and therefore turned them into objects of U.S. missions. Claiming that Cubans seemed ungrateful and did not seem to understand that Americans were playing a generous and humanitarian role, some U.S.

officers compared Cubans to black men in the United States in 1863, "because so many of them did not seem to understand, or be grateful for, what had been done to them."[45]

Many African Americans identified with the Cuban struggle, and the mulatto general Antonio Maceo's fight against the Spanish forces inspired many black Americans.[46] To them, the fight for freedom of "colored Cubans" paralleled their struggle for full citizenship in the United States. But many others argued that they should not fight under the American flag when black people in the United States were denied civil and political rights, segregated, and lynched. An armed conflict with Spain, they asserted, would not promote racial justice in the United States.

A week after the explosion of the *Maine*, Frazier Baker, a black postmaster in Lake City, South Carolina, was lynched by a white mob, and his house and post office were set on fire. Given Baker's position as a federal employee, the black community hoped the government would take a stance against this violence. A mass meeting was held in Chicago, where Ida Wells-Barnett, the well-known antilynching activist, lived. She then went to Washington to represent the black community, arriving shortly before war was declared with Spain. Several congressmen from the Chicago district and several prominent citizens of Washington, D.C., accompanied Wells-Barnett to meet McKinley. The president listened courteously, accepted the resolutions of the citizens of Chicago, and told Wells-Barnett that he had already placed some of the best secret agents at work to find and prosecute the lynchers. She spent five weeks in Washington, visiting the Capitol daily. When war was declared, Wells-Barnett was advised to go home. "I returned home and found that the publicity which had come to me by reason of this effort militated against the cooperation which I had hoped for among my own people, and the matter was never brought up again." The movement to mobilize the black community to raise the Eighth Regiment of colored men, which the governor of Illinois had promised to send to Cuba as a state unit, had begun. Like Wells-Barnett, the majority of African Americans in Chicago wanted their young men to have such an opportunity.[47] Her story exemplified the ambivalent response black Americans gave to the expansionist trend in foreign policy: they looked at Cuba through the lenses of their own desire of freedom and their unresolved double consciousness, or "two-ness," as W. E. B. Du Bois eloquently defined it in *The Souls of Black Folk* (1903).[48]

African Americans continued to be divided over this issue, particularly
after Postmaster Baker was lynched. With the number of lynchings steadily
increasing, the *Afro-American Sentinel* noted that it seemed ludicrous for the
U.S. government to be waging a war in the interest of humanity and "to bring
about the cessation of Spanish outrages in Cuba, when it has such a record at
home." Making explicit the horrible irony between the horrors of lynching
and the justification of intervention in Cuba as a humanitarian rescue, the
St. Paul (Minn.) Appeal reported that an Arkansas convention of Democrats
had passed resolutions endorsing the war "now being waged to assist an oppressed people struggling for liberty," but that at the end of the convention,
some of the delegates "returned to their homes and assisted in the lynching of
an Afro-American charged of stealing a pig." The *Richmond Planet* continued to receive letters from readers stressing that the war was bringing North
and South together again at the expense of the African Americans: "The War
Department does not allow anything to be done for the Afro-American that
will antagonize the prejudice of the South."[49] This was a keen perception,
as the experience of racial segregation and political disfranchisement in the
South became the model the American military forces brought with them to
Cuba during the first U.S. occupation of the island.[50]

By the time the war in Cuba ended and a joint resolution between North
Americans and Cubans was signed, their tenuous alliance was already faltering. Many U.S. officers and war correspondents held that Cubans had contributed nothing to the victory over Spain, that they were weak allies "of
another race," and unable to understand "the steady nerve and the business-
like habits of their American rescuers." By the end of July 1898, the *New York
Times* had already reached the conclusion that "there is no Cuba. There is
no Cuban people. There are no freemen here to whom we could deliver this
marvelous island."[51] While breaking their alliance with the Cubans, Americans began to build a bond with the Spaniards, their erstwhile enemies, finding that they had "fought courageously against insuperable odds" and had
shown "courage, valor, and honor."[52] The *New York Times* reported that in
the streets of Santiago the former enemies drank together, chatting and ex-
changing souvenirs and war stories, and the correspondent of the *New York
Tribune* found it hard "to tell whether there is more rejoicing among the vic-
tors or the vanquished." The American change of heart was so sudden that
it seemed "as if the Spaniards and not the Cubans had been the allies of the
United States in the recent campaign around this city."[53]

During their military occupation, North Americans came to believe that the previous Spanish rule had prevented Cuban insurgency from turning into a race war and felt morally obligated to take over Spain's "burden." The U.S. general William Shafter candidly admitted to the *New York Times* reporter: "As I view it, we have taken Spain's war upon ourselves." In August 1898, the *New York Times* reported on the Cuban upper classes made up of Spanish merchants and landowners who were afraid that independence of the island would result in "a long reign of terror," and were "in favor of American annexation, or at least of a permanent American protectorate." In Havana, several hundred planters signed a petition to President McKinley appealing for the annexation of Cuba to the United States. The *New York Times* concluded: "if we are to save Cuba, we must hold it. If we leave it to the Cubans, we give it over to a reign of terror—to the machete and the torch, to insurrection and assassination." Cubans were now portrayed as children of a primitive race and, as such, incapable of self-government. In Senator Orville H. Platt's terms, Spain had deprived Cubans of their "manhood," and what remained was their "childhood."[54] The American sanitary commissioner of Santiago found the Cubans "stupid" and yet "docile, willing, careful," but under American supervision they might become "a useful race and a credit to the world." He advised against independence: "We must await until the children of to-day are old enough to think for themselves, and absorb American ideas."[55] In the words of an American resident of Havana, "the Cuba Libre of the blacks would be a veritable hell upon earth, a blot upon Christian civilization."[56] Others believed that an improper concession of independence would result in a mass exodus of whites from the island, creating conditions similar to the black republic of Haiti. Posing the alternatives as civilization or chaos, North American military forces felt the moral responsibility to continue their occupation. In General Oliver O. Howard's terms, Americans were committed to uplifting Cubans as a God-given mission.[57]

Although this notion of uplifting did not go uncontested, Anglo-Saxon racial ideology penetrated the island during the first U.S. military occupation. The results of the 1899 census showed that those designated as "black race" or "Ethiopian race" constituted one-third of the Cuban native population. Americans saw the remedy to such a pervasive blackness in the alliance and promotion of the Spanish elite. To "de-Africanize" the island, the U.S. governor, Leonard Wood—a former leader of the Rough Riders—put forward, with the support of the Cuban Planters Association, an immigration project to whiten the Cuban population by favoring colonization programs of white families from southern Spain or the Canary Islands.[58]

The U.S. military occupation of Cuba ended in 1902 with the Platt Amendment attached to the Cuban constitution. The importance of this period (1898–1902) as a laboratory of American imperial nationalism should not be underestimated.[59] The profound changes in Cuban institutions and culture, the interaction between local elites and the U.S. government, experiments of uplifting carried out by American reformers, forms of cultural resistance to the Americanization of the island, and the filtering of the overall experience in U.S. national culture still need to be explored further. During that time, most U.S.-educated and Americanized (white) members of the Cuban community in New York ceased to care about José Martí's vision of "racial unity" as a means of realizing social justice for all in Cuba Libre.[60]

In New York, *el cronista* and prophetic leader Martí had tried to forge a strong identity for "Nuestra America" by interpreting Latin America for Anglo-Americans. In Cuba, New York "action journalists" like Richard Davis had interpreted Cuba Libre in the racial language of imperial nationalists like Theodore Roosevelt. In the aftermath of the war of 1898, Americans were divided over their new role in expanding American freedom. A large majority were convinced that an American protectorate of Cuba was a reasonable solution, but a growing minority saw the danger of imposing American democracy in the United States' brutal occupation of the Philippines. Many joined the Anti-Imperialist League, a rather nebulous coalition of antiexpansionist interests. Jane Addams, one of the founders, was one of the few who saw in the celebration of Kiplingesque militarism the failure "to distinguish between war and imperialism on the one hand and the advance of civilization on the other." She was convinced that the appeal to the fighting instinct "does not end in mere warfare" but arouses "brutal instincts latent in every human being." Addams reminded her compatriots that to "protect the weak" was always the excuse of the ruler and the tax gatherer, of the king and the baron, and that now it had become the excuse of "the white man." In her view, the Spanish war "with its gilt and lace and tinsel" confused moral issues "with exhibitions of brutality." Her thoughtful, provocative conclusion is still relevant today: "National events determine our ideals, as much as our ideals determine national events."[61]

NOTES

1. Four years before his arrival in New York City as a member of that community of exiles, Cuban refugee José Martí commented on that event from Mexico in the *Revista Universal*, stressing the great support that Cuban marchers received in the streets of New York. *La Voz de la Patria*, New York, July 7, 1876, in Enrique López Mesa, *La comunidad cubana de New York: Siglo XIX* (Habana, 2002), 25. See Mary Ryan, "The American Parade: Representations of the Nineteenth-Century Social Order," in *The New Cultural History*, ed. Lynn Hunt, 144 (Berkeley, 1996).

2. Cubans marched as a subdivision of the Italian parade because of the solidarity and commonality that existed between Italians and Cubans living in New York at that time. Fernando Ortiz, *Italia y Cuba* (Habana, 1998). Black men marched in separate divisions according to post-Reconstruction racial codes, and women were not allowed to participate in public celebratory events. See Alessandra Lorini, *Rituals of Race: American Public Culture and the Search for Racial Democracy* (Charlottesville, 1999), 30–31.

3. Cubans settled in Boston, New York, Baltimore, and Philadelphia, as well as in Florida, where they started the tobacco industry. According to the 1870 U.S. Census there were 5,300 Cuban residents in the United States; by the 1890's their number had doubled.

4. See Louis A. Pérez Jr., *The War of 1898: The United States and Cuba in History and Historiography* (Chapel Hill, 1998). No modern historian who deals with the Spanish-American war can leave out the complex Cuban movement that had been fighting Spanish colonialism for more than thirty years (with a war [1868–78] and other endeavors) before the 1898 U.S. intervention. Historians Louis Pérez Jr., Ada Ferrer, Francisca López Civeira, Marial Iglesias, and others have shown that the U.S. intervention of 1898 blocked the real independence of Cuba. In recent years an extensive scholarship has explored the motivations of the U.S. intervention in geopolitical terms, connecting expansion to domestic politics. See Pérez, *The War of 1898*; Ada Ferrer, *Insurgent Cuba: Race, Nation, and Revolution, 1868–1898* (Chapel Hill, 1999); Marial Iglesias Utset, *Las metáforas del cambio en la vida cotidiana: Cuba, 1898–1902* (Bogotá, 2003). See also Amy Kaplan, *The Anarchy of Empire in the Making of U.S. Culture* (Cambridge, Mass., 2002).

5. David Blight in *Race and Reunion: The Civil War in American Memory* (Cambridge, 2001) has convincingly argued that national reunion between the North and South was made in the name of the military courage that both sides of the Civil War had shown.

6. Emilia Casanova became the wife of patriot novelist Cirilo Villaverde, the author of *Cecilia Valdes*. Published in New York in 1879, the novel is the masterpiece of nineteenth-century Cuban literature. Cirilo Villaverde, *Cecilia Valdes* (Habana, 2002).

7. *Emilia Casanova de Villaverde, Apuntes Biográficos de Emilia Casanova de Villaverde: Escritos por un contemporáneo* (New York, 1874), 60–61; Enrique Pertierra Serra, *Italianos por Cuba* (Habana, 2000), 34–36.

8. *Casanova de Villaverde, Apuntes Biográficos*, 167, 170–71, 175–76.

9. By 1880 the New York community included between two thousand and five thousand Cubans (probably the largest Spanish-speaking community in New York). See Mesa, *La comunidad cubana de New York*; Gerald E. Poyo, *"With All and for the Good of All": The Emergence of Popular Nationalism in the Cuban Communities of the United States, 1848–1898* (Durham, 1989); Louis Pérez Jr., *On Becoming Cuban* (Chapel Hill, 1999).

10. Martí produced most of his literary work during the years of his exile in New York. He also translated the works of several North American authors into Spanish and edited newspapers, political and economic journals, and children's magazines. His collected works total 12,500 pages in twenty-seven volumes. Colectivo de autores, *José Martí y los Estados Unidos* (Habana, n.d.); Pedro Pablo Rodriguez, *De las dos Americas. Aproximaciones al pensamiento martiano* (Habana, 2002); *José Martí Reader: Writings on the Americas*, ed. Deborah Shnookal and Mirta Muniz (New York, 1999); *José Martí: Selected Writings*, ed. and trans. Esther Allen (New York, 2002). On the strength of Martí's myth in Cuban history and national identity, see Lillian Guerra, *The Myth of José Martí: Conflicting Nationalisms in Early Twentieth-Century Cuba* (Chapel Hill, 2005).

11. Such a crowd of international polyglot activists and intellectuals included a Bakunian journalist delivering his speech in English, German, and Russian; a long list of refugees from Germany, France, Italy, Ireland; the choral singing societies,; and many women. *La Nación*, May 13 and 16, 1883, in *José Martí*, ed. Allen, 132–33.

12. "Letter to General Máximo Gómez," *José Martí*, ed. Allen, 258–59.

13. On the making of the Partido Revolucionario Cubano and Cuban political clubs in New York, see Francisca López Civeira, "Relaciones controversiales y la construcion del Partido Revolucionario Cubano en Estados Unidos a la fin del siglo 19," in *An Intimate and Contested Relation: The United States and Cuba in the Late Nineteenth and Early Twentieth Centuries*, ed. Alessandra Lorini (Florence, Italy, 2005).

14. See *New York Times*, Oct. 11, 1891 March 7, 1892; Archivo Nacional, Habana, Inventario General del Archivo de la Delegacion del PRC a Nueva York (1892–98), 14, 448; *New York Times*, May 6, 1893; *New York Tribune*, Apr. 29, 1895.

15. See Paul Estrade, "Los clubes femininos en el Partido Revolucionario Cubano (1892–1898)," *Anuario del Centro de Estudios Martíanos* 10 (1987): 177, 181.

16. As in U.S. mainstream culture at that time, women in public meetings were "represented" by men. Lorini, *Rituals of Race*, 1–15.

17. Estrade, *Los clubes femininos*, 188.

18. Martí deeply admired Helen Jackson Hunt—he translated her *Ramona* into Spanish at his own expense (*José Martí*, ed. Allen, 427)—Harriet Beecher Stowe, and several other women reformers.

19. "Our America," in *José Martí*, ed. Allen, 290.

20. Ibid., 294–97. What Martí called "natural statesmen" were those leaders who "read in order to apply what they read, not copy it."

21. "My Race," in *José Martí*, ed. Allen, 319–20. In early independent Cuba, however, such a "national antiracism" constituted a legacy that silenced any attempt made by people of color to gain social and economic equality, and gave negative connotations to African heritage, similar to those that blacks were confronting in the United States. Historian Ada Ferrer has questioned the "silence of patriots" on racial categories as an ambivalent transcendence leading to a concept of national unity "forged in manly union during war." Martí spoke more of a mestizo America than a mestizo Cuba, and racial union "was less the product of miscegenation than of masculine heroism and will." Ferrer, *Insurgent Cuba*, 126.

22. The "redeemed" South disfranchised black voters, and mobs were left free to lynch an average of at least 140 people each year, 75 percent of them black, a percentage that rose the following decade. By the early 1890s, the collective memory of the Civil War as a war of ideas between those who fought for freedom and those who fought for slavery, as Frederick Douglass had put it, had disappeared from national public discourse. Blight, *Race and Reunion*; Lorini, *Rituals of Race*.

23. See Jacqueline Dowd Hall, *Revolt against Chivalry* (New York, 1979).

24. "A Vindication of Cuba," in *José Martí*, ed. Allen, 263–67.

25. Hundreds of articles appeared in daily papers, and many pamphlets were privately published speaking in favor of or against Cuban independence and the possibility of U.S. involvement. See, for example, *New York Tribune*, June 27, 1897, Dec. 3, 1895, and May 26, 1896. On Washington's cooperation with the Spanish government, see Louis Pérez Jr., *Cuba and the United States: Ties of Singular Intimacy* (Athens, Ga., 1997), 85.

26. A few years later American forces used another version of this cruel practice in the Philippines; the British employed it in South Africa during the Boer War, and the United States in Vietnam (the so-called strategic hamlets).

27. Examining a century of American historiography of events leading to McKinley's message to Congress of Apr. 11, 1898, Pérez has shown how the ·

imminence of a Cuban triumph has been erased from the narratives, Pérez, *The War of 1898*, 14.

28. *New York Times*, Oct. 17, 1897.

29. See Kristin Hoganson, *Fighting for American Manhood: How Gender Politics Provoked the Spanish-American and Philippine-American Wars* (New Haven, 1998).

30. W. Joseph Campbell, "Not a Hoax: New Evidence in the New York Journal's Rescue of Evangelina Cisneros," http://academic2.american.edu/wjc/wjc2/cisnerospaper.html

31. *New York Journal*, Aug. 18, 1897; *New York World*, Aug. 27, 1897.

32. The message was that women across the country had to mobilize because men had failed to put an end to Spanish atrocities in Cuba. Hoganson, *Fighting for American Manhood*, 58–61.

33. *New York World*, Oct. 14, 1897; *New York Times*, Oct. 9, 12, 14, 1897; Hoganson, *Fighting for American Manhood*, 61.

34. *New York Times*, Oct. 17, 1897; *New York Journal*. Oct. 15, 16, 1897.

35. Campbell, "Not a Hoax," 10.

36. As Máximo Gómez put it, "We are for liberty, not for Spanish reforms." Quote in Pérez, *The War of 1898*, 9.

37. *New York World*, Oct. 8, 1897.

38. Pérez, *The War of 1898*, 79.

39. Michael Schudson, *Discovering the News: A Social History of American Newspapers* (New York, 1978), 61–62; Ferdinand Lundberg, *Imperial Hearst: A Social Biography* (New York, 1936), 68–69; W. A. Swamberg, *Citizen Hearst: A Biography of William Randolph Hearst* (New York, 1961).

40. Richard Harding Davis, *Cuba in War Time* (Lincoln, Neb., 2000), 55, 129–30, 133.

41. Ibid., introduction by Matthew M. Oyos, x.

42. Quote in Hugh Thomas, *Cuba, or, the Pursuit of Freedom* (New York, 1998), 418.

43. Theodore Roosevelt, *The Rough Riders*, **I. "Raising the Regiment," 30–36, 47; II. "To Cuba," 20–21, 37. http://www.bartleby.com/51/.

44. **Ibid., IV. "The Cavalry at Santiago": 50.

45. Quote in Pérez, *The War of 1898*, 98.

46. See William B. Gatewood Jr., *Black Americans and the White Man's Burden, 1898–1903* (Urbana, 1975); Manning Marable, "Race and Revolution in Cuba: African American Perspectives," in *Dispatches from the Ebony Tower*, ed. Marable, 90–107 (New York, 2000); Lisa Brock, Digna Castaneda Fuentes, *Between Race and Empire: African Americans and Cubans before the Cuban Revolution* (Philadelphia, 1998).

47. Alfreda M. Duster, ed., *Crusade for Justice: The Autobiography of Ida B. Wells* (Chicago, 1970), 252–54.

48. On this point, see, Alessandra Lorini, "Race and Reconciliation: The United States and Cuban Independence," in *Reconstructing Societies in the Aftermath of War*, ed. Flavia Brizio-Skov, 215–32 (Boca Raton, 2004).

49. *Richmond Planet*, July 16, Aug.6, 1898; *Afro-American Sentinel*, July 9, 1898; *Cleveland Gazette*, July 16, 1898.

50. See Alejandro de la Fuente, *A Nation for All: Race, Inequality, and Politics in Twentieth-Century Cuba* (Chapel Hill, 2001); Iglesias Utset, *Las metáforas del cambio*.

51. Andrew S. Draper, *The Rescue of Cuba* (New York, 1899), 176; O. O. Howard, "The Conduct of Cubans in the Late War," *Forum* 26 (1898): 153–55; *New York Times*, July 29, 1898.

52. Such a language evoked the rhetoric of sectional reconciliation in the United States of the 1880s and 1890s, when former enemies reunified at the expense of African American freedom and full citizenship. Joseph Edgar Chamberlain, "Spanish Bravery at Caney," *Review of Reviews* 18 (Sept. 1898): 325. Lorini, "Race and Reconciliation."

53. *New York Times*, July 21, 1898; *New York Tribune*, Aug. 7, 16, 1898. Cubans were now puzzled about the real aims of the U.S. intervention. Cuban leaders came to accept "reconciliation" with the Spaniards and complied with North American requests to obtain independence as a "civilized nation." In late nineteenth-century language this meant erasing any form of savagism or barbarism that coincided with African traits and deploying powerful gender connotations. Ferrer, *Insurgent Cuba*, 182.

54. *New York Times*, Dec. 19, Aug. 5, July 29, 1898; Pérez, *Cuba between Empires*, 216–17, 272.

55. George Kennan, *Campaigning in Cuba* (New York, 1899), 1021–22.

56. *New York Times*, 24 Aug. 1898

57. Thomas Gold Alvord Jr., "Is the Cuban Capable of Self-Government?" *Forum* (Sept. 1898): 119–20; John R. Brooke, *Civil Report of Major-General John R. Brooke, U.S. Army, Military Governor of Cuba, 1900* (Washington, D.C., 1900). Howard, "The Conduct of Cubans in the Late War," 155; Lorini, *Rituals of Race* and "Race and Reconciliation."

58. "Los restos de Maceo y Panchito Gómez," *La Lucha* (Sept. 19, 1899); Aline Helg, *Our Rightful Share: The Afro-Cuban Struggle for Equality, 1886–1912* (Chapel Hill, 1995), 105.

59. The amendment, which preserved the appearance of Cuban independence and granted self-government, blocked any possibility of Cuban self-determination by giving the United States the right to intervene in the internal affairs of the island to preserve Cuban independence and protect "life, property, and individual liberty." David F. Healy, *The United States in Cuba, 1898–1902: Generals, Politicians, and the Search for Policy* (Madison, 1963).

60. Iglesias Utset, *Las metáforas del cambio*; Poyo, *"With All, and for the Good of All."*

61. Jane Addams, "Democracy or Militarism," address before the Chicago Liberty meeting, Apr. 30, 1899. http://www.boondocksnet.com/ai/ailtexts/addams.html.

Chapter Ten

* * * * * * * *

Transnational Solidarities

The Sacco and Van{etti Case in Global Perspective

LISA McGIRR

In August 1927, high in the mountainous region of the Andes in Bolivia, more than sixty thousand peasants and mine workers paraded through small towns and villages to protest wage reductions and land seizures. Led by Tristan Maroff, a Marxist-inspired radical leader, these impoverished men and women denounced the power of the mine companies and large land owners while railing against the impending execution of two formerly obscure anarchists in the United States, Nicola Sacco and Bartolomeo Vanzetti. Speakers drew parallels between the plight of the two men with workers' experiences in Bolivia: both were linked to a global web of labor exploitation. The "assassination," they declared, was meant to demonstrate the power of capitalists to workers throughout the world. Echoing these concerns, a small group of men in the capital of La Paz, including Angel Oroso and Beautista Gomez, the latter an electrician and a Communist, plotted to bomb U.S. targets to protest the death sentences. When local police uncovered these threats, the U.S. government requested police guards to protect its consulate and U.S.-owned businesses.[1]

Between 1921 and 1927, as Sacco and Vanzetti's appeals progressed, occurrences like the one in the Andes were replayed again and again throughout Latin America and Europe. Over those six years, the Sacco and Vanzetti case had gone from being a local robbery and murder trial into a global event.[2] Building on earlier networks, solidarities, and identities and impelled by a short-lived, but powerful sense of transnational worker solidarity, it crystallized a unique moment of international collective mobilization. Although the world would never again witness an international, worker-led protest of comparable scope, the movement to save Sacco and Vanzetti highlighted the ever denser transnational networks that continued to shape social movements throughout the twentieth century.[3]

The "travesty of justice" protested by Mexican, French, Argentinean, Australian, and German workers, among others, began just outside Boston in 1920. On April 15, the payroll of the Slater and Morrill Shoe Company in south Braintree, Massachusetts, was stolen and the paymaster and guard murdered. Acting on a hunch that the crime was the work of local anarchists, a veteran police officer arrested two radicals, charging them with robbery and murder. Unsurprisingly, the arrest of the two Italian anarchists, at a time of heightened political repression in the United States, quickly attracted the attention of leftist sympathizers. When, on July 14, 1921, a Dedham, Massachusetts, jury declared the two men guilty of murder, anarchists and radicals in the United States and abroad moved into action. Declaring the trial a mockery, they called for justice for the two men and mobilized support for their cause. Such appeals were heard in Boston, New York, and Chicago. The verdict also galvanized protest in more distant locales. In Mexico City and Buenos Aires, Montevideo, Marseille, Casablanca, Caracas, and elsewhere, workers attended vigils and rallies to express their solidarity with Sacco and Vanzetti. Indeed, so widely did concerns spread, by 1927, Sacco and Vanzetti had become household words even in remote areas of Latin America. In Venezuela, according to the U.S. consul there, "practically all the lower classes regarded them as martyrs." One old servant of a well-to-do family had even "arranged a newspaper picture of Sacco and Vanzetti surrounded by burning candles and was praying for them before it." The storms of protest that raged in Europe and Latin America led the conservative French newspaper *Le Figaro*, to ask, "to what kind of folly is the world witness?"[4]

In recent years, scholars have called for historians to embed U.S. history in a global context. Historians, including Akira Iriye and Daniel Rodgers, have revealed identities, networks, and processes that extend beyond the nation-state.[5] Yet, thus far, those studies, largely focused on economics, policy-makers, social elites, and institutions, have neglected transnational social movements.[6] Reexamining the history of the Sacco and Vanzetti case through a global lens reveals an important moment of transnational movement building.[7] Although preceded by earlier transnational mobilizations—such as abolitionism and woman's suffrage—the "passion" of Sacco and Vanzetti brought the popular masses to the forefront of international protest for the first time. Never before had global radical institutions and global mass communications played such a central role in collective popular mobilization. This new form of protest revealed a shift in the boundaries of belonging that came to characterize the twentieth century. The international social movement around Sacco and Vanzetti also highlights transformations in the dynamics of global radicalism and of class. Some class dynamics, of course, can only be understood by looking at the historical contingencies within individual nation states. But only by moving beyond individual nations can we understand what dynamics were not particularly "French," "American," or "Argentinean," but instead part of broader trends with repercussions in many countries.[8] It is precisely such trends that the history of the social movement in support of Sacco and Vanzetti reveals.

This essay first lays out the factors that set the stage for the international prominence of Sacco and Vanzetti, then charts the global trajectory of the case itself. The men's global presence points to a moment in history when radical labor movements in Europe, Latin America, and North America had a deeply internationalist vision. Building on the roots of the massive migration of European workers in the late nineteenth and early twentieth centuries, radicals had forged transnational networks and identities.[9] Anarchists, Communists, and socialists, while deeply divided, shared a vision of international worker solidarity that sought to transcend national allegiances. There was an ideological proclivity to support comrades in faraway lands. The international labor outcry during the Haymarket affair in 1886, as well as the protests to free the "class war prisoners" such as Tom Mooney and Warren Billing (radicals sentenced for murder after a bomb was thrown in San Francisco in 1916) and Arturo Giovannitti and Joseph Ettor (labor leaders arrested for murder in the midst of a fierce textile strike in 1913), demonstrate that commitment.

The Sacco and Vanzetti case gained global visibility because it arose at a transitional moment in radical politics. The 1920s were a time when anarchism—a significant current of radical politics in the late nineteenth and early twentieth centuries—was declining, and its supporters were seeking a new lease on their political life.[10] At the same time, the international Communist parties had just been born. Both groups, in effect, vied to strengthen their cause by championing Sacco and Vanzetti. While the global mobilization in support of Sacco and Vanzetti was inspired by international proletarianism, ethnic solidarity also contributed to the wave of support for the two men. Indeed, Italians, more than any other group of workers in the late nineteenth and early twentieth centuries, experienced transnationalism as a way of life.[11] Thus, the fact that Sacco and Vanzetti were Italians mattered a great deal, as even Italians opposed to their politics were sympathetic to their plight as fellow nationals.

The Sacco and Vanzetti case took place at a moment when the world was more closely connected through mass communications than ever before. Revolutions in print and communications technology enabled far-flung communities to follow the case as it unfolded..[12] As part of this new density of communications, labor and radical movements in different parts of the world had established their own newspapers, put out their own pamphlets, and made their own films, democratizing access to knowledge and thus facilitating global protest.

At first, working-class solidarity and ethnic identification served as the core for the emerging mobilization in favor of Sacco and Vanzetti. But their cause was eventually adopted by a much wider array of intellectuals, politicians, and newspaper reporters. Intellectuals, in particular, provided the supporters of Sacco and Vanzetti with a stamp of legitimacy the labor movement alone could not, both in the United States and abroad. By 1926, these intellectuals had transformed the case into a symbol for what they perceived as global threats to individualism and free expression—making Sacco and Vanzetti heroes of bourgeois individualism in an age of "the mass man." Indeed, their anarchism, sheared of its militancy, was romanticized and heroized by men as disparate as the American writer John Dos Passos and the Italian Fascist Benito Mussolini.[13]

The fact that the trial took place in the United States is critical to understanding its international repercussions. Hundreds of injustices of equal weight occurred in other parts of the world, but the United States claimed to stand as a beacon of freedom. This stance, coupled with global resentment over the increasing power of the United States in the wake of World War

I, encouraged radicals and bourgeois intellectuals to mobilize in solidarity with Sacco and Vanzetti. These factors, taken together, laid the seeds for mobilization. The global social movement to free Sacco and Vanzetti evinced a new contentious form of protest and politics across the globe.

While this set of factors contributed to the case's resonance, it was the activities of individual men and women that led to the organization of a global social movement. To chart the blossoming of this movement, this essay sketches the first moments of mobilization in the United States and abroad, looking at how, why and where the movement mushroomed. Second, it explores how the mobilization came to transcend its original social base to become a broad popular front. And last, it looks at the way the men were memorialized after their execution and the legacy of the case in distinct parts of the world.

It was quite evident as early as 1921 that reactions to a guilty verdict would not be confined to the United States. Sacco and Vanzetti were part of a broader, worldwide network of anarchists with pockets of strength stretching from Switzerland, France, and Italy to Uruguay and Argentina. Anarchism had long vied with socialism as a significant strand of radicalism. While the growing strength of socialist parties and, in particular, the founding of the Third International in 1919, signified the declining influence of anarchism, some radicals continued to subscribe to the anti-statism, absolute individualism, and international proletarianism set out by theorists like Bakunin, Kropotkin, and others.[14] Sacco and Vanzetti were among them. Since immigrating to the United States in 1908, the two young men had become increasingly radical, and by the time of their arrest they were committed men of action. Indeed, they had become part of the ultramilitant circle of Italian anarchists around Luigi Galleani, a charismatic man who romanticized what he saw as the cleansing force of violence as a response to injustice.[15] Men like Galleani and his anarchist compatriots moved in international circles. Galleani himself had lived in Italy, France, Switzerland, England, Egypt, the United States, and Canada. And while Sacco and Vanzetti had lived in the United States for most of their adult lives, they had spent a year in Mexico with a group of Galleanista militants in 1917. Sacco and Vanzetti themselves, in fact, enjoyed personal contacts with militant anarchists beyond the borders of the United States. Some of the sixty or so anarchists with whom they had lived in Monterey moved to Italy, hoping to spark revolution there, while still others migrated to other parts of Latin America, setting in place a worldwide network of contacts. Throughout Sacco and Vanzetti's long years of imprisonment, they maintained their international contacts, writing to anarchist compatriots in places like France and Italy, requesting aid for their cause, and receiving news of the worldwide activities on their behalf.[16] Sacco and Vanzetti's political and mental world was framed as much by the community of militant Italian anarchists as by the local communities in which they lived and the Grupo Autônomo, the local Italian anarchist organization in Boston they belonged to.

The strong internationalist bent was not the terrain of anarchists alone. Other radicals, especially socialists and Communists, also espoused strong internationalism. With the Soviet Union not yet out of its infancy, supporters of the newly emerging "worker-state" took up the banner of Sacco and Vanzetti as victims of bourgeois class warfare and as a means of bolstering support for their ideologies. In such a world of global radical politics, it is hardly surprising that once Sacco and Vanzetti were convicted of robbery and murder shortly after the infamous Palmer raids in 1919, workers in many parts of the world would come to their aid. Those comrades who were part of the close-knit circle of Italian militants in the United States spread the first news of their arrest. But the antiorganizational thrust of the sect meant that it was left to other groups to forge the institutional networks necessary to build a broad social movement. In the United States, Fred Moore, one of the original defense lawyers, undertook a lengthy and energetic correspondence with labor union leaders, socialists, and Communists in the United States and abroad, tapping the far-flung political connections he had developed through his years in U.S. labor circles.[17]

Outside of the United States, Italy was the main focus of the U.S. defense team's initial effort to drum up support for the men. Fred Moore found a receptive audience in his Italian contacts.[18] Debates in the Italian parliament, led by Leonardo Mucci, a socialist whom Moore knew, linked the case to the poor treatment that Italian immigrants consistently received in the United States, expressed, most recently, in the campaign for immigration restriction. He called on Italians to "stand up to America."[19] The Italian foreign minister soon ordered the U.S. ambassador Rolando Ricci to "take every possible step toward the [U.S.] government to secure a pardon for our nationals Sacco and Vanzetti," In Italy, as in the Italian diaspora, anarchists and their enemies were united on one point: Sacco and Vanzetti's plight was due, in no small part, to their status as foreigners "whose deaths would mean little because of their nationality." Even after the Fascists took power in 1922 and crushed the socialist, Communist, and anarchist opposition, Mussolini bowed to public sentiment and his own nationalist predilections in calling for the commutation of the men's sentence.[20] But Mussolini, much to the relief of the U.S. officials there, was quick to repress popular outpouring of protest. U.S. embassy officials repeatedly expressed their thanks for the Fascist police, who saw to it that public support for the men did not lead to mass demonstrations and violence against U.S. targets as it did elsewhere.[21]

With Italians broadly supportive of Sacco and Vanzetti but unable to express their support in public manifestations, it fell to radicals elsewhere to take to the streets. France was foremost among them. On October 23, 1921, in Paris, two thousand demonstrators confronted police detachments of infantry. In Le Havre, brilliant red posters were displayed throughout the city protesting the verdict.[22] And in Marseille, French police protected the U.S. embassy because of the "quite formidable" demonstrations in front of it. In the earliest stages of the case, U.S. visitors such as the radical journalist Eugene Lyons and anarchist friends of Sacco and Vanzetti, like Mario Buda, spread the word about the men's plight. The anarchist paper *Le Libertaire* also announced news of their fate.[23] But it was the French Communist Party (PCF) that took the lead in calling for the liberation of the two men. The PCF, founded only one year earlier by radicals with deep anarcho-syndicalist traditions, was quick to pick up on a call to save the two Italian anarchists.[24] Not only did the traditions of French working-class radicalism provide a favorable terrain for a mass campaign of solidarity, but in some regions large numbers of Italians filled the ranks of syndicalist organizations like the Confédération Général du Travail. For these workers, a sense of class and of ethnic solidarity mobilized them to action.[25]

A burst of violence signaled the militancy of a segment of Sacco and Vanzetti supporters in France. In October, U.S. ambassador Myron Herrick was the target of a mail bomb. In another incident that same month at the Salle Wagram, protesters threw a bomb at the police.[26] On November 8, 1921, an explosion damaged the U.S. consulate in Marseille. Bombings were not limited to France. The front of the U.S. consulate general in Zurich was blown out; an explosion damaged the embassy in Lisbon; and another bomb destroyed the front of the U.S. embassy in Rio de Janeiro.[27] While these bombings no doubt hardened a segment of public opinion against the two men, they also brought the Sacco and Vanzetti case prominently onto the international stage. As one radical wrote to Fred Moore after the bombings in France, "I can appreciate the difficult position you were placed in by the Paris happening. However, a byproduct of that event is far greater international interest then before."[28]

While French radicals took the lead in Europe in bringing the case to international prominence, Mexico and Argentina stood at the forefront of Latin American protest. In the wake of the Mexican Revolution, with resentments toward the Yankee neighbor to the north running high and a sympathetic left-leaning revolutionary government in power, Sacco and Vanzetti's supporters found a breeding ground of dissent favorable to their cause. Anarchism, moreover, had formed a dominant current of left politics. Indeed, the strength of anarchist currents within Mexican radical circles had provided a hospitable temporary home for Sacco and Vanzetti in Monterey a few years earlier, their small circle of Galleanist militants swimming in a broader tide of Mexican anarchist currents. Even while the Mexican Communist Party struggled to dominate and differentiate itself from the largely anarcho-syndicalist-influenced radical milieu from which it sprang, the Sacco-Vanzetti issue provided one point of unity with the anarchists. While the Mexican Communist Party boasted a membership of only a few hundred in the early 1920s, by the end of the decade, it had become the most successful of the Latin American Communist parties. Their support of the agrarian cause played a large role in their success, but it is quite likely that, for some anarchists, the party's championing Sacco and Vanzetti helped to smooth the road toward an embrace of Communism.[29]

Mexican radicals mobilized early and powerful support for Sacco and Vanzetti. By 1921, the U.S. consulates in Tampico, Merida, and Veracruz were besieged by demonstrations and protests. The Truck Drivers of the Port of Veracruz syndicate wrote a threatening letter. "Free Sacco and Vanzetti or the proletarian world will rip out your guts. We do not ask pity. . . . If you are implacable we also will be implacable. An eye for an eye! . . . The law of retaliation will be served if our brothers are not freed."[30] Mexico, which provided a militant early seedbed of mobilization, was eventually surpassed by Argentina, where protest bubbled up from Cordoba to Patagonia. Much to the consternation of the Argentinean elite, anarchism proved attractive to the immigrant workers who constituted most of Argentina's working class. But by the 1920s, a period of stasis had set in in the once powerful radical labor movement. State repression helped quell the earlier class conflict, but the lessening of confrontational tactics and general strikes was also due to the increasing integration of workers into Argentinean society, with populist politicians fostering cross-class appeals.[31] By the 1920s, anarchism was losing its hold on the loyalties of workers. Anarchist newspapers railed against a working class "unwilling to break its chains."[32] The Sacco-Vanzetti case revived the movement, providing discouraged anarchists with a new mission. For well over a year, the sole preoccupation of Argentinean radicals was the liberation of Sacco and Vanzetti. The cause galvanized the anarchists' base, expressing, however, not so much a revived faith in anarchism as an attachment to a broader working-class and ethnic identity. Argentinean workers followed the twists and turns of the case through newssheets and small anarchist papers, as well as through *La Protesta*, the large and well-established newspaper in Buenos Aires, which linked the case to "yanqui plutocracia."[33]

But the strength of anarchist traditions alone does not explain the overwhelming resonance of Sacco and Vanzetti in Argentina. The men's cause resonated not only in radical circles but also with a large segment of the vibrant middle-class Italian community, engendering a cross-class appeal. Italians made up a large portion of the working class; they also formed an important segment of the urban employing class. The Grand Committee of Protest that mobilized "monster meetings" on the men's behalf in 1925 was organized at the Colonia Italiana, an Italian immigrant society.[34]

Specific national conditions clearly contributed to the extensive efforts on behalf of Sacco and Vanzetti. Countries with powerful labor movements and steeped in anarchist tendencies stood at the forefront of protest. At the same time, these core countries spread protest throughout the world. Protest, in effect, begot more protest. By 1924, U.S. consulates from countries as diverse as China, Paraguay, Germany, Sweden, Norway, and England wrote to their superiors reporting protests against the verdict of the two men—highlighting the truly transnational reach of the case. But the extent of the protests differed significantly by region. At the height of the "Sacco and Vanzetti crisis" as some embassy officials called it, the U.S. ambassador in Java asked to be taken off the list of embassies receiving notifications about the case, since it had generated "no interest what so ever . . . in this country."[35]

Meanwhile, Communists, anarchists, and socialists continued to closely follow the Sacco and Vanzetti case and worked to build momentum for the men's release. From 1921 to 1926, radicals took the lead in calling for their freedom. In doing so, they told their own versions of the Sacco and Vanzetti story. Different stories circulated about the men's plight depending on the purpose of the teller. The specifics of the case, not surprisingly, were elided—nuances and complexities were jettisoned. Both those on the left and the right often mischaracterized the men's politics for their own purposes. *Le Figaro*, quickly cast them as "Communists." And Communist parties in different countries portrayed the two men as revolutionary leaders condemned because of their "beloved ideals of social renovation."[36]

The meanings of "Sacco and Vanzetti" were shaped not only by international radical institutions but also by local circumstances. Protest meetings in China, for example, highlighted police and government corruption. Radicals claimed that Sacco and Vanzetti's possession of "documents" that could compromise police authorities resulted in their "persecution." In many countries, the claim was made that the judge and jury had been bribed.[37] While these stories had little basis in fact, they kept the cause alive, and they resonated with their respective audiences because of their plausibility.

While Communist Party literature tended to heroize the two men as revolutionary leaders, other representations portrayed them as simple working men caught up in the wheels of an unjust legal system. In the United States, for example, Fred Moore sought to link the two men to the cause of organized labor, making the case "the pivot around which class struggle in America is to swing." Elizabeth "Rebel Girl" Gurley Flynn contended that this strategy undermined its power. "The case," she said, benefited by "its very isolation. . . . Being unknown, they had no labor enemies. The simple cry 'Save Sacco and Vanzetti,' has power. . . . It is a dynamic slogan. For heaven's sake, don't lose it in a mass of other issues. Europe . . . respond[ed] to the human appeal and simple pathos of Sacco and Vanzetti. Their very obscurity and helplessness made them powerful."[38] Gurley Flynn's words were prescient. The two men became malleable symbols for different groups drawn to the case. The civil libertarians, intellectuals, and artists who eventually became Sacco and Vanzetti's leading champions rallied around the cause of the "poor fish peddler and good shoemaker." In doing so, their advocates increasingly defanged the men's politics. As they did so, the case transcended its original social base, bringing the global history of the case to a second stage.

Between 1926 and 1927, a successful popular front movement drew in the middle class and intellectuals in Europe and Latin America. The prejudiced climate in which the trial took place, the deep animosity toward anarchists and foreigners expressed by the judge and the foreman, and the shaky and contradictory evidence of the prosecution cast doubts that the men had received a fair trial. With request after request for a retrial failing, prominent intellectuals eventually labeled the verdict a judicial outrage. By early 1927, an increasingly broad swath of "respectable opinion" around the world had become deeply critical of the U.S. justice system, the verdict and sentencing, and the "deafness" of U.S. government officials to international opinion about the case.

In the United States and abroad, the men's plight took on the urgency of high moral drama, and writers, artists, and intellectuals increasingly embraced their cause. Defenders like Fred Moore had tried to involve them early on. In 1921, he contacted Felix Frankfurter, who was then a law professor at Harvard; he also urged the writer Upton Sinclair to visit Bartolomeo Vanzetti in prison. That meeting deeply touched Sinclair, leading him to publish an account of the encounter that painted Vanzetti with a halo of "childlike" innocence.[39] Scholars and writers such as Sinclair, Dos Passos, and Frankfurter had a visibility and respectability that extended beyond labor and radical circles, and they influenced and shaped opinion abroad. Newspaper editorials and journals around the world printed Frankfurter's arguments, often in full detail, for why the men should receive a new trial.[40]

Intellectuals in other countries amplified the concerns of U.S. advocates, emphasizing the unfair trial proceedings, weak evidence, and atmosphere of political intolerance and prejudice. For them, the U.S. justice system itself was on trial. Many intellectuals abroad had already spoken out in favor of the two men: Anatole France, Henri Barbusse, and Romain Rollan lent their names to the cause soon after Sacco and Vanzetti were convicted. By 1927 this roster included such distinguished names as H. G. Wells, Diego Rivera, Albert Einstein, Marie Curie, Bernard Shaw, and Thomas Mann. While some of their concerns mirrored those of U.S. intellectuals, foreign critiques went further. Intellectuals and newspapers abroad often raised questions not only about the nature of U.S. justice but also about the growth of the U.S. empire.

The discourse abroad highlights deep currents of anti-Americanism as well as new concerns with U.S. power in the wake of World War I. In Latin America, the arrogance of "yanqui" power had long been a concern of the elites and the lower classes. The persecution of Sacco and Vanzetti seemed to highlight the hypocrisy of a country that claimed to uphold tolerance and justice while refusing the men a fair trial. In Europe, at a time when the United States was replacing Great Britain as the major world power, the United States was under great scrutiny. The intolerance, prejudice, squashed civil liberties, and inefficient justice system revealed by the case seemed to challenge its claims about bringing freedom and democracy to the world. This led to "violent hostility" in countries like Denmark, where the media generally expressed strong criticism of U.S. judicial methods and "assumed the innocence of both these criminals."[41] But critiques of the United States were framed in a more complex manner then the reductionist term "anti-Americanism" might imply. As one paper in Denmark put it, "If it were only in Russia or some other barbaric country that such a judicial murder were committed for political reasons. But America, the United States of America! If such a thing happens there the wholesome sense of justice of mankind will . . . feel deeply wounded." As the *Ekstrabladet*, a liberal Danish paper proclaimed, "America, which formerly was the country of liberty has begun a new role: that of reaction . . . which is preparing to assume world hegemony."[42]

In August 1927, these sentiments culminated in a wave of outrage and indignation as the time of the execution drew near. World press opinion was united in its hostility toward the United States. As a U.S. legation official remarked, virtually all the Danish newspapers and perhaps "all the press of the civilized world" opposed the execution. In Germany, demonstrations in Hamburg, Berlin, and Leipzig turned violent and bloody. In Berlin, a wide spectrum of the press expressed doubts that justice had been done, with Social Democrats declaring the men's sentence "Justizmord" (judicial murder).[43] Influential politicians like Paul Loebe, president of the Reichstag, joined the loud chorus of dissent. In France, protest bubbled up from Lille to Marseille. It reached its height in Paris as the execution day approached: hundreds of protesters were arrested and hundreds more injured in a day of rioting. In neighboring Switzerland, mobs attacked the U.S. consulate. According to the U.S. ambassador to Denmark, U.S. embassy officials there only escaped mob violence because of the considerable "forces of police" offering them protection.[44] While in Europe the names of Sacco and Vanzetti fueled the fires of political conflict, in Latin America hostility toward the powerful neighbor to the north rose to critical levels.

Sacco and Vanzetti sympathizers mobilized from Mexico to Argentina. In Mexico City and in Montevideo, Uruguay, general strikes brought business and traffic to a standstill when the men were executed. Movie theaters in Mexico City suspended their performances for half an hour to protest the men's fate.[45] By then the trial and sentencing were making headlines around the world. "Whether one likes it or not," wrote the French *Journal des Débats* in 1927, "the fate of Sacco and Vanzetti has assumed international importance." In Munich a weekly magazine depicted on its cover an agitated crowd. The caption remarked on the "storms" of protest that raged in Germany and throughout Europe. Even in distant Uruguay, according to a U.S. embassy official, the press followed the trial to "an unbelievable extent."[46]

U.S. government officials expressed deep concerns about this vast agitation. As the State Department put it in 1922, "in view of the many inaccurate reports which have appeared in the foreign press regarding the cases of Messrs. Sacco and Vanzetti, the department has deemed it advisable to obtain from the authorities of Massachusetts a brief statement of the facts of the case as brought out upon the trial of the two men."[47] The State Department closely followed the progress of appeals. To help embassies and consulates prepare for the expected threats and acts of violence and protest, the State Department sent them copies of judicial decisions. These circulars were quite detailed. One memorandum in 1926 stated that the "Attorney General of Massachusetts informs Department that the seventh motion filed for a new trial of Sacco and Vanzetti cannot be heard before the second week in September at the earliest because of Judge Thayer's illness."[48] This was sent to such diverse countries as Argentina, Uruguay, Brazil, Chile, Peru, Cuba, Albania, Austria, Belgium, Japan, Bulgaria.

That same year the State Department determined that notification of decisions after they were handed down did not offer embassies and consulates abroad sufficient time to prepare. They appealed to Massachusetts authorities for advance notification. As the assistant secretary of state wrote, "I think that we should inform our various Missions by telegraph not only that the men have been sentenced because that news will go all around the world promptly enough, but we should be able to inform them in absolute confidence two or three days in advance in order that proper precautions can be taken to protect them before it is too late. . . . I should be very grateful if you will tell me . . . that I shall get this information in plenty of time." Massachusetts authorities assured department officials that this would, indeed, be possible.[49] These efforts in the United States were mirrored by consulates abroad. In Argentina, embassy officials went so far as to publish an updated history of the case in order to correct again "misperceptions." U.S. businessmen operating there took out advertisements in newspapers publishing in full the history that embassy officials had earlier released to the press.

U.S. officials were deeply concerned about the agitation surrounding the case. Ironically, international protest seems to have hardened officials' determination to carry out judicial decisions. William Borah (R, Idaho), chairman of the Senate's Foreign Relations Committee, pointed out that "it would be a national humiliation, a shameless, cowardly compromise of national courage, to pay the slightest attention to foreign protest. . . . The foreign interference is an impudent and willful challenge to our sense of decency and dignity and ought to be dealt with accordingly." Lawrence Abbott Lowell, president of Harvard University, who headed the committee charged by Governor Fuller to review the case, wrote to the governor shortly after the execution commending him for his refusal to commute the sentences. Clemency, Lowell wrote, would "have kept the agitation for a pardon open indefinitely." Nonetheless, he called on the governor to produce an extensive report "of one hundred or two hundred pages," which would be "of great value . . . for people in this country . . . and for its influence upon foreigners who have gotten a wholly distorted idea of the case."[50]

As Lowell's remarks suggest, the struggle over the legacy of the case began soon after Sacco and Vanzetti were executed. Having already become worldwide symbols of U.S. prejudice and injustice, the men were elevated to a sacred, almost religious status as martyrs. Protests and demonstrations disappeared but the case was not forgotten. The men became tragic figures memorialized in poetry, novels, music, and film throughout the world. In Germany, Switzerland, Austria, and Russia films were produced shortly after the execution, dramatizing the lives and deaths of the men. These movies were shown in such places as Montevideo and Morocco.[51] In some countries, articles of commerce began to appear registered with the names of "Sacco and Vanzetti." Indeed, shortly after the execution, the U.S. ambassador to Argentina protested the registration of articles of commerce "bearing the names of two convicted criminals in the United States" to the foreign minister. He was particularly distressed by the appearance on the Argentine market of a "Sacco and Vanzetti" cigarette brand.[52]

The case has long functioned in symbol and myth in radical folklore and in perceptions of the United States in far-flung places. The men's names have been bestowed on streets in towns and cities in France, in Italy, and in the former Soviet Union. Since 1988, the Museum of Modern Art in Frankfurt has had a Sacco and Vanzetti "reading room," created by the Iranian-born artist Siah Armajani as a tribute to the men's "dedication to the rights of working people and to the goal of universal education."[53] In these memorializations, the details of the case have been lost. The case has been transformed into a grand symbol of the struggle of the weak, the poor, and the working class for social and economic justice, and of efforts to achieve tolerance of political minorities.

Given that after eighty years historians still have failed to come to a consensus on the question of whether the two men were guilty or innocent of the murder and robbery for which they were convicted, it might seem odd that they have achieved this global status as working-class martyrs. After all, the twentieth century witnessed its share of innocent women and men persecuted and even executed by repressive states because they held unpopular political opinions. Yet, when considered in the particular historical moment and set of historical contingencies that brought the two Italians to prominence, their staying power makes sense. The Sacco and Vanzetti case coincided with the birth of the modern world in the 1920s. It took place at a moment when the dynamics of global radicalism were being reworked, when class relations were being altered in significant parts of Europe and Latin America, and when the mass media was making the world a more connected place. These factors, along with deepening anxieties over the rise of the United States to a position of world power, and the linkage of different groups into one movement to save the two men, unleashed the global passion for Sacco and Vanzetti. And although the story of Sacco and Vanzetti—a moment of worker-led global protest—is unique, the sense of increasing global connectedness it revealed has influenced international social movements ever since.

ACKNOWLEDGMENT

A different version of this essay was published by the *Journal of American History*. Permission to reprint has been granted by the Organization of American Historians.

NOTES

1. Letter from Jesse S. Cottrell, Legation of the United States of America, La Paz, Bolivia to Secretary of State, September 1927, File Number (hereafter FN) 311.6521 Sa1, 924, Record Group 59, State Department Records, National Archives 2, College Park, MD (hereafter SD). The document lists "Tristan Navarro or Tristan Maroff" as the leader of the demonstrations. This is a reference to Gustavo Navarro, who took the name Tristan Maroff and later became a prominent radical leader. See, for example, Herbert Klein, *Bolivia: The Evolution of a Multi-Ethnic Society* (New York, 1982), 197–98.

2. On "transnationalism," see Linda Basch, Nina Glick Schiller, and Cristina Szanton Blanc, *Nations Unbound: Transnational Projects, Postcolonial Predicaments, and Deterritorialized Nation-States* (Amsterdam, 1994), 21–48.

3. See Paul Avrich, *Sacco and Vanzetti: The Anarchist Background* (Princeton, 1991); Louis Joughin and Edmund M. Morgan, *The Legacy of Sacco and Vanzetti* (New York, 1948); Roberta Feuerlicht, *Justice Crucified: The Story of Sacco and Vanzetti* (New York, 1977); Francis Russell, *Tragedy in Dedham: The Story of the Sacco-Vanzetti Case* (New York, 1962), and Michael Topp, *The Sacco and Vanzetti Case: A Brief History with Documents* (Boston, 2005).

4. Willis C. Cook to Secretary of State, September 28, 1927, FN 311.6521, SD; *Le Figaro*, August 11, 1927.

5. For example, Thomas Bender, *Rethinking American History in a Global Age* (Berkeley, 2002).

6. See, for example, Daniel Rogers, *Atlantic Crossings: Social Politics in a Progressive Age* (Cambridge, Mass., 1988); Sven Beckert, "Emancipation and Empire: Reconstructing the Worldwide Web of Cotton Production in the Age of the American Civil War," *American Historical Review* 109 (Dec. 2004): 1405–38; Akira Iriye, *Global Community: The Role of International Organizations in the Making of the Contemporary World* (Berkeley, 2002); Kristin Hoganson, "Cosmopolitan Domesticity: Importing the American Dream, 1865–1920," *American Historical Review* 107 (Feb. 2002): 55–83. A number of studies have examined transnational social movements. These include Bonnie Anderson, *Joyous Greetings: The First International Women's Movement, 1830–1860* (New York, 2000); Penny Von Eschen, *Race against Empire:*

Black Americans and Anticolonialism, 1937–1957 (Ithaca, 1997); Winston James, *Holding Aloft the Banner of Ethiopia: Caribbean Radicalism in early Twentieth-Century America* (London, 1998); James A. Miller, Susan D. Pennybacker, and Eve Rosenhaft, "Mother Ada Wright and the International Campaign to Free the Scottsboro Boys, 1931–1934," *American Historical Review* 106 (Apr. 2001): 387–430; Jeremi Suri, *Power and Protest: Global Revolution and the Rise of Detente* (Cambridge, Mass., 2003). On global cultural movements, see Michael Denning, *Culture in the Age of Three Worlds* (London, 2004). On global labor history, see Marcel van der Linden, *Transnational Labour History: Explorations* (Burlington, 2003), esp. pp. 143–53.

7. The shelves of books on this subject have largely focused on the legal aspects of the case and its domestic ramifications. The one author who has advanced an explanation for the dynamic international protest remarked in a patronizing and unconvincing vein: "The most conservative of Europeans found it easy to believe that the authorities had conspired to murder two innocents. In the first place, such phenomena were not unknown in the history of Europe. In the second place, the Europeans have the greatest difficulty with the simplest events." David Felix, *Protest: Sacco and Vanzetti and the Intellectuals* (Bloomington, 1965), 170. Others like Robert Montgomery have reduced the international mobilization to a protest orchestrated by Moscow. Such portraits are far too reductionist to explain the vast and divergent groups that supported the campaign to rescue the two men. See Robert Montgomery, *The Murder and the Myth* (New York, 1960). See also Avrich, *Sacco and Vanzetti*, 9; and Topp, *Sacco and Vanzetti Case*, 46.

8. Marcel van der Linden argues for this approach. See Marcel van der Linden, *Transnational Labour History: Explorations*, esp. intro. and 143–53.

9. Marcel van der Linden, *Transnational Labour History*, 20. See also Frits van Holthoon and Marcel van der Linden, eds., *Internationalism in the Labour Movement, 1830–1940* (Leiden, 1988).

10. On anarchism see George Woodcock, *Anarchism: A History of Libertarian Ideas and Movements* (Cleveland, 1962); Giampietro D. Berti, *Errico Malatesta e il Movimento Anarchico Italiano e Internazionale, 1872–1932* (Milano, 2003); Geoff Eley, *Forging Democracy: The History of the Left in Europe, 1850–2000* (New York, 2002), 85–123; See also Benedict Anderson, *Under Three Flags: Anarchism and the Anticolonial Imagination* (London, 2005).

11. See Donna Gabaccia, *Italy's Many Diasporas* (Seattle, 2000), and Donna Gabaccia and Fraser Ottanelli, eds., *Italian Workers of the World: Labor Migration and the Formation of Multiethnic States* (Urbana, 2001).

12. See Stephen Kern, *The Culture of Time and Space, 1880–1918* (Cambridge, Mass., 1983), 240.

13. On Dos Passos, see David Sanders, "The 'Anarchism' of John Dos Passos," 122–35, and Alfred Kazin, "Dos Passos and the 'Lost Generation,'" 12, both in

Dos Passos, the Critics, and the Writer's Intention, ed. Allen Belkind (Carbondale, Ill., 1971). On Mussolini see Philip Cannistraro, "Mussolini, Sacco-Vanzetti, and the Anarchists: The Transatlantic Context" *Journal of Modern History* 68 (March 1966): 43–44.

14. George Woodcock, *Anarchism: A History of Libertarian Ideas and Movements* (Cleveland, 1962).

15. On the Galleanistas in the United States, see Nunzio Pernicone, "Luigi Galleani and Italian Anarchist Terrorism in the United States," *Studi Emigrazione/Etudes Migration* 30 (Sept. 1993): 469–89.

16. See, for example, letters from Bartolomeo Vanzetti to Luigi Bertoni, Paris, October 10, 1926, April 3, 6, 7, 1927, Luigi Bertoni papers, International Institute for Social History, Amsterdam, the Netherlands (hereafter IISH). See also "Un Saludo de Vanzetti al Pueblo de la Argentina," *Brazo y Cerebro,* July 31, 1927, and "Una Nueva Carta de Sacco," *La Antorcha,* August 27, 1926; letter from Nicola Sacco and Bartolomeo Vanzetti, "Solo con la Vita cessera la nostra fede," reprinted in *Agitación: Publicación del Comité de Agitación Pro Libertad de Sacco Y Vanzetti,* August 1926, Ar 308, IISH.

17. See, for example, letter from Fred Moore to Elizabeth Gurley Flynn, August 26, 1920, and December 15, 1921; Fred Moore to Selma Maximilion, May 24, 1922, in Fred Moore Correspondence (hereafter FMC), 4A, Sacco-Vanzetti Papers (hereafter SV), Boston Public Library (hereafter BPL). See, for example, Fred Moore to Ben Legere, Amalgamated Textile Workers Union in Lawrence Massachusetts, September 4, 1920; F. S. Merlino, Esq., Rome, October 26, 1920; letter from Fred Moore to Morris Gebelow, October 26, 1920, in FMC, 4A, SV, BPL.

18. Letter from Fred Moore to Leonardo Mucci, January 16, 1922, FMC, 4A, SV, BPL; letter from Leonardo Mucci to Fred Moore, December 3, 1921, FMC, 4A, SV, BPL.

19. See Atti Parliamentari, 3342, legislature 26, March 20, 1922.

20. Philip Cannistraro, "Mussolini, Sacco-Vanzetti, and the Anarchists: The Transatlantic Context" *Journal of Modern History* 68 (March 1966): 43–44.

21. Memorandum from H. Roderick Dorsey to Secretary of State, American Consulate, Florence, October 22, 1921, 311.6521 Sa1 57; memorandum from Embassy of the United States, Henry Fletcher to Secretary of State, June 26, 1926, FN 311.6521 Sa1 270; memorandum from American Consulate, Genoa to Secretary of State, August 1927, FN 311.6521 Sa1 893; memorandum from H. P. Starrett, American Consul, Genoa to Secretary of State, August 1927, FN 311.6521 Sa1 893, SD.

22. *Figaro,* October 21, 1921. Memorandum from American Consulate to Secretary of State, November 8, 1921, FN 311.652 Sa1 85, SD; "Impartial Havrais," poster in memorandum from the American Consulate, Le Havre, "Protest of Chambre

Syndicale des Ouvriers," to Secretary of State, October 27, 1921. FN 311.6521 Sa1 44, SD.

23. See *Le Libertaire*, various issues. See also Anne Rebayal and Jean-Paul Roux, "L'Affaire Sacco et Vanzetti vue par *L'Humanité* et *Le Libertaire*" (Paris, 1971); Louis Lecoin, *Le cours d'une vie* (Paris, 1965), 103–20; Sylvain Garel, *Volonté Anarchiste: Louis Lecoin et le Mouvement Anarchiste* (Paris, n.d.).

24. Edward Mortimer, *The Rise of the French Communist Party, 1920–1947* (London, 1984), 19–98. See also Annie Kriegal and Robert Wohl, *French Communism in the Making, 1914–1924* (Stanford, 1966). See also issues of *L'Humanité*, which on October 6, 1921, titled a column "Pour Sacco & Vanzetti"; the column traced events around the case and publicized news of demonstrations and meetings.

25. See Pierre Milza, "L'immigration italienne en France d'une guerre à "l'autre: interrogations, directions de recherche et premier bilan," in *Les Italiens en France de 1914 a 1940*, ed. Milza, 18–29 (Rome, 1986). See also Pierre George, "L'immigration italienne en France de 1920–1939: aspects démographiques et sociaux," 45–67, and Pierre Guillen, "Le rôle politique de l'immigration italienne en France dans l'entre-deux-guerres," 323–41, both in *Les Italiens en France*, ed. Milza.

26. *Journal des Débats*, Oct. 21, 22, 23, 1921; *Le Figaro*, October 24, 1921. W. R. Castle, State Department to Dean Wigmore, Northwestern University School of Law, FN 311.6521 Sa1 518; memorandum from W. Stanley Hollis to Secretary of State, November 1, 1921, Dispatch 338, FN 125.1, SD.

27. American Consulate, Lisbon, Portugal, November 3, 1921, to Secretary of State and letter from W. R. Castle, State Department to Dean Wigmore, Northwestern University School of Law, FN 311.6521 Sa1 518, SD.

28. Letter from Arthur Shields to Fred Moore, November 8, 1921, FMC, 4A, SV, BPL.

29. John M. Hart, *Anarchism and the Mexican Working Class, 1860–1931* (Austin, Tex., 1978), 14; Barry Carr, "Marxism and Anarchism in the Formation of the Mexican Communist Party, 1910–1919," *Hispanic American Historical Review* 63 (May 1983): 277–305. See also Barry Carr, *Marxism and Communism in Twentieth-Century Mexico* (Lincoln, 1992), 1–46; Max Nettlau, "Anarchisten in LateinAmerika," MS (n.d.), 443, IISH.

30. Translation of letter from "Torch of Liberty Guard," Vera Cruz, November 9, 1921, FN 311.6521 Sa 1 99, SD; Gaylord March, American Consul, Progreso, Mexico, November 14, 17, 1921, FN 311.6521 Sa1 94 SD; memorandum from American Consul to Secretary of State, Veracruz, November 30, 1921, FN 311.6521 Sa1 106; memorandum from American Consul to Secretary of State, November 15, 1921, FN 311.6521 Sa1 78, SD.

31. Ronaldo Munck, *Argentina: From Anarchism to Peronism: Workers, Unions, and Politics, 1855–1985* (London, 1987), 12–59, 103; Matthew B. Karush, *Workers or Citizens: Democracy and Identity in Rosario, Argentina, 1912–1930* (Albuquerque, 2002), 43–58; Leandro H. Gutierrez and Luis Alberto Romero, *Sectores Populares, Cultura y Política: Buenos Aires en la Entreguerra* (Buenos Aires, 1995).

32. Karush, *Workers or Citizens*, 157.

33. *La Protesta*, February 9, 1923; May 6, May 26, 1921. *La Protesta*, suplemento semenal, November 8, 1926; suplemento quincenal, August 20, 1926; suplemento quincenal, June 20, 1927. See, for example, *Agitación: Publicación del Comité de Agitación Pro Libertad de Sacco Y Vanzetti*, May 1926; *La Antorcha*, 1923–29; *Brazo y Cerebro* and *El Libertario*, various issues; and "El Caso Sacco y Vanzetti." See also "Notas de Agitación Para Salvar a Sacco y Vanzetti," *Humanidad*. The Biblioteca Jose Inginieros has an extensive collection of these materials.

34. *La Protesta*, October 25, 28, 1925. Letter from Chamber of Commerce of the United States of America in the Argentine Republic to Philander L Cable, U.S. Charge d'Affaires. Embassy of the United States, August 22, 1927, FN 311.6521 Sa1 873, SD. The General Federation of the Italian Societies of the Argentine Republic, cablegram, August 9, 1927, FN 311. 6521 Sa1 621, SD.

35. Memorandum from Charles L. Hoover, American Consul to Secretary of State, March 7, 1927, FN 311.6521 Sa 1 395 SD.

36. *Le Figaro*, October 22, 23, 1921; memorandum from American Consulate the Hague to Secretary of State, November 18, 1921, the Hague, FN 311.6521 Sa1, 105, SD; Internationale Presse-Korrespondenz, 1921, v. 13, 112, cited in Zelt, *Proletarische Internationalismus*, 43. See also *L'Humanité*, October 19, 1921; memorandum from American Consulate in the Hague to Secretary of State, November 18, 1921, FN 311.6521, Sa1, 105.

37. Memorandum from the American consulate, Harbin, China, to Secretary of State, December 18, 1924, 331.6521, Sa1, 195. SD; "American Foreign Service Report, Stockholm, Legation to United States, February 13, 1925, FN 311.6521 Sa1 20, SD.

38. Letter from Elizabeth Gurley Flynn to Fred Moore, December 14, 1921, FMC, 4A, SV, BPL.

39. Letter from Upton Sinclair, May 22, 1922, to Fred Moore, FMC, 4A, SV, BPL, later reprinted in *Appeal to Reason* (June 17, 1922). See also Upton Sinclair, *Boston* (1928; reprint, Boston, 1978), xx; Leon Harris, *Upton Sinclair: American Rebel* (New York, 1975).

40. See, for example, Felix Frankfurter, *El Caso Sacco y Vanzetti* reprinted in *La Protesta*, supplemental quincenal, September 5, 1927; remarks by Frankfurter in *Giornale D'Italia*, Buenos Aires, July 15, 1927; comments on Frankfurter in *Mercury*, Leeds, England, April 26, 1927, in "Editorial Comments on the Sacco-Vanzetti

case," April 26, 1927; memorandum to Secretary of State from American Consulate, Leeds, England. FN 331. 6521 Sa1 440 SD; *Frankfurter Zeitung*, July 3, 1927; Zelt, *Proletarischer Internationalismus*, 26, 169; Lehning, *De Feiten en de Beteekenis Van de Zaak Sacco en Vanzetti*, 1; *Nationaltidende*, August 4, 1927.

41. See memorandum from H. Percival Dodge, American Minster, American Legation in Copenhagen, August 1927, FN 311.6521 Sa1 744, SD.

42. *Nationaltidende*, August 4, 1927, See translations in Legation of the United States of America, Copenhagen, Denmark to Secretary of State, August 1927, 311.6521 Sa1 774. SD.

43. See memorandum from H. Percival Dodge, American Minster, American Legation in Copenhagen, August 1927, FN 311.6521 Sa1 744, SD; *Vorwärts*, Berlin, August 4, 1927.

44. See *Le Figaro*, August 8, 1927; August 9, 1927; memorandum from H. Percival Dodge, American Legation, Copenhagen to Secretary of State, December 1927, 311.6521 Sa1 960, SD; *Journal des Débats*, Paris, August 24 1927; *Simplicissimus*, Stuttgart, September 5, 1927.

45. Memorandum from U. Grant-Smith, American Legation, Montevideo to Secretary of State, August 1927, FN 311.6521 812 SD; memorandum from Joseph C. Satterwaite, American Vice-Consul, Guadalajara, Mexico to Secretary of State, August 12, 1927 FN 311.6521 Sa1 710, SD; memorandum from Joseph C. Satterwaite, American Vice-Consul, Guadalajara, Mexico to Secretary of State, August 11, 1927 FN 311.6521 Sa1 708, SD; letter from Grant-Smith, American Legation in Montevideo to Secretary of State, August 8, 1927, FN 311.6521 Sa1 598, SD; letter from Grant-Smith, American Legation in Montevideo to Secretary of State, FN August 10, 1927, 311.6521 Sa1, 633, SD; memorandum from H.F. Schoenfeld, Embassy of the United States to Secretary of State, August 26,1927, FN 311.6521 Sa1 813. SD.

46. *Journal des Débats*, Paris, August 24, 1927; *Simplicissimus*, Stuttgart, September 5, 1927; Memorandum from U. Grant-Smith to Secretary of State, August 1927, FN 311.6521 812 SD.

47. Henry P. Fletcher, Department of State to "Diplomatic Officers of the United States of America," January 27, 1922, FN 311.6521 Sa1 86.

48. W. R. Castle Jr., Department of State to Robert O. Dalton, Adjutant General's Office, State House Boston, July 1, 1926, FN 311.6521 Sa1272, 284 SD. Philander L. Cable, Chargé d'Affaires, Embassy of the United States, Buenos Aires to Secretary of State, August 13, 1927 and Philander L. Cable, Chargé D'Affaires, Embassy of the United States, to Secretary of State, August 24, 1927 FN 311.6521 Sa1 873, SD.

49. W. R. Castle Jr., Department of State, to Robert O. Dalton, Adjutant General's Office, State House Boston, July 1, 1926, FN 311.6521 Sa1272, 284 SD.

50. August 18, 1927, telegram; "Borah Amazes Sacco Vanzetti Forces," newspaper clipping, August 18, 1927, and "Jane Addams' Plea," *Washington Post*, n.d., newspaper clippings in Jane Addams Papers, Swarthmore College Peace Collection, series 1, microfilm, Ann Arbor, 1985. Letter from A. Lawrence Lowell, Harvard University President to Governor A. Fuller, September 9, 1927 in A. Lawrence Lowell Papers, Harvard University Archives, Harvard University.

51. Teatro Artigas, handbill enclosure, Legation of the United States, Montevideo, Uruguay, enclosure in memorandum from Grant-Smith, Legation of the United States, Montevideo to Secretary of State, December 29, 1927, Fn 311. 6521 Sai 959, SD. Enclosure in memorandum from H. Percival Dodge, American Legation, Copenhagen, to Secretary of State, December 29, 1927, FN 311.6521 Sai 959, SD; letter from H. Percival Dodge, American Legation, Copenhagen to Secretary of State, September 1, 1927, FN 311.6521 Sai 868, SD; letter from Robert Woods Bliss, Embassy of the United States, Buenos Aires to Secretary of State, December 28, 1927, FN 311. 6521 Sai 957, SD; memorandum from Grant-Smith, Legation of the United States in Montevideo to Secretary of State, December 29, 1927, FN 311.6521 Sai 959 SD; J. C. W to Secretary of State, Embassy of the United States, Berlin, December 1927, FN 311.6521 SA 955, SD.

52. Letter from Robert Woods Bliss, American Embassy in Buenos Aires to Secretary of State, November 28, 1927, FN 311. 6521 Sai 954, SD.

53. Siah Armajani, "Sacco und Vanzetti—Leseraum," Museum für Moderne Kunst, Frankfurt am Main (Frankfurt, 1988).

Chapter Eleven

"An Ironic Testimony to the Value of American Democracy"

Assimilationism and the World War II
Internment of Japanese Americans

MAE M. NGAI

The internment of Japanese Americans during World War II stands as one of the most extreme cases of "alien citizenship" in American history. During the era of Asiatic exclusion (1882–1952), Chinese, Japanese, and other people of Asian descent were not only excluded from immigration but were denied the privilege of naturalized citizenship as well. The legal logic that declared Asians racially unassimilable and doomed them to permanent foreignness led to the widespread perception that even people of Asian descent who were born in the United States, and who were therefore birthright citizens, were aliens.[1]

During World War II the U.S. government did not formally strip Japanese Americans of their citizenship, but it effectively nullified their citizenship on exclusive grounds of racial difference. Presuming all Japanese in America to be racially inclined to disloyalty, the United States removed 120,000 people of Japanese descent—two-thirds of them U.S. citizens—from their homes on the Pacific Coast and interned them in ten concentration camps in the U.S. interior.[2] Military orders, posted on telephone poles in early March 1942, called for the evacuation of "all persons of Japanese

ancestry, both aliens and non-aliens"—"non-aliens" the rhetorical effacement of citizenship of some 70,000 Americans. Today we call this racial
profiling. In 1942 it was said, "A Jap is a Jap."[3]

Earl Warren, then the attorney general of California, explained the difference in policy toward people of German and Italian descent, which was
based on individual investigation, and the Japanese: "We believe that when
we are dealing with the Caucasian race we have methods that will test the
loyalty of them. . . . But when we deal with the Japanese we are in an entirely
different field and cannot form any opinion that we believe to be sound."[4]

But while internment rested on a fairly simple, straightforward racism—
in General John DeWitt's famous words, "the Japanese race is an enemy
race"—that racial logic was complicated by the administration of the camps
by the War Relocation Authority (WRA).[5] WRA officials in fact did not
believe all Japanese were racially inclined to disloyalty. So they practiced a
coercive assimilationism, which used culture to both measure and produce
Japanese Americans' loyalty.

The conflation of culture and loyalty was not a new phenomenon in the
United States. During World War I, American war nationalism had pressured German Americans to forswear their native language and religious
cultural practices in order to demonstrate their loyalty to the United States.[6]
During World War II, Japanese Americans came under similar pressures to
assimilate, but under radically different conditions: citizenship nullification
and internment.

Nullification and internment, and the racism that animated them, have
obscured from view the assimilationist policies that were pursued by those
in charge of the camps. In this essay I argue that the internment was shaped
as much by assimilationism as it was by racial exclusion. In fact, the most
incendiary and disastrous aspects of the internment—the "loyalty test" and
the segregation of "disloyals"—were impelled principally by coercive assimilationism. Usually understood as opposite vectors of immigration and
racial policies, assimilationism and exclusion were closely entwined during internment. The conventional view of the internment as an expression
of official racial animus against Asian Americans, indeed, as its apotheosis,
while certainly accurate, nevertheless seems to me incomplete. That render-
ing tends to be too flat, too simple. It positions the internment as an anach-
ronism in an era of emerging racial liberalism, whereas it might profitably
be considered, instead, a constitutive element of racial liberalism. A more

nuanced analysis that examines both the execution and reception of assimilationism, I argue, helps situate the internment more clearly in the broader context of the racial politics of the day and in a longer trajectory of Americanization policies from the Progressive Era to the 1960s.

THE WAR RELOCATION AUTHORITY'S AMERICANIZING VISION

Although the U.S. Army executed the exclusion and evacuation orders that removed Japanese Americans from their homes, the camps were administered by a civil agency, the War Relocation Authority. The WRA was part of the Department of Interior, the secretary of which was Harold Ickes, one of the New Deal's most renowned liberals. The WRA's director, Milton Eisenhower, and his successor, Dillon Myer, had both served in FDR's Department of Agriculture.[7] Unlike the unapologetic racists and nativists that wanted to rid the country of all Japanese Americans, these liberals considered themselves antiracist.

The antiracism of the officials in charge of the WRA was part of a growing trend in American social politics. Shorn of the Social Darwinism and scientific racism of the late Victorian age and the Progressive Era that had animated the Asiatic exclusion movements, these liberals were more likely to have been influenced by intellectuals like Franz Boas and Louis Brandeis than by the shrill racism of the Pacific Coast exclusion lobby. Although the New Deal was arguably more concerned with economic rights than with racial equality, these New Dealers were cut from the cloth of racial tolerance, not racial nativism. Moreover, as government bureaucrats they were less vulnerable to the popular racism that excited voters than were elected officials in the western states and in Washington, D.C.

Eisenhower and Myer brought to the WRA another legacy from the New Deal: an obsession with social planning. WRA leaders believed they had an opportunity to turn an unfortunate incident of war into a positive social good. Ever optimistic about the potential of mass social engineering, they envisioned the camps as "planned communities" and "Americanizing projects" that would speed the assimilation of Japanese Americans through democratic self-government, schooling, work, and other rehabilitative activities. Comparing their own experiment with the Nazis' concentration camps, WRA officials believed their "community building" project was, as one anthropologist described it, "ironic testimony to the value of American democracy."[8]

To be fair, Eisenhower initially envisioned the camps (or "relocation centers," as they were euphemistically called) as open, not closed, facilities, where Japanese Americans could freely come and go for shopping, recreation, and work, including "private employment." He advocated that centers comprise public works, agriculture, and small industry, which would provide the evacuees with employment and allow them to contribute to the national war effort. However, Eisenhower's proposals were quickly scuttled in the face of opposition from the army, the governors of western states where the camps were situated, and manufacturers opposed to "subsidized" competition. Yet even as the camps were built with barbed wire fences and guard towers and WRA officials became "committed to [a policy of] detention," they persisted in their belief that theirs would be a democratic experiment.[9]

Other liberals, who were skeptical about the necessity of relocation, nonetheless believed, or wanted to believe, that Japanese Americans would benefit from the internment. Endorsing the WRA's strategy to use internment to Americanize and modernize the Japanese, the social scientist Everett Stonequest wrote that a "farsighted and just handling [of the internment] may turn what is now a great national problem into some kind of asset. . . . [W]ith a wise and skillfully executed policy of resettlement, the Japanese-Americans, instead of continuing as an isolated collection of 'Little Tokyos' in one section of the country, might be more thoroughly woven into the texture of American life on a national scale."[10]

Writing in 1942, the California journalist Carey McWilliams, a champion of cultural pluralism, similarly hoped internment would break Japanese Americans' clannishness and push them to assimilate. Despite the "painful and distressing experience" of internment, McWilliams argued, the camps were potential "demonstrations of democracy" that would situate Japanese Americans in a "far more satisfactory position in American life" after the war.[11]

By 1943, McWilliams had concluded that the camps were not "normal communities" but "a type of prison complex." Others, such as photographer Ansel Adams, remained more hopeful. Adams's 1943 book *Born Free and Equal* presented photographs of internees at Manzanar to demonstrate Japanese Americans' humanity and Americanness. The book can be read as an effort to educate the American public to accept Japanese Americans as fellow citizens in anticipation of resettlement after the war. Like other liberals, Adams believed that ethnic dispersal was the solution to race prejudice. He wrote, "The scattering of loyal Japanese Americans throughout the country is far better for them than re-concentration into racial districts and groups."[12]

Adams portrayed the internment as benevolent, as "but a detour on the road to citizenship." He seemed to believe that the camps, both in their administration by the WRA and in their very physicality, enabled Japanese Americans to imbibe and perform loyal citizenship. He read Manzanar's desert landscape, with its "acrid splendor" and "ringed with towering mountains," as a site for democracy. "Out of the jostling, dusty confusion of the first bleak days in the raw barracks," he said, Japanese Americans "have modulated to a democratic internal society and a praiseworthy adjustment to conditions beyond their control. The huge vistas and the stern realities of sun and wind and space symbolize the immensity and opportunity of America."[13]

For Japanese Americans, however, Manzanar was a harsh and desolate and internment; they saw it for what it was: a deprivation of their liberty. How could the liberals not understand this fundamental point? WRA officials viewed Japanese Americans as racial children in need of democratic tutelage, infantilizing them in much the same way that the government constructed Filipino colonial subjects and Native American Indians as dependent wards not yet fit for democratic citizenship.[14] In this sense, nullifying Japanese American citizenship was a precondition for properly rehabilitating it. As the school superintendent at Minidoka claimed, Japanese Americans "had little opportunity [before the war] to practice the principles of democracy but here . . . is a chance ready-made to live such experiences and thus be made aware of the advantages to our country." This was similar to the logic of President McKinley's program of "benevolent assimilation" for the Filipinos, which rested on American military conquest and colonial possession.[15]

As in the Philippines and on Indian reservations, the assimilationists in the WRA believed traditional cultures were not conducive to liberal citizenship. They frowned on the use of native language, kinship structures of leadership, and other manifestations of alleged cultural backwardness. In the case of the Japanese, the pressure for cultural assimilation was freighted with the demand for loyalty. Liberals thus considered certain "types" to be particularly prone to disloyalty based on a cultural reading of their social status. These included, for example, the Kibei, U.S.-born Japanese who had been raised and schooled in Japan, and Buddhist and otherwise "Japanesey" Nisei.[16]

The conflation of culture and loyalty was not absolute and was sometimes contradictory. For example, WRA policy embraced freedom of religion, but officials suspected those who practiced Shintoism, which worshipped the emperor.[17] WRA administrators also took a laissez-faire policy toward recreational activities, allowing for both Japanese and American leisure practices. But in the areas deemed most important for citizenship construction—work, schooling, and self-government—WRA policy was pointedly assimilationist.

Following long-established concepts of liberal citizenship, the WRA considered productive labor the cornerstone of its Americanizing project. But this was not easily implemented. Eisenhower's initial plans to turn the camps into agricultural and industrial centers failed on account of stiff resistance from inland politicians and businesses. But the centers needed internees' labor in order to function. There were some ten thousand internees at each camp, which necessitated the infrastructure and operations of a large town—housing and road construction and repair, maintenance, kitchens and mess halls, hospitals, policing, and the like. While white American staff held all supervisory and administrative positions, internees performed the myriad jobs that made the camps run and farmed the crops that kept the camps' population fed.

The WRA insisted that work be voluntary and paid, lest it resemble forced prison labor. Initially, officials announced it would pay internees according to wage guidelines of the Works Progress Administration. After public protest because the proposed wages exceeded those of the average American soldier, the WRA dropped the idea in favor of a monthly "cash allowance" of nineteen dollars for professionals and sixteen for highly skilled workers. Eisenhower himself deemed it a "miserably low" amount. Yamato Ichihashi, a Stanford professor interned at Tule Lake, believed the pay system, along with barracks living and other "communalist" ways of life were actually counterproductive to liberal individualism.[18]

The WRA had ambitious plans for schooling in the camps. It made schooling compulsory for all internees under the age of seventeen and aimed at putting students through school in keeping with state and college requirements. Officials did not trust Japanese American teachers, despite their professional certification and experience, and mandated that only white American teachers could teach in the centers' schools. Instruction was in English only; Japanese language classes, whether in the center schools or extracurricular classes organized by internees, were forbidden.[19]

WRA education officials pursued the "progressive education" model, which it hoped would be an "effective instrument of community building" and an "Americanizing factor." Lucy Adams, a WRA education planner who was the former director of education for the Navajo reservation, believed schools should teach students in "behavior or generalized controls of conduct which, if developed, will lead to the realization of the democratic ideal." Schools would be "democracy in action," with PTAs, student councils, clubs, and citizenship classes. The assimilationist orientation also prompted teachers to try to break students from the strictures of parental authority and traditional custom. They aggressively used the classroom to agitate against arranged marriages, to promote normative domestic habits, and to reform students of "incorrect habits and incongruous ways." According to the historian Thomas James, "culture and kinship were in danger of becoming symbols of disloyalty. . . . In the minds of many administrators, the enemy became the family itself."[20]

Self-government was perhaps the most important element in the WRA's plan for the camps as Americanizing projects. Officials designated the block, comprising fourteen barracks and housing 250 internees, as the basic unit of representation for elected "community councils." All internees over the age of eighteen could vote, but only U.S. citizens could serve on the councils, and all business was conducted in English. The councils' mandate was to prescribe and provide penalties "on all matters (except felonies) affecting the internal peace and order of the project and the welfare of the residents," but all decisions were subject to review and veto by the project director. In fact, the councils functioned more like a liaison between administrators and internees. As one account described it, "Usually at the meeting of the Council the members do little more than listen to new rules, new plans of WRA, handed down from Washington or the local director. The block representatives are expected to pass on this information to all the people."[21]

DUALISM AMONG THE JAPANESE AMERICANS

Most Japanese Americans did not subscribe wholly to the WRA's assimilation program; they took from it selectively those aspects that they wanted, most notably, schooling and work. But even these were sites of conflict. Workers continually complained and petitioned the authorities about labor conditions, such as a lack of work clothes and supplies, unsafe equipment, and pressure from administrators to produce. Work stoppages and strikes were not uncommon. Internees also ignored or resisted programs that they considered not in their best interest. For example, they refused to participate in social surveys and family counseling, which they associated with forced relocation.[22]

Most notably, internees regarded the WRA's requirements for participation in the community councils to be affronts to the adult generation (Issei), which comprised noncitizens and many non-English-speakers. To categorically exclude the Issei from leadership was seen as a sign of extreme disrespect. In addition, the second generation was quite young—the median age was seventeen and only a handful were older than twenty-five—and few believed the Nisei had the maturity or experience to provide responsible leadership.[23]

The imposed "realignment" in the community's leadership structure led to a great many conflicts between the internees and WRA officials and among the Nikkei themselves. In some camps, internees boycotted the community council elections. The Issei—who wanted "voting power" more than anything else—asserted their authority by creating alternate bodies of leadership and self-governance. They turned block meetings into venues for "instructing" representatives to the community councils, and appropriated other camp structures to wield influence, notably block planning boards and the cooperative stores.[24] The Nisei who served on the community councils tended to be associated with the JACL (Japanese American Citizens League) and were deemed proassimilationist and—worst of all, in the eyes of most Nikkei—proadministration. Internees called them "power crazy" and "pushy" Nisei and generally ostracized all real and suspected collaborators and informers as *inu* (dog).[25]

Contrary to the Americanizing schema promoted by the WRA, everyday life in the camps involved both Japanese and American culture and politics.[26] Leisure and recreational activities were bicultural, including such activities as flower-arranging, sock hops, go tournaments, cutting trees at Christmastime, and baseball games. Internees observed Lincoln's, Washington's, and the emperor's birthdays. At Poston, they gave nicknames to the streets running through camp: Tojo Road (a big street) and Roosevelt Lane (a little one). The Issei, neither monolithic nor passive, argued about the war at meetings and informally. War talk and political debate in the camp were ubiquitous, especially among Issei men, for whom daily kibitzing about the war was a major activity.[27]

Yet even as internees obsessed over news and rumors from the outside, for many Nikkei the import of political developments lay more in the practical realm of what the war meant for their individual and family future. Many Japanese Americans believed that after the war they would be deported en masse or if not forcibly repatriated, they would be unable to remain in the United States, where they were hated. These scenarios could be imagined no matter which side won the war. Many wished to stay in America—they regarded the United States as their adopted country and as the native homeland of their children. They had built a life in America and did not want to sacrifice their property. While some internees left the camps during the war to repatriate to Japan or to resettle in areas outside the West, most Japanese Americans wanted to remain in camp until the war ended. They preferred to await the peace and keep their options open.[28] The pragmatic strategy required a certain balancing of their dual nationalisms and allegiances—or avoiding politics as much as possible. But their efforts were thrown into crisis in the early months of 1943, when the WRA required all adult internees to fill out a lengthy registration form to ascertain their loyalty to the United States.

THE LOYALTY TEST

This famous intervention was officially called "application for leave clearance." Its genesis lay in two initiatives—the volunteer combat unit and resettlement—that the War Department and the WRA designed in order to promote Japanese Americans' citizenship and assimilation, respectively.

After Pearl Harbor, the military had dismissed Nisei serving in the armed forces on the mainland with "honorable discharge" at the "convenience of the government." The Selective Service reclassified Nisei who had I-A status (fit for duty) to IV-C (enemy alien) and soon ceased inducting Japanese Americans into the military altogether.[29] The JACL protested these policies and vigorously lobbied the government for the Nisei's right to enlist, in order to prove their loyalty. By late 1942, a few officials in the War Department had begun to argue for inducting the Nisei, citing the need to counter Japan's war propaganda and to rehabilitate Japanese Americans' citizenship and public image.[30]

In January 1943, the War Department decided to organize an all-Nisei volunteer combat unit as a "symbol of [Japanese Americans'] loyalty, which can be displayed to the American public and to those who oppose the Japanese Americans." To determine the loyalty of prospective volunteers and to effectuate their release from camp, it developed a questionnaire for male internees within the age range for military service and various investigative procedures.[31]

The WRA proposed that the loyalty questionnaire be extended to all internees over the age of seventeen. The WRA, committed to its assimilationist goal of returning Japanese Americans to the mainstream of American life, desired a mechanism to separate the truly disloyal from the loyal majority in order to relocate the latter out of the camps. It was disappointed in the slow progress of its program of "voluntary leave clearance," by which internees determined to be loyal could move to an area outside the West Coast, provided they had personal sponsorship and an offer of employment or education. By the end of 1942, only 866 internees had relocated, mostly Nisei college students and young adults with ambition and without familial responsibilities.[32] In the fall and winter of 1942, the WRA debated segregating the camp population by class—"Kibei, aliens, old bachelors, parolees, repatriates . . . although few people could agree on the same set of categories." Some within the WRA, including Eisenhower, argued that categorical segregation was inherently unjust and advocated for individual examination. The War Department's loyalty questionnaire addressed this concern, providing the WRA with "a basis for forming judgments as to an individual person's loyalty that may be reasonably sound."[33]

Registration, as it was called, was compulsory. The questionnaire comprised some eighty questions about religious affiliation, educational and occupational background, and the like. Many questions concerned cultural knowledge and practices, evincing the WRA's use of culture as an index of loyalty; for example, "Will you conform to the customs and dress of your new home?" "Do you think you are 'losing face' by cooperating with the U.S. government?" and "Do you believe in the divine origin of the Japanese race?"

The most incendiary questions were question 27, asked of all males of military age, "Are you willing to serve in the armed forces of the United States on combat duty, wherever ordered?" and question 28, asked of all adult internees, "Will you swear unqualified allegiance to the United States of America and faithfully defend the United States from any or all attack by foreign or domestic forces, and forswear any form of allegiance or obedience to the Japanese emperor, or any other foreign government, power or organization?"[34]

The registration program provoked widespread confusion, resentment, and opposition. Not without reason, internees believed they would be forced or pressured to relocate to unfamiliar and hostile areas, without means and without their sons, whom many believed would now be drafted. Answering "yes" to question 28 would have made the Issei, who were barred from American citizenship, stateless people. Moreover, expressing disloyalty to their country of birth connoted a lack of personal integrity. An Issei explained, "No Issei would disobey the laws of the United States. . . . In that sense they can be called loyal to the United States. On the other hand, none of them are disloyal to Japan."[35]

In every relocation center there were mass meetings, some of them "extremely turbulent," where internees debated and argued over what to do. Family relations were also strained. Some Issei pressured their children to answer "no" in order to keep the family together or to keep their sons out of the military. Other Nisei militantly refused to register, contrary to their parents' wishes. Yamato Ichihashi noted that "the young people are very serious this time, and do not yield very easily. . . . Their parents are worried over the twenty year sentences" that they risked for refusing to register.[36]

In all, 87 percent of the eligible internees gave an unqualified "yes" answer to the loyalty questions. Those who answered "yes" represented a range of motivation and belief. While many undoubtedly welcomed the opportunity to state their loyalty to the United States, others trod the path of least resistance and hoped that a "yes" answer would shield them from further accusations of disloyalty.[37]

Thirteen percent either refused to register or answered "no" to one or both questions. Fully 20 percent of Nisei males answered "no." Refusal to register or "no" answers were highest at Tule Lake (42 percent) and at Manzanar and Jerome (26 percent each). Even among Nisei who answered "yes," there was widespread opposition to the combat team. The War Department had hoped for five thousand volunteers, but fewer than twelve hundred signed up. By contrast, more than three thousand internees applied for repatriation or expatriation to Japan during the registration period.[38]

The low rate of resettlement after the registration also disappointed the WRA. Over the next two years barely one-third of the total camp population (36,000) left the camps for cities in the Midwest and East, despite the WRA's aggressive campaign to promote resettlement through incentives that were both positive (job recruiters and "welfare counselors") and negative (making life in camp less comfortable).[39] The other two-thirds remained in the camps until the end of the war, either segregated at Tule Lake as "disloyal" (18,000 who answered "no" to the loyalty questions or requested repatriation to Japan) or through passive resistance to resettlement (62,000).[40]

"THE SALVAGE"—ASSIMILATION'S SUCCESS?

Berkeley sociologist Dorothy Swaine Thomas called these three groups "salvage," "spoilage," and "residue," respectively. During the war Thomas conducted the Japanese American Evacuation and Resettlement Study (JERS), collaborating with sociologists Frank Nishimoto and Charles Kikuchi and Nisei graduate students—all interned in the camps—as field researchers.[41] JERS offered a sociological portrait of the "salvage," "spoilage," and "residue" according to criteria that it believed indexed assimilation. Accordingly, male Buddhist Kibei from agricultural backgrounds had the highest incidence of "spoilage" (78.9 percent), whereas female Christian Nisei from nonagricultural backgrounds had the lowest (1.1 percent). The "salvage" included a preponderance of college-educated, urban Nisei either Christian or secular.[42]

Whereas Thomas viewed the "spoilage" as tragedy, she saw in the "salvage" a hopeful future for the Nikkei. Presumptively loyal (only those who answered "yes" qualified for leave clearance) and already highly assimilated, the resettlers were pioneers of a sort. They assumed the "same burdens" as other Americans living and working on the home front. They also bore "special risks and uncertainties inherent in their close physical resemblance to the Japanese enemy." Their reward would be a "range of contacts and career possibilities" that were denied to Japanese in prewar California. More broadly, the project promised a new kind of race relations that was predicated on an end to racial prejudice and discrimination through ethnic dispersal and effacement. Some resettlers embraced this idea. A "restaurant keeper" who left Minidoka for Chicago did not want to see a Japanese community form there: "[T]hat would ruin the whole resettlement program," he said. If the Nisei "can lose themselves, they may be taken as individuals . . . and find a place in American society."[43]

This view, of course, rehearsed the intentions expressed in the WRA's original strategy to Americanize the Nikkei by cleansing them of their Japaneseness. Thomas was highly critical of the WRA's management of the camps, which she believed resulted in the high rate of "spoilage." She also understood that many who were segregated as "disloyal" were not really disloyal but were embittered, confused, or trying to avoid resettlement or family separation. Nevertheless, Thomas's sociological portrait, which correlated assimilation with social type (occupation, religion, education), gave statistical authority to the ideological premises of the WRA's benevolent assimilation.

The aggregated statistics, however, obscured many subtleties in the internment experience. There is a curious dissonance between the sociological generalizations presented in the first part of Thomas's *Salvage* (1952) and the fifteen "life experience" narratives that follow in the second part. Thomas selected the narratives from more than sixty interviews with resettlers, which were conducted by Charles Kikuchi in Chicago in 1944–45. Kikuchi interviewed Nisei from diverse backgrounds (urban and rural, Buddhist and Christian, college-educated and not), so they do not comprise a sample consistent with the statistical claim that most resettlers were highly assimilated, urban, Christian, and college-educated Nisei.

Interestingly, however, the narratives reveal other lines of commonality among the resettlers that might be understood as psychic, rather than sociological. Consider the reasons they gave for wanting to leave camp. Only a few chose resettlement for strategic purposes. For example, a "countergirl" explained that she and her husband believed "there would be a grand rush to leave the camp after the war and we wouldn't have so much chance if we did not go earlier." The young couple, who had gotten married on the eve of the evacuation and had their first child in Gila, "wanted to save some money before the war [was] over."[44]

Most, however, seem to have resettled because they found being in camp unbearable. Some found camp life boring, an utter "waste of time."[45] But most describe being deeply depressed. The reasons were manifold—loss of their homes and property, violation of their rights as citizens, the dust and desolation of camp. "I just existed," said one. Some young Nisei men joined gangs, gambled at cards, and chased girls, but then sought greater escape.[46]

The political conflicts among the Nikkei, especially during the registration, also angered and depressed these resettlers. Nearly all described themselves as having been apolitical before the war. Yet, even as they criticized the Issei and Kibei "agitators," they expressed their own ambivalence about the war and about the choices that were forced upon them. "Civil servant," an employee of the state of California who was fired from his job after Pearl Harbor, considered himself "pro-U.S." but said he understood why the Issei were pro-Japan. He conceded that he wanted Japan "to make a good showing in the war, but not win." The agitation led him to "withdraw into my private life and do as little as possible for the community. . . . We [he and his wife] were anxious to get out as soon as possible."[47]

A Nisei "errand-boy" joined a gang that "cussed the government" but also fought with the Kibei, whom he considered "too damn fresh." His sentiments are hard to capture without quoting him at length:

> I never thought about the war very much so I didn't have too many arguments about this with them [Kibei]. I kept up with Japan's conquests and I thought it wouldn't last long. Hell, I didn't care because we were discriminated against anyway. I couldn't bother about these things as I was having more fun anyway. To tell the real truth, I did not give a damn who won the war, but I hoped that it would be over quick. At times I thought that Japan would win and I thought of going back to the old country. I didn't think I could get a good job here afterwards. I thought we'd all get shoved around and we would never be treated right again. But then, I figured what the hell, I could go back to Japan any time and I wanted to stick around the U.S. for a while to see how things turned out. I felt pretty close to the people in camp, except for the Kibei. They were too much for Japan, and they talked too much against everything American, even though I felt the same way as them

at times. Maybe it was the way they said these things that griped me. They didn't even know how to speak English. . . .

I registered in camp in February 1943, and I just wrote down what they told me to. Afterwards I wondered whatta hell I was answering Yes-Yes for. The older folks reacted in a different way. They didn't want us Nisei to be in a combat unit. They said we would all get stuck in the front line and get killed off like pigs. . . . We used to argue about it in our gang and nobody knew what to believe. I had no intention of volunteering. I felt that they would have had to come and get me if they wanted me for the Army. We forgot about this right away and went on playing poker. I did not pay any more attention to all the yelling about registration that was going on.[48]

"Errand boy" had drifted from one menial job to another before the war, and during the internment he did the same thing: he signed up for seasonal leaves to work in the sugar beet fields (to escape the dust storms at Topaz) and then moved from Salt Lake City and small towns in Utah to Idaho, working in coal mines, at a peach ranch, a "Jap noodle shop," and other jobs. He finally relocated to Chicago in January 1944 and, after a series of job failures, settled into a position as a welder in a factory. He said,

I just know it's going to be hard for the Nisei after the war no matter who wins. We will all be in the same boat. . . . I still don't think much of the war yet. I never read the newspapers and I don't like to listen to the war news over the radio. I worry more about myself and what is going to become of us. . . . I think I have reformed a little out here. . . . Back in camp, I had a zoot suit but I don't wear it anymore. . . . I don't know if I'm better off now than I was before the evacuation. I think that maybe I am. . . . [I]f I was back in Frisco, I'd probably be an errand boy yet. Now I can say that I am a welder. . . . I got a trade now so I got some chance for after the war.[49]

Strictly speaking, "errand boy" fit the sociological profile of the "salvage"—he was urban (he grew up in San Francisco), he had some college education (he dropped out of junior college after one year), and he was not religious (although his parents were Buddhist). Resettlement enabled him to develop some ambition and with it, some hope. "Errand boy's" story, however, does not read as that of an assimilating subject, at least not insofar as assimilation implies affective and political attachment to the host society, in addition to socioeconomic incorporation. As with many Nikkei, "errand boy's" attachments and loyalties were mixed, pulled in different directions, and often sublimated. Under the duress of internment, these conflicting impulses were often difficult to bear. Some became 100 percent super-American patriots; others renounced their American citizenship and repatriated to Japan. The majority, however, struggled to survive as "hyphenated" ethnic Americans—as Japanese Americans—with attenuated attachments to both nations and both cultures. This characterized the majority of Nikkei, whether "spoilage," "salvage," or "residue."

During the 1940s, a new trend of racial liberalism emerged in American politics and social science that stressed equal citizenship based on civil rights, assimilation, and integration. It was continuous with older forms of liberal and cultural pluralism, dating from the Progressive Era through the Chicago school of sociology in the interwar period, which assumed that "backward" minority cultures were rooted in agricultural and rural life and would be overcome in the milieu of the modern city, in its neighborhoods, factories, and schools. Although it may seem odd that Thomas's analysis was based on a model in which "residue" was the analytical category for more than half the data, in fact her interpretation resonated with and reproduced the dominant sociological theory of immigrant assimilation as normative and inevitable.

At the same time, the racial liberalism of World War II and the postwar years exhibited new features, notably a vision of an activist role for the federal government and an emphasis on cultivating ethnically and racially unmarked citizen-subjects.[50] It urged white Americans to be tolerant and accepting of minority groups but also demanded that the latter behave according to the cultural and ideological norms of mainstream white society. These concepts, which would become prominent in the civil rights era, had an early rehearsal in the Japanese American internment and resettlement.[51]

NOTES

1. I use the term "Japanese American" to refer to all persons of Japanese ancestry in the United States regardless of their generational or citizenship status. The ethnoracial community of Japanese in America (Nikkei) comprised the Issei (first generation immigrants), who were legally barred from naturalized citizenship, and the Nisei (second generation), born in the United States and birthright citizens. Some 15 percent of the Nisei were Kibei-Nisei, Nisei who had been sent to Japan for schooling and then returned to the United States as young adults. There were very few Sansei (third generation) at the time of the war. On the racial ineligibility of Asians to become naturalized citizens, see Mae M. Ngai, *Impossible Subjects: Illegal Aliens and the Making of Modern America* (Princeton, 2004), chap. 1.

2. In Hawaii the government imposed martial law but did not evacuate Japanese Americans owing to the large size of the Japanese American population and its centrality to the local labor force. However it sent 1,875 "dangerous" Japanese aliens and citizens to Department of Justice and WRA camps on the mainland. Report of the [U.S.] Commission on Wartime Evacuation and Relocation of Civilians, *Personal Justice Denied: Report of the Commission on Wartime Relocation and Internment of Civilians: Report for the Committee on Interior and Insular Affairs* (Washington, D.C., 1983; reprint, Seattle, 1997), 268–77.

3. In fact, as with all race classifications, it was not so easy to determine who was a person of "Japanese ancestry." A Catholic priest who ran an orphanage in Los Angeles inquired which children he should send—for he had under his charge some who were "half Japanese, others one-fourth or less"—and was told by Colonel Karl Bendesten, "if they have one drop of Japanese blood in them, they must go to camp." Father Hugh Lavery quoted by Michi Weglyn, *Years of Infamy: The Untold Story of America's Concentration Camps* (New York, 1976), 76–77.

4. Warren testimony at House Select Committee Investigating National Defense Migration hearings (Tolan Committee), quoted by David O'Brien and Stephen Fugita, *The Japanese American Experience* (Bloomington, 1991), 47.

5. *Personal Justice Denied*, 6, 85–88. In fact, the Office of Naval Intelligence had concluded categorically in October 1941 that both Issei and Nisei were loyal to America. The ONI report was circulated at the highest levels of government and was seen by President Roosevelt in November 1941. Weglyn, *Years of Infamy*, 40–44. See also Greg Robinson, *By Order of the President: FDR and the Internment of Japanese Americans* (Cambridge, Mass., 2001).

6. Frederick C. Luebke, *Bonds of Loyalty: German-Americans and World War I* (DeKalb, Ill., 1971).

7. Richard Drinnon, *Keeper of the Concentration Camps: Dillon S. Myer and American Racism* (Berkeley, 1987).

8. Orin Starn, "Engineering Internment: Anthropologists and the War Relocation Authority," *American Ethnologist* 21 (1986): 709, 715. On camps as "community building" projects, see Dorothy Swaine Thomas and Thomas Nishimoto, *The Spoilage*, vol. 3 of *Japanese American Evacuation and Resettlement* (Berkeley, 1974), 57, and John Provinse and Solon Kimball, "Building New Communities during War Time," *American Sociological Review* 11:4 (August 1946): 396–409. On liberalism and the internment, see also Gordon H. Chang, "'Superman Is about to Visit the Relocation Centers' and the Limits of Wartime Liberalism," *Amerasia Journal* 19:1 (1993): 37–60; Colleen Lye, "Model Modernity: The Making of Asiatic Racial Form, 1882–1945" (PhD diss., Columbia University, 1999), 280–81.

9. Provinse and Kimball, "Building New Communities," 399; Thomas and Nishimoto, *The Spoilage*, 25–26, 33.

10. Stonequest quoted by Starn, "Engineering Internment," 715.

11. Carey McWilliams, "Moving the West-Coast Japanese," *Harpers* (September 1942): 359–69, cited in Lye, "Model Modernity," 281. See also McWilliams, "Japanese American Evacuation: Policy and Perspectives," *Common Ground* (August 1942).

12. Ansel Adams, *Born Free and Equal: Photographs of Japanese Americans at Manzanar Relocation Center, Inyo County, California* (New York, 1944), 24, 84, 103; McWilliams quoted at 51. The book was published with the approval of the WRA and included a preface by secretary of the interior Harold Ickes.

13. Ibid, 9.

14. In fact, WRA officials included the former superintendent of the Navajo Indian reservation and the head of the Navajo school system. See Thomas James, *Exile Within: The Schooling of Japanese Americans, 1942–45* (Cambridge, Mass., 1987), 36–38; Raymond Okamura, "'The Great White Father': Dillon Myer and Internal Colonialism," *Amerasia Journal* 13:2 (1986–87): 155–60.

15. Indeed, the same duality of violence and paternalism continued to mark the United States' engagement with non-European nations and peoples in the twentieth century, even in the contexts of national self-determination following World War I and decolonization in the post–World War II era. See for example, Mary Renda, *Taking Haiti: Military Occupation and the Culture of U.S. Imperialism* (Chapel Hill, 2001); Mark Bradley, *Imagining Vietnam and America: The Making of Post-Colonial Vietnam* (Chapel Hill, 2000).

16. James Sakoda, "'The Residue': The Unresettled Minidokans, 1943–1945," in *Views from Within: The Japanese American Evacuation and Resettlement Study*, ed. Yuji Ichioka, 249 (Los Angeles, 1989).

17. *Rabbit in the Moon*, dir. Emiko Omori (Public Broadcasting System, 1999).

18. Thomas and Nishimoto, *The Spoilage*, 33, 35; Gordon H. Chang, ed., *Morning Glory, Evening Shadow: Yamato Ichihashi and His Internment Writings* (Stanford, 1997) (hereafter Ichihashi diary), 215–16.

19. James, *Exile Within*, 36–37.

20. Thomas and Nishimoto, *The Spoilage*, 37; James, *Exile Within*, 40, 88–89.

21. Thomas and Nishimoto, *The Spoilage*, 37; "Issei, Nisei, Kibei," *Fortune*, vol. 24 (April 1944), 78.

22. Ibid, 41; James, *Exile Within*, 104.

23. James, *Exile Within*, 104; Dorothy Swaine Thomas, *The Salvage*, vol. 2 of *Japanese American Evacuation and Resettlement* (Berkeley, 1952), 19; Provinse and Kimball, "Building New Communities," 406.

24. Thomas and Nishimoto, *The Spoilage*, 44–45; Provinse and Kimball, "Building New Communities," 407; Thomas, *The Salvage*, 79, 443.

25. Thomas, *The Salvage*, 173; Arthur A. Hansen and David A. Hacker, "The Manzanar Riot: An Ethnic Perspective," *Amerasia Journal* 2 (Fall 1974): 112–57, esp. 133–34; Lon Kurashige, *Japanese American Celebration and Conflict: Ethnicity and Festival in Los Angeles, 1934–1990* (Berkeley, 2001), 75–118.

26. For firsthand accounts of camp life, see Ichihashi diary; Mine Okubo, *Citizen 10366* (New York, 1946); Takeo Kaneshiro, ed., *Internees: War Relocation Memoirs and Diaries* (New York, 1976); John Modell, ed., *The Kikuchi Diary: Chronicle from an American Concentration Camp: The Tanforan Journals of Charles Kikuchi* (Urbana, 1973). There are many published personal accounts of the internment but these are among the few that are contemporaneous; most are memoirs written after the war. See, for example, Yoshiko Uchida, *Desert Exile: The Uprooting of a Japanese American Family* (Seattle, 1982); Minoru Kiyota, *Beyond Loyalty: The Story of a Kibei* (Seattle, 1997).

27. Ichihashi diary, 202; "Diary and Memoir of Takeo Kaneshiro" 38, 47, 49, 54, 73, 78, 80; "Diary of Kasen Noda," 12, 15, 17, both in Kaneshiro, ed., *Internees*; Summary of Monthly Reports [Tule Lake]," December 1944, Japanese American Evacuation and Resettlement Study Papers, Bancroft Library, University of California, Berkeley (hereafter JERS), microfilm reel 161, frame 448. Kaneshiro ("Diary and Memoir," 71, 79–80) describes "boiler room conferences" of Issei men that took place daily in his block. See also Ichihashi diary, 188–93.

28. John Embree, "Resistance to Freedom: An Administrative Problem," *Applied Anthropology* 2:4 (1943): 14; Thomas and Nishimoto, *The Spoilage*, 184–220; Sakoda, "The Residue," 254.

29. *Personal Justice Denied*, 187. Two thousand Nisei serving in two infantry units in Hawaii were not discharged but put in a segregated unit, even though they had defended Pearl Harbor. The segregated unit, the 100 Infantry Battalion, was transferred to mainland bases and eventually sent to fight in North Africa and Italy. Ibid, 187, 265.

30. Weglyn, *Years of Infamy*, 140; *Personal Justice Denied*, 187–88.

31. *Personal Justice Denied*, 189–90; Scobey quoted in Muller, *Free to Die for Their Country*, 55.

32. *Personal Justice Denied*, 190–91; Thomas, *The Salvage*, 615.

33. Memo from Director WRA to Secretary of War, March 12, 1943, cited in [Morton Grodzins], "Segregation: Development of the Policy," [October 1943], JERS 93/160, 164. Not only did the WRA conflate assimilation and loyalty but Mike Masaoka of the JACL recommended that the WRA should segregate "Kibei who had studied in Japan five or more years, all or part of that time falling after 1930 or all or part experienced after the age of 12." Ibid, 93/160.

34. Questions 27 and 28, Thomas and Nishimoto, *The Spoilage*, 57–58; the rest of the questionnaire is reprinted in Weglyn, *Years of Infamy*, 196–99.

35. Thomas and Nishimoto, *The Spoilage*, 65–71, 100–101, quote at 100.

36. Ichihashi diary, 190. The Espionage Act made it a felony to interfere with military recruitment or induction, punishable by up to twenty years in prison and a ten thousand dollar fine.

37. Kurashige, *Japanese American Celebration and Conflict*, 104. (Issei "yes" answers improved when WRA reworded question 28: "Will you swear to abide by the laws of the United States and to take no action which would in any way interfere with the war effort of the United States?")

38. *Personal Justice Denied*, 195–97, 203. By contrast, in Hawaii some ten thousand Nisei volunteered for service. Ibid, 197.

39. Thomas and Nishimoto, *The Spoilage*, 61; Thomas, *The Salvage*, 111–12; Sakoda "The Residue," 262.

40. Thomas, *The Salvage*, 115.

41. For more on the work of Nisei social scientists as native informants for JERS see *Views from Within*; Henry Yu, *Thinking Orientals* (New York, 2000).

42. Thomas, *The Salvage*, 102, 124–25.

43. Ibid, 106; interview with restaurant keeper, 340; see also interview with mechanic, 360. The descriptors refer to the individual's occupation at the time of the evacuation. Resettlement agencies soon realized that prohibiting ethnic congregation made adjustment much more difficult and bred other social problems. For more on resettlement see Charlotte Brooks, "In the Twilight Zone between Black and White: Japanese American Resettlement and Community in Chicago, 1942–1945," *Journal of American History* 86:4 (March 2000): 1655–87; Ellen D. Wu, "Zoot Suiting, Swing Dancing, and Ball Playing: Nisei Leisure and Citizenship, 1943–53" (typescript, 2000, in author's possession); Meredith A. Oda, "Interpreting Assimilation: The Chicago Resettlers Committee and Nikkei Resettlement in Chicago, 1945–1954" (typescript, 2002, in author's possession).

44. Thomas, *The Salvage*, interview with counter-girl, 379.

45. Ibid, interview with music teacher, 497.

46. Ibid, interview with mechanic, 352; interview with agricultural student, 198.

47. Ibid, interview with civil servant, 557, 560.

48. Ibid, interview with errand boy, 277, 281.

49. Ibid, 289–90, 297.

50. Indeed, the internment narrative departed from Robert E. Park's foundational theory of the "race relations cycle" in this respect. Contrasted with Park's view that assimilation was an organic process, the Nikkei achieved assimilation only through state-sponsored internment and rehabilitation. See Robert Ezra Park, *Race and Culture* (New York, 1950), 149–50.

51. On racial liberalism, see Nikhil Pal Singh, *Black Is a Country: Race and the Unfinished Struggle for Democracy* (Cambridge, Mass., 2004); Mary Dudziak, *Cold War Civil Rights* (Princeton, 1999); Matthew Jacobson, *Whiteness of a Different Color* (Cambridge, Mass., 1999).

Chapter Twelve

• • • • • • • • • •

Student Protest, "Law and Order," and the Origins of African American Studies in California

MARTHA BIONDI

Student participation in the civil rights movement is usually associated with the lunch counter sit-ins of 1960 and with the subsequent campaigns of the Student Nonviolent Coordinating Committee (SNCC) in Mississippi and Alabama. But the student component of the black liberation movement actually grew much later in the decade. By the late 1960s, SNCC veterans, along with newly established black student unions, had built a student movement across the nation that was pushing open the doors of elite white universities, transforming black colleges, and insisting on the right of the urban working class to obtain a free or very low cost college education. Political activity in the black power era is typically located on the urban streetscape: Malcolm X's rallies outdoors in Harlem, the urban uprisings summer after summer, Black Panther street patrols, gun battles with police. And the archetypical protagonist of the black power era is the defiant black militant with signature black sunglasses, beret, and assault weapon. While there is certainly much truth to these images, they have tended to obscure the importance of the college campus as an arena of struggle for African American radicals. Here we find not only the neglected intellectualism of the black liberation movement but also a generation of black students who took bold steps to redesign structures of opportunity that would be pivotal in expanding the black middle class. To be sure, student activists also used the rhetoric of revolution and engaged in confrontational tactics, and this radicalism has likely helped to obscure the legacy of their activism.

Organized protest by black students in the late 1960s—sit-ins, strikes, building takeovers, and rallies—occurred on literally hundreds of campuses, public, private, northern, southern, eastern, western, black, and white. On white campuses, students protested the lack of black faculty, administrators, coaches, and staff; the absence of courses that addressed African American politics, culture, and history; the small number of black students; and the lack of multicultural services or programming on campus. Before 1968 it was rare for a four-year college or university to have more than 1 percent black students. After the assassination of Martin Luther King in April 1968, black student protest escalated. Coming on the heels of four summers of serious urban insurrection, universities were in a mood to make concessions, and the most common ones they made were pledges to create black studies programs and to implement affirmative action in admission. Lost in the media coverage of black power, the desegregation and democratization of American higher education was arguably the most significant breakthrough of the era. While African American studies has existed since the nineteenth century as a subject of scholarly interest, before 1969 there were no black studies departments or programs. Within five years, there were about 250.[1]

This generation of black student activists saw themselves as "Malcolm's children." Influenced by the black nationalist idea that previous generations of college-educated "Negroes" had sold out their people for the perks of integration, these young men and women set out to remake the black collegiate experience. They envisioned college not only as a route to individual upward mobility but also as a place to acquire useful skills they could "bring back" to the black community. Since an ethos of community service and racial uplift is in fact deeply rooted in the historical formation of the African American middle class, this generation's self-fashioning is better understood as marking a rejection of the antiradical, conformist pressures of the Cold War era as well as individualist, or conservative, renderings of the civil rights movement. This formative moment of social commitment had profound consequences. However one judges the extent to which the black student movement changed society or higher education, the movement indisputably changed the lives of its participants. Nearly forty years later, many of the leading student activists of this era remain deeply committed to an ideal of civic engagement. For them, the responsibility to stay engaged in a struggle for social justice is a lifelong commitment. And whether they have chosen law, medicine, higher education, the ministry, or some other profession, their desire to serve black communities has shaped their entire adult lives.[2]

There were important regional differences in the black student movement of the late 1960s. The extensive system of urban public higher education put California campuses in the vanguard of this struggle. Many of the protests were initiated and led by black students but came to have a multiracial following—and ethnic or third world studies was added to the list of demands. Moreover, the Black Panther Party gave California activism a particular character. But in addition to an active and visible left, California had a powerful and influential right. They were people in high office, including the governor, and, for the purposes of this story, the mayor and district attorney of Los Angeles. Conservative leaders made astute use of the (white) public's antipathy for student protesters. Many self-described California "taxpayers" recoiled at the intemperate language, the bold critique of authority, indeed, the direct challenge to their own values and belief systems. Elected officials made student activism, and black student activism in particular, the pivot for a politics of "law and order" and racial resentment. In the gubernatorial campaign of 1966 Ronald Reagan had skillfully and successfully mobilized public anxiety about the Watts riot and white radicals at Berkeley. The black student movement appeared to fuse these insurgencies, and while some college administrators were trying to manage and interpret student discontent, conservative politicians eagerly rushed to condemn it. African American student activists faced considerably harsher sanctions than their Euro-American counterparts. Governors, mayors, state legislatures, local police forces, and the U.S. Congress joined forces to stop the student rebellions and punish the participants. Black student unions became a target of COINTELPRO (Counter Intelligence Program) and other federal counterinsurgency programs. Ironically, this legal crackdown and public ridicule of protesters occurred at the same time that progressive reforms were actually being won on many college campuses. This paradoxical conjuncture of victory and defeat, and the negative portrayal of many black student activists by the media and elected officials, has blocked a fuller appreciation of the innovations and successes of the black student movement. This essay examines the student movement at San Fernando Valley State College in Northridge, California. (It is now called California State University at Northridge.) That protest produced many significant reforms, but in the short term the students were assailed by the state leaders and indicted on seventy felony charges.

Bill Burwell was one of about 23 black students when he entered Valley State in the fall of 1967. "The thing I felt more than anything else," he recalled of the campus of 18,500 whites in an affluent Los Angeles suburb, "was a sense of isolation." Extracurricular activities—plays, concerts, and other performances were designed for white students; the curriculum ignored black history and culture; and the professors, counselors, coaches, and other adult supervisors were virtually all white. The twenty-four-year-old Burwell was already a seasoned activist. He led a black nationalist organization called Afro-Pac in his nearby hometown, Pacoima. That fall Burwell and fellow students Jerome Walker, Genie Washington, and Archie Lee Chatman formed a black students union—BSUs were the principal vehicle of black student activism in the nation during the 1960s and 1970s. At Valley State, the tiny BSU lobbied the administration to introduce courses in black literature and history and to increase the numbers of African American students. Archie Lee Chatman, a student-athlete from a poor family, was a transfer from Los Angeles City College in 1967. Chatman soon quit the Valley State football team and became a vocal critic of the exploitation of black student-athletes. According to his friend Les Johns, Chatman "had an enlarged photograph in his dormitory room. It was taken at a football game, and Archie had his arms around this white boy's neck. Underneath the picture he had an inscription, `My name is Archie Chatman. I don't answer to "boy" and I don't eat watermelon.'"[3]

Ever since the creation of the master plan for education in 1960, California had implemented a "tracking" system in its three tiers of public higher education that offered affordable higher education for every high school graduate, but black students were overwhelmingly relegated to junior colleges, the lower rung. The eighteen California state colleges had a policy that 2 percent of students admitted did not have to meet its admissions standards. This was traditionally applied to students with special skills, such as musicians and athletes, but it also included students, labeled as "culturally

disadvantaged," who had the talent to succeed in college but had been deprived of an adequate secondary education. After the April 1968 assassination of Dr. Martin Luther King Jr., the board of trustees doubled the quota
to 4 percent and promoted it as a way to increase the numbers of African
American and Mexican American students. Governor Ronald Reagan's immediate criticism of this extremely modest affirmative action policy threatened its success from the start. Voicing a core tenet of southern segregation-
ists and northern conservatives, the governor questioned the intellectual
capacity of people of color. "We have more than 80 community colleges
in this state, and this is the place where these students should be admitted.
There is a danger in putting them into the state colleges. There's a high
likelihood of failure in this, with the most noble of intentions, may result in
a very real psychological crippling."[4]

In the fall of 1968, 223 black students entered Valley State. Most hailed
from poor or working-class families. Eddie Dancer grew up in Texas,
where he missed schooldays to pick cotton. He came to Valley State on a
basketball scholarship but Chatman soon talked him out of playing sports.
"He told me I was making a mistake, that most black brothers came to white
schools with illusions of being great stars, then get exploited for their abili-
ties while the school makes money and gains prestige, and then the school
lets the brother out on his own and he doesn't have the academic training he
needs to make it in the world."[5] The new Educational Opportunities Program (EOP) offered an alternative means of financing his education. As on
other campuses, the students' political views were diverse but were strongly
influenced by the rising cultural nationalism in the Los Angeles area. Robert
Lewis first encountered Maulana Karenga and the US organization in 1965
while a student at San Fernando Valley High School in Pacoima. "They
had tight discipline," Lewis remembered. "They came to Pacoima, and they
were uniformly dressed in bubas and walked in formation. I was impressed
by this." He was also drawn to Karenga. He seemed "invulnerable." "I had
never heard anybody talk like that against the white man, and the symbols
of white culture—like Christianity—and get away with it."[6]

Lewis said that he joined US after he and two friends, high on marijuana
and alcohol, were in a car accident on the way to a pro baseball tryout in San
Diego. He quit smoking and drinking, took the name Uwezo, which means
"power" in Swahili, and began studying Swahili and karate. He shortly left
US and founded his own group in Pacoima called House of Umoja.[7] But he

said the police harassed him and pressured local black businesses to cease supporting him, so he closed the House of Umoja and went to college in 1968. Although Lewis's narrative of rejecting drugs and finding purpose in an organization with a strict moral code and discipline is usually thought to apply to former convicts or high school dropouts, he was raised in a middle-class family. His parents had the kind of unionized working-class jobs that brought middle-class lifestyles—his father worked for the post office and his mother was employed at an airplane factory. Like so many students who hailed from middle-class backgrounds and were drawn to black nationalist ideas, Lewis saw himself as forging a new racial identity that eschewed the assimilationist tendencies that—he claimed—had characterized his parents' generation.[8]

African American student activists of the late 1960s have generally been portrayed as having more pragmatic goals than white student activists, particularly those in SDS (Students for a Democratic Society) who were seeking a revolutionary transformation of society. As Robert Lewis told *Life* magazine, "Listen, we've got a thing going. We're gonna get an education and take it home to our people. Don't give me any of that crap about revolution for revolution's sake." Still, this reform versus revolution dichotomy may not be the best way to understand the black student movement. Lewis's statement, for example, shows the influence of thinkers who saw Afro-America as a colony. The goal of getting an education and taking it "home to our people" was part of the rejection of integration—and of individualism; it was a call to the black middle class to use their skills and resources to serve "the people." To nationalists, the civil rights movement was encouraging assimilation into a white dominated culture. Their vision was for the college-trained not to "leave behind" the colony/ghetto for personal advancement but to devote themselves to its transformation and empowerment. In an emblematic exchange, an African American female student occupying a building at Brandeis University in January 1969 was pressed by a white female student to explain why the demand for Afro-American studies was not simply another form of integration. Their goal, she replied, was to create a new black middle class that would be oriented toward helping the masses of the people. A "relevant" education was absolutely vital to this process of identity transformation. The students at Brandeis, as at most other campuses where such protest occurred, envisioned that an Afro-American studies department, controlled by black people, would "instill the values that we need" to carry out this mission.[9]

During the 1968–69 academic year black students on many campuses turned to confrontational tactics to pressure the administration to implement their demands, but these confrontations always had a history of negotiation between students and administrators. San Francisco State gained attention as the first college to formally commit to a black studies department for the fall of 1968, although Yale, in the winter of 1969, seems to have been the first to actually implement a black studies program. San Francisco State stayed in the national media spotlight for most of the academic year after black and third world students launched a student strike on November 6, 1968, that led to repeated campus closures, police occupation, mass arrests, a faculty walkout, and the resignation of the president, before a settlement was finally reached in March. While every campus had its own political dynamics, student leaders strove to create solidarity networks across campuses. Archie Chatman visited San Francisco and Berkeley and spoke to activists at various Los Angeles campuses, while activists from San Francisco State attended rallies at Valley State. "We were caught up in the spirit of that time," Chatman recounted in an interview two years later. "The black students on campus were ready—like all other black people—and this spirit of being ready to take whatever means were necessary to change our plight was infectious. It spread from city to city, from campus to campus."[10]

The catalyst for the Valley State protest was racism in the athletic department, an extremely common source of campus racial conflict in this era. There were an estimated thirty-seven protests by black student-athletes in 1968 alone, and California launched what Harry Edwards called "the revolt of the Black athlete." Edwards helped ignite the sports struggle in 1967 at San Jose State College, where student athletes caused the cancellation of the opening day football game. This set in motion a series of protests that culminated with the black power salute by San Jose State students Tommie Smith and John Carlos on the medal podium at the Mexico City Olympics in the fall of 1968.[11]

On October 18, 1968, when a scuffle broke out during a football game at Valley State, George Boswell, an African American freshman, ran onto the field to help his teammates. The white assistant coach, who happened to be an off-duty police officer, ordered him to run off the field. Boswell walked off instead. The coach went after him. "He grabbed me around the neck, turned me around, and kicked me in the groin," Boswell later testified in court. During the preceding several months, the BSU had accused officials

in the athletic department of using racial slurs and practicing racial discrimination in athletic assignments and financial support of players. The twenty
or so BSU members at the game that day organized quickly to demand the
dismissal of the coach, Don Markham. On November 4, a group of students
waited in the hallway while Chatman, Eddie Dancer, and Robert Lewis met
with the athletic director. Running through subsequent white testimony
about the events of this day is the premise that a group of black youth, who
had banded together and were angry or determined, constituted a threat of
violence. A white administrator said that the sight of BSU members standing in the lobby wearing T-shirts saying By Any Means Necessary "scared
the hell out of everyone there." When the athletic director said only the
president had the power to fire the coach (who was actually a volunteer),
the students decided to go to the Administration Building and find the president. Their walk across campus, with twenty-five BSU members surrounding the head football coach and two administrators, would later be cited as
felonious false imprisonment.[12]

The emboldened students decided to occupy a floor of the building. "We
took over the fifth floor," Art Jones recalled. "We moved all of the staff
into one room. The young brothers were running up and down the halls
just letting off steam, waiting for Archie and the others to work out the
plan on how to fire Markham. The sisters were in the room watching the
staff." Seizing the opportunity to address racial conditions on campus more
fully, BSU leaders quickly formulated a list of demands. As it happened,
the "veteran" student activist Bill Burwell was in Pacoima on November 4,
so leadership mostly fell to Archie Chatman. "It was an excellent opportunity," he said later; "the administration wasn't in a position to procrastinate,
they had to deal with the problems then. So we worked up a list of twelve
demands." The students went well beyond athletic grievances and pushed
for a broad transformation of the college. "We realized," Chatman said,
"that—black studies, [a] large black student populace, black faculty, and [a]
black tutorial program—were needed if we were going to develop a body
of black intellectuals—not Negro intellectuals—at Valley State, who would
become a positive force in the black community." Many student-activists
of this era held similar ideas about the mission of collegiate desegregation:
that it should not unleash a brain drain but should train and inspire African
Americans to serve their own communities. In the meantime, BSU members
began to more or less "guard" thirty-four workers on the floor—holding

them hostage the state would contend, although the students did not have weapons or make verbal threats. The only physical confrontation occurred when Eddie Dancer pushed or kicked Vice President Harold Spencer after Spencer defended Markham's physical attack on George Boswell. Workers said they were "subjected to lectures on how the white people were responsible for the Negro's condition." Lewis told a secretary who asked how long the protest would last, that "we've been waiting for 400 years" so surely she could wait a little longer.[13]

The president at first agreed to sign their demands along with a pledge not to prosecute them. He agreed to dismiss the coach, set up a black studies department, admit five hundred black students each semester, and hire more black faculty. The whole protest lasted less than four hours. But at a press conference the next day, the president suspended the students, called for their arrest, and retracted the agreement. The Los Angeles County district attorney moved quickly to identify and arrest the students. Expressing a wish that police had been called in to forcibly evict the students the previous day, Governor Reagan said the students "should have been taken out of there by the scruffs of their necks." The students, who had all been unarmed and had caused no damage or injuries, were charged with the most serious crimes ever in the history of campus protest. Twenty-seven students were charged with more than seventy counts each of conspiracy, assault, kidnapping, false imprisonment, robbery, and burglary. The state contended that the takeover had been planned in advance and therefore constituted a criminal conspiracy. Bill Burwell, who was in Pacoima on November 4, always insisted that the protest "was an absolutely spontaneous event." The students faced the prospect of life imprisonment. The NAACP, alarmed at the severity of the charges, announced that it would defend the students. The Los Angeles Police Department remained on alert for the rest of the academic year and periodically appeared on campus.[14]

Most white students and faculty initially condemned the takeover, but many would come to support the BSU, seeing their demands as reasonable and the charges against them as excessive. Even many administrators would eventually support this view. As early as December, administrators were warding off a grand jury's call for longer student suspensions and an investigation of the Educational Opportunities Program, which had been accused of stimulating militant student action. Indeed, the events of November 4 quickly led Valley State down unexpected pathways. Even as the students were being crucified by elected officials up and down the state of California, they precipitated and helped guide a transformation of campus life.[15]

The turning point came in January when the police were called in and forcibly broke up a protest. As on other campuses, this tactic backfired. Among the protestors who were injured or arrested was the Reverend James Hargett of the California Southern Christian Leadership Conference (SCLC), who had come to offer support. Seeking to identify with the concerns of the younger generation, he embraced black power and called it "the power to disrupt." This SCLC minister illustrated a fact whites often overlooked: the black student rebellion had significant support among adult black leadership. "We will stop disrupting," Reverend Hargett declared, "when we get a share of freedom and when every college has a significant share of black students." The students vowed to hold another rally the following day. But the president abruptly declared a state of emergency and banned all campus demonstrations and rallies. The rally was held anyway, and the anger over the administration's heavy-handed tactics galvanized students. Two to three thousand came to the rally. One hundred LAPD officers converged on campus and arrested 286, including nine faculty members and ministers. Very soon after this, the administration abruptly shifted course and pursued negotiations with the students. One observer felt that the recent shooting deaths of EOP students Bunchy Carter and John Huggins on the UCLA campus was "a catalyst" in settling the dispute at Valley State.[16]

The negotiating team included representatives from the faculty, administration, BSU, United Mexican American Students (UMAS), and leaders from the nearby Mexican American and African American communities. The UMAS had not played a prominent role in the student movement nor had they participated in the November 4 occupation, but Chicanos suffered from the same exclusionary policies and limited curriculum as African Americans, and the two groups worked together during the negotiations. The three-day negotiating sessions were tape-recorded, and they reveal a familiar clash between discourses of tradition and fiscal prudence on the one hand and ones of access and social justice on the other. As administrators stressed the cost of admitting large numbers of students, Burt Corona, a veteran Chicano activist, forcefully reminded the group that "anything below mass entry of our people into these colleges is unacceptable. I don't care how it's done." As Valley State representatives pondered whether the board of trustees would permit them to exceed the 4 percent quota, Corona pushed them to rethink the definition of standards: "Are you finding creative and innovative ways to test the uncut diamonds that exist in the Chicano and Black communities?" An African American leader from Pacoima similarly tried to shift the focus away from negatives, from limits, from rationales as to why more minority students couldn't come. "If you show us and prove to us that they cannot come here, you are telling us that you will continue to rob us of our tax monies and to support something that does not include us. And I want to let you know," he declared, "that we're tired of being robbed." Community support was important to the successes of the black student movement. But so was the leadership of the students themselves. Journalists may have captured the more sensational aspects of late 1960s campus protest, helping to shape a public image of youthful extremists, but black student activists worked diligently behind the scenes—often assuming adult responsibilities, especially in schools that had few or no black faculty and administrators. They proposed new courses, attended department meetings, and formulated the first generation of affirmative action policies in college admissions. A faculty member credited Archie Chatman and Bill Burwell with helping keep the group on track. "On at least ten occasions, the talks came close to breaking down," but the two BSU leaders intervened. "Wait a minute," they'd insist. "Let's get together again."[17]

Student demands in this era ranged from calls for open admissions for all high school graduates—activists at San Francisco State attacked the SAT, which had been implemented in the early 1960s and had quickly precipitated a sharp drop in black student admissions—to calls for black and Latino admissions that reflected their proportion of the population. At the predominantly white City College in Harlem, New York, black and Puerto Rican students occupied a building demanding that City admit the same percentage of black and Puerto Rican students that were in nearby public high schools. Instead, the City University of New York adopted an open admissions policy that had the effect of increasing black and Puerto Rican representation in the senior colleges. The protests at Valley State were similarly motivated by opposition to the tracking system in public higher education that had kept the state's four-year colleges and universities predominantly white. The goal was not simply diversity but a commitment to afford an opportunity to those who had been systematically denied it.

On January 15, Valley State announced a landmark agreement that mirrored many of the demands from November 4. The college agreed to set up departments of African American and Chicano studies, with students having a formal role in selecting the chairs. They agreed on a flexible approach to hiring that incorporated the students' perspective: "The criteria for qualified instructors will not be limited to academic background but will recognize areas of expertise in the field." The heads of the new departments would be black and Chicano, and the administration also pledged to recruit faculty of color in all departments. They agreed to "vigorously pursue the recruitment of Chicano and Black students," and to a fall 1969 goal of 350 new students in each group. A striking feature of African American student activism of this era was the attention given to workers, whether service workers on campus or in the surrounding community, reflecting the students' desire to link their struggle with the broader needs of the black community. At protests around the country students typically included a demand pertaining to staff hiring practices or wages. At Valley State, the administration agreed to call in the state Fair Employment Practices Commission to determine the racial/ethnic breakdown of the college's workforce. The settlement vindicated the black student leaders, who had been denounced in the strongest possible terms by virtually every campus and state authority. The president of the faculty assembly now declared that "the militancy of these students is the best thing that has happened to this campus."[18]

The settlement softened campus anger over the November 4 protest. Many felt that the university should have protected its students from such severe charges, and they launched a campaign for amnesty for the twenty-seven students awaiting trial. One petition with three thousand signatures said, "All that they demanded has now been achieved through negotiation, yet their futures, their very lives, hang in senseless jeopardy." The students, they argued, had already made considerable sacrifices "in grades, mental anguish, the trauma of arrest and physical injuries." Another petition for amnesty was equally passionate. "The single most important problem now before us is the need to recognize that punitive force will solve nothing," it declared. "When King called for forgiveness we did not charge him with being a muddle headed sellout who kowtows to violence. Why do we levy this charge against the whites who call for compassion? Can it be that we hailed this man only because the forgiveness on which he insisted was for us?"[19]

But off-campus public opinion was running strongly against student protesters in California. Indeed, the nation was convulsed in campus rebellion. Universities, and even high schools, exploded in protest in the spring of 1969, and violence was escalating as the National Guard increasingly joined police in stamping out student protest. While opposition to the U.S. war in Vietnam and the draft fueled much of the protest, racial issues were increasingly becoming catalysts. By 1969, they were at the forefront of more than half the campus protests, and black student activists were the focus of media attention, especially at Cornell where protesters emerged from a building takeover carrying rifles and ammunition. (The fact that they had armed themselves in response to threats by white males to forcibly retake the building was downplayed.) Reagan, who was up for reelection in 1970; the superintendent of public instruction, Max Rafferty, who was running for the U.S. Senate; and the Los Angeles district attorney Evelle J. Younger, who was running for state attorney general, all demanded stern reprisals against student protesters at Valley State and other California campuses. Reagan, who would soon see to it that state funding for the EOP was slashed, accused college presidents who negotiated with student protesters of "appeasement." And in another remarkable throwback, Los Angeles mayor Sam Yorty issued a report claiming that an international Communist conspiracy was behind the campus turmoil. Unrest in the Los Angeles area, including at San Fernando Valley State, the mayor claimed, has "been masterminded, instigated and sponsored" by Communist front groups as a way to "promote urban violence and social turmoil." One week before the trial of the Valley State students began, Reagan signed into law several bills that stiffened penalties for student demonstrators, including cutting off financial aid.[20]

The trial began in September 1969. The "audience consisted mainly of friends of the defendants, young Negroes with bushy Afro hairdos and defiant faces," the *New York Times* reported. The prosecutor, Vincent Bugliosi, told the press that a stiff sentence would set a much-needed example to campus radicals "who've gotten away with murder and might think twice before doing it again." The defense attorneys, who included veteran civil rights lawyer Loren Miller, argued that the students' protest was spontaneous and born of their frustrated attempts to end institutionalized racism at the college. Most of the accused, the defense stated, had only stood around and watched; the state provided no evidence that the staff was prevented from leaving the building. That the Los Angeles NAACP was defending student "militants" who were endeavoring to win an autonomous black studies department was ironic, because national NAACP leaders, especially Roy Wilkins, derided the black studies movement as separatist. And there were evidently tensions between the attorneys and a few of the student leaders. According to Robert Lewis, the attorneys had advised the students to waive their right to a jury trial, a decision that Lewis, Chatman, and Eddie Dancer opposed. "This co-option lasted throughout the trial," Lewis claimed. "They wanted us to act like pseudo-Negroes, who weren't aware of what we had done. Most of us on trial, being young and politically immature, were convinced by the NAACP lawyers that that was the way the case should be handled." Roy Wilkins came to observe the trial one day and meet the students but found that some of them "cursed out the NAACP." They said, "I'm an old-fashioned Uncle Tom and the white folks' mouthpiece and that sort of thing," declared Wilkins, who was undoubtedly used to this charge. "But these kids need a defense," he maintained, "and my organization is going to defend them."[21]

In November the judge handed down the first and only mass felony convictions resulting from campus protest. He concluded that a conspiracy did indeed exist. Wearing T-shirts emblazoned with Malcolm X's slogan By Any Means Necessary showed, according to the judge, that the students "were prepared to, and did use, violent, felonious means." The judge rejected a recommendation for probation and fines. At the sentencing hearing he quoted from speeches made by some of the students at a campus rally calling him "senile," "a fascist pig," and "a lackey for Reagan."[22]

For their part, the more militant students made their disdain for the judge evident. Public, contemptuous challenges to authority were emblematic of 1960s protest. For African American college students, this marked a stark departure from the deeply entrenched strategy of racial respectability employed by generations of African American community leaders. For all that the black power generation's desire to "give back" to the community resonated with a long tradition of black middle-class service or a commitment to racial uplift, it broke from that tradition in its tactics and style. Just before sentencing, Archie Chatman made a statement, telling the judge, "I did not get a fair trial. This court is a racist court." According to the media, the sixty or so spectators "applauded vigorously," and Robert Lewis raised his fist and shouted the slogan of the Black Panther Party, "power to the people!" Chatman, Lewis, and Eddie Dancer were sentenced to state prison for one to twenty-five years. Eight others were given sentences of three months to a year; eight received lesser penalties; and five students were acquitted of all charges. Loren Miller insisted that the only reason the students were prosecuted, convicted, and given jail time was because they were black. They were "a frustrated group of young people," he said, "who were only trying to improve their lives." Fellow defense attorney Morgan Moten also countered the judge's harsh condemnation of the students: "These kids are not out to overthrow the government by any violence. You should hope that every black kid in America is like these kids." But this was not the image projected to the citizens of California. While civil rights attorneys, the majority of the African American public, and, increasingly, most people at Valley State saw the students as part of a venerable American civil rights tradition of direct action protest, the judge and conservative politicians deployed the authoritarian rhetoric of "law and order" and the image of themselves as cracking down on wild-eyed youth in order to tarnish and discredit the students' activism. In 1970, D. A. Evelle Younger won the election for California attorney general, and he highlighted the injustice of the Valley State convictions in his campaign advertising. In Robert Lewis's view, Younger was "saying to the racists, the conservatives of California, that he won't stand for any shit."[23]

A judge released Dancer, Lewis, and Chatman on probation after they had spent three months in jail. But his ruling barred them from reenrolling at San Fernando Valley State and prevented them from participating in efforts to develop the black studies program. In the spring of 1969, the college hired Bill Burwell to help set up the program. Students in the BSU played a significant role in interviewing and hiring faculty. The "basic test" for hiring, Burwell later said, was "sensitivity, commitment and understanding of the black problem." Instructors "were expected to be black nationalists." Whether the new African American studies units on campuses across the country would be structured as programs or departments was hotly contested. Many, if not most, of the architects of black studies desired the autonomy, budget, and stature of a department, but some colleges favored setting up programs, since they were cheaper and put control over faculty and course content in the traditional disciplines. The politicization of this issue was such that even Governor Reagan weighed in, taking the occasion to question the scholarly competence of faculty and students in African American studies. "One really must ask," the former actor remarked, "whether the demand for a completely autonomous department is not in reality a request for a sanctuary from the rigors of the institution, a sanctuary from the normal standards." According to Burwell, Valley State initially sought a program. After he was sent on a national tour to investigate models for black studies, he pushed hard for a department. "What I discovered was that the only way to have any permanence and have any power was that I had to have an academic department." The administration relented after the students threatened another round of demonstrations.[24]

The students' success in building a department in such a short period of time is striking. Within a couple of years sixteen faculty members had been hired. But the direction the department traveled in its first decade turned out to be more mainstream academic and less political than some student-activists had envisioned. The reasons for this are varied. It was certainly shaped by the fallout of the criminal convictions, which by barring Chatman, Dancer, and Lewis from campus, created a gulf between the students who had struggled for the department and the department itself as it was forging an identity and striving for permanence. But it was also an outgrowth of professional educators assuming leadership of the new discipline and needing to fight for its survival and legitimacy in an academic environment that remained suspicious, if not hostile, to its existence. Still, the idea that an academic unit could become a permanent agent of political activism, even if idealistic or naive, reflected this generation's belief that they were on the vanguard of major social change—what they called the "black revolution."

Chatman changed his name to Adewole Umoja, taught African culture in Guyana for two years, returned to Pacoima in the late 1970s, and tried to convince the United Nations to charge the United States with genocide. Umoja became a critic of the Pan-African Studies Department and accused Burwell of settling "for the crumbs that white America is willing to throw out when it's in a good mood." For his part, Burwell experienced many internal conflicts over his new insider role. "Within those first three years, I probably never slept one night when I didn't have to grapple with it. I'd wake up and start thinking about whether there was a conspiracy out for my life, if the system was out to get me, or if some revolutionary brother was standing behind a bush waiting to blow my brains out." In a pattern replicated on many campuses, the Pan-African Studies Department at Valley State gradually moved toward hiring faculty with traditional academic qualifications, which often caused serious ruptures. Jerome Walker, president of the BSU in 1968, taught in the department for several years after graduation but was ultimately let go in a dispute over credentials.[25]

Those who built the department also had mixed feelings about the outcome of the black studies struggle. Burwell had hoped that African American studies would counteract the lure of integration by instilling a new racial consciousness and commitment. Instead, he lamented, African American students at Valley State regarded college as "a way to get out of the community rather than come back and strengthen it." He also complained that most black students "assimilated much too quickly and readily and took on the same values that I had fought against." This suggests that the black nationalists' analysis of the connections between race, culture, and career choice may have been flawed, but if one examines the career aspirations of African American studies majors, not just black students in the aggregate, the idea of "giving back" to the community remains salient to this day. In another unexpected outcome, institution-building quickly eclipsed political struggle as the focus of faculty and departmental energies. This was true on many other campuses as well, which sometimes led, ironically, to complaints by the next cohort of African American students that black studies had sold out. "The changeover of talk from revolutionary violence to the more staid pursuits of academe was extraordinary," Burwell recalled. Barbara Rhodes, who took over the chair's position from Burwell in 1975, agreed that "the department has not continued to push as strongly in areas of social change as it should. . . . So much energy has gone into just staying on the campus."[26]

A *Los Angeles Times* reporter concluded that after its first decade the "Pan-African Studies Department failed to become an aggressive agent for social change and instead evolved into merely an accepted part of mainstream academics." This interpretation reflects the disappointment of many, like Chatman, who thought the new departments had strayed from their roots, but it misses the significance of the academic mission. The rise of black studies was part of a broader sea change in the U. S academy in the wake of the social movements of the 1960s. The department at Northridge grew into the largest in the California state college system, with seven tenured faculty and ten instructors who offered a phenomenal fifty to sixty courses each semester.

The incorporation of African American studies on many campuses, although still partial and incomplete, has inspired ambivalent feelings about its origins. For some, its activist roots are a blemish. A white professor at Valley State observed twenty years later that "we hired people who did not always have a full understanding of the academic community. . . . They came in somewhat as revolutionaries, and we didn't have the time to go out and find the best people." His view that political pressures slowed the academic development of African American studies and that with more time black scholars would have been actively recruited is probably shared by many others, but it elides the critical point: these departments only came into existence because of political pressures. Indeed, this scholar also makes the highly questionable claim that even without student activism universities would eventually have created black and Mexican American studies departments, ones that would have had more institutional support. Bill Burwell insists that the tactics students resorted to on November 4 were understandable in light of the "insensitive, intolerant and unyielding" administration. "We had to go to a by-any-means-necessary [strategy] because peaceful means were simply not being responded to."

Like other participants in the civil rights movement, black student activists at Valley State—as well as those at Howard, UCLA, Harvard, Alabama State, San Mateo Junior College, Cornell, Northwestern, Southern, and many other colleges—took risks and suffered reprisals to expand the rights and opportunities for people of color in the United States. But they have been omitted from the pantheon of movement icons, and the sites of their climactic struggles have been left off the movement's map.

The student activists of the late 1960s and early 1970s helped establish affirmative action policies in college admissions across the country. If the legal gains of the early 1960s helped push open the door to higher education, black student activism later in the decade ensured that it would stay open—and be open wide enough for children from every class and walk of life. The black student movement also transformed academic scholarship in the United States by inaugurating African American studies and ultimately pushing scholars across disciplines to seriously incorporate race, class, and gender into their research endeavors. The "identity politics" that black nationalism unleashed and the attention to class that its proponents insisted on turned out to be far more effective than integrationist discourses in actually desegregating the academy. While many features of the student-led black revolution were never realized, access to higher education was critical to black social mobility—especially as deindustrialization put large numbers of African Americans permanently outside of the labor market. Armed with Title 7 and a liberal federal judiciary, these students would translate educational attainment into occupational mobility. To a great extent, the success of this generation of student activism laid the foundations for the modern black middle class.

NOTES

1. Historians are beginning to document case studies of black student activism and the black studies movement. See Joy Ann Williamson, *Black Power on Campus: the University of Illinois, 1965–1975* (Urbana, 2003), and Wayne Glasker, *Black Students in the Ivory Tower: African American Student Activism at the University of Pennsylvania, 1967–1990* (Boston, 2002).

2. Take Chicago for example. Many leading African American activists in the city today were student activists in the late 1960s. Lewis Myers, an attorney who has represented Rainbow/PUSH and Louis Farrakhan, was an undergraduate student leader at Howard. The student cohort that successfully fought to change the name of one of the city colleges to Malcolm X College have been important antiracist activists ever since. Standish Willis, past president of the National Conference of Black Lawyers, has been a leader in the fight against police brutality, and following Malcolm X, has brought the issue to the United Nations. Henry English and Calvin Cook, also student activists at Malcolm X College, were founders of the National Black United Fund. Edward "Buzz" Palmer, who provided campus security, was a founder of the Afro-American Patrolman's League. Interview with Standish Willis, Chicago, June 13, 2006.

3. John J. Broesamle, *Suddenly a Giant: A History of California State University at Northridge* (Northridge, Calif., 1993), 46; Earl Anthony, *The Time of the Furnaces: A Case Study of Black Student Revolt* (New York, 1971), 29.

4. Broesamle, *Suddenly a Giant*, 45; "Summary of Interview with Governor Reagan of 2–18–69," Records of the National Commission on the Causes and Prevention of Violence, Series 57: Records Relating to the San Francisco State Investigation, box 12, Lyndon B. Johnson Library, Austin, Texas. For the racial views of conservatives, see Nancy MacLean, *Freedom Is Not Enough: How the Struggle for Jobs and Justice Changed America, 1955–1980* (Cambridge, Mass., 2006.)

5. Anthony, *Time of the Furnaces*, 22.

6. Ibid., 23–24.

7. "I split with Karenga in '67 for reasons I don't want to go into," Lewis said. Others broke from Karenga in a similarly mysterious fashion. See Scot Brown, *Fighting for US: Maulana Karenga, the US Organization, and Black Cultural Nationalism* (New York, 2003).

8. Anthony, *Time of the Furnaces*, 21–23. At the same time, Lewis's parents conveyed their skepticism of expressive politics and the way their generation was being constructed. An afro hairstyle, in their view, did not signify black consciousness or political commitment, and conversely, straightened hair did not signify their

absence. See David Nevin, "Uneasy Peace at Valley State," *Life Magazine*, March 14, 1969.

9. To be sure, there were also many African American student activists, including Bill Burwell at Valley State, who considered themselves revolutionaries. Burwell later stated that he had kept "an arsenal" in his house and led "guerilla training up in the mountains" in preparation for the eventual overthrow of the system. David Nevin, "Uneasy Peace at Valley State," *Life Magazine*, March 14, 1969; Broesamle, *Suddenly a Giant*, 45 and 51; Brandeis student quoted from "Black Power on University Campuses," program 24 of *Say Brother* (air date, January 16, 1969), WGBH Archive, Boston.

10. Chatman quoted in Anthony, *Time of the Furnaces*, 120. For the San Francisco State strike, see Dikran Karagueuzian, *Blow It Up! The Black Student Revolt at San Francisco State and the Emergence of Dr. Hayakawa* (Boston, 1971) and William H. Orrick, *Shut It Down! A College in Crisis*, Staff Report to the National Commission on the Causes and Prevention of Violence, June 1969.

11. See Harry Edwards, *The Revolt of the Black Athlete* (New York, 1969), and Douglas Hartmann, *Race, Culture, and the Revolt of the Black Athlete: The 1968 Olympic Protests and Their Aftermath* (Chicago, 2003), 178–79.

12. Anthony, *Time of the Furnaces*, 35, 51, 54; Broesamle, *Suddenly a Giant*, 49.

13 Anthony, *Time of the Furnaces*, 62, 78.

14. Ibid., 96; Broesamle, *Suddenly a Giant*, 50; *San Fernando Valley Times*, November 5, 1968, Campus Unrest Collection, box 1, California State University at Northridge (CSUN).

15. *Los Angeles Herald-Examiner*, November 5, 1968, Campus Unrest Collection, box 1; "Repression at Valley State," *Crisis and Action* (December 1968), Campus Unrest Collection, box 5; *Los Angeles Times*, December 21 and 22, 1968, Campus Unrest Collection, box 1, all in CSUN.

16. *Los Angeles Times*, January 9 and 10, 1969, Campus Unrest Collection, box 1, CSUN; Records of the National Commission on the Causes and Prevention of Violence, series 57, box 12, "Interview No. 2."

17. *Los Angeles Times*, January 11, 1969; "Student Unrest Negotiations," January 12–14, 1969, tape no. 5, CSUN.

18. Broesamle, *Suddenly a Giant*, 58; "Student Unrest Negotiations, January 12–14, 1969, tape no. 4, CSUN; *Van Nuys News*, January 24, 1969, and *Los Angeles Times*, January 24, 1969, Campus Unrest Collection, box 1, CSUN.

19. *Van Nuys News*, June 5, 1969 Campus Unrest Collection, box 1; M. M. Auerbach and J. Richfield, "The Case for Amnesty," n.d., Campus Unrest Collection, box 2, both in CSUN.

20. *Van Nuys News*, n.d, Campus Unrest Collection, box 1, folder 39, CSUN.

21. *New York Times*, clipping, n.d., *Los Angeles Times*, September 20, 1969, Campus Unrest Collection, box 2, CSUN.

22. *Van Nuys News*, November 20, 1969; *San Fernando Valley Times*, January 27, 1970, and *Los Angeles Times*, January 28 and 29, 1970, Campus Unrest Collection, box 2, CSUN; Anthony, *Time of the Furnaces*, 89–90.

23. *Los Angeles Times*, January 29, 1970, Campus Unrest Collection, box 2, CSUN; Anthony, *Time of the Furnaces*, 99, 89–90.

24. "Summary of Interview with Governor Reagan of 2–18–69," Records of the National Commission on the Causes and Prevention of Violence, series 57, box 12; Broesamle, *Suddenly a Giant*, 51.

25. Broesamle, *Suddenly a Giant*, 85–87; "Did CSUN Takeover Win?" *Los Angeles Times*, June 24, 1979, Campus Unrest Collection, box 2, CSUN.

26. "Did CSUN Takeover Win?" *Los Angeles Times*, June 24, 1979, Campus Unrest Collection, box 2, CSUN.

Chapter Thirteen

· · · · · · · · · · ·

Duke Ellington Plays Baghdad

Rethinking Hard and Soft Power from the Outside In

PENNY VON ESCHEN

On April 11, 2003, over the caption "Palace of Rubble: American Soldiers Yesterday Inside a Ruined Palace in Baghdad That Belongs to President Saddam Hussein's Son Uday," the front page of the *New York Times* displayed a picture of a grand piano, legs collapsed, top smashed, lying in the rubble of a bombed palace. Looking at the demolished piano, two American soldiers, surrounded by chunks of rock, wall, and marble, ascended the palace's winding staircase.[1] The photograph appeared amid criticism of official indifference to Iraqi cultural treasures, as U.S. forces failed to protect museums and priceless archaeological artifacts from extensive looting and destruction. As the seeming triumph of Saddam's overthrow yielded to an increasingly violent and chaotic U.S. occupation, I labored to understand a moment forty years earlier when at least some U.S. officials experienced a very different (if far from unproblematic) relationship with Iraq. While researching cold war era jazz tours, I had discovered that in November 1963, the internationally renowned American pianist, composer, and bandleader Duke Ellington had performed with his orchestra in Baghdad under the auspices of the U.S. State Department. Ellington and his organization began their visit to Iraq with a performance at a party celebrating the founding of the U.S. Marine Corps, hosted by U.S. Ambassador Robert C. Strong. Noting that the party for the 188-year-old military institution took place in a city twelve centuries old, a giddy U.S. official reported that "the ambassadorial residence rocked," as four hundred Iraqis and Americans danced to "such old favorites as 'Take the A Train,' 'Mood Indigo,' 'Sophisticated Lady' . . . or crowded around the orchestra for a closer look at the ageless Duke."[2] Local sponsors' fears of a low turnout proved groundless when the first concert on November 12 easily sold out. It was also broadcast live by Iraqi state television. U.S. officials reported that as "[a]n enthusiastic first-night audience" watched the concert at Khuld Hall near the presidential palace, "all over the city thousands sat around television sets in open air cafes and restaurants or in the comfort of their own homes and enjoyed the artistry of one of the great contemporary figures in American music."[3] While we cannot know the depth of the American official's appreciation of the ancient cultural heritage of Baghdad and Iraq, he understood the richness of its tradition enough to revel in juxtaposing it with the newness of the U.S. Marines. Moreover, the U.S. official portrayed a modern nation, with a vibrant public culture, as citizens unable to attend the actual performance partook of the experience through broadcast television in cafes, restaurants, and in one another's homes.

I begin with this story *not* to suggest that the United States once had a more complex and nuanced relationship with Iraq, but because I think Ellington's performance in Iraq offers a glimpse into a hidden history: a long and tangled involvement of the United States with Iraqi regimes that not only belies the claims of disinterested benevolence asserted by the Bush administration as the United States invaded Iraq in 2003 but also challenges ingrained habits and assumptions in our study of post-1945 U.S. history.

After more than a decade of rigorous calls for internationalizing U.S. history and broadening the field "formerly known as diplomatic history," the tragedy of the U.S. war and the occupation of Iraq has made understanding the hegemonic projects of post-1945 America all the more urgent. In his 2001 presidential address to the AHA (American Historical Association), Eric Foner invoked Louis Hartz's "brilliant and sardonic" observation in *The Liberal Tradition in America* that the internationalism of the postwar era seemed "to go hand in hand with self-absorption and insularity." For Foner, "the unfinished story of American freedom must become a conversation with the entire world and not a complacent monologue with ourselves."[4] As the American monologue has become a nightmare for many Americans and untold Iraqis, it is hardly surprising that others have echoed Hartz's mid-twentieth-century observations. Perry Anderson has characterized the United States as a Janus-faced power, at once unprecedented in its world-ordering ambitions and "terribly insular in its self-conception." According to the historian Michael H. Hunt, American policy-makers have been "too self-absorbed even to grasp the dimensions of those gargantuan ambitions."[5] Anderson, Hunt, and others maintain that a belief in the uniqueness of American political culture, if not its superiority to other nations, has often blinded citizens, scholars, and policy-makers to the ways in which the United States is deeply enmeshed in the violent history of the twentieth century.

In this essay, I take up the challenge posed by these critics to disrupt the American monologue and read U.S. history in conversation with the rest of the world. I also take up their challenge of analyzing the paradox of insularity and ambition by suggesting that a pervasive separation of "culture" from "political economy" in historical writing, further incarnated in the concept of what Joseph Nye has termed "hard and soft power," remains an obstacle to understanding American culture as well as the exercise of U.S. power in the world. [6] The arresting photograph of a smashed piano, made all the more disturbing in my case by the image of Ellington at such a piano in Baghdad forty years earlier, demonstrates the appeal of "soft power" as a noncoercive form of communication and exchange. Yet further scrutiny of the presence of Ellington in Iraq during the attempted coup d'etat, suggests that hard and soft power are not the diametrical opposites they are routinely made out to be.

The story of Ellington in Iraq opens with a birthday party, but continues with jazz concerts, coups d'etat, nightclubs, and the U.S. sale of military helicopters to Iraq's first Baathist regime, pointing us forty years ahead to bombings, smashed pianos, looted museums, massive civilian casualties, and torture. According to journalistic and diplomatic lore, months before Ellington's Iraqi visit, the CIA had masterminded a February coup, led by General Ahmad Hassan al-Bakr, a mentor of Saddam Hussein. That coup had ousted 'Abd al-Kaim Qassim and brought the Baathist party to power.[7] Qassim had come to power in 1958 in an earlier coup that had challenged Western oil interests, dealing U.S. officials a setback only five years after the CIA had deposed the democratic nationalist leader Musaddiq in Iran.

After the February 1963 coup in Iraq, Roy Melbourne, U.S. chargé d'affaires, gloated, "the Russians give every sign of knowing what we do, namely, that they have received a serious defeat in the Middle East."[8] President Kennedy, anxious to see Iraq's dependence on the Soviet Union reduced, had asked his National Security Council staff six months earlier "what we're doing for the new Iraqi regime." While Kennedy's advisers were probably more involved with the possible sale to the Bakr regime of twelve helicopters for use against pro-Qassim insurgents than with the jazz bands, the Ellington visit in November was part and parcel of the U.S. strategy, as "White House Middle East expert Robert Komer told Kennedy" in July, of "making [the] most of [this] Iraqi opportunity."[9]

Three months after the U.S.-backed coup, early on the morning after Ellington's first concert, with the musicians asleep in their hotel across the bank of the Tigris, the presidential palace was attacked by Iraqi air force jets in an attempted coup d'etat. The attempt by rightists in the Baathist party to overthrow the moderate Baathist government created a ctiywide emergency and an imposed curfew.[10] While most of the musicians and their State Department escort officer welcomed the unplanned hiatus at a point when the physical demands of the tour were taking their toll, two members of the band insisted on visiting a local nightclub. "They could only have been prevented by force," lamented the escort officer, "and all Marines were at the Embassy." The musicians later recounted an enjoyable outing: "two men and twenty girls, shaking like leaves, and 'all those cats with sub-machine guns sitting around outside.'"[11] The Iraqi capital quickly returned to normal. When phone service was restored at the U.S. embassy, "they were swamped with calls from Iraqis who had to wait twenty-four hours to congratulate them on the Duke's dazzling first-night performance."[12] The scheduled concert went on and, like the first, was a sellout.[13] On November 15, Ellington left the country. Three days later, the Iraqi army revolted and overthrew the Baathist government.[14]

While this second 1963 coup might best be characterized as factional Baathist infighting in which the military wing of the party had colluded with the government to form a military dictatorship, the Baathist Party and the ousted Ahmed Hassan al-Bakar did not regain power until the 1968 coup, and then, only with the help of Saddam Hussein.[15] American policy-makers could not halt the evaporation of the opportunities represented in the first coup. But it was not for lack of trying. Clandestine CIA involvement in Iraqi politics had further undermined stability in the country, and prior and subsequent interventions in the region would sabotage the goodwill exemplified by the Ellington orchestra's visit. Recent scholars have wisely emphasized the limits to U.S. power and control in the Middle East. Yet the enormous scope of political and military involvement, from the CIA role in ousting Qassim in 1963 to the later funding of Saddam Hussein's regime to counter the Iranian revolution against the U.S.-backed shah, should serve as a reminder that the United States is deeply implicated in this troubled history.

Despite the depth and duration of U.S. involvement in Iraqi politics, I found it enormously difficult to construct even the most rudimentary narrative context for Ellington's sojourn in Iraq. Despite fine histories of the United States in the Middle East such as *American Orientalism* by Douglas Little and excellent work by Iraqi specialists, it is an understatement to note that for scholars of U.S. foreign relations, Iraq has been very much on the periphery, in spite of extensive U.S. involvement in the region. The sheer scope of jazz tours in the region underline the importance of U.S. interests as well as the complexity of U.S. attempts at influence in the region. In 1958, on the verge of the coup that first brought Qassim to power, Dave Brubeck and his quartet performed in Iraq. Indeed, as I researched the history of State Department cultural-presentation tours, I found that musicians were sent with remarkable frequency to countries and regions that have eluded the scrutiny of U.S. historians (or have been at the far periphery), but have been constantly in the news since the United States attacked Iraq in 2003. To mention only examples from Middle Eastern and adjoining states, in addition to Brubeck's and Ellington's performances in Iraq, Dizzy Gillespie was sent to Afghanistan, Pakistan, Syria, and Lebanon, in 1956; Dave Brubeck was in Afghanistan, Pakistan, and Iran in 1958; and Ellington was in Afghanistan, Pakistan, Iran, Jordan, and Syria in 1963.

If Hartz regarded America's self-absorption and insularity as characteristic of its culture as well as foreign policy in the early cold war era, much of the recent literature on U.S. foreign policy and international relations has focused on economic globalization and the transformations in the global political economy since the early 1970s, and the collapse of the Fordist economy of mass production and mass consumption.[16] I do not wish to minimize the importance of this epochal shift. But in rightly emphasizing the collapse of the industrial/manufacturing-based economy and the concomitant increased mobility of capital and labor, scholars have lost sight of an equally epochal shift. The ascendance of the United States as a hegemonic power at precisely the moment of the collapse of formal European colonialism and the formation of more than forty nominally independent nation-states remains only partly understood. Indeed, some of the most compelling and insightful analyses of twentieth-century globalization processes, such as Charles Bright and Michael Geyer's "Where in the World Is America? The History of the United States in a Global Age," take for granted the broad legitimacy of U.S. power and underestimate the challenges to that legitimacy from what was initially conceived as a nonaligned bloc and has more recently coalesced in the form of north-south divisions in global trade policy.[17] It is imperative that we focus on what was, and remains, at stake in the epochal collapse of European colonialism, namely, trade relationships and access to and control of the world's resources.

Contemporary struggles over control of oil reserves in the Middle East have their origins in the accelerated race for U.S. control over global resources that accompanied the collapse of European colonialism and the postwar rise of the nonaligned bloc of Afro-Asian nations. Such questions remained largely unexplored as Americanists concentrated on the well-worn history of the cold war with the Soviet Union, with barely a nod to the global anticolonial revolution against European colonialism and its unfulfilled promise, an era that has bequeathed to us the vexed and challenging world in which we live. Despite careful work by diplomatic historians that has detailed U.S. involvement in every corner of the globe, and much recent work on multinational and transnational perspectives, including work focused on U.S. interaction with and responses to anticolonial and nation building projects, this work sits uneasily outside of a still-dominant cold war paradigm that continues to obscure an understanding of the complexity and the character of U.S. hegemonic projects in the early cold war era.[18]

The consolidation of global hegemony by the United States in the wake of the collapse of European colonialism through programs of global economic integration, covert action, and proxy wars throughout Asia, Africa, and Latin America is essential to our comprehension of the contemporary world. As Pransenjit Duara reminds us, historical periodization need not be seen as an "ontological condition." Scholars of the cold war must broaden their vision, engaging the contradictions and conflicts produced by anticolonialism and decolonization.[19] For Americanists, this means that the cold war must be read alongside of, and often in collision with, other dynamics and trajectories.[20] Rather then yield to the temptation of insularity, Americanists can benefit from recent scholarship that enables them to engage the history of the postwar world from the outside in.

Americanists have been concerned primarily with narrating the story of landmark cold war events such as the Cuban missile crisis and the Vietnam War (often though not always asserting a variety of American exceptionalism) and have tended to work in a bipolar frame that reads the post-1945 period through the lens of U.S.-Soviet conflict. But as Duara has argued, "decolonization was one of the most important political developments of the twentieth century because it turned the world into the stage of history." For Duara, questions of what replaces colonial control after independence and the extent to which current historical approaches are adequate to describe the transformative processes of decolonization remain paramount.[21] In the case of Iraq, as Rashid Khalidi has pointed out, "there had never been a state, empire, or nation of Iraq before British statesmen created it in the wake of World War I."[22] Yet if Iraq, along with much of the Middle East, does not have the same historical trajectory of colonization and decolonization as much of Asia and Africa, it nevertheless remains at the center of the era's struggle over controls of the resources of the formerly colonized world. The crucial issue of control of resources at the moment of the consolidation of U.S. hegemony can link regions with disparate political trajectories, connecting Asia, the Pacific, Africa, the Middle East, and Latin America, where U.S. imperialism had long plagued formally independent states.[23]

A powerful challenge to the neglect of U.S. responses to postcolonial nation-states, Mahmood Mamdani's *Good Muslim, Bad Muslim: The Cold War and The Roots of Terror*, locates the roots of current global crisis in the U.S. anticommunist policy of containment but inverts the story to center U.S. relations with formerly colonized countries. Mamdani explores the proxy wars of the later cold war that led to U.S. officials' support of the anti-Soviet Mujahadeen fighters in Afghanistan (including Osama Bin Laden) and enlisted Iraq and Saddam Hussein as allies against Iran after the shah's overthrow. He also reminds us of the era's aborted democratic projects, as exemplified by the 1953 CIA-backed coup ousting Mussadiq in Iran. Tracing the history of the arming of Africa and the Middle East by the United States and the Soviet Union, Mamdani exposes the dubious alliances with third world "strongmen" undertaken by the United States and other Western powers, including the arming of Idi Amin in Uganda. Mamdani challenges the "culture talk" of Samuel Huntington and others who have framed contemporary discussions of "the war on terror" and finds the roots of contemporary terrorism in politics, not the "culture" of Islam. Like Tariq Ali's riposte to Huntington, *The Clash of Fundamentalisms*, Mamdani's account of the post-1945 world takes us through those places where U.S. policy has supported and armed military dictatorships, such as Pakistan and Iraq, or intervened clandestinely, such as Iraq, Afghanistan, and the Congo. Foregrounding this history provides a context for what otherwise gets posed as an "Islamic threat," demonstrating, for example, that the current alliance with Pakistan in the "war on terror" is part of a history of U.S. military support for Pakistan that reaches back to partition and U.S. hostility toward India and nonalignment.[24]

As scholars grapple with the abuse and suspension of human rights at Abu Ghraib prison in Iraq and at Guantanamo, work by international feminist scholars that explores the sexual and racial violence endemic to U.S. military base communities provides critical context. Yoko Fukumora and Martha Matsuoka's "Redefining Security: Okinawa's Women's Resistance to U.S. Militarism" analyzes the human and environmental destruction wrought by U.S. military bases in Asia by tracing the work of activists who are demanding redress of the toxic contamination and U.S. military violence against women endemic to base communities.[25] Fukumora and Matsuoka also outline an alternative definition of security, based on a decentralized and sustainable global order, rather than the "slash-and-burn of rampant development."[26] Their engagement with the history of racial and sexual oppression within the military is a corrective not only to the inattention to race and sexuality within foreign policy studies but also to claims that the sexualized abuse of Iraqi prisoners is "un-American." Attention to the development of exploitative sex industries allows us to place such recent horrors as the abuse, torture, and sexual debasement at Abu Ghraib prison in Iraq within a history of military conduct toward nonwhite peoples.

Taken together, these studies survey the effects of U.S. power in Asia, the Middle East, and Africa, regions where that power has been instrumental in creating undemocratic military regimes. Placing the work of those who have viewed U.S. hegemony "from the outside in" in dialogue with the increasing number of U.S.-based scholars producing transnational work will further contribute to disrupting the self-absorption that has been an abiding feature of U.S. political culture.[27]

In foregrounding the issue of control of resources in the post-1945 world, I do not intend to make an "economics in the last instance" argument. Instead, a focus on resources raises questions about the constitution of U.S. citizens as imperial subjects that address the paradox of insularity and ambition posited by Louis Hartz. Scholars such as Amy Kaplan, Laura Wexler, and Christina Klein have helped us understand the complex mix of sentimentality, paternalism, class, and national privilege that has informed U.S. citizens' self-image as unique vessels of democracy and freedom with the right and responsibility to order the world in their own image. Far from insular, in a simple sense, Americans have long been engaged with the world.

In their important introduction to *Political Culture in the Shadow of Capitalism*, Lisa Lowe and David Lloyd attribute the bifurcation of culture from political economy, in part, to the assumptions and languages of modernity. Lowe and Lloyd argue that within modern intellectual traditions, the sphere of culture has been defined by its separation from the economic and political. Against this, they insist on elaborate imbrications of culture, politics, and economics. At the same time, they employ a fluid sense of culture—as work, pleasure, consumption, spirituality, "aesthetic production," and reproduction—that allows us to see culture itself as a site of power and contests over power. Michael Denning's *Culture in the Age of Three Worlds* also argues against the bifurcation of politics and culture.[28] Denning challenges approaches in cultural studies that read "the cultural commodities of postmodernism without interrogating the labor processes of post-Fordism."[29] Without taking up the challenge posed by Denning, Lowe, and Lloyd to transcend this fundamental modern dichotomy, we cannot possibly grasp, let alone confront, the paradox of a dominant American political culture whose global reach is matched by its self-absorption at home.

By rejecting the false dichotomy of culture and politics in the realm of foreign policy and the study of the United States' relationship to the non-American world, scholars such as Emily Rosenberg and Amy Kaplan have demonstrated that methodological approaches traditionally seen as in the sphere of "culture" provide a rich understanding of the workings of power and political economy. Scholarship that emerged in the 1950s and 1960s that was highly critical of U.S. dominance and revived the use of the term imperialism—namely the work of William Appleman Williams and his students—focused heavily on issues of political economy. In arguing that empire was a way of life, Williams emphasized that U.S. policy was motivated by the pursuit of economic advantage. America's departure from its isolationist past was undertaken by those policy-makers who sought to create and maintain an open door for overseas trade and investment. But as numerous historians have since shown, selling this policy to a public divided by moral and political objections to expansion was a complicated debate waged on terrains as varied as World's Fairs, the labor movement, and the pages of the rival Hearst and Pulitzer newspaper syndicates. Within such debates, racialized and gendered assumptions about manliness and civilization proliferated, bridging policy-makers and public opinion.[30] Mary Renda's *Taking Haiti* examines the processes of meaning-making among U.S. elites and working-class soldiers alike, brilliantly demonstrating that racial hierarchies were constitutive of Wilsonian liberalism. For the post-1945 era, Melanie McAlister's *Epic Encounters: Culture, Media, and U.S. Interests in the Middle East, 1945–2000*, charts U.S. media and cultural constructions of the Middle East while providing an account of U.S.-Iranian relations in her analysis of the political significance of mass media constructions of terrorism.[31]

Such studies are critical for grasping the scope and the limits of America's global reach, for they demonstrate that however gargantuan, U.S. ambition did not arise from a unitary aim but reflected a *multiplicity* of projects rife with internal tension and contradictions.[32] The United States' global ambition was not orchestrated by any one group of people but was shaped by multiple and often contradictory interests, from the State Department and the Pentagon, to such publishers as Time-Life owner Henry Luce, who coined the term "American century" to describe his vision of the post–World War II world. Indeed, Luce's career illustrates the blurry boundaries of hard and soft power. Luce castigated Harry Truman for inaction in Iran and the oil-producing nations of the Middle East, sponsoring Dwight Eisenhower's presidential campaign. And, as John Foran has demonstrated, *Time*'s forty-three articles on Musaddiq in 1951, when oil was nationalized, and the dozens that would appear each year until his ouster in 1953 "would go far beyond following the lead of the foreign policy establishment" to portray Musaddiq as an irrational fanatic who must be removed from office.[33] The analytic separation of culture and political economy has made it difficult to interrogate the deeply entangled relationships between the culture industries and the ascendance of the United States as an economic, cultural, and military power over the course of the twentieth century. From the Wilsonian legislation that freed Hollywood industries, along with banks and other corporations, from Progressive Era restrictions with the explicit intent of providing U.S. industries with a competitive global advantage, to the postwar circulation of Coca-Cola, Hollywood, and comic books, many people of the globe have encountered what we commonly think of as "private industry" in the context of U.S. economic dominance, U.S. government sponsorship, and an overt military presence.

The connection between the spread of U.S. film, music, comics, and other consumer products and military and other government agencies by no means implies that such cultural productions and artifacts were part of a unitary corporate, military, or government project. But neither does this imply, as often happens in cultural histories of Americanization, that one can neatly separate a nice, unproblematic history of the circulation of film or comics from the economic, political, and military conditions that informed and shaped that circulation. Drawing on the important insights of historian Bruce Cumings about the U.S. "archipelago empire," characterized by military bases throughout the Pacific, we can note that such bases were one of the major vehicles for the circulation of U.S. culture.[34] In the post-1945 world, many Asians and Pacific Islanders encountered rock 'n' roll music, Coca-Cola, and U.S. comic books for the first time in and around U.S. bases. Indeed, attention to the conditions of production, distribution, and circulation allow us to appreciate contradictions and contingencies in U.S. relations abroad. In corporate-state insistence on controlling access to resources from oil to uranium along with the numerous minerals critical for everything from refrigerators to vacuum cleaners to jet engines and the material technologies of radio and film, it becomes impossible to discern lines of hard and soft power.

If attention to culture has led to more nuanced understandings of politics and the origins of contemporary conflicts, the wide-ranging emphasis on culture as a process of meaning-making and an emphasis on the resistance of cultural forms to political manipulation has also at times contributed to a retreat from interpretive ambition and a deemphasis on questions of state power. Within the U.S. academy, the rejection of U.S. exceptionalism has tended to come not through an engagement with rest of the world per se, but from a well-placed skepticism toward the master narratives of U.S. history, a rejection of grand narrative, and a far-reaching cultural turn. Geoff Eley has trenchantly outlined the impact of the crisis of the enlightenment project, with its "commitment to grasping society as a whole" and "conceptualizing its underlining principles of unity." In many ways, this crisis has been enormously productive for our understanding of politics and has helped us confront the multifaceted nature of U.S. power. But however productive the focus on meaning-making and the rejection of reductive material analyses have been, historians have too often thrown in the towel prematurely, so to speak. If we want to understand change or power, obviously we cannot return to a grand, unitary narrative—in the sense of something that professes to give us the all-encompassing "real" story. But, for Eley, the untenability of a correspondence theory of truth does not mean that history is pointless or undoable. Rather, history's value is as a site of difference and contestation, "partly because it is always *de facto* being fought over (i.e., invoked and appropriated in conflicting and contradictory ways) and partly because it affords the contexts by which the ever seductive unities of contemporary social and political discourse, the naturalizing of hegemonies, can be upset."[35]

The story of Ellington in Iraq not only reveals history as a site of contests, unraveling myths about the disinterested spread of democracy that rest on denial of the long U.S. entanglement in the region, but also refuses to honor boundaries between culture, foreign policy, and political economy. The itineraries of American jazz musicians as cultural ambassadors for the State Department during the cold war followed the hard power of economic resources in Africa, Asia, and the Middle East, targeting those emergent "uncommitted" nations that comprised the nonaligned world. The early jazz tours were an expression of the expansive internationalism of U.S. policy-makers during the postwar period, as well as the boisterous one-upmanship of the cold war and the masculinist adventurism espoused by journalists and U.S. officials that, over the course of the 1950s, elevated covert action into a cult of counterinsurgency.[36] On the one hand, jazz tours embodied what Christina Klein has described as an outward-looking, open, popular internationalism. Reflected in such government programs as people-to-people exchanges, as well as in middlebrow mass media from magazines to movies to novels, this emphasis on positive global connections as opposed to the ominous preoccupation with containment was critical in forging domestic support for the ambitious global agendas of the American century.[37] On the other hand, jazz was consistently represented as a stealth weapon, and many State Department jazz tours navigated through a world of espionage and counterinsurgency, challenging us to question the relationships between hard and soft power—between force and belligerence and the connective bonds forged through languages of modernization, modernism, and egalitarianism.

One reason the musicians ended up in close proximity to coups and wars was simply because there were so many of them taking place. U.S. policy-makers did not seek to take over European forms of colonialism as they withered in the face of anticolonial challenges and the straitened conditions of wartime. Asserting instead the right of the United States to lead the "free world," they pursued a project of global economic integration through modernization and development. Those American policy-makers committed themselves to making sure that the West had privileged access to the world's markets, industrial infrastructure, and raw materials. They preferred to see the project of global economic integration as "benevolent supremacy."[38] But in the face of persistent attempts on the part of formerly colonized peoples to regain control of their resources, U.S. policy-makers made repeated use of (often covert) military force, making the term "cold war" a misnomer for the peoples of Asia, Africa, Latin America, and the Middle East, where democratic challenges often met with violent suppression by either proxies or covert operatives or both.[39] The CIA was so involved in behind-the-scenes Middle East scheming that an officer in Beirut wondered if "we'd soon be out of key politicians for CIA personnel to recruit. These included the so-called million dollar agents who steadily received six-figure subsidies."[40] By the time the jazz tours began, the CIA had already carried out covert actions in the Middle East, Southeast Asia, and Latin America.[41] Certainly many policy-makers viewed these actions as a necessary evil. The "common sense" of covert action depended on a worldview that viewed the Soviet Union as a dangerous enemy that fundamentally threatened "the American way of life." But in seeing an ubiquitous Soviet threat, American policy-makers repeatedly conflated nationalism and communism. Moreover, as several scholars have shown, the ouster of leaders throughout the Middle East, Africa, Asia, and Latin America often depended on ethnocentric assumptions about non-Western leaders that prohibited American policy-makers from viewing them as independent political agents. U.S. policy-makers tended to see leaders in these regions as pawns or potential pawns of the Soviets.[42] Despite the intricacy of America's global interdependence, with control of global resources at stake, American policy-makers rarely tolerated ambiguity or complexity when it came to assessing the allegiances of national leaders. And the self-absorption of these policy-makers, combined with a remarkable confidence in their ability to shape the world to their liking, made them unable to imagine the ramifications of such actions as the overthrow of democratic secular governments, which they perceived as threatening U.S. access to resources. Hence, an understanding of the processes of meaning-making and the particular racial and gender constructs of the post-1945 era are critical to understanding the paradoxes of insularity and ambition that characterize U.S. foreign policy.

The question of who controls the world's resources in the face of the collapse of European colonialism—and how U.S. policy-makers constructed the questions and answers about the place of the United States in the post-1945 world—has been entirely absent from celebratory accounts of the United States' "winning" of the cold war. Since the collapse of the Soviet Union, there has been an outpouring of interest—popular as well as scholarly—in the role of "culture" in the cold war. Paralleling the claims occasioned by the death of Willis Conover, the Voice of America jazz broadcaster, about his singular role in the U.S. triumph over the Soviet Union, it has become commonplace in post–cold war discourse to claim that the cold war was ultimately won by Levi's blue jeans and jazz.⁴³ To be sure, the world witnessed an arms buildup, "low-intensity" conflict here and there, but the appeal of American consumer culture could only be held at bay for so long, and in the end, consumer capitalism triumphed over state socialism. There are grains of truth that have made this view compelling. Conover *was* important in internationalizing jazz and no doubt helped shaped the contours of the cultural cold war. And demonstrably, aspects of American culture were attractive, if not seductive, for many of the world's people. But the actual history of the jazz ambassadors and the jazz tours belies the American exceptionalism of this contemporary replication of the 1950s celebration of jazz as the uniquely American contribution to world culture.

The story of jazz and the State Department is not the story of a nation standing apart from and unsullied by the exercise of imperial power. From a *longue durée* perspective, it is the story of an America deeply implicated in the machinations and violence of global modernization: from the slave trade that forced millions of Africans to the Americas, to U.S. involvement in coups from Iran to Iraq to the Congo and Ghana, and the arming of such military states as Pakistan that set the context for the tours. The itineraries of the jazz ambassadors force us to contend with entangled relationships between cultural and military interventions. Not only were artists deployed in proximity to covert and overt military campaigns, but in the broader sense of culture as structures of feeling and material life, this separation ignores the extent to which the material affluence of the United States in the post-1945 era was dependent on the domination of global resources. And in the face of persistent attempts by formerly colonized peoples to reclaim control of their resources, U.S. control of such resources was in turn necessarily dependent on militarism.[44] As Dave and Iola Brubeck so astutely pointed out in their musical collaboration with Louis Armstrong, *The Real Ambassadors*, "no commodity is quite so strange, as this thing called cultural exchange." What made cultural exchange so strange, in part, was that it closely pursued the quintessential cold war commodities, oil and uranium, along with many others critical to America's material abundance, which was so seductive for overseas audiences.[45] Then, as now, the material affluence of American life and the conditions of the daily reproduction of its culture of abundance were deeply dependent on U.S. foreign relations. In more ways than we may care to consider, our access to and consumption of resources implicate all of us in a global web of power relations.

Commenting on continued British denial of its colonial past and present, Stuart Hall has wryly noted that one doesn't have to look farther than the bottom of the ubiquitous "cuppa tea" for evidence of how colonialism fundamentally structured British society. The structuring of the United States as an imperial power can be discerned in comparable examples. Americans consumed millions of TV dinners in the 1950s and 1960, no doubt for the most part unaware of the Jamaican bauxite mines, acquired by the U.S.-based Reynolds Metals corporation during World War II, from which the aluminum tins originated, or the dismal working and living conditions of the undocumented immigrants in southern poultry factories who slaughtered and prepared the fried chicken, or the western migrant labor harvesting the fruit desert. Then, as now, the classic American freedom of the open road depended on oil and the Middle East. U.S. oil dependence was exposed in the 1970s energy crisis and is evident again in high gas prices in the aftermath of U.S. intervention in Iraq. And current debates on the interrelated commodities of oil, gas, and automobiles only begin to point to America's deeper global dependencies. Today, U.S. dependence within a web of global labor relations, as well as in the shadows of U.S. wars and global entanglements, is reflected in a myriad of seemingly mundane consumer decisions such as whether to order Vietnamese or Cambodian takeout. In our extremely privileged status as a nation, as the consumer of the lion's share of the world's energy and natural resources, much of what we see, think, and eat is shaped by the history of the expansive American global involvement.[46]

By suggesting that the United States has prevailed through the example of material success and democratic values, historians ignore fundamental conflicts within the United States, suggesting a shared, core adherence to material abundance that ultimately transcended differences. However, the story of the jazz tours is one of often-substantial differences in the aims of artists and government officials, particularly over the meaning of American national culture. Those who overtly challenged a dominant American culture of self-absorption were often in favor of a critical cosmopolitanism that proved most appealing to disparate groups in various parts of the globe.[47] If jazz fostered an anticommunist counterculture in the Eastern Bloc, as Miles Davis and Charles Mingus became symbols of cultural rebellion, they were identified as much with African American freedom struggles as with the government's ideas of democracy. In Africa and its diaspora, this dynamic was perhaps even more pronounced through a reciprocal process by which jazz, soul, and rhythm and blues inspired emerging African popular music styles, which, in turn, influenced American musicians.

In their attempt to deploy jazz musicians as agents of U.S. foreign policy, U.S. officials got a lot more than they bargained for. The State Department tours illuminated connections between domestic and foreign policies, and tensions between race, nation, and modernism. As representatives of a nation, musicians didn't simply sing its praises or soberly acknowledge its faults. They criticized its inequities, laughed at its foibles, and made fun of its pretensions. They spoke to the world through their horns and with their voices in the language of democracy and equality. On Ellington's 1963 Middle Eastern tour, when the musicians protested that they were only playing for elites already familiar with jazz when they had expected to play for "the people," the escort officer for Ellington's band, Thomas Simons, contrasted his official role with the musicians' view of "the people." The orchestra members, Simons explained, had a "different conception of what they were to do" than the State Department. Simons reported: "The orchestra members had misunderstood the word 'people,' and were disagreeably surprised."[48]

Positioning himself as a mediator between the musicians and the State Department, Simons adopted the third person in his report:

He could point out that societies in that part of the world are less fluid and more highly stratified than American society, . . . that the "people," the lower classes[,] do not in fact "count" as much as they do with us, and that we are trying to reach out to those who did count. . . . Few of these arguments made any real impression. Band members continued to feel that they would rather play for the "people," for the men in the streets who clustered around tea shop radios. More rationally, they believed that the lower classes, even if unimportant politically, were more worthy of exposure to good western music than the prestige audiences for whom they played.[49]

But it was U.S. government officials who had misunderstood the word people, *not* the members of Duke Ellington's orchestra. And that misreading of "the people" as Middle Eastern neocolonial elites allied with Western oil interests has cost the people of the region and the world dearly. Following these musicians *through* culture to an engagement with politics takes us to the heart of our task as historians. Not only did the members of Ellington's band insist on raising the question of who gets to count as "the people" but also, by contesting State Department priorities and focusing on those "who clustered around tea shop radios," they remind us that training as Americanists or a location in the U.S. academy does not create a privileged site from which to write about democracy or U.S. history. Taking the musicians seriously demands that we interrogate the assumptions that we bring to our study of history, and that we *listen*, in a global conversation about "who owns history?"

NOTES

1. "Palace of Rubble: American Soldiers Yesterday Inside a Ruined Palace in Baghdad That Belonged to President Saddam Hussein's Son Uday," photo, *New York Times*, April 11, 2003, 1.

2. Memo from anonymous U.S. official in Baghdad, to United States Information Service [USINFO], Washington, D.C., November 11, 1963, Bureau of Educational and Cultural Affairs Historical Collection, J. William Fulbright Papers, University of Arkansas at Fayetteville, hereafter cited as BHC; "The Duke Ellington Orchestra, September 6–November 28, 1963," sixteen-week synopsis, series 2, box 9, BHC. See also, Penny Von Eschen, *Satchmo Blows Up the World: Jazz Ambassadors Play the Cold War* (Cambridge, Mass., 2004).

3. Memo from anonymous U.S. official in Baghdad, to United States Information Service, Washington, D.C., November 11, 1963, BHC.

4. Eric Foner, *Who Owns History? Rethinking the Past in a Changing World* (New York, 2002), 73.

5. Michael H. Hunt, "In the Wake of September 11: The Clash of What?" *Journal of American History*, 89, no. 2 (March–April 2002): 416–25. In the depiction of the United Sates as a Janus-faced power, I am drawing on Perry Anderson, "Internationalism: A Breviary," *New Left Review* 14 (March–April 2002): 23, and Nikhil Pal Singh, *Black Is a Country: Race and the Unfinished Struggle for Democracy* (Cambridge, Mass., 2004), 136.

6. Joseph S. Nye, *Soft Power: The Means to Success in World Politics* (Washington, D.C., 2004).

7. Tariq Ali, *The Clash of Fundamentalism: Crusades, Jihads, and Modernity* (London, 2003), 110–13; Con Coughlin, *Saddam: King of Terror* (New York, 2001), 39.

8. Douglas Little, *American Orientalism: The United States and the Middle East since 1945* (Chapel Hill, 2002), 205.

9. Little, *American Orientalism*, 205–6.

10. Baghdad to USINFO, Washington, D.C., November 14, 1963, BHC.

11. Thomas W. Simons Jr., "General Report on the Ellington Tour," series 1, box 2, 20. See also series 2, box 9, BHC. Baghdad to USINFO, Washington, D.C., November 14, 1963, BHC.

12. Baghdad to USINFO, Washington, D.C., November 14, 1963. BHC

13. "Complete Itinerary of Ellington's 1963 Mid-East Tour," post-comments, 14, BHC.

14. "Army Said to Oust Baathists in Iraq: President Reported to Lead Revolt—Communications from Baghdad Cut," *New York Times*, November 18, 1963, 1.

15. Little, *American Orientalism*, 206.

16. Perhaps the most influential and widely debated example of this is Michael Hardt and Antonio Negri, *Empire* (Cambridge, Mass., 2000).

17. Charles Bright and Michael Geyer, "Where in the World Is America? The History of the United States in a Global Age," in *Rethinking American History in a Global Age*, ed. Thomas Bender, 64–99 (Berkeley, 2002). See Michael Denning's discussion on this point in Denning, *Culture in the Age of Three Worlds* (London, 2004), 49.

18. Akira Iriye has argued that a multinational perspective would "characterize immediate post-war years, not in terms of the origins of the Cold War, but the time when the forces of globalization and internationalism renewed themselves after they had been subverted by the Cold War," "Internationalizing International History," in *Rethinking American History*, 56; Akira Iriye, *Global Community: The Role of International Organizations in the Making of the Contemporary World* (Berkeley, 2002).

19. Prasenjit Duara, "Transnationalism and the Challenge of National Histories," in *Rethinking American History*, 30; Rashid Khalidi, *Resurrecting Empire: Western Footprints and America's Perilous Path in the Middle East* (New York: Beacon, 2004).

20. Fred Cooper's skeptical approach to the concept of globalization is useful for thinking about these trajectories. Fred Cooper, "What Is the Concept of Globalization Good For? An African Historian's Perspective," *African Affairs* (2001): 100, 189–213.

21. Pransenjit Duara, *Decolonization: Perspectives from Then and Now* (London, 2004), 1. On African American interaction with the anticolonial world, see, Penny M. Von Eschen, *Race against Empire: Black Americans and Anticolonialism 1937–57* (Ithaca, 1997); Winston James, *Holding Aloft the Banner of Ethiopia: Caribbean Radicalism in Early Twentieth-Century America* (London, 1998); and Kevin K. Gaines, *American Africans in Ghana: Black Expatriates in the Civil Rights Era* (Chapel Hill, 2006).

22. Rashid Khalidi, *Western Footprints and America's Perilous Path in the Middle East* (New York, 2004,) 92.

23. See, for example, Gilbert M. Joseph, Catherine C. LeGrand, and Ricardo D. Salvatore, eds., *Close Encounters of Empire: Writing the Cultural History of U.S.-Latin American Relations* (Durham, 1998). In *Post-Nationalist American Studies* (Berkeley, 2000), John Carlos Rowe has brilliantly challenged insular studies of the United States by offering a profoundly transnational and comparative volume ranging from Latin America to the Pacific and from women and war to the commodification of culture.

24. Mahmood Mamdani, *Good Muslim, Bad Muslim: The Cold War and Roots of Terror* (New York, 2004).

25. Yoko Fukumora and Martha Matsuoka, "Redefining Security: Okinawa's Women's Resistance to U.S. Militarism, " in *Women's Activism and Globalization: Linking Local Struggles and Transnational Politics*, ed. Nancy Naples and Manish Desai, 239–63 (New York, 2002).

26. Ibid., 260.

27. Viewing the United States from the outside in can also entail focusing on the subjectivities and transnational projects of marginalized peoples within the United States. A focus on black subjectivity and black political projects and cultural production has already provided an important model for bringing Americanist concerns into conversation with the rest of the globe and continues to point in critical directions for the re-visioning of historical scholarship. For recent scholarship see Brent Edwards, *The Practice of Diaspora* (Cambridge, 2003); Singh, *Black is a Country*; Gaines, *American Africans in Ghana*.

28. Frederick Cooper and Ann Laura Stoler, eds., *Tensions of Empire: Colonial Cultures in a Bourgeois World* (Berkeley, 1997).

29. Michael Denning, *Culture in the Age of Three Worlds* (New York, 2004).

30. Emily Rosenberg's superb essay "Turning to Culture" charts multiple turns toward culture, emphasizing the way in which they offer more refined insights into political contestation. Rosenberg surveys examples of the analysis of popular culture as a site of struggle, studies of transnational cultural interactions, "symbolic systems that comprise the languages of power," the "representational technologies of U.S. predominance," and investigations of identity formation that erase the difference between domestic and international history. Rosenberg, "Turing to Culture," in *Close Encounters of Empire*, 497–514.

31. Melanie McAlister, *Epic Encounters: Culture, Media, and U.S. Interests in the Middle East, 1945–2000* (Berkeley, 2001), 49, 210–11.

32. It was indeed, what Catherine Hall has characterized in the British context as a "cacophony of imperial voices" rife with internal tensions and contradictions. Catherine Hall, *Civilising Subjects: Metropole and Colony in the English Imagination, 1830–1867* (Chicago, 2002).

33. John Foran, "Discursive Subversions: *Time Magazine*, the CIA Overthrow of Musaddiq, and the Installation of the Shah," in *Cold War Constructions: The Political Culture of United States Imperialism, 1945–1966*, ed. Christian G. Appy, 165 (Amherst, 2000).

34. Bruce Cumings, "Is America an Imperial Power?" *Current History* (November 2003).

35. Geoff Eley, "Is All the World a Text: From Social History to the History of Society Two Decades Later," CRSO no. 445 (October 1990): 213, 216. See also,

Geoff Eley, *A Crooked Line: From Cultural History to the History of Society* (Ann Arbor, 2004).

36. See Christina Klein's elegant discussion of what she calls the "global imaginary of integration." Klein, *Cold War Orientalism: Asia in the Middlebrow Imagination, 1945–1961* (Berkeley, 2001), 19–60.

37. Klein, *Cold War Orientalism*; Singh, *Black Is a Country*.

38. McAlister, *Epic Encounters*, 43–55.

39. See Bruce Cumings, "The Wicked Witch of the West Is Dead: Long Live the Wicked Witch of the East," 87, and Walter LaFeber, "An End to Which Cold War?" both in *The End of the Cold War: Its Meanings and Implications*, ed. Michael J. Hogan (New York, 1992).

40. Quoted in Derek Leebaert, *The Fifty-Year Wound: The True Price of America's Cold War Victory* (Boston, 2002), 206. While I disagree with many of the political assumptions and analytic perspectives presented by Leebaert, his meticulous study on the cost of America's extensive cold war engagements is an important contribution.

41. Ibid. Uadrey R. Kahin and George McT.Kahin, *Subversion as Foreign policy: The Secret Eisenhower and Dulles Debacle in Indonesia* (New York, 1995); Robert J. McMahon, *Colonialism and the Cold War: The United States and the Struggle for Indonesian Independence, 1945–1949* (Ithaca, 1981).

42. Thomas Borstelmann, *The Cold War and the Color Line: American Race Relations in the Global Arena* (Cambridge, Mass., 2003); Michael Hunt, *Ideology and U.S. Foreign Policy* (New Haven, 1988).

43. Robert McG. Thomas Jr., "Willis Conover, 75, Voice of America Disc Jockey," *New York Times*, May 19, 1996, 35. In his nuanced discussion of U.S./Soviet cultural exchange, the historian Walter Hixson has rejected what he has termed "the crude and parochial triumphalist perspective on the end of the Cold War." Yet in his view, the role of culture remains decisive. For Hixson, it was the modern version of old-fashion idealist diplomacy with its belief in the inevitability of "the nation serving as a model of material success and democratic values," not militarism, that "ultimately proved more effective in combating the Soviet Empire. Walter L. Hixson, *Parting the Curtain: Propaganda, Culture, and the Cold War, 1945–1961* (New York, 1997), 231–32.

44. Irene L. Gendzier, "Play It Again, Sam: The Practice and Apology of Development," in *Universities and Empire: Money and Politics in the Social Sciences during the Cold War*, Christopher Simpson, 57–95 (New York, 1998).

45. Dave Brubeck, "Cultural Exchange," *The Real Ambassadors*, Columbia LP, 1961.

46. Kristin Hoganson, "Cosmopolitan Domesticity: Importing the American Dream, 1865–1920," *American Historical Review* 107 (February 2002): 55–83. Much

of the recent work on consumption has brilliantly linked shifts in consumer habits to politics and race relations but has not likewise considered the foreign relations undergirding the extraction and production of the materials required for such abundance. See, Lizabeth Cohen, *A Consumers' Republic: The Politics of Mass Consumption in Postwar America* ((New York, 2003).

47. Reinhold Wagnleitner, "The Empire of Fun, or Talkin' Soviet Union Blues: The Sound of Freedom and U.S. Cultural Hegemony in Europe," *Diplomatic History* 23, no. 3 (summer 1999): 499–524.

48. Thomas W. Simons Sr., Effectiveness Report, Ellington Tour 1963, series 2, box 9, 15–17, BHC.

49. Ibid. See also Von Eschen, *Satchmo Blows Up the World.*

Chapter Fourteen

· · · · · · · · · · ·

The Story of American Freedom— Before and After 9/11

ERIC FONER

Keynote address for "Contested Democracy: Freedom, Race, and Power in American History," a conference in honor of Eric Foner, October 14, 2005, Columbia University, New York

It is a great source of pride to be honored this weekend and to see again this brilliant group of students who came to Columbia fifteen to twenty years ago. It is a remarkably diverse group, hailing from six countries (China, Germany, India, Israel, and Italy, along with the United States) and writing on issues and time periods that range across the entire two centuries of American nationhood. Nothing gives a teacher greater pleasure than seeing his students fulfill their early promise and become prominent and widely admired scholars in their own right. This event has led me to reflect on my own education as a historian. I think of my late father, Jack Foner, himself a historian, and how pleased he would have been on this occasion. Deprived of his livelihood while I was growing up because of McCarthyism, he worked as a freelance lecturer on history and current affairs. If his lectures had an overriding theme, it was how present concerns can be illuminated by the study of the past—how the repression of the McCarthy era recalled the days of the Alien and Sedition Acts, the civil rights movement needed to be viewed in light of the great struggles of black and white abolitionists, and how in the suppression of the Philippine insurrection at the turn of the century could be found the antecedents of American interventions in Iran, Guatemala, and Vietnam. I also imbibed a way of thinking about the past in which visionaries and underdogs—Tom Paine, Wendell Phillips, Eugene V. Debs, and W. E. B. Du Bois—were as central to the historical drama as presidents and captains of industry.

I think about my experiences as an undergraduate history major here at Columbia and then, after an interval of two years at Oxford, as a graduate student, and the great teachers who inspired me. First was Jim Shenton, legendary at Columbia for his dramatic lecturing style and the personal interest he took in his students—down to introducing us to the city's culinary attractions. His yearlong seminar on the Civil War era was the first history class I took here, and ever since, this pivotal period of our history has been the major focus of my historical scholarship. Among the department's American historians at that time were the witty, incisive William Leuchtenberg and the deeply thoughtful Eric McKitrick, in whose lectures one could observe a first-rate intellect examining a subject from every possible angle. And the one from whom I learned the most, Richard Hofstadter, the foremost historian of his generation. At that time, the history department was still divided into graduate and undergraduate branches, the former with offices in Fayerweather, the latter in Hamilton. Hofstadter taught mainly graduate courses but chose to keep his office in Hamilton, perhaps, one of his colleagues speculated, because years before there had been opposition to his receiving tenure and he was grateful for the strong support of Harry J. Carman, dean of the college.

Hofstadter was not a particularly accomplished lecturer. He was a modest man who hated performing for an audience. His forte lay in leading discussions and subjecting written work to penetrating criticism. He played brilliantly the role of intellectual mentor so crucial to any student's career. He did not try to impose his views on his students; instead he pushed them to do the very best work they were capable of doing, on subjects and with outlooks of their own choosing. I well recall his graduate colloquium on the Progressive historians. Hofstadter remarked almost apologetically at the outset that studying Charles Beard, Frederick Jackson Turner, and Vernon Parrington must seem hopelessly arcane to us, but that each scholar must at some point try to come to terms with his or her formative influences. And Hofstadter's books directed me toward the subjects that have defined so much of my own writing—the history of political ideologies and the interconnections between social development and political culture. I sometimes feel that although I have come up with very different answers than he did, my career has been devoted to addressing the same questions Hofstadter posed about American history.

One of those questions has to do with the history of freedom in the United States, as an idea, a reality, and a mythology. No subject has been more central to my work as a historian. From my dissertation, "Free Soil, Free Labor, Free Men," to my latest publication, *Forever Free*, no fewer than seven of my books have had the words "free," "freedom," or "liberty" in the title. The history of this idea was the subject of *The Story of American Freedom*, published in 1998. No idea is more fundamental to Americans' sense of themselves as individuals and as a nation than freedom. The central term in our political vocabulary, freedom—or its twin, liberty—is deeply embedded in the documentary record of our history and the language of everyday life. The Declaration of Independence lists liberty among mankind's unalienable rights; the Constitution announces as its purpose to secure liberty's blessings.

Freedom has been a rallying cry to mobilize public support for American wars. The United States fought the Civil War to bring about a new birth of freedom, World War II for the Four Freedoms, the Cold War to defend the Free World. The current war in Iraq has been given the title Operation Iraqi Freedom. Americans' love of freedom has been represented by liberty poles, liberty caps, and statues of liberty. It has been acted out by burning stamps and burning draft cards, by running away from slavery, and demonstrating for the right to vote. Obviously, other peoples also cherish freedom, but the idea does seem to occupy a more prominent place in public and private discourse in the United States than elsewhere. "Every man in the street, white, black, red or yellow," wrote the educator and statesman Ralph Bunche in 1940, "knows that this is 'the land of the free' . . . [and] 'the cradle of liberty.'"

Perhaps because of its very ubiquity, the history of what the historian Carl Becker called this "magic but elusive word" is a tale of debates, disagreements, and struggles rather than a set of timeless categories or an evolutionary narrative toward a preordained goal. Rather than seeing freedom as a fixed category or predetermined concept, I view it as what philosophers call an "essentially contested idea," one that by its very nature is the subject of disagreement. Use of such a concept automatically presupposes an ongoing dialogue with other, competing meanings. And the meaning of freedom has been constructed not only in congressional debates and political treatises, but on plantations and picket lines, in parlors and even bedrooms.

If freedom has been a battleground throughout our history, so too has been the definition of those entitled to enjoy its blessings. It is hardly original to point out that the United States, founded on the premise that liberty is an entitlement of all humanity, blatantly deprived many of its own people of freedom. Efforts to delimit freedom along one or another axis of social existence have been a persistent feature of our history. More to the point, perhaps, freedom has often been defined by its limits. The master's freedom rested on the reality of slavery, the vaunted autonomy of men on the subordinate position of women. I could elaborate further on these ideas, which are explored in depth in my book published in 1998. But what I want to do today is to suggest how an appreciation of the history of freedom—as a contested idea and a lived experience—can help us understand some of the changes American society has undergone since September 11, 2001.

The events of that tragic day, and the way Americans and our government have responded over the past four years, rudely placed certain issues on the historical agenda. Today, I want to speak about three of them and their implications for how we think about the American past: the invocation of freedom as an explanation for the attacks and a justification for the ensuing war on terrorism; widespread acquiescence in significant infringements on civil liberties; and a sudden awareness of considerable distrust abroad of American actions and motives. The first step in thinking about these developments is to historicize them—to understand that they all have histories. I argue that it is our responsibility to bring a historical perspective to bear on the challenges America faces today and to try to counterpose a historical mode of thinking to the mythmaking so prevalent in our public debates.

In the aftermath of September 11, the language of freedom once again took center stage in American public discourse, as an all-purpose explanation for both the attack and the ensuing war against "terrorism." "Freedom itself is under attack," President Bush announced in his September 21 speech to Congress, and he gave the title Enduring Freedom to the ensuing war in Afghanistan. Our antagonists, he went on, "hate our freedoms, our freedom of religion, our freedom of speech, our freedom to assemble and disagree with each other." In his June 2002 speech to the International Brotherhood of Carpenters, the president asked why terrorists attacked

America. His answer: "Because we love freedom, that's why. And they hate freedom." In mid-September 2002, in calling for increased attention to the teaching of American history so that schoolchildren can understand "why we fight," Bush observed, "ours is a history of freedom, . . . freedom for everybody."

One of the key expressions of this public embrace of freedom—and of the ways the invocation of freedom has become a way of closing rather than opening debate—appears in the 2002 National Security Strategy, the document that announced the doctrine of preemptive war. This opens not with a discussion of weaponry or global geopolitics but with an invocation of freedom, which it defines as political democracy, freedom of expression, religious toleration, and free enterprise. These, the document proclaims, "are right and true for every person, in every society." There is no sense that other people may have given thought to the question of freedom and arrived at their own conclusions. In addition, the document proclaims the existence of a "single sustainable model" of social organization based on freedom: that of the United States. It is worth stopping for a moment to reflect on this language. The idea of a single social model is a profoundly illiberal idea—not in the sense of today's liberals and conservatives, but in terms of Sir Isaiah Berlin's definition of a liberal society as one in which many models compete for acceptance. And sustainable? How sustainable would life on earth be if the entire world consumed energy and emitted carbon dioxide into the atmosphere at the American rate?

The high point of the president's identification of his administration's policies with freedom came in his 2005 inaugural address. In its 2001 predecessor, he used the words liberty or freedom seven times. Four years later, by my count, they appeared forty-seven times, in a fifteen-minute speech. President Bush affirmed God's plan for history and for using the United States as His special agent in carrying out this plan. How do we know that freedom is the plan of history? Because "history . . . has a visible direction, set by liberty and the Author of Liberty." Today, more than ever, we debate contemporary issues in a landscape shaped by ideas of freedom. But historians will recognize that there is nothing unusual in the invocation of freedom as an American rallying cry.

The Revolution gave birth to a definition of American nationhood and national mission that persists to this day, in which the new nation defined itself as a unique embodiment of liberty in a world overrun with oppression.

The Civil War and emancipation reinforced the identification of the United States with the progress of freedom. In the twentieth century, the discourse of a world sharply divided into opposing camps, one representing freedom and the other its antithesis, was reinvigorated in the worldwide struggles against Nazism and communism. The sense of American uniqueness, of the United States as an example to the rest of the world of the superiority of free institutions, remains very much alive as a central element of our political culture. Freedom is the trump card of political discourse, invoked as often to silence debate as to invigorate it. The very ubiquity today of the language of freedom suggests that we need to equip students to understand the many meanings freedom has had and the many uses to which it has been put over the course of our history.

Calling our past a history of freedom "for everybody" makes it impossible to discuss seriously the numerous instances when groups of Americans have been denied freedom or the ways in which some Americans today enjoy a great deal more freedom than others. It makes it impossible to appreciate how battles at freedom's boundaries—the efforts of racial minorities, women, and other groups to secure freedom as they understood it—have both deepened and transformed the meaning of freedom. The modern idea that freedom is equally an entitlement of all Americans regardless of race, for example, owes as much to slaves and abolitionists who insisted that liberty is a truly human ideal as to the founders, who spoke of freedom as a universal entitlement but established a slaveholding republic.

The post-9/11 "war on terrorism" also raises timeless issues concerning civil liberties in wartime, the balance between freedom and security, the rights of noncitizens, and the ethnic boundaries of American freedom. As has happened during previous wars, the idea of an open-ended global battle between freedom and its opposite has justified serious infringements on civil liberties at home. Legal protections such as habeas corpus, trial by impartial jury, the right to legal representation, and equality before the law regardless of race or national origin have been curtailed. At least five thousand foreigners with Middle Eastern connections were rounded up in the aftermath of September 11, and more than one thousand arrested and held without charge or even public acknowledgment of their fate. To this date, not a single one has been charged with involvement in the events of 9/11. (Zaccarias Moussaoui, the so-called twentieth hijacker, was already in custody on that day.)

An executive order authorized the holding of secret military tribunals for noncitizens deemed to have assisted terrorism, and in June 2002 the Justice Department argued in court that even American citizens could be held indefinitely and not allowed to see a lawyer, once the government designates them "enemy combatants." After 9/11 the United States set up a worldwide system of detention centers for the purpose of holding and interrogating captured people and suspects. There were no charges or trials—this was not a system of imprisonment for crimes. Evidence soon surfaced of the abuse of prisoners, some killing, and much torture, especially at Abu Ghraib prison in Iraq.

The "age of human rights," optimistically proclaimed in the 1990s, in which nations would conduct themselves on the basis of respect for the rights of all persons, came to an abrupt end. Memos to the president by his legal advisers, including the current attorney general, argued that the government is not fully bound by the Geneva conventions. The release of documents related to torture in 2005 revealed lawyers and other officials laying the groundwork for using torture in the war on terrorism. After much adverse publicity, at the end of December 2004 the Department of Justice announced that torture was unacceptable—but reports of abuse continued to circulate. This was not the first time torture by American soldiers inspired outrage—it had happened in the Philippine War and in Vietnam. But in those cases, torture was not an official policy.

The photographs that shocked the world do not represent the values of American society. But they are the inevitable consequence of the outlook that says that because we represent freedom, those who oppose us are by definition the enemies of freedom; that because of our self-evidently noble motives we are not like other countries—they must abide by time-honored conventions of behavior but we can set our own rules of conduct for ourselves. In 2004, the Supreme Court rejected important parts of the Bush administration position on the detention and trial of "unlawful combatants." This was partly a question of the division of powers—the courts are extremely reluctant to approve the creation of places where the law does not apply. But despite some judicial resistance to the sweeping restraints on civil liberties initiated by the government, one "surprise" of the last four years has been how willing the majority of Americans are to accept them, especially when they seem to apply primarily to a single, ethnically identified segment of our population.

This was brought home to me last spring when I visited the International Spy Museum, in Washington, D.C. I wanted to see the exhibit The Enemy Within: Terror in America 1776 to Today. What I found was a hodgepodge of people and movements—John Brown, the KKK, anarchists, Timothy McVeigh, even the British burning Washington in the War of 1812 (an act that qualifies as uncouth but hardly terrorism). The exhibit contained computer screens where visitors could vote on various propositions. One asked for a response to this statement: "The government should have the authority to deport or indefinitely detain people suspected of supporting groups hostile to the United States." This language needs to be read carefully—it proposes the indefinite detention of people neither accused nor convicted of any crime, and offers no definition whatever of "hostile to America" (a phrase that some would apply to environmentalists, opponents of the Iraq war, indeed any critic of administration policies). As of January 2005, thirty thousand people had voted—not a scientific sample, but a large group nonetheless. The result: 54 percent, yes; 32 percent, no.

Like other consequences of September 11, this willingness to suspend traditional notions of fair play and individual rights needs to be understood in its historical context. That history suggests that strong protection for civil liberties is not a constant feature of our "civilization" but a recent and still fragile historical achievement. Our civil liberties are neither self-enforcing nor self-correcting. America, of course, has a long tradition of vigorous political debate and dissent, an essential part of our democratic tradition. But until well into the twentieth century, a broad rhetorical commitment to this ideal coexisted with stringent restrictions on speech that was deemed radical or obscene, or that challenged the racial status quo.

In our teaching we ought to recall previous episodes—the Alien and Sedition Acts of 1798, the massive repression of dissent during World War I, the victimization of civil rights activists, Japanese American internment during World War II—to emphasize the dangers of stigmatizing unpopular beliefs or particular groups of Americans as unworthy of constitutional protections. We need to remind our students of obscure Supreme Court decisions—Fong Yue Ting (1893), the Insular Cases of the early twentieth century, Korematsu during World War II—in which the Court allowed the government a virtual carte blanche in dealing with aliens and in suspending the rights of specific groups of citizens on grounds of military necessity. But we should not forget the ringing dissents in these cases. In Fong Yue Ting, which authorized the deportation of Chinese immigrants without due process, Justice Brewer warned that the power was now directed against a people many Americans found "obnoxious," but "who shall say it will not be exercised tomorrow against other classes and other people?" In Korematsu, which upheld Japanese American internment, Justice Robert Jackson wrote that the decision "lies about like a loaded weapon ready for the hand of any authority than can bring forward a plausible claim to an urgent need."

In the aftermath of September 11, it seemed for a time that the Bush administration had put aside the unilateralism that marked its first months in office in favor of a cooperative approach to international affairs. But the idea that the United States as the world's predominant power can ignore the opinions of other nations soon reappeared. This has been a special temptation in the wake of September 11, which has produced a spate of historical and political commentary influenced by Samuel P. Huntington's mid-1990s book *The Clash of Civilizations*. It is all too easy to explain September 11 as a confrontation between Western and Islamic civilizations. But the notion of a "clash of civilizations" is monolithic, static, and essentialist. It reduces politics and culture to a single characteristic—race, religion, or geography—that remains forever static, divorced from historical development. It denies the global exchange of ideas and the interpenetration of cultures that has been a feature of the modern world for centuries.

It also makes it impossible to discuss divisions within these purported civilizations. The construct of "Islam," for example, lumps together over a billion people in diverse societies stretching from East Asia to the Middle East and Africa. And the idea that the West has exclusive access to reason, liberty, and tolerance ignores both the relative recency of the triumph of such values within the West and the debates over Creationism, abortion rights, and other issues that suggest that commitment to such values is hardly unanimous. The difference between positing civilizations with unchanging essences and analyzing change within and interaction between societies is the difference between thinking mythically and thinking historically.

It certainly seems to be true that the various ideas of freedom with which we are familiar have not sunk deep roots in Islamic societies. But to explain terrorism as the inevitable outcome of the pathologies of Islamic civilization—or to suggest, as the president does, that democracies do not produce terrorism—ignores the fact that many societies, including our own, have spawned terrorists. The Ku Klux Klan during Reconstruction murdered more innocent Americans than Osama bin Laden has. The Oklahoma City bombing of 1995 and the post-9/11 circulation of anthrax through the mails were both initially attributed to foreign terrorists, yet both were home grown. Terrorism springs from specific historical causes and can emerge in many times and places. Its roots require historical analysis.

Ironically, September 11 highlighted not only America's vulnerability but our overwhelming power. Never, perhaps, since the days of the Roman empire has one state so totally eclipsed the others. In every index of power—military, economic, cultural, scientific—the United States far exceeds any other country. It is not surprising in such circumstances that many Americans feel that the country can operate as it sees fit. Since September 11, the word "empire," once a term of opprobrium, has come back into unembarrassed use in American political discourse. The need to shoulder the burdens of empire is a theme in discussion among the foreign policy elite. Like other responses to September 11, the idea of the United States as an empire has a long history, one linked to the belief that the country—by example, force, or a combination of the two—can remake the world in its own image.

Jefferson spoke of the United States as an "empire of liberty." This might seem an oxymoron, since empire means domination over others, but Jefferson insisted that America's would be fundamentally different from the oppressive empires of European powers. When the nation stepped onto the world stage as an imperial power in the Spanish-American War, President McKinley insisted that ours was a "benevolent imperialism." Woodrow Wilson maintained that only the United States possessed the combination of military power and moral righteousness to make the world safe for democracy. In 1942, Henry Luce, the publisher of *Time* and *Life* magazines, called for the United States to assume the role of "dominant power in the world" in what he famously called "the American century."

The history of the idea and practice of empire might help Americans understand why other countries sometimes resent our tendency to pursue our own interests as a world power while proclaiming that we embody universal values and goals. A recent Gallup poll revealed that few Americans have any knowledge of other countries' grievances against the United States. But the benevolence of benevolent imperialism lies in the eye of the beholder. Indians and Mexicans did not desire to surrender their lands to the onward march of Jefferson's empire of liberty. Many Filipinos did not share President McKinley's judgment that they would be better off under American rule than as an independent nation. A candid study of the history of our relationship with the rest of the world might enable us to find it less surprising that despite the wave of sympathy for the United States that followed September 11, there is widespread fear outside our borders, including among many longtime allies, that the war on terrorism is motivated in part by the desire to impose a Pax Americana in a grossly unequal world.

Local situations and complex motives throughout the world cannot be subsumed into a single either-or dichotomy of friends and enemies of freedom or terrorists and their opponents. It is worth remembering that anti-Americanism in the Middle East is a recent phenomenon, not a primordial hatred, and that it is not confined to Islamic fundamentalists but can be found among secular nationalists and democratic reformers. It is based primarily on American policies—toward Israel, the Palestinians, oil supplies, and the region's corrupt and authoritarian regimes—not distaste for freedom. Indeed, despite all the rhetoric to the contrary, there is no reason to believe that 9/11 was motivated primarily by hatred of freedom. "They hate us because we are free" cannot explain why terrorists are not attacking other free societies, like Canada or Denmark.

Back in the eighteenth century, Anthony Ashley Cooper, the Earl of Shaftesbury and a key Enlightenment figure in Great Britain, commented on the growing xenophobia and insularity that empire seems to produce: "Our best policy and breeding is, it seems, to look abroad as little as possible, contract our views within the narrowest compass and despise all knowledge, learning or manners which are not of a home growth." More than two centuries later, 9/11 seems to have produced an odd combination of cosmopolitanism and myopia—a recognition that we exist as part of a wider world, coupled with demands that we once again emphasize what sets us apart from the rest of mankind.

Shortly before Richard Hofstadter's death in 1970, *Newsweek* published an interview with him on the state of American life. It was a melancholy reflection on a society confronting what he called a "crisis of the spirit." Young people, said Hofstadter, had no sense of vocation, no aspirations for the future. The causes of their alienation were real—"You have a major urban crisis. You have the question of race, and you have a cruel and unnecessary war." He rejected young radicals' stance of "moral indignation" as a kind of elitism on the part of those who did not have to face the day-to-day task of earning a living. But ultimately, he went on, it was American society itself, not just its children, that had to change. "I think that part of our trouble is that our sense of ourselves hasn't diminished as much as it ought to." The United States, he seemed to be saying, would have to accept limitations on its power to shape the world.

Today, Hofstadter's call for Americans to listen to the rest of the world, not simply seek to impose its will upon it, seems more relevant than ever. This may be difficult for a nation that has always considered itself a city upon a hill, a beacon to mankind. Yet American independence was proclaimed by men anxious, as they wrote in the Declaration of Independence, to demonstrate "a decent respect to the opinions of mankind." It is not the role of historians to instruct our students on how they should think about our turbulent world or to define their ideas of freedom for them. But it is our task to insist that the study of history should transcend boundaries rather than reinforcing or reproducing them. In the wake of September 11, it is all the more imperative that the history we teach must be a candid appraisal of our own society's strengths and weaknesses, not simply an exercise in self-celebration. If September 11 makes us think historically—not mythically—about our nation and its role in the world, then perhaps some good will have come out of that tragic event.

Afterword

"From the Archives and from the Heart"

DAVID W. BLIGHT

Remarks on Eric Foner, October 15, 2005, Columbia University, New York

It was not the first time I had met Eric Foner, but it was the first time I had the pleasure of spending any time with him. We were gathered as part of the Milan Group, in June 1992. That group of historians and other scholars, a mixture of Americans, Europeans, Australians, Israelis, and others who tended to write from a left, social-political history perspective, had been formed back in the 1970s by Herbert Gutman and Loretta Mannucci. Eric was chair and commentator on a session where I gave my first-ever paper on the memory of the Civil War. He was gentle in his criticisms, enthusiastic and encouraging about the overall project (which I had hardly figured out at that point), and a little suspicious of just what I meant by "cultural and social memory" and how that was supposed to be any different from versions of history possessed by the broader public. He did have one specific piece of advice that I remember. "Whatever you do with this problem of Civil War memory," he said, "don't leave out the politics." It was one of the most memorable and formative conference sessions of my life. In the wrap-up session, after a vigorous discussion regarding Leon Litwack's paper about the dark and terrible story of the Jim Crow South at the turn of the twentieth century, Eric challenged us all to be careful that our work and our interpretations did not merely buttress the tragic, dead-end, victimized vision of African American history (which was reviving in a way in the late 1980s and early '90s and lending itself to a new kind of racial separation and conservative black nationalism). I distinctly remember his saying something like: "We can't change the world that way; we have to change it together." I remember thinking silently, my God, he really means it—the history we write might actually *change the world*.

From his parents' blacklisting in the 1940s and '50s, to recognizing that W. E. B. Du Bois and Paul Robeson were family friends, picketing Woolworth stores and attending civil rights marches as a teenager with his parents, and growing up with Frederick Douglass as a household name due to his uncle Philip's magisterial editing of the great abolitionist's writings, Eric came to this craft of history assuming that past, present, and future were always and everywhere intertwined, however we may be trained to keep those three senses of time in their proper compartments. Eric ends his autobiographical essay movingly with the story of lecturing in South Africa in 1994, where at the end of his talk, a torch was lit symbolizing the new birth of freedom in the wake of apartheid. This illustrated, he writes, "the interconnectedness of past, present, and future." Even more moving to me, though, is Eric's poignant description in the same essay of the meaning of his magnum opus on Reconstruction. After recognizing that *Reconstruction: America's Unfinished Revolution* had garnered book awards and gratifying reviews, he stopped for one moment of self-revelatory commentary that may strike the central theme, even the purpose, of all of Eric's work and of those of us who have so long claimed him as a model. "Ultimately," he writes, "the book's merits derive from the fact that I care deeply about the issues of racial justice central to Reconstruction and to our society today. If *Reconstruction* was born in the archives, it was written from the heart."[1] Have not all of us, for better or worse, in varying degrees of success, tried to do just that: to find the ways to research and write history that makes a difference, to connect our endless hours on microfilm and in dusty file boxes to the experiment we live every day in American society. Especially in the field of the Civil War and Reconstruction, but in American history more generally, who has led our profession any better than Eric in showing us how to connect the academy to the real world, where versions of the past are part of the daily struggle to determine policy, curriculums, elections,

Supreme Court decisions, and the ways the vast public forges its identities? Who has helped us better to successfully link scholarship to society, the archives to our hearts?

This is, of course, somewhat of a tradition in American historical studies, but we have all needed leadership on this front. Eric surely had that with his father, and ultimately from his doctoral mentor, Richard Hofstadter, who once wrote that all his own books had been "in a certain sense, topical in their inspiration . . . I have always begun with a concern with some present reality."[2] We have all heard and even probably issued the warnings to our own students to beware the "perils of presentism." Good history, as we can tell from reading Eric's work, must begin with deep research. As the culture wars and history wars raged in the 1990s, and perhaps are raging again, we may have found ourselves on both sides of this clichéd dilemma. But the rub, of course, is all in the doing. To me, Foner has always been like the great, radical preacher who succeeds with audiences not because of homiletic style, or the mere force of voice or personality, but with deeply informed theology, a relentless pursuit of hard truths, and what Protestants would call "tough grace." He is the trial lawyer who does not merely outwit his opponents and persuade a jury with the cleverest story; he simply reads and knows the law, and how it ought to work in life, better than the opponent. He is the writer who persuades not with dazzling metaphors but with a narrative laced with the best examples, a story that convinces by altering the angle of vision from top to bottom and then back again. And he is the social critic who writes history that vividly reminds us of our current condition.

The Freesoilers and Republicans (in *Free Soil, Free Labor, Free Men*) had much to teach us about how political coalitions are formed, about how the political, moral, and economic motives in life can forge a transforming movement larger than any one part of an ideology of reform. Tom Paine had much to tell us about how and why ideas matter in changing history, indeed, that radical challenges to existing, formidable systems can, over the long run, actually win some tenuous victories, however their authors may be sacrificed or exiled. *Reconstruction* was above all an extraordinary work of synthesis about an era not easily summarized or packaged in a general narrative. It demonstrated through the richness of detail, a brilliant eye for selection of quotations and voices, and a faith that a narrative of a whole and its parts is not only possible but essential. Eric's *Reconstruction* also reflected a determination to see the story on the ground in the South among real people, that the Civil War's consequences may always be with us—as measures of the democracy we say we cherish. What is *Freedom's Lawmakers* but a startling collection of the generation of black leadership—most of them forgotten—that forever serves as the prototype of all who aspired to that complicated title of "black leader." And in *The Story of Freedom*, Eric listened to his own call to take on big ideas, dig out their roots in the larger political culture, and then write their history for a general audience—thereby, in the end, showing that nothing, especially this most ubiquitous of American ideas, is static, unchanging, continuous, reassuring, or safe in our comfortable pockets of national mythology. In short, the present is illuminated in the past and the past in the present. Eric seems to have been deeply aware of Du Bois's claim that a people who lack an informed historical consciousness will also lack "moral foresight."[3] And his work has always reminded us that cold-blooded *interests* are forever entangled with concepts and *ideas*, human moral choices with intractable social structures.

In his autobiographical essay, Eric says that an "unexpected twist" came in his career when he became "something of a public historian." Well, *something of* indeed. Eric has done much to teach us how a scholar can be a public historian and what such an effort means. What happens when we leave our guild hall and enter that wilderness of public memory? How are we to compete for the public's sense of history against all the forces that shape it every day? Well, we learn that not everyone can be an oncologist or a heart surgeon, but everyone can claim to be a historian. It means facing Carl Becker's famous admonition that "Mr. Everyman is stronger than we are, and sooner or later we must adapt our knowledge to his necessities."[4] Becker did not say his tastes, his habits, his ignorance, his personal memory per se. He said his necessities. And by that I think he meant the need for story, the need for history that appeals to Mr. Everyman's innate sense of narrative and to his belief that nations still have discernable histories whatever becomes the fashion at academic conferences where social histories that reject master narratives altogether may reign. In museum exhibits, documentary films, textbooks, on public commissions, and on the op-ed pages of newspapers, Eric has led by example. If we don't speak up for and about history, Lynne Cheney and her narrow-minded, exclusionary, triumphalist minions surely will. If we don't help make the documentary films and craft the exhibits and imagine the national narrative in the civic arena, then we can't complain when those who do get it all wrong. If we don't write new master narratives, someone else surely will, and they are not likely to be anything we would call new. If we don't monitor how presidents use the word "freedom" in inaugural rhetoric as a way of forging a particular sense of history, and if we don't call a Supreme Court majority on its "sophistry" as it interprets the meaning of slavery and race in the American past, then we should not be surprised when even our friends don't understand "revisionism." H. L Mencken was right about never underestimating the ignorance of the American people, but Eric's work in public history (from the Disney controversy on down to the recent exhibits on slavery at the New-York Historical Society) has drawn many of us along to the realization that the millions who "love" history are also eager to know more than the standard sanitized tale of national progress. They can handle complexity; they can understand pluralism and tragedy; and they are not all believers in inevitability and an inherent righteousness born of the English settlers of North America.

In answer to his own question posed in the title of his most recent book of essays *who owns history?* Eric wisely declares: "Everyone and no one."[5] This is exactly what we all quickly learn when we venture forth into the realm of public history. Social memory is much larger than the history we write and teach, its power more sacred than our secular craft of scholarship. Memory is possessed as either personal heritage or perhaps the foundation of a political worldview. Memory is often owned, while history is interpreted; memory is passed down from generation to generation, while history, in that word of recent ill repute, gets *revised*. Eric has been a leader ushering us across this swinging, unstable, sometimes dangerous bridge between academic history and public memory. It is a bridge that needs constant repair, constant vigilance; the sentries on one side are always firing shots at the skirmishers on the other. With others, Eric has shown us that we can make a difference on the balance sheet kept in the marketplace of history where the battle rages between those who would keep America's story comfortable, pleasing, and traditional, and those who will write a history in the service of critical self-understanding.

"We can forget the past," Eric wrote in his essay about his visit to South Africa, "but the past, most assuredly, will not forget us." There is a lesson apparently not yet learned in the effort to try to build a memorial at Ground Zero in New York, a project with which Eric has been closely involved. But neither will the future forget us. Another unusual mentor in my own career

was Nathan Huggins, a former colleague of Eric's here at Columbia in the
1970s and '80s, and a huge, if all too brief, influence on me before he died in
1989. In his entry in *Who's Who*, Huggins fashioned a simple but elegant explanation for the study of history that may also be a fitting description of Eric's lasting impact. "I find in the study of history," wrote Huggins, "the special discipline which forces me to consider people and ages not my own. . . .
It is the most humane of disciplines, and in ways the most humbling. For
one cannot ignore those historians of the future who will look back on us
in the same way."[6] It is humbling to say the least to have the opportunity to
pay tribute to a professional historian I so admire with the words of another
I also admired. But as Huggins warns, it is doubly humbling to know that
we too will be studied, we will be examined and judged, not only for what
we wrote about our world, but for what we did to change it.

NOTES

1. Eric Foner, *Who Owns History? Rethinking the Past in a Changing World* (New
York, 2002), 19, 24.

2. Hofstadter, quoted in Foner, *Who Owns History?* 41.

3. W. E. B. Du Bois, *The Suppression of the African Slave Trade to the United
States of America, 1638–1870* in *W. E. B. Du Bois: Writings* (New York, 1986),
197.

4. Foner, *Who Owns History?* 20; Carl Becker, "Everyman His Own Historian,"
in *The Vital Past: Writings on the Uses of History*, ed. Stephen Vaughn, 34 (Athens,
Ga., 1985).

5. Foner, *Who Owns History?* xix.

6. Foner, *Who Owns History?* 108; Huggins, quoted in David W. Blight, *Beyond
the Battlefield: Race, Memory, and the American Civil War* (Amherst, 2002), 258.

Notes on Contributors

TYLER ANBINDER is professor of history and chairman of the History Department at George Washington University, where he teaches Civil War–era political history and the history of American immigration. His first book, *Nativism and Slavery: The Northern Know Nothings and the Politics of the 1850s* (New York, 1992), won the Avery Craven Prize of the Organization of American Historians. In 2001 he published *Five Points*, the story of a New York City neighborhood that was once the world's most notorious slum.

SVEN BECKERT is professor of history at Harvard University, where he teaches the nineteenth-century U.S. history. He is the author of *The Monied Metropolis: New York City and the Consolidation of the American Bourgeoisie* (New York, 2001). Currently his work focuses on the history of nineteenth-century capitalism. He is writing a global history of cotton during the "long" nineteenth century and a history of the nineteenth-century world economy.

MARTHA BIONDI is an associate professor of African American studies at Northwestern. She is the author of *To Stand and Fight: The Struggle for Civil Rights in New York City* (Cambridge, Mass., 2003) and of a forthcoming book on the black student movement and the origins of African American studies.

DAVID W. BLIGHT is Class of '54 Professor American History at Yale University and author of the Bancroft Prize–winning *Race and Reunion: The Civil War in American Memory* (Cambridge, Mass., 2001), as well as the forthcoming "Seizing Freedom: The Civil War and Emancipation of Wallace Turnage and John Washington."

ERIC FONER is DeWitt Clinton Professor of History at Columbia University. He has served as president of the Organization of American Historians, the American Historical Association, and the Society of American Historians. Among his best-known books are *Free Soil, Free Labor, Free Men: The Ideology of the Republican Party before the Civil War* (New York, 1970; reissued with new preface, New York, 1995); *Tom Paine and Revolutionary America* (New York, 1976); *Nothing but Freedom: Emancipation and Its Legacy* (Baton Rouge, 1983); and *Reconstruction: America's Unfinished Revolution, 1863–1877* (New York, 1988), which won, among other awards, the Bancroft Prize, Parkman Prize, and Los Angeles Times Book Award. His books have been translated into Chinese, Korean, Italian, and Portuguese.

MARTHA S. JONES is assistant professor in the Department of History and the Center for Afroamerican and African Studies and visiting assistant professor in the Law School at the University of Michigan. Her first book, *"All Bound Up Together": The Woman Question in African-American Public Culture, 1830–1900,* an intellectual and cultural history of black women's public lives in nineteenth-century America is forthcoming from the University of North Carolina Press. Her current work explores the relationship of African Americans and the Atlantic world legal culture in the pre–Civil War period.

MELINDA LAWSON teaches in the Department of History at Union College. She is the author of *Patriot Fires: Forging a New American Nationalism in the Civil War North* (Lawrence, Kans., 2002). She is currently working on a book about the remaking of American culture in the Civil War.

ALESSANDRA LORINI teaches comparative history of the Americas at the University of Florence, Italy. She is the author of *Rituals of Race: American Public Culture and the Search for Racial Democracy* (Charlottesville, Va., 1999), *Ai confini della libertà: Saggi di storia americana* (Roma, 2001), and many essays and articles on U.S. cultural history; she is the editor of several volumes including *An Intimate and Contested Relation: The United States and Cuba in the Late Nineteenth and Early Twentieth Centuries* (Firenze, 2005).

LISA MCGIRR is associate professor of history at Harvard University, where she teaches twentieth-century U.S. history. Her book *Suburban Warriors: The Origins of the New American Right* (Princeton, 2001), examines the national Right's rise from the grass roots. Her current research is focused on the 1920s, revisiting the Sacco and Vanzetti case and writing a social and cultural history of national prohibition.

MAE M. NGAI is professor of history at Columbia University. She is the author of *Impossible Subjects: Illegal Aliens and the Making of Modern America* (Princeton, 2004), which won the Frederick Jackson Turner Prize from the Organization of American Historians, among other prizes. She received her PhD from Columbia in 1998 and has held fellowships from the Radcliffe Institute for Advanced Studies at Harvard, NYU School of Law, and Social Science Research Council.

MARTHA SAXTON is associate professor of history and women's and gender studies at Amherst College. She is the author of a biography of Louisa May Alcott (New York, 1995) and of *Being Good: Women's Moral Values in Early America* (New York, 2003). She is also an editor of the *Journal for the History of Childhood and Youth*.

MANISHA SINHA is associate professor of Afro-American studies and history at the University of Massachusetts Amherst. She is the author of *The Counterrevolution of Slavery: Politics and Ideology in Antebellum South Carolina* (Chapel Hill, 2000) and coeditor of the two-volume *African American Mosaic: A Documentary History from the Slave Trade to the Twenty-first Century* (Upper Saddle River, N.J., 2004). Currently, she is working on a book on African Americans and the movement to abolish slavery, which is under contract with Harvard University Press. She has held fellowships from the N.E.H., the American Philosophical Society, the Rockefeller Foundation and the W.E.B. Du Bois Institute of Afro-American Research and the Charles Warren Center in American History at Harvard University.

PENNY VON ESCHEN is professor of history and American culture at the University of Michigan. She is the author of *Race against Empire: Black Americans and Anticolonialism, 1937–1957* (Ithaca, 1997) and *Satchmo Blows Up the World: Jazz Ambassadors Play the Cold War* (Cambridge, Mass., 2004). She is currently working on a book entitled "Soul Call: Black Artists on a World Stage."

XI WANG is professor of history at Indiana University of Pennsylvania. He is the author of *The Trial of Democracy: Black Suffrage and Northern Republicans, 1860–1910* (Athens, Ga., 1997) and *Principles and Compromises:*

The Spirit and Practice of the American Constitution (Beijing, 2000). He is the translator of the Chinese edition of Eric Foner's *Story of American Freedom* (Beijing, 2002). Currently he is the editor of the *Chinese Historical Review* and holds a Chang Jiang Scholar Professorship in World History at Peking University, China.

MICHAEL ZAKIM is the author of a political history of the business suit, *Ready-Made Democracy: A History of Men's Dress in the American Republic, 1760–1860* (Chicago, 2003). He is currently writing a book entitled "Accounting for Capitalism: The Business Clerk as Social Revolutionary" of which "Free Soil, and Free Labor, Free Markets" is a part. Zakim teaches history at Tel Aviv University.

Index